D1453527

Theater of Disorder

Theater of Disorder

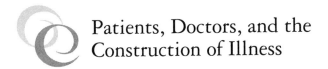

Patients, Doctors, and the
Construction of Illness

Brant Wenegrat

OXFORD
UNIVERSITY PRESS

2001

OXFORD
UNIVERSITY PRESS

Oxford   New York

Athens   Auckland   Bangkok   Bogotá   Buenos Aires   Cape Town
Chennai   Dar es Salaam   Delhi   Florence   Hong Kong   Istanbul   Karachi
Kolkata   Kuala Lumpur   Madrid   Melbourne   Mexico City   Mumbai   Nairobi
Paris   São Paulo   Shanghai   Singapore   Taipei   Tokyo   Toronto   Warsaw

and associated companies in
Berlin   Ibadan

Published by Oxford University Press, Inc.
198 Madison Avenue, New York, New York 10016

Oxford is a registered trademark of Oxford University Press.

Library of Congress Cataloging-in-Publication Data
Wenegrat, Brant.
Theater of disorder : patients, doctors, and the construction of illness
    p. cm.
Includes bibliographical references and index.
ISBN 0-19-514087-7
1. Sick—Psychology. 2. Social influence. 3. Physician and patient.
4. Psychotherapist and patient. 5. Social psychiatry.   I. Title.
R726.5.W46   2001
610.69'6—dc21   00-053760

9 8 7 6 5 4 3 2 1

Printed in the United States of America
on acid-free paper

Preface

In recent years, even as scientists have made progress in the treatment of serious mental disorders, such as schizophrenia and depression, some odd events have occurred in the field of mental health. In the late 1970s, multiple personality disorder, a hysterical illness once consigned to the dustbin of history, suddenly reappeared in many American clinics. Within a decade, hospital wards were filled with patients said to have "alters," or alternate personalities, able to seize control of their voices and bodies. The nineteenth-century antecedent of psychoanalysis, recovered memory therapy, also reappeared. Patients began to remember being abused by parents they had once thought were loving. Some clinicians specialized in the treatment of patients whose parents had supposedly involved them in satanic rituals. Patients remembered ritually killing and cannibalizing babies, orgiastic sexual rites, incest, and molestation. Professionals made public statements attesting to the importance of satanic abuse as a cause of illness. As if that weren't enough, by the end of the century, a psychiatrist teaching at Harvard had publicized his belief that abduction by extraterrestrials was a cause of much mental illness. Earthbound covens suddenly seemed passé.

The outrageous statements and practices of multiple personality specialists and recovered memory therapists have badly wounded the reputations of mental health practitioners and the interests of the psychologically ill. Citing such statements and practices, some authors condemned the practice of so-called depth psychotherapy, from which the multiple personality and recovered memory movements ostensibly emerged. According to these authors, insofar as it spawns absurdities, the process of depth psychotherapy must itself be flawed. Unable to make fine distinctions in a field they don't understand, some people in need of assistance may reach the same conclusions.

Fascinated by the seeming temporary insanity of a profession devoted to treating, not imitating, the mentally ill, I and many others have tried to place the events of the past 30 years in larger conceptual frameworks. The framework that I develop in this book is that of "invented illness." As I show, other instances of invented illness include possession disorders, medieval lovesickness, early-modern and modern-day European tarantism, the various forms of hysteria recognized by eighteenth- and nineteenth-century European physicians, and most of the many recent cases of chronic fatigue syndrome and multiple chemical sensitivity. Hypnotism, an offshoot of early-modern European demon possession, is a closely related phenomenon, as I describe. I develop the view that invented illnesses are shaped by patients or patients together with healers in pursuit of hidden but nonetheless intelligible motives. In creating invented illnesses, patients may act independently, but they often take stage directions from their physicians or healers.

As I try to show, several things seem clear when the recent events I have cited are viewed in this larger context. First, the excesses recently exhibited in relation to multiple personality disorder and recovered memory therapy are more than just millennial madness on the part of a few clinicians in a particular field. Similar phenomena have occurred in other areas of medicine, in the historical past, and in other cultures entirely. Whatever such events signify, they say something about the healer-patient relationship and illness behavior in general. Second, these events can be understood only within the framework of modern-day social psychology. In fact, multiple personality disorder, recovered memory therapy, and alien abduction provide the most powerful illustrations of social psychological principles at work available outside the laboratory. They are worthy of serious study on that count alone. It is impossible to learn about multiple personality disorder or recovered memory therapy without developing a new respect for social influence processes. Finally, the events of the past 30 years pose a particular challenge to the commonsense views of what it means to be human, to have a particular personality or identity, and to be conscious of one's beliefs and motives. The study of multiple personality disorder, for instance, turns out to be the study of every man and woman, not just of those who enact the particular role.

Many individuals contributed to this book. Lynda Malavanya first suggested this project and made some important suggestions concerning its structure and content. She first directed me to many of the social psychological studies described in this book. Robert Baker, Arthur Kleinman, Elizabeth Loftus, Harold Merskey, Edward Shorter, Phillip Slavney, Alan Young, and Phillip Zimbardo generously read earlier drafts of this manuscript and made crucial suggestions regarding particular points and the manuscript as a whole. They pointed out factual errors, important conceptual issues, and critical findings of which I had been unaware. They helped me identify the important, as opposed to the peripheral, issues and to better understand their own published work. They are not responsible for errors that might be found in this book, but they did prevent me from making many others.

James Hawkins, Georg Alpers, and Walton T. Roth found a number of helpful references, which are cited in subsequent pages.

Phillip Laughlin and his successor at Oxford University Press, Catharine Carlin, helped make this book a reality.

Finally, I would not have been able to write this book without the support of Anne Wenegrat and Jacob Wenegrat, Adolf Pfefferbaum, Bert Kopell, and a Stanford academic's essential friend, Pete McCloskey.

Contents

Theater of Disorder

1

The Theater of Disorder

In *As You Like It*, William Shakespeare likened the world to a stage and people to "mere players." Four hundred years later, many social scientists appear to have taken him literally. In social psychology, sociology, and anthropology, social life is frequently likened to theater and specific social interactions to performances. People are said to use cues, play roles, and manage and stage the impressions they hope to make on others.

Although it is familiar to social scientists, the modern-day "theatrical" view of social life has largely failed to penetrate psychiatry or medicine, in spite of the fact that medical interactions have clear theatrical elements, with roles, costumes, and props. Doctors are taught in medical school to appear authoritative and to interact with patients in a "professional" manner. They wear white coats regardless of whether they need protection from bodily fluids, and they work in offices furnished to convey their status and special powers. Patients for their part are expected to be deferential, to describe their symptoms in a standard format, and to follow physicians' advice. Some of the most troubling moments for physicians are caused by patients who do not play their role. Of course, medicine is more than theater, and its theatrical elements often take a back seat to practical concerns. But theater is still present, and often dominant. It is especially prominent in the histories of illnesses described in this book. For example, the book jacket shows André Pierre Brouillet's painting of Jean-Martin Charcot, the nineteenth-century neurologist. Charcot was a dramatist and stage director par excellence. His carefully directed clinical demonstrations, one of which is shown here, were attended not only by doctors but also by artists and intellectuals from throughout Europe. Brouillet depicted Charcot standing before such an audience. Next to him, a swooning, partially undressed woman is supported by two attendants. The woman depicted was Blanche Wittman, one of Charcot's so-called grand hysterics (see chapter 5). Her behavior, including her swoon, conformed to an illness role directed by Charcot and his colleagues in the Salpêtrière, the Parisian women's asylum. Today's patients do not swoon in lecture halls because we do not expect them to, or give them cues to do so. Imperial and assured, Charcot is pictured gesturing calmly toward his stricken patient.

The purpose of this book is to systematically apply a theatrical model of social relations to certain well-known mental and physical illnesses. As I hope to show, a theatrical model raises important questions about these disorders that would not otherwise be asked. It illustrates certain important aspects of human nature and consciousness, and it puts illness behaviors in their larger, cultural context. As the reader will see, some of the most influential twentieth-century theories regarding the human mind grew out of the study of illnesses discussed in later chapters. When viewed as dramatic enactments, these same illnesses show the way to new views of mental life. Although they may seem strange, these new views are consistent with modern-day experimental findings from the field of social psychology and with observational studies conducted on small groups.

To analyze a disorder in theatrical terms implies that it is a social role or, more specifically, an illness role. Like a theatrical role, a social role in general is a purposive behavior pattern consistent with a character, or character type. An illness role is a purposive behavior pattern consistent with a character in poor health. Enacting an illness role involves giving proper responses to various prompts and contingencies. For example, a patient playing the illness role called multiple personality disorder (see chapter 6) has to prove she has this illness by changing her voice and diction in the role of a child "alter." A patient playing the illness role corresponding to what we call conversion paralysis (see chapter 5) may have to fall to the floor when his doctor requests that he stand.

At least in modern theater, roles are learned by reading and studying scripts. Illness roles, by contrast, are learned less formally. In subsequent chapters, I show how patients learn illness roles from healers or medical doctors, from lay practitioners, and from their communities. Acquired through multiple channels and not through canonical scripts, illness roles tend to evolve. As I show, eighteenth- and nineteenth-century "hysteria" was modeled on late medieval forms of demon possession. Several disorders today are derivatives of hysteria. Today's multiple personality disorder was modeled on demon possession and on early mesmeric phenomena (which also mimicked possession). The false memory syndrome has roots in seventeenth-century witchcraft accusations, early mesmerism, and nineteenth-century hysteria. The evolution of illness roles leads to thematic consistencies that are often overlooked: Like their medieval forerunners, some modern-day patients with multiple personality disorder (see chapter 6) claim to have commerce with witches or even to have demon alters, and, while nineteenth-century physicians attributed hysteria to sexual frustration, modern-day physicians attribute hysteria's offshoots to sexual abuse.

The theatrical viewpoint suggests that others, and not just the actor, are involved in the illness production. At the least, actors need an audience. Family, friends, coworkers, and authorities of all kinds make up the audience for most illness roles. Sometimes, as with modern-day somatization disorder (see chapter 5), the physician is in the audience, often unwillingly. Certain roles need supporting actors or even directors. In subsequent chapters I show

how healers and doctors act to direct some illness roles or play supporting roles required for full enactments.

Finally, just as in the theater actors work for pay, those enacting illness roles expect to be rewarded. Like their theatrical counterparts, illness enactments are rational, goal-directed behaviors. To some extent, all illness roles produce the same set of benefits: attention, care, concern, and relief from work or burdens. However, some illness roles serve additional functions, such as allowing the actor to voice complaints, embarrass family members, or avoid culpability for past misbehavior.

Numerous authors have likened illness behavior to theater. Spirit possession (see chapter 3), mesmerism (see chapter 4), petit and grand hysteria (see chapter 5), and multiple personality disorder (see chapter 6) have all been compared to theater or theatrical roles.[1] The events in Charcot's Salpêtrière, as depicted in Brouillet's painting, were often likened to theater by the French popular press.[2] Nonetheless, this metaphor has not been explored as systematically or as deeply as it deserves. In this book I hope to show that a whole class of well-known illnesses, examples of which are found in diverse cultures and times, is best understood as theater and that the likeness to theater runs very deep. By taking the comparison between illnesses and theater more seriously than it has been taken in the past, we can achieve some insights that are otherwise not apparent, not only about these illnesses but about human nature.

In fact, while cancers, infections, and even seeming mood disorders occur in many species, the illnesses discussed in this book occur only in humans. Two aspects of homo sapiens may have, so to speak, set the stage for the appearance of illnesses that resemble dramatic productions. First, only human beings appear to be capable of the sustained and complex role-playing that these disorders entail. In his well-known book describing chimpanzees living in a colony at the Arnhem zoo, Frans de Waal described incidents in which individual chimpanzees pretended to be injured or to have friendly intentions and, in one case, to not know where some fruit was hidden.[3] As the closest living relatives of homo sapiens, with whom they shared a common ancestor about 7 million years ago, chimpanzees have social lives similar to those of humans. But each of the feigned behaviors observed by de Waal and his colleagues was simple and transitory in comparison with the role-playing behaviors typical of humans (see chapter 2). The proverbial thousand monkeys may be able to type out *Hamlet*, but no monkey or chimpanzee is likely to play the lead.

Second, whenever they can, humans give special attention, privileges, and care to their ill or disabled, often for very long periods of time. Care for the ill and disabled most likely evolved from what evolutionary theorists call kin altruism, or the evolutionarily advantageous tendency to aid those who carry one's genes by virtue of common descent.[4] Chimpanzees, too, show concern for their ill or disabled, but here again there is a major difference between the two species: While chimpanzees do what they can, only human societies are structured so as to provide prolonged care and dispensations for the chronically ill. Furthermore, prolonged care and dispensations for the ill or injured go far back in human prehistory: Neanderthals and modern humans evolved from a common hominid ancestor more than 100,000 years ago, but Neanderthal remains show that individuals who had suffered severe, crippling fractures were able to survive them.[5] Those who had suffered such injuries must have required prolonged care and, later, long-term assistance.

That humans care for their ill explains the existence of illness roles. Care, attention, and privileges lavished on the ill or disabled motivate illness roles, rendering them intelligible. As long as illness or disability leads to special care, privileges, and attention, some individuals will be tempted to enact illness or disability to garner the care, privileges, and attention for themselves. Looked at in this way, illness roles are the flip side of care of the ill and disabled. Moreover, given the ancient provenance for care of the ill and disabled, it seems likely that illness roles existed in the earliest, now unknown human societies. Also, whatever the historical fate of today's illness roles, illness roles will exist in the last societies, too, unless we become so brutal that we fail to care for the ill.

There are, of course, other models than the theatrical one to account for some of the illnesses described in the following chapters. For example, several of the disorders considered in later chapters are currently explained in terms of "dissociation." Dissociation, according to the American Psychiatric Association Diagnostic and Statistical Manual, Fourth Edition (hereafter called DSM-IV), is a "disruption in the usually integrated functions of consciousness, memory, identity, or perception of the environment."[6] This disruption, moreover, can be "sudden or gradual, transient or chronic." Multiple personality, now called "dissociative identity disorder," is listed in DSM-IV under the rubric "dissociative disorders," and conversion symptoms, such as hysterical blindness or paralysis, are considered "dissociative symptoms." Dissociation has also been been widely applied to hypnosis (see chapter 4), which has sometimes been called a "dissociated" state.

The concept of dissociation has two major weaknesses when it is used to explain the disorders discussed in this book. First, as a causal account, dissociation leads to circular reasoning. Since "consciousness, memory, identity, [and] perception of the environment" are not directly observable, their disrupted integration is generally inferred by taking patients' illness behaviors at face value. The patient with multiple personality disorder, for example, is said to have a disrupted sense of identity because he or, more commonly, she acts as if she does. People with the disorders discussed in later chapters are said to have fallen ill because they "dissociate," and the fact that they "dissociate" is deduced from the fact they are ill. This is not a recipe for scientific progress, and, in fact, it was evident early on that not much would be made.[7] The only area in which dissociation has really proven testable as a causal theory is with respect to the so-called hidden observer phenomenon in hypnosis (see chapter 4), and with respect to this phenomenon it has fallen short.

Second, unlike the theatrical model, dissociation theory fails to account for the obvious functions of illness behavior. In the following chapters, many examples are given in which patients use illness behavior to achieve social goals. To say that such behavior results from dissociation is to overlook the obvious functions it serves. From the theatrical viewpoint, the ability to "dissociate," at least in the sense of ignoring contradictions between roles assumed, may equip patients for enactments such as hypnosis (see chapter 4) or for illness behaviors such as multiple personality disorder (see chapter 6), which invoke roles at odds with normal modes of action, but it cannot be said to "cause" the enactments or illness in question. By way of analogy, the actor who can isolate the feelings evoked by playing Lear from his mundane emotional preoccupations may thereby be better equipped to play the part convincingly, but this ability does not "cause" his performance. This issue is discussed more in following chapters.

Arthur Kleinman, a well-known authority on cultural aspects of illness, studied neurasthenic patients in mainland China.[8] (Neurasthenia and chronic fatigue, to which it is closely related, are discussed extensively in chapter 5.) Kleinman found that neurasthenic patients were generally unhappy with their situations. Some patients, for instance, had been assigned to lifetime factory jobs that they found intolerable. Others had been assigned to live in cities distant from families or loved ones, and still others had suffered devastating losses during the Cultural Revolution from which they had never recovered. In the United States, patients with such problems might say they were depressed, but Chinese patients generally do not report mood problems. In the 1960s and 1970s, when Kleinman worked in China, depressed mood could also be taken as proof of a bourgeois mentality. In the worker's paradise, all people had to be happy, at least with their living conditions. According to Kleinman, some depressed Chinese were even sentenced as dissidents. Unwilling to say that their situations depress them, Chinese patients complain of protean physical symptoms. If they admit to depression, they say it is a result of their illness, which is acceptable. Chinese physicians attribute these physical symptoms to neurasthenia and prescribe rest, vacations, and other privileges that may at least partly redress the cause of their patients' distress.

Kleinman argued that in China, neurasthenia is an "idiom of distress,"[9] or a locally understood means of expressing unhappiness, and he likened neurasthenia, in this respect, to certain illnesses (most of them petit hysterias) once commonly seen in the West (see chapter 5). At times, Kleinman refers to "idioms of distress" as if they are what I will call illness roles, or enactments of ill health, that serve patients' and sometimes also physicians' interests. For example, Kleinman suggests that an "illness career" can lead to financial compensation, disability, or love or attention from others. He writes of neurasthenia, in particular, as a "coping pattern" and notes that illness behavior is adaptive only if it conforms to the models accepted by health professionals. Kleinman's case examples, which I cite in chapter 5, show a keen eye for the everyday uses of illness behavior.

However, as a general descriptive term, "idiom of distress" may have misleading connotations with regard to some of the illness roles discussed in later chapters. Most important, to say that the patient's behavior is an "idiom of distress" can be taken to mean that the function of illness is largely declarative and that the healer's role is to interpret the statement made in the form of an illness. The patient, that is, may be thought to declare his distress to the healer, who is expected to listen and act on what he hears. Yet, rather than being declarative, as the term "idiom" may imply, illness behavior also can directly serve some functions. The functions that a role serves may determine the form it takes, whereas the form might be arbitrary if its purpose were merely declarative. In chapter 6, for instance, I argue that one of the functions served by multiple personality disorder (MPD) is to excuse misbehavior on the patient's part. The patient is not held responsible for past acts reinterpreted as the work of alter personalities. Obviously, this specific illness function can be served only by disorders that have specific forms. Also, the healer is not just the audience but takes a more active role in staging some illness enactments. Charcot and his colleagues, for instance, "directed" the grand hysterics in the Salpêtrière (see chapter 5), while those who treat MPD at the least act supporting roles (see chapter 6). These points should become more evident as the theatrical model is applied to specific disorders.

In the following chapters, I argue that certain disorders are really illness roles. Other disorders, such as tuberculosis, diabetes, cancer, and schizophrenia, to name a few, are not mentioned at all. In deciding which disorders to study as illness roles, I employ the following principles.

First, illnesses not associated with objective physiological or anatomical abnormalities are more likely than other disorders to be illness roles. I take it for granted that illness roles affect only behavior and subjective experience. This is not to deny that social factors can have adverse physiological effects. Social stress, for instance, is known to raise the risk of several chronic diseases. It is only to say that such diseases are more than illness roles, as I define them here. This is also not to deny the limits of present-day methods of physical diagnosis. In some cases, present-day methods and knowledge may be inadequate to demonstrate physical findings that accompany real diseases. This is an important issue with regard to chronic fatigue (see chapter 5). This criterion alone eliminates most disorders as candidate illness roles.

Second, narrowly distributed illnesses are more likely than other disorders to be illness roles. Illness roles tend to be scripted in particular societies or by limited groups of practitioners. Grand hysteria, for instance, was seen in its fully developed form only in the precincts of the Salpêtrière (see chapter 5). Multiple personality, which is discussed in chapter 6, is diagnosed almost exclusively by a small group of practitioners and is not seen at all by other practitioners. Likewise, only a few practitioners diagnose alien abduction syndrome or satanic ritual abuse (see chapter 7). This criterion helps to eliminate some widespread mental disorders, such as schizophrenia or bipolar disorder, as candidate illness roles, but it is not absolute. For instance, disorders that resemble chronic fatigue syndrome or somatization disorder occur in many societies, but other evidence suggests that these are illness roles. *Kuru*, on the other hand, occurs only among the Foré tribesmen of New Guinea, but it is an infectious illness, not a role.

Third, new syndromes or syndromes that increase in incidence are more likely than other disorders to be illness roles.[10] The reason is that illness roles are subject to fads and fashions. Physicians in particular sometimes meet their own needs by stage-directing new illnesses, which—human imagination being somewhat limited—often turn out to be modeled on older disorders. This was the case in the Salpêtrière and is still true today, as later chapters illustrate. This criterion, too, is only relative. AIDS is a rather new and rapidly spreading disorder that is not an illness role. Somatization disorder, or something akin to it, has been around for a long time, but it nevertheless reflects unwarranted illness behavior.

Finally, some disorders may be real for most patients and illness roles for others. Chronic fatigue syndrome and so-called Gulf War syndrome may belong in this category. As discussed in chapter 5, some of the Gulf War veterans who complain that they are disabled (and perhaps some patients with chronic fatigue syndrome, too) may have real disorders that account for their complaints, while others are enacting a popular illness role. Insofar as art is based on real life, we should expect to see emulation of all kinds of real disorders, especially if these are the object of publicity and attention.

This study is not comprehensive. Many disorders that might really be illness roles, at least for many patients, are not discussed. The class of illnesses to which the theatrical model might usefully be applied is simply too broad to be covered in a single work. The disorders discussed in this book were chosen because they exemplify key aspects of the theatrical model being presented. In particular, some readers may be surprised to find that so-called factitious disorders, such as malingering and Munchhausen's syndrome, are not discussed in this book, except insofar as they relate to other topics. Although factitious disorders can be described as role playing, they fail to fully illustrate the concept of illness roles developed in later chapters. As will become evident later, the power of social roles over thought and behavior is realized when the actor loses himself in his role, a transition not characteristic of these particular syndromes.

Henry Sigerist and Talcott Parsons, both well-known sociologists, also used the term "role" in connection with illness.[11] According to Parsons, for instance, ill people assume a "sick role." This is a deviant role, in the sense of being other than the usual role of an adult group member. The sick role confers certain privileges, such as exemption from everyday responsibilities, and also certain burdens, such as cooperation with healers. The ill are expected to recognize that their sick role behavior deviates from group norms. Though the concept of role used here and the concept used by these authors share certain features in common—both types of roles, for instance, can be viewed as scripted and stereotyped—these concepts are also fundamentally different. Sigerist and Parsons were interested mainly in how disease changes social performance. The topic of this book is disease itself as performance.

The disorders discussed in this book might be called "social constructions," rather than illness roles. The problem, as the philosopher Ian Hacking observed, is that this frequently heard term is really an empty one.[12] Buildings, corporations, nations, and systems of faith are also social constructions, but calling them this does little to clarify either their qualities or the differences among them. The question is not whether the disorders discussed in this book are social constructions of sorts but rather what kind of social constructions they are, and this question is more meaningfully addressed in the language of roles.

Some readers may object that the model developed here stigmatizes patients and physicians. To say patients "play" illness roles, that physicians "direct" such roles, or that patients and healers cooperate to stage illness enactments seems to cast doubt on the honesty of everyone involved. This seems especially unkind in respect to patients who suffer from obvious misfortunes and social "ill health," if not from bodily woes, as do many of the individuals described in later chapters.

Although the illness role model questions patients' integrity, and healers' as well, the research on which it is based (described in chapter 2) suggests that the type of "dishonesty" involved in illness roles is in fact pervasive in human social transactions. People play whatever roles promise them benefits, often quite unknowingly. Self and other delusion is rampant in human affairs. In this general context, the self and other deceit inherent in illness roles is really less extraordinary than it might seem, and the indictment, if any, must be issued against humanity, not against individuals. None of us is entirely free from this type of dishonesty.

However, the fact that we can't cast the first stone doesn't mean we have to close our eyes entirely. Patients frequently do deceive themselves and others, and the illness roles discussed in later chapters offer some of the clearest examples of such deceit. As I hope to show, patients are ill served if we ignore the facts or obfuscate them with vague references to social ill health. Whatever is really wrong with them, patients lead lives that are being ruined as the result of illness roles described in later chapters. A humane but skeptical attitude, not patronizing collusion, is the best way to help them. I hope that readers with the patience to read through this volume will come away convinced that kindness and compassion are best served by truthfulness.

Similar remarks apply to some clinicians. The truth is that some psychologists, psychiatrists, and physicians have made their careers directing role enactments. I assume that the vast majority of them sincerely believe in the reality of the illness roles in which they have specialized, but I argue that this belief depends on self-deception. Like everyone else, clinicians are inclined to believe fervently those things that promise them advantage, in this case over colleagues who take more cautious views.

The plan of this book is as follows: In chapter 2, I describe some experiments conducted by social psychologists that show the extent to which humans respond to role cues from others. Playing a social role changes beliefs and attitudes; these become consistent with the role enacted. Since people are often unaware of the causes of their own behaviors, they may not know that they are responding to cues from others, or even that they are role playing. I also cite some modern studies of social groups—in this case, religious cults— that show the extent to which role cues can change behavior in real-life settings, with subsequent effects on attitudes and beliefs. Individuals differ in responsiveness to role cues. I review the bases for these differences in responsiveness to role cues in general and to cues that suggest illness roles in particular.

In chapter 3, I describe "culture-bound" disorders, disorders found only in certain cultures. Since ethnographers and historians have long made a point of addressing the functions such illnesses serve, their study can help to illustrate some uses of illness behavior. I start by reviewing the work of the anthropologist I. M. Lewis, who studied possession illnesses in traditional societies.[13] Lewis described in detail the functions such illnesses serve and the role of shamans in helping to stage possession. Then I describe a number of culture-bound syndromes: the *negi negi* syndrome among the Bena Bena tribesmen of New Guinea, *latah* among the Malays, "acute psychoses" among students in Swaziland, *bebainan* in Bali, *ataques de nervios* in Latin-Caribbean cultures, and tarantism, lovesickness, and demon possession in Europe. Some aspects of demon possession survived in the guise of hysteria, an entirely secular illness.

In chapter 4, I describe the social role view of hypnosis. According to this view, hypnosis is not a "state of mind" but a culturally sanctioned role. Hypnotist and subject collude to enact a drama in which something out of the ordinary appears to happen but that in fact manifests everyday role-playing skills. Mesmerism, the original form of hypnosis before it slowly evolved into its modern form, was, like hysteria, modeled on demon possession. Just as belief in spirits provides the logical basis for belief in possession disorders, so the belief that hypnosis corresponds to a special state has provided the logical basis for belief in most Western illness roles for the past hundred years. Just as loss of faith in the existence of spirits exposes possession as a social role, so loss of faith in hypnosis exposes these modern disorders to a more critical view.

In chapter 5, I describe the various forms of hysteria. Contrary to popular view, there is in fact little evidence that hysteria as a concept antedated the seventeenth century. In its earliest form, hysteria was an attempt to medicalize possession. By the end of the nineteenth century, several forms of hysteria were recognized by physicians. First, there was grand hysteria as described by Charcot and his colleagues in the Salpêtrière Hospital. There was also petit hysteria, a much more common form. Most of the famous cases of hysteria were petit. Then there was neurasthenia, which was not called hysterical so that upper-class men could have it but which was nonetheless closely related to petit hysteria. Neurasthenia is still diagnosed outside the United States but in the United States it appears now in the guise of so-called chronic fatigue syndrome. As described in chapter 5, petit hysterias have been transmogrified into Briquet's syndrome and, more recently, into somatization disorder, and also into conversion disorder. The last two of these are found in the DSM-IV. So-called environmental illness, which tips its hat to modern-day concerns with air pollution, is also closely related to petit hysteria and to neurasthenia.

In chapter 6, I address multiple personality disorder, a secularized possession illness that has recently been epidemic, at least in North America. As I show in this chapter, the nineteenth-century patients who are said to have had MPD actually had a disorder quite different from that seen today. The speed with which MPD has recently been evolving is on the same order of magnitude as that shown by grand hysteria in the Salpêtrière. It seems likely that MPD will meet the same fate, too: Those enacting the MPD role have gotten so carried away—some now have hundreds of alters, including animals and demons—that professionals and lay observers in effect jeer at their performances. Increasingly, observers refuse to believe MPD illness enactments. There is no worse fate for an illness role than to play to a critical audience.

In chapter 7, I describe the recovered memory syndrome, which is closely related to multiple personality disorder and has elements of hysteria but can stand on its own as an illness role. Here, too, role inflation, for lack of a better term, has led to a backlash, sometimes from those accused of having abused their children. In recent years, patients with supposedly recovered memories have closed the historical circle by claiming they were victimized by devil worshippers. In this way they hearken back to late medieval times and witchcraft accusations. Others, more futuristic than historically minded, claim to have been sexually abused by extraterrestrials, usually on spaceships and sometimes in outer space. There is a small but adequate audience for such enactments.

In chapter 8, I discuss the issue of unconscious attitudes. Some subjects who enact illness roles may come to believe they are sick. Others, however, may be aware they are well and therefore might be called malingerers. Although the DSM-IV distinguishes between some disorders discussed in this book and malingering on the basis of whether or not the symptoms appear intentional, in actual practice there is no basis for this distinction. In chapter 8, I argue that the social psychological data suggest that there is a spectrum of belief in illness roles; at one end are those who frankly disbelieve in their illness behavior, and at the other end are those who have come to believe they are ill. Most people are in between. The concept of "the unconscious," which developed as an attempt to understand petit hysteria, has recently come under fire because of the antics of patients (and their therapists) as they enact recovered memories. The theatrical model suggests a new view of "the unconscious." This accounts for the clinical findings in role-playing patients in general while avoiding the pitfalls that vexed the older, discredited concept. In chapter 8, I present results from modern studies that suggest that role enactments, carried to their logical conclusion, may sometimes really "split consciousness." In a limited sense, multiples may have alters and the possessed their demons, in spite of the fact that their illnesses are really role enactments.

The recent evolution of novel illness roles suggests that the modern environment is conducive to the development of such disorders. Just as poor sanitary conditions spread infectious diseases through nineteenth-century cities, so the modern mass media now spread illness roles. To counter these conditions, practical steps should be taken to slow down the spread of future epidemics of illness behavior. At the very least, physicians and other professionals have to become more aware of illness-role enactments. Every medical student learns the precept *primum non nocere* (first, do no harm) attributed to Hippocrates, in the fifth century B.C. As this book shows, some traditional illness roles may serve useful functions, but modern-day illness roles are often extremely destructive. By ignoring theatrical aspects of modern-day illness roles, health professionals have been complicit—as stage directors, supporting actors, or audience members—in illness-role enactments that are harmful to their patients. The theatrical model, and knowledge of the research on which this model rests, can help health professionals follow Hippocrates' rule.

2

Basic Research and Observations

The theatrical model is rooted in research and observations from social psychology, sociology, and anthropology. First, modern studies show that human behavior is strongly controlled by social cues. Since people may be unaware of the causes of their behavior, they may be unaware that they are responding to cues. People also enact social roles, sometimes in response to cues. Researchers have shown that enacting a particular social role can change beliefs and attitudes so that these become consistent with the role enacted. Finally, individuals differ with respect to their propensities to enact new social roles in general and illness roles in particular. To lay the foundation for the study of illness behaviors, I briefly describe some research from social psychology and sociology that pertains to each of these points. Anthropological research is cited in chapter 3.

Types of Social Cues

People obtain several types of social cues from others. Social psychologists distinguish, for example, informational (or descriptive) and normative cues or influence.[1] Informational cues suggest accurate judgments and/or effective behaviors in a particular situation. If you are lost in the woods and you follow another hiker who is walking ahead of you, you are using the course she takes as an informational cue. You are hoping that her directional judgment is better than yours and hence that her choice of path will lead you both somewhere. Normative cues, by contrast, point out socially skilled behaviors. If you are uncertain which dining utensil to use and you follow the lead of another diner at your table, you are using his choice of utensil as a normative cue. Any utensils might be effective for moving food, but what you are seeking are cues to socially favored choices. Obviously, some cues may be both normative and informational. If the only effective way to get something done is to do it in the normative fashion, then the cues that indicate how it could be done are also cues that indicate how it should be done.

Additional types of social cues that might be distinguished are cues that convey demands or social incentives and cues that invoke and direct enactments of social roles. Such cues are informational, in the sense that they

serve to inform us about the state of the world, but the information conveyed concerns the desires of others, their willingness to reward certain
types of behavior, and the roles that they want us to play. However, such
cues may also be normative, in the sense that they serve to inform us of how
others want us to act if we are to have their approval.

Sherif, a social psychologist, performed a famous experiment to demonstrate how people use informational cues.[2] Sherif seated subjects in a completely darkened room. One after another, pinpoints of light became visible
on a wall, appeared to move, and then vanished. The movement, however,
was only apparent; the lights were actually stationary and their movement
an illusion—the "auto-kinetic effect"—caused by lack of any visible frame
of reference. Subjects were asked to estimate how far each light had traveled.

Since Sherif's subjects lacked objective means for determining distance of
movement—no actual movement had occurred—they might be expected to
be especially attuned to informational cues from the responses of others. In
fact, this was the case. Whenever two or more subjects were placed in the
room together and informed of each other's responses, they began to give
similar estimates. Groups of subjects settled on very different estimates, but
estimates within each group converged on a group mean.

Sherif varied this study by introducing research confederates posing as
subjects. By making estimates very much higher or lower than those that
most naive subjects would make, these confederates induced Sherif's subjects to change their estimates in the expected direction. Thus, subjects in
the room with a confederate who was making high estimates began giving
high estimates themselves; subjects in the room with a confederate who was
making low estimates began giving low estimates. Sherif also showed that
group means were stable, once they had developed. Old members could be
gradually removed from groups and new ones introduced without much
change occurring in group means.

In support of the hypothesis that the social cues provided by others' distance estimates were primarily informational, Sherif found that group means
determined individual subjects' estimates even when the subjects were later
tested alone. The subjects must have thought the group means were correct,
rather than just the proper thing to say in the group context. Group means
even determined individual subjects' responses one year later, when subjects
were tested alone, and they determined responses when subjects were placed
in new groups, with completely different subjects.

Another famous study, in this case by Solomon Asch, illustrates how people use normative social cues.[3] Asch introduced subjects into groups of six
to eight research confederates. The subjects were told to indicate which of
three "comparison" lines displayed to all the subjects was closest in length to
a so-called standard line. Subjects were told to make their judgments independently, but they gave their answers out loud in front of all the others.
During noncritical trials, research confederates gave correct answers. During
critical trials, though, the confederates unanimously gave answers that were
clearly incorrect. For example, instead of matching a two-inch standard line

with a two-inch comparison line, they matched it with a line only one inch long.

Confronted with unanimous, obviously wrong confederate estimates, a large proportion of subjects also gave wrong answers. Insofar as the correct responses were obvious, subjects who responded to wrong cues given by others must have been using these cues for their normative content. That is, they used these cues to fit in with the group, rather than because the judgment was uncertain. Consistent with this hypothesis, many subjects laughed nervously or fidgeted in their seats before giving in to the group consensus. Also, allowing the subjects to answer out of the confederates' earshot greatly reduced conformity with erroneous answers.

From introspection and memory, readers can supply their own data on cues that convey demands or incentives. All of us have responded to such cues and know how imperative responding to such cues can feel. In chapter 4, I argue that hypnosis is a role temporally bounded by an induction ritual on one side and a wakening ritual on the other. The induction and wakening rituals, as well as instructions given during the hypnotic "trance," fall under the rubric of role cues.

Some of the most famous social psychological experiments have as their theme the ease and extent of control of behavior by social cues. In a well-known study by Stanley Milgram, for instance, a variety of informational, normative, demand, incentive, and role cues were used to induce peaceful, law-abiding subjects to give extremely painful and, for all they knew, harmful or even lethal electrical shocks to other people.[4] In another study, Zimbardo showed that normal male college students were quickly induced to brutality or to cowed submission by placing them in a context—a simulated prison—that provided numerous role cues.[5] Darley, Latané, and others staged simulated emergencies in laboratories, stores, elevators, and subways as well as on the street.[6] Helping behaviors were shown to be highly determined by cues from bystanders and confederates. The reader should note that these studies show cue-based control of behaviors—moral and altruistic—that are normally thought to reflect internal motives and standards.

Awareness of Cues

In a classic paper on the issue of self-awareness, Richard Nisbett and Timothy Wilson argued that people often have little or no information about the real causes of their own behavior.[7] For example, in one experiment conducted by these authors, the subjects were shown nightgowns and asked which they preferred. The nightgowns were displayed left to right on a table. In the absence of substantial differences among the objects displayed, people generally prefer the object farthest to the right in this type of task, and that finding was replicated in Nisbett and Wilson's experiment. However, when asked why they preferred that particular garment, Nisbett and Wilson's subjects referred to the garments themselves, rather than to their position. They appeared unaware that position had influenced their decision. In another experiment, subjects memorized word pairs and then were asked to name category members. The word pairs were such as to increase, through their associations, the naming of certain targets in the categories. The pair "ocean-moon," for instance, would increase the chance that the subjects would say "Tide" when asked to name a detergent. In fact, the word pairs doubled, from 10 to 20 percent, the naming of target items in the categories. In spite of the fact they remembered the word pairs they had been taught, almost no subjects cited the word pairs as cues in their thinking. Instead, when asked why they had given the target responses in question, subjects concentrated on qualities of the target. They claimed, for example, that they had thought of Tide detergent because it is the best-known brand, because their mother used it, or because they liked the box. In still another experiment, subjects watched an interview with a college teacher who had a European accent. Half the subjects saw the teacher anwer the questions, which dealt with educational philosophy, in a pleasant and agreeable manner, and the other half saw him answer the questions in an autocratic, rigid manner. Subjects then rated the teacher's likability, appearance, mannerisms, and accent. The subjects who saw the pleasant, agreeable interview tended to like the teacher as well as his appearance, mannerisms, and accent more than the students who saw the autocratic, rigid version. Subjects later denied, though, that their like or dislike of the teacher had affected their ratings of his characteristics. In fact, subjects who observed the second interview believed that their dislike of the teacher's appearance, mannerisms, and accent had caused them to dislike him more generally.

If subjects do not know the real reasons for their behavior, how do they nonetheless invent the reasons they do cite? Nisbett and Wilson's subjects seem to have cited reasons chosen for their convenience. That is, the subjects who cited the characteristics of the garment they chose, the popularity of Tide detergent, or the salient accent of the teacher they disliked were all in some sense seizing on obvious explanations. In other cases, though, the process is more complex. "Self-attribution" theorists argue that people attribute the causes of their own behavior using the very same processes they apply to others.[8] That is, they observe their own behavior, look for environmental factors that might have influenced them, and draw their conclusions accordingly. A substantial body of research seems to support this hypothesis.[9]

Insofar as the general principal described by Nisbett and Wilson applies to social cues, people may be unaware of the role such cues play in their own behavior. Evidence that this can occur emerged from some of the studies cited in the previous section. In Sherif's perception experiment, for example, subjects thought visual evidence had led to their distance estimates. We know, however, that estimates made by other persons were the critical factors. In Darley and Latané's studies, subjects explained their behaviors—helping or failing to help—by citing aspects of the apparent emergency that suggested to them that help was or was not needed. We know, however, that responses by other persons were the critical factors.

In subsequent chapters, I argue that powerful role cues, sometimes from physicians, prompt and shape illness enactments. The extent to which patients are cognizant of their responses to role cues is a theme that emerges repeatedly in the study of illness roles.

Social Roles

Like a theatrical role, a social role is a purposive behavior pattern consistent with a character, or character type. Social role enactment was observed in Zimbardo's experiment, in which subjects took on the personae of guards or prisoners. Similar examples of enactments of normally shunned roles in response to social incentives have been observed in small groups such as college fraternities and among groups of sports fans.[10] Here I cite examples from religious cults.

In 1978, Marc Galanter, a New York University psychiatrist, suggested that individuals join religious cults for comaraderie.[11] Galanter had studied 119 converts to the Divine Light Mission, an Eastern religious group whose members report having visions and other mystical experiences. He found that members obtained relief of negative mood and psychosomatic symptoms by joining this cult and that relief was correlated with the extent to which members experienced the Mission as a socially cohesive group. Subsequent studies supported Galanter's thesis.[12] Galanter himself, for example, studied individuals who attended weekend retreats offered by the Reverend Sun Myung Moon's Unification Church.[13] Lack of camaraderie was the sole predictor of which individuals would go on to join the church.

Consistent with Galanter's theory, cult groups attract new members by offering them comaraderie, not by impressing them with theological arguments.[14] Potential recruits are sought from populations likely to be socially alienated, such as students on large campuses at the beginning of new terms or the elderly living alone in single apartments. They are invited to dinners or other social events and are showered with attention and offers of practical help from friendly, concerned cult members. If they appear to enjoy themselves, they are invited to a lengthier weekend retreat, which is usually held in an isolated location. This is the kind of retreat in which Galanter's study was set. In the course of the weekend retreat, potential recruits are given still more friendly attention. Potential recruits who express interest in joining the group are urged to take up residence in communal quarters, which, for student recruits, are located near campuses.

As individuals go from being dinner guests to weekend visitors to residents in a cult home, they have increasing incentives to conform to group norms. Once they have become members and have cut their outside ties, the whole of their social world rests on their ability to behave as committed cultists. How far will cultists go in enacting the devotee role?

The answer seems to be "however far is needed." Members of the Unification Church, for example, cut their ties to family, live in dormitories, and work long hours without pay at church-run enterprises. Church members seek the honor of acting as servants to Moon, his wife, or his numerous children, who are viewed as semidivine. Thousands of American followers of Moon have, at Moon's behest, married other devotees they had not even met. Followers of the Bhagwan Shree Rajneesh, 30 percent of whom had advanced university decrees, labored dawn to sunset in the fields of Rajneeshpuram, the commune he founded in Oregon in the 1970s.[15] The Bhagwan, who lived in luxury, was most often seen by his followers being driven through the fields in one of his many Rolls Royces. As the Bhagwan's car approached, his followers put down their implements and bowed to the ground respectfully.

Cult group members will play the devotee role literally to death. In 1978, 700 followers of Jim Jones, an obviously psychotic man who considered himself the Messiah, killed themselves and their 200 children in the Guiana jungle.[16] Before moving to Jonestown, these had mostly been normal adults who behaved as adults behave in a large American city. Nearly 15 years later, David Koresh's followers died in a confrontation with federal marshals in Waco, Texas.[17] In March 1997, police in Rancho Sante Fe, California, discovered that 39 members of Heaven's Gate, a millennarian cult that had focused its attention on the approaching Hale-Bopp comet, had committted mass suicide with lethal doses of sedatives.[18] Still more recently, more than 50 members of a sect calling itself the Solar Temple were found dead in Switzerland and Quebec. Some may have been murdered, but most of them killed themselves.[19]

The Effect of Social Role Enactments on Beliefs and Attitudes

A long line of research shows that subjects who play a social role change their beliefs and attitudes to make them consistent with the role they are playing. For example, in the earliest of these studies, published by Janis and King in 1954, male college students were asked to make several predictions, such as the extent to which the nation's meat supply would increase in subsequent years.[20] Approximately four weeks later, the subjects were divided into groups of three, allegedly for the purpose of helping researchers to develop an aptitude test to measure speaking ability. One at a time, each group member gave a speech to the others that pertained to one of the predictions the subjects had made, on the basis of an outline of arguments he and the other group members had been given just minutes before. The speaking student was told to play the role of a sincere advocate of the point of view expressed in the outline from which he was speaking, while the nonspeaking students were told to judge how well the speaker was doing in presenting the arguments outlined. All subjects were later given additional questionnaires, ostensibly for the purpose of rating how each of them had performed. In the midst of some filler items, subjects were asked to make new predictions like those they had made before.

Janis and King found that subjects who delivered an outlined speech showed a sizable change in their second predictions, compared to their first, in the direction of the positions for which they had publicly spoken. By contrast, subjects who had read the outlines and heard others talk on an issue failed to show much change in their second predictions. The different effects of speaking and hearing a speech were not due to inattention in the latter condition. Subjects who took notes on arguments voiced by others were nonetheless less affected than were the speakers themselves, in spite of the fact that the notes they took were oftentimes highly detailed. Other studies like Janis and King's are cited in chapter 8.[21]

Role-induced attitude change may account for extreme commitments to real-life social roles. For example, some of Jim Jones's followers wholeheartedly believed that Jones was the Messiah. Unaware of their real reason for following Jones to Guiana—which, if Galanter is correct, was largely their need for camaraderie—they had come to explain their behavior with a set of consistent beliefs. These beliefs made suicide appear a rational choice.

Illness roles are purposive behavior patterns consistent with poor health. Insofar as these are like other roles, and thus change attitudes and beliefs, people who enact such roles may come to believe they are ill. As I discuss in chapter 8, this outcome is especially likely if they are unaware of the real causes of their enactments.

Who Plays an Illness Role?

Some individuals are more prone than others to take on illness roles. Characteristics of patients with particular illness roles are discussed at length in subsequent chapters. People with high role malleability, those who are unable to meet their needs more directly, and those who have certain personality types appear to be most likely to assume illness roles. What follows is an overview of these several causes.

Regarding role malleability, sociologists and psychologists have long been aware that individuals differ in their ability and willingness to adopt social roles in response to transient cues. For example, authors in the "impression management" tradition, such as the sociologist Erving Goffman, distinguished between competent and less competent impression managers.[22] Competent impression managers, according to these theorists, attend to cues from others and vary their self-presentations according to their situation. They are aware of how they appear to others, have a large repertoire of potential roles, and are able to learn new roles when they enter new social settings. Less competent impression managers have difficulty interpreting role cues or varying their self-presentations and are slow to learn new roles in new social settings. In *The Lonely Crowd*, David Riesman described two personality types, which he called "inner-" and "other-directed."[23] According to Riesman, inner-directed types chart their social courses according to their own values, standards, and self-conceptions. Other-directed types chart their social courses according to expectations and social cues given by others. The former, Riesman analogized, are guided as if by a gyroscope; the latter rely on radar.

Goffman, Riesman, and others have noted that people differ in the flexibility of their role playing, but it was left to Mark Snyder, a psychologist, to try to measure this difference.[24] Snyder's so-called self-monitoring scale consists of 25 self-descriptive items, which subjects can mark as either true or false. Subjects who obtain high scores on this scale are likely to change their social roles to conform with role expectations, at least in everyday settings. Subjects who obtain low scores on this scale are likely to act much the same, regardless of their social settings or the expectations of others. Items that might be endorsed by high self-monitoring subjects include: "I would probably make a good actor"; "In different situations and with different people, I often act like very different persons"; and "When I am uncertain how to act in social situations, I look to the behavior of others for cues." Items that might be endorsed by low self-monitoring subjects include: "I have trouble changing my behavior to suit different people and different situations"; "I can only argue for ideas which I already believe"; and "I would not change my opinion (or the way I do things) in order to please people or win their favor." Scores on Snyder's scale are stable over time.

Experimental studies confirm that high and low self-monitors differ in their responses to real role demands. In one study, for instance, students were placed in a group defined so that nonconformity was an important value. There were cameras and microphones, and students signed releases allowing themselves to be videotaped for possible future viewing by other psychology students. In another setting, salient values were defined by group members themselves. There were no cameras or microphones, and the discussions were understood to be private. In the public setting, when a premium had been placed on nonconformity, high self-monitors presented themselves as individualists. In the private setting, by contrast, they tended to conform to whatever group norm evolved. They adjusted their self-presentation to fit the values defined by the group they were in. By contrast, low self-monitors presented themselves as equally conforming or nonconforming in both situations.

Being dependent on role cues, high self-monitors like social situations with clearcut role demands. For example, high self-monitors generally prefer to join conversations characterized by agreement between the conversing parties. Divergent beliefs and attitudes might pull them in different directions: Should they agree with the atheist or the religious zealot, the liberal or the conservative, the pacifist or the hawk? By contrast, low self-monitors prefer to join conversations in which there are participants with whom they identify. Liberal low self-monitors will want to join conversations in which other liberals take part; religious low self-monitors will want to join conversations that other faithful have joined. While low self-monitors have more or less similar friends who are like themselves, high self-monitors tend to form indiscriminate friendships, as long as they can keep their different types of friends, who impose different role demands, separate from one another. Segregation of friends with disparate values and attitudes allows high self-monitors to keep their varied roles separate. Because they interact with particular others only in limited ways, high self-monitors tend to form less intimate long-term relationships.

High self-monitors tend to see material items as props for roles they play. Hence, they are responsive to image-based advertisements, which emphasize how products appear to other persons. Marlboro cigarettes were marketed on the basis of the masculine look they created. Rolex watches are marketed as symbols of status and wealth. Products presented this way are attractive to high self-monitors. Low self-monitors respond to quality claims, which emphasize worth or value. Laundry detergents, for instance, not being of much use as props, are generally marketed on the basis of their effectiveness. Seeing clothes, haircuts, and jewelry as props for their self-presentations, high self-monitors are also much concerned with fashions.

Snyder explicitly used dramaturgical language in describing high self-monitors. According to Snyder, high self-monitors "treat interactions with others as dramatic performances designed to gain attention, make impressions, and at times entertain."[25] Low self-monitors, according to Snyder, are "unable or unwilling to engage in histrionics in social situations," nor do they "use dramatic performances to impress others or to gain their attention."

According to Snyder and others who have studied this issue, differing levels of willingness to give dramatic performances are not necessarily related either to mental health or to success in life. Although high self-monitors can be viewed as shallow, low self-monitors can be seen as rigid. Low and high self-monitors are equally likely to be mentally ill. High self-monitors tend to do well in positions that require skilled social performances in front of different groups, but low self-monitors may do better in jobs that are task-oriented.

In chapter 4, I argue that commonly used hypnotizability scales also measure differences in role-cue responsiveness. At the very least, those who are most hypnotizable—so-called hypnotic virtuosos—appear to be highly responsive to role cues of diverse kinds.[26] Such individuals are overrepresented among patients who present with the illness roles discussed in later chapters, such as grand hysteria, somatization disorder, and multiple personality.

People may play illness roles because they cannot meet their needs by being well. For example, many of Charcot's grand hysterics had nowhere to go outside the Salpêtrière and no way to gain attention and privileges within it except by acting the part of the grand hysteric. It must have been far from easy or pleasant to act this particular illness role (see chapter 5), which suggests the desperation these patients must have felt. More recent case histories, too, along with data cited in later chapters, show that patients with illness roles objectively lack other ways of meeting either their emotional or material needs. Illness roles meet these needs when no other means are available. Anthropological studies cited in chapter 3 show that illness roles in traditional cultures are often the province of those who lack power in their particular group. Most victims of possession illnesses, for example, are women in patriarchal tribal societies, who use their illness roles to gain concessions from men.

Theorists and researchers have pointed to a lack of options for meeting personal needs as an important factor causing depressed mood.[27] It comes as no surprise, then, that depressed mood is common in patients who enact illness roles. Case reviews of hysterical nineteenth-century patients show that depression was a prominent feature, as it is today in patients with somatization or multiple personality disorders (see chapters 6 and 7). Kleinman's observations of Chinese neurasthenics, together with anthropological studies in traditional societies (chapter 3), also show how depression and illness roles co-occur.[28] Significantly, Kleinman observed the responses of depressed neurasthenics treated with antidepressants. These patients' moods improved with antidepressant treatment, but not their illness behavior. Neurasthenic complaints were relieved only by changes in social situations so that these complaints no longer served a function. Similar findings with antidepressants have been described for depressed patients with somatization disorder, with multiple personality disorder, or with others of the syndromes discussed in later chapters. For example, antidepressants may relieve depressed mood in patients with somatization disorder, but they are unlikely to effectively curb care-seeking behavior in the absence of changes in the social setting.

Finally, many of the patients who present with illness roles in our society have features of antisocial, borderline, histrionic, or narcissistic personality disorders. These are the so-called cluster B personality disorders listed in the DSM-IV.[29] Cluster B personality disorders are all characterized by dramatic, overly emotional, and erratic behavior, and they often appear in mixed forms. Patients with these disorders are, to variable degrees, deceitful, manipulative, emotionally unstable, histrionic, and socially disinhibited. Some of them show vague, impressionistic styles of thinking.

Why do patients with illness roles tend to have cluster B traits? First, cluster B traits themselves may increase the chance that patients will take on illness roles. Manipulative and antisocial patients may gravitate toward illness enactments that are inherently deceitful (see chapter 8). Emotional lability, vague cognitive styles that render individuals blind to their own self-contradictions, histrionic tendencies, and disinhibition may make it easier to stage convincing illness performances. Alternatively, factors that produce cluster B traits may directly predispose to illness role enactments. A number of studies, for example, suggest that borderline and antisocial patients tend to have been raised in abusive families (see chapter 6), a factor that may also sharpen role-playing skills (see the discussion in this chapter).

Consistent with the hypothesis that particular types of persons tend to play illness roles, patients can be observed switching from one illness role to another in response to changing role cues. Instances of switching are cited in later chapters.

Human Behavior and Social Control

Responsiveness to social cues, social role enactments, lack of insight into effective causes, and role-induced attitude change together place human behavior under tight social control. The several examples of group-induced social roles that I have mentioned suggest that social control can lead to severe exploitation. The Rajneeshees, for instance, worked as agricultural laborers so that the Bhagwan could drive around in his Rolls Royces. The long, unpaid hours Moonies put in working have filled church coffers to overflowing. The residents of Jonestown, the Branch Davidians, and the members of Heaven's Gate and the Solar Temple supported their cults with their work and their personal wealth and eventually lost their lives.

The apparent disadvantages that accrue from social control of human behavior must be only part of the story. Given that social control of human behavior is part of evolved human nature, and not just a cultural artifact, then a willingness to follow social cues and to play social roles, a lack of real insight, and a tendency to vary attitudes with role changes must have been advantageous to ancestral humans. Two possible advantages readily come to mind.

The first advantage might lie in more efficient groups. That is, groups composed of persons who share attitudes and beliefs and who respond to one another's cues by enacting social roles might function more effectively than groups that are more fractious. Like humans today, ancestral humans lived in groups that competed for game, territory, and trophies of war. Better-functioning groups could have succeeded against less-effective groups, leading to the evolutionary strengthening of social control of behavior such as we see today.

Some evolutionary theorists doubt that behavior can evolve due to advantages conferred on social groups, as opposed to individuals.[30] Their reasoning is complex and need not concern us here. Suffice it to say that, given certain conditions, better functioning groups can confer advantages on those individuals who play contributing roles. The conditions that need to be present include honest negotiations for division of costs and benefit that accrue from playing roles, enforceable agreements, and freedom from coercion. These conditions may have been satisfied in human ancestral groups, at least a good part of the time.

Second, social control of behavior may have evolved because it reduces the risk that one will be harmed by others. Modern groups ostracize members who fail to behave as they are expected to or who espouse unpopular views. A famous study by Schachter illustrates this process.[31] Schachter assembled groups of college students to determine appropriate punishment for a juvenile delinquent dubbed Johnny Rocco. In each group, Schachter had three research confederates. One of the confederates was instructed to agree with the majority of the real subjects; a second, the "deviant," was instructed to take the opposite position; and a third, the "slider," was instructed to first oppose the majority of subjects and then to agree with them. Schachter observed that initially many of the subjects tried to change the deviant's mind by way of friendly arguments. As he resisted, however, the arguments became hostile and eventually ceased entirely, giving way to silent emnity. After the discussion, subjects were asked to rate how much they liked the confederates. They liked best the confederates who had always agreed with them. They liked the sliders somewhat less and the deviants least of all. When they were asked to pick members for future discussion groups, the subjects omitted the deviants from groups they considered important. The deviants had been ostracized for espousing unpopular views!

In chapter 4, I cite evidence that responsiveness to role cues may be increased in people raised in abusive environments. Growing up in a home with a threatening adult possibly sensitizes children to subtle social cues. Increased social responsiveness may be a way such children fade into the social woodwork. If, by way of example, a usually contrarian subject in the "Johnny Rocco" study realized that other group members were likely to physically harm him, rather than to just give him the cold shoulder, he might consider it prudent to better attend to their cues. Instead of ignoring the acerbic tone of their voices as they tried to change his mind, such a subject might begin to espouse their views. Janis and King's findings, moreover, suggest that the subject might come to believe in his new position.

The Biological Basis of Role Playing

Insofar as role-cue responsiveness is part of evolved human nature, then individual differences in responsiveness to such cues may have biological causes.

This hypothesis has both clinical and experimental support. Clinical support comes from studies of individuals who lack normal role-cue responsiveness, the most numerous of whom are those with schizoid or schizotypal personality disorders. These disorders belong in the "odd and eccentric" personality cluster, designated "cluster A" in the DSM-IV.[32] Schizoid individuals are socially aloof and unemotional. They lack the normal desire for intimacy with others, and they are usually indifferent to others' opinions of them. They frequently fail to notice or respond to social cues, and their behavior thus appears inept or self-absorbed. Schizotypal individuals are similar to schizoids, but their thinking is also magical and idiosyncratic. Failing to perceive or respond to social cues, they often strike others as stiff, cold, or withdrawn. Schizoid and schizotypal individuals are found in excess numbers in families of schizophrenics and sometimes go on themselves to develop outright psychoses, suggesting that these personality disorders result from the same genetic factors that produce schizophrenia. Schizotypal patients, moreover, have been shown to have visual tracking deficits like those observed in schizophrenics.[33] Visual tracking deficits are thought to reflect abnormalities in cerebral integration of sensory cues and movements.

Asperger's syndrome, which may be a mild form of infantile autism, is similar in some ways to schizoid or schizotypal personality disorder.[34] Unlike these disorders, though, it becomes evident early in childhood, is often associated with neurological symptoms or signs of slowed maturation of the nervous system, and is not found in excess in families of schizophrenics. Like schizoid and schizotypal individuals, patients with Asperger's syndrome show little appreciation for or use of emotional expressions, they prefer solitary activities to those involving others, and they generally are unresponsive to social cues from others. Their social behavior is thus exceedingly rigid. Apparently, more than one type of nervous system insult may result in loss of social-cue responsiveness.

Experimental evidence that role-cue responsiveness varies with brain function, or at least with genes, comes from studies of self-monitoring and hypnotizability. Self-monitoring, for example, is unrelated to social or economic class, regional, religious or ethnic origin, geographic mobility, or any other demographic variable. Such negative findings led Dworkin to study twin pairs to see whether genetic factors could help explain who becomes a high or low self-monitor.[35] Identical twins raised in their families of origin are alike in both their genes and their early environments. Fraternal twins raised in their families of origin are less alike in their genes but share the same early environment. Thus, if identical twins are more alike in self-monitoring than are fraternal twins, genetic factors are likely to be responsible. Dworkin found that identical twins were much more alike than fraternal twins, suggesting that levels of self-monitoring are determined in part by genes.

Gangestad performed a similar study, but, instead of studying raw scores on the self-monitoring scale, he studied the extent to which twin pairs fell into the same self-monitoring category, that is, the extent to which twin pairs were both either high or low self-monitors.[36] Ninety-five percent of 149 identical twin pairs were both either low or high self-monitors, compared with just 74 percent of 76 same-sex fraternal twin pairs. Only 55 percent of randomly formed pairs of subjects were both either high or low self-monitors. Inevitably, some twins who are thought to be identical on the basis of their appearance are really fraternal twins who just happen to look alike. Therefore, Gangestad separately studied identical twin pairs whose identical status had been confirmed by blood typing. Of these pairs of certain identical twins, 99 percent were both either high or low self-monitors.

There are several promising lines of research concerning the biological correlates of hypnotizability, but I will mention just one, which seems especially pertinent to the concerns of this book. Helen Crawford, an experimental psychologist, joined a long line of theorists, stretching back to the nineteenth-century, by positing that attention is the key to hypnotic phenomena.[37] Crawford and colleagues hypothesized that individuals who are readily hypnotized differ from those who are not susceptible to hypnosis by virtue of their greater ability to sustain focused attention on some stimuli while disattending to others. Focused attentional skills are thought to reflect brain functions.

Consistent with her hypothesis, Crawford and her coworkers observed that tasks that require heightened selective attention predicted hypnotizability scale scores. For example, so-called dichotic listening tasks require subjects to disattend to distracting or confusing information presented to them through one ear, while attending closely to information presented through the other. In Crawford's study, superior performances on dichotic listening tasks predicted hypnotizability scale scores.

A connection between hypnosis and focused attentional skills makes sense from a social-role viewpoint. Role enactments, as I have discussed, generally entail beliefs and attitudes. Therefore, quick changes in social roles require selective attention to current beliefs and attitudes, as opposed to beliefs and attitudes congruent with old roles. As the DSM-IV might put it, rapid wholehearted role changes involve "dissociating" the roles of just moments ago, and their attendant beliefs and attitudes, from the roles being played in the present. Focused attentional skills may be one of the factors that make hypnotizable subjects such facile responders to role cues (see chapter 4).

The frontal cerebral cortex plays an important role in selective attention.[38] Patients with damage to the frontal cerebral cortex show impaired concentration, heightened distractibility, and difficulty maintaining their attentional focus. Children with attention deficit disorder, who also lack normal ability to maintain an attentional focus, have been shown to have abnormalities of brain structures functionally connected with the frontal cortex.[39] These findings point to a dysfunction of the frontal cortical regions as the cause of this common disorder. Hypnotizable subjects, on the other hand, may show increased blood flow in prefrontal regions during hypnotic tasks.[40] Increases in cerebral blood flow accompany increases in neural activity. Thus, hypnotizable subjects may be invoking frontal-cortical selective-attentional processes in order to play the role of the hypnotized subject.

3

Anthropological and Historical Studies

Medical anthropologists and historians have described a number of "culture-bound" syndromes, disorders found only in certain cultures or during certain eras. Many of these appear to be illness roles. Since anthropologists and historians have long made a point of addressing the functions such illnesses serve, their study can help to illustrate how people use illness behavior. Several themes emerge with respect to these disorders. First, enactments of culture-bound syndromes are used to obtain attention and care that would otherwise not be forthcoming. They are also used to seek redress for grievances that cannot be stated directly. They may also serve as a ticket to membership in groups. Enactments of culture-bound syndromes may be used to excuse misbehavior or to gain relief from work and other burdens, and sometimes they are used to allow the patient to harm other people. Consistent with these functions, culture-bound syndromes are generally enacted by those who lack power to meet their needs more directly and by those who are not allowed to directly express their anger, hostility, or frustration, whether because of their station or because their society is decorous and strict.

I. M. Lewis on Possession Illness

I. M. Lewis, a cultural anthropologist, divides possession illness into two broad types: "Central" possession illnesses affect upper-class persons, especially upper-class males.[1] Possession by ancestor spirits or the spirits of group totems may mean the possessed has been chosen to become a "central" shaman, or channel, for such spirits. Central shamans command great respect and authority. By contrast, "peripheral" possession illnesses, which illustrate several aspects of illness roles in general, affect mainly lower-class men and women in socially stratified societies or women of any class in highly patriarchal societies, and they are attributed to mischievous or malign spirits. In these cases, rather than being chosen, victims are thought to be made susceptible to possession by frustrations in their lives or family relationships. Health is restored through treatments by "peripheral" shamans, who, having been possessed by the same malign spirits, have learned to communicate with them. Although less influential than central shamans, peripheral shamans are credited with expertise in dealing with particular spirits. The treatment aim is not just to exorcise spirits but to strenghten the victim's resistance by alleviating frustrations.

According to Lewis, the victim of peripheral possession benefits from his or her illness in three distinct ways. First, the possessing spirit often voices complaints and accusations on the victim's behalf or even attacks those who have angered the victim. The victim is held blameless for saying and doing things that are strictly forbidden except in the grip of possession. Second, treatment of possession necessitates that concessions be made to the victim in order to bolster his or her resistance to spirit possession. Thus, the complaints and accusations voiced by possessing spirits are likely to be acted on in some way or another. Finally, many victims go on to experience further possessions, which makes them eligible for membership in healing cults that offer them social support. Those who learn to control and even to summon spirits go on to become shamans, assuring themselves of important positions in their community.

To illustrate these points, Lewis cites the case of Somali women, who are prone to possession by malevolent spirits called *sars* (or elsewhere, *zars*).[2] Somalis believe that *jinns*, of which *sars* are but one example, are constantly lurking about looking for human victims, possession of whom will provide them with access to luxury foods, perfumes, and consumer goods. Women are the most common victims of these spirits. The typical victim is married and struggling to provide the basic necessities of life to her children. Her husband is often absent or inattentive to her, and he may favor his other wives. Her ability to complain is sharply circumscribed by her husband's ability to divorce her whenever he wants. According to Lewis, most cases of *sar* possession follow identifiable stresses in married life, such as a husband's move to take an additional wife.

When possessed by *sars*, Somali women demand clothes, perfume, food, and other considerations. They require ritual dances ("beating the *sar*") directed by female shamans from the local *sar* cult. These are expensive and time consuming and may yield only temporary relief. Most husbands pay for these rituals and modify somewhat their treatment of a possessed wife, but if a woman has been possessed several times before, their patience may wear thin. In such a case, they try to cure the victim by beating her, which Lewis states may be effective, or threaten divorce. Apparently, some Somali wives who want a divorce can obtain it only by driving their husbands away by claiming repeatedly to be possessed.

According to Lewis, Somali men are not entirely unaware of the way their women use possession and, hence, negotiate with them regarding such illnesses. He recounts the story of the wife of a well-to-do man who, whether to have a good party or to vex her husband, spent a good deal of his money mounting a curative ritual for her possession illness. The following day, when his wife was out of the house, her husband sold her gold and silver jewelry and used the proceeds to mount a feast for some local holy men.

When his wife returned to the house, she found the door barred and heard loud hymns from inside. After the feast, her husband explained that he had suddenly been taken ill and had had to sell her jewelry to entertain holy men who would pray for him. She promised never again to "beat the *sar*" with his money, and he promised never again to entertain holy men at her expense.

Sar possession is widespread in the Middle East.[3] It has been described in Ethiopia, where it is believed to have originated, in the Sudan, Egypt, other parts of North Africa, and the Arabian Gulf. In all these areas, relatively powerless wives apparently use illnesses ascribed to *sars* in order to gain concessions from their husbands. Among Ethiopian Christians, the disease is known as "creditor," for the debts husbands incur to cure it, and in the Egyptian countryside it is called the "excuse," since victims are excused from their routine chores. In Khartoum, the Sudanese capital, malignant *sar* spirits are known to caustically criticize husbands in terms that would not be accepted if they came from the victims themselves.

Lewis cites other examples of peripheral possession illnesses outside the Muslim world. Among Kamba tribesmen in Africa, for example, mischievous spirits from neighboring tribes or from Europe are thought to cause women's disorders.[4] Affected women speak in what are thought to be foreign tongues and demand gifts and attention from men. The specific gifts required vary somewhat with the provenance of the possessing spirit. Swahili spirits demand embroidered hats, while European spirits require items identified with Europe.[5] These spirits are known to increase the wardrobes of their victims. One woman with cravings for meat could obtain her husband's consent to slaughter an animal only by becoming possessed with a meat-craving spirit. In Tanzania, Swahili women are prone to so-called devil's disease, which is attributed to spirit possession.[6] As in the Kamba tribe, the spirits indicate their foreign provenance by the kinds of gifts they demand. Treatment consists of expensive curative ritual dances, and a shaman must also move in with the victim's family. Not only is attention thus focused on the wife, but also the family's treatment of her is altered.

The Swahili of southern Kenya recognize possession illnesses triggered by marital conflict.[7] Afflicted women are treated with ritual exorcisms, in the process of which male spirits voice demands for goods. Gifts that were refused when the wife requested them may be granted when requested by spirit voices. Husbands are bound by custom to make good on promises made to spirits. The Luo people of Kenya recognize foreign spirits that afflict unhappy women.[8] These spirits are held responsible for everything from constipation to more flagrant disorders. Treatment consists of ritual dancing and feasting, during which female shamans summon the spirit responsible to find out its demands. Sometimes victims live briefly with the treating shaman, thus enjoying a respite from the stresses of family life. Spirits are not expelled but merely brought under control, and, victims may quickly relapse if they are not treated well.

Syndromes like these are found in Asia, too. As many as 20 percent of

Havik Brahmin women in the state of Mysore in India are diagnosed with possession at some point in their lives.[9] Women are thought to be prone to possession because they are weak and because spirits are attracted by their beauty. Since the status of Brahmin women is secured by fertility, it comes as no surprise that possession illnesses occur most often among young brides, who have not yet borne children and among women past childbearing age. Possessing spirits demand expensive curative rituals, along with some consideration for the victim. Since the illness is considered likely to relapse, possession ensures that the victim will receive greater attention and consideration than would otherwise be the case. In Sri Lanka, women are prone to possession by demons that state demands on their behalf.[10] Historical records show that spirit possession occurred in Japan during the Heian period (784–1185).[11] Once again, the victims were women, especially concubines or second wives, and the possessing spirits gave voice to their domestic complaints. Yap, a Chinese psychiatrist, showed that possession syndromes seen in modern Hong Kong conform to the same general pattern: Being possessed by spirits serves the victims' interests in difficult situations.[12]

As I have noted, peripheral possession also occurs in lower-class men in socially stratified societies and serves much the same functions that it does for women. In this regard, Lewis cites Mafia Island, off the coast of Africa.[13] Mafia Island is peopled by several ethnic groups, which occupy different positions in a status hierarchy. The least powerful group is the indigenous Pokomo tribe, while the more powerful groups claim an Arabian heritage. Pokomos are excluded from governmental and Islamic offices but not from their own spirit cults. Both men and women are prone to possession by "land spirits," or *shaitani*, which cause illnesses with varied presentations. Pokomo shamans diagnose and treat such illnesses and initiate victims into their healing cults. Those members of healing cults who rise to the rank of shaman are guaranteed status and influence and often become wealthy. Mafia Island women from higher-status groups are also prone to possession, but not by Pokomo *shaitani*. Instead, they are afflicted by Arabic-speaking spirits that come from across the sea. The upper-class women most prone to possession are those whose positions are insecure; their treatment is expensive and requires that concessions be made to them. A woman's spirit society arranges the treatment rituals and provides victims with fellowship and status.

Upper-class men may also be afflicted by peripheral spirits, but the disorder is then attributed to witchcraft, rather than to the victims' weak defenses. This pattern of attribution, in which personal weakness is held responsible for illness enactments by women while external circumstances are held responsible for the same symptoms in men, was also evident with respect to hysteria, during the nineteenth-century (see chapter 5). The witches, of course, are those women, and sometimes lower-class men, who as spirit familiars have specialized in treating peripheral possession illnesses. If they can cast spirits out, the reasoning goes, they can as easily cause them to seek a new victim. According to Lewis, witchcraft accusations are used to control the behavior of overly aggressive shamans in the peripheral cults, who are effectively leaders of subversive movements. The Somali *sar* healer, for instance, can be seen as colluding with victims to gain concessions from men. She diagnoses possession, interprets the spirits, if need be, to state the victims' demands, insists that husbands and fathers shoulder exorbitant costs, and even encourages victims to join the spirit cult, thereby ensuring a threat of recurrent possesion. Swahili specialists in the treatment of devil's disease move into the victim's household and serve as her advocate. Mafia Island shamans in the upper-class women's cult meet every Friday with victims and parody male activities, including religious rites that occur in the mystical brotherhoods to which upper-class men belong. When an upper-class man is thought to be afflicted by a peripheral spirit, then, in addition to whatever steps are taken against the suspected witch, ritual exorcisms are mounted to cure the disorder. Here there is no question of learning to live with the spirit, which is not of the proper class.

In the following sections, I describe selected culture-bound syndromes in greater detail. In each case, a thorough analysis of the context in which these illness enactments occur reveals their social functions.

The *Negi Negi* Syndrome

In a famous paper, Langness, an anthropologist, described the *negi negi* syndrome as it occurs among the Bena Bena tribesmen of the Eastern Highland region of New Guinea.[14] Langness notes that forms of temporary insanity essentially identical to *negi negi* are widely distributed among Highland tribes and in coastal New Guinea, suggesting that the syndrome is part of a cultural complex that the Bena Bena share with other peoples. A few anthropologists have suggested that these illnesses result from ingestion of plant toxins indigenous to the region, but Langness notes that the evidence for this is scarce and that there is reason to disbelieve it. Among the Bena Bena, for example, *negi negi* is limited to males, but, in some neighboring tribes, syndromes like *negi negi* appear in women as well.

Bena Bena tribesmen, of whom there were approximately 14,000 at the time Langness visited them, are identified by their language. They live in a remote region that was believed uninhabited until 1930 and that was isolated from the outside world until after World War II, when a town and coffee plantations were established. There are no large-scale Bena Bena political or administrative groups; instead, the people live in villages with 50 to 300 inhabitants, where they survive by horticulture and by raising pigs. Warfare is endemic, and males are subjected to painful initiations. Marriages are polygynous, and ancestor worship is practiced. Physical illnesses are attributed to sorcery, and mental illnesses are attributed to ghosts of the recently dead, who are greatly feared. Bena Bena tribesmen refuse to go out alone at night for fear of ghost attacks.

Negi negi occurs in men between the ages of 22 and 32, and it is understood to be caused by an attack by ghosts, which is related to but different from possession in the usual sense. Consistent with the notion that ghosts are responsible for this syndrome, it often appears when recent deaths have occured in the subclan to which the victim belongs. The episodes start at night and may extend into the next day, but they do not last longer than 24 hours. The afflicted person reports losing his hearing at the beginning of the illness, but he later regains it when he has recovered. In fact, *negi negi* means both deaf and insane in the local language. Langness describes several episodes of *negi negi*, which give a good picture of how it is manifested. The first case Langness described, which he witnessed himself, occured in a 30-year-old man named Abio. After hearing a woman's cry, Langness observed Abio run silently toward his kinsmen, making threatening gestures with a wooden club. Four men were required to wrestle him to the ground, and he made repeated efforts to escape until he was bound with vines. According to Langness, Abio's eyes appeared glazed, his skin was cold, and his breath was deep and panting. He appeared not to understand or hear others, even when they crept up behind him and shouted in his ear. After a while, Abio was able to sit up, but he remained mute. When untied, he leaped to his feet, ran off, and then returned, brandishing a stick. Then he ran through a garden and disappeared in the dark. What Langness called "insane cackling" could be heard near the village. Once again, Abio appeared, carrying a large stick. He ran round and round a group of villagers, sometimes reversing himself and running backward for no apparent reason. While running, he held himself very straight, with his arms hanging down at his sides. This went on for about half an hour, until he started running backward and forward and running in one spot with his legs raised high. At the end, Abio fell over backward, striking his head on the ground. After 10 minutes of immobility, he sat up and took a cigarette. Although he was still dazed, the villagers divined that the attack had ended. When questioned the next day, Abio seemed very nervous. Rather than join the other men in the communal garden, he stayed close to home and spent the day mending a fence. He gave no explanation of what had occurred the night before, nor was he concerned that he would be held responsible. Later, he explained that he had been walking on a path by the cemetery when he saw the ghost of a recently deceased kinswoman. The ghost spoke to him and suggested they go off together. When he objected, a sudden wind hit his ears, making him lose his hearing. The ghost then got into his big toe, making him *negi negi*.

Men with *negi negi* often attack their wives and children. One man, for instance, had an episode of *negi negi* after seeing the ghost of his recently deceaséd nephew. The ghost wanted to walk with him, and, when he refused, hit him on the ears, making him *negi negi*. In this state, he tore down the wooden door on the house of one of his wives, dragged her out by the legs, and demanded that his clansmen have intercourse with her. When they did not respond, he pointed to his three-year-old son and loudly declaimed, "He is not my son; take him away and throw him in the treetops. Throw him in the water." This particular victim had had previous episodes, as had his father before him.

Langness cites several aspects of male Bena Bena life that he believes are relevant to this syndrome. Severally and together, they suggest that young Bena Bena men who are susceptible to *negi negi* are subjected to extreme achievement and family pressures but are prevented by strong social mores from giving voice to their frustrations or hostility. The *negi negi* syndrome serves as a means for expressing otherwise taboo feelings without fear of retribution. Many of the pressures that impinge on young men are related to their need to become what they call *oropavoyave* or, later, "men with names." *Oropavoyave* are men, ages 30 to 50, who have completed the last of many initiation rites, have taken at least one wife and possibly raised children, have their own houses and gardens, and have started paying back monies lent to them by the clan to buy their brides and pigs. They must participate in the pig exchange, be successful gardeners, and have proven themselves responsible and influential clan members. In addition to being *oropavoyave*, so-called men with names have earned prestige in war. Success in war, which boys are taught to value from an early age, is thought by the Bena Bena to depend on arduous rituals. To become *oropavoyave* and, hence, to later have a name, young men must also pay for ritual feasts, contribute to funeral expenses if the deceased is related, and maintain their families in an appropriate manner.

Marriage customs, too, place pressure on young men. The clan buys brides for 17- to 23-year-olds, but, because of a year-long avoidance taboo following betrothal as well as other delays demanded by custom, the marriages are unlikely to be consummated until the man is at least 23. During the waiting period, young men are excluded from the life of the group. Sometimes they are even sent to neighboring villages or must live in the bush near their own. Since women raise the pigs and do the heavy gardening work, such as clearing and breaking the ground, men cannot have large gardens and many pigs—essential to their becoming *oropavoyave*—unless they have at least one and preferably two hard-working wives. Unless he is fortunate enough to inherit a wife or to find one at bargain rates, a man may go deeply in debt in order to marry twice.

Young men without names, who are not *oropavoyave*, are subject to public shamings by their elders. According to Langness, a young man who dares to argue with an elder male is told, "You are not a man. You don't have pigs and gardens. You don't have a name. When you do, then you can talk; until then, be quiet." Elders control the clan pursestrings, and young men are forced to plead with them if they want any money. Expression of anger toward elders is, of course, strictly taboo.

To show how these pressures provide the background for *negi negi*, Langness gave an account of Abio's situation at the time he fell ill. Abio was having problems getting his way with his wives. He was infatuated with his senior wife, but she had borne no children. His clan, who disliked her, suspected her of eating a local plant believed to prevent conception. Because she was not a good worker, she threatened Abio's efforts to become *oropavoyave*. Abio had inherited his second wife from his brother, who had died while working on the coast. Abio disliked her, but she had borne him a son, who was five years old at the time. More recently, he had avoided intercourse with her, paid her little attention, and failed to care for her in the customary fashion. Other clan males wanted Abio to divorce her so that they could marry her themselves, a fertile female being extremely valuable to the clan, but Abio could not make up his mind to do so. At the time of his illness, Abio wanted to take his son away from his mother and move the boy into the house he shared with his first wife. Public opinion, however, prevented his making this move.

If this impasse was not bad enough, Abio was also under material stress. In spite of the fact that he was not caring for his second wife, he was making little progress toward becoming established. Because of his first wife's deficiencies, he owned few pigs, the measure of wealth among the Bena Bena. Also, his five-year-old son was overdue for a *yapifana*, an expensive ceremony in honor of a child that requires that gifts be given to one of the mother's brothers. Performing obligations like the *yapifana* are obligatory for a man who wishes to become *oropavoyave*. Men who do not perform this particular ceremony are considered rubbish by friends and relatives. Also, only a month before Abio's episode of *negi negi*, the wife of one of his kinsmen had unexpectedly died. Abio's relation to this kinsman was such that his own status had required him to help put on the funeral. He had spent much of his time preparing the funeral feast and had had to kill two of his pigs as his contribution. The gifts he dispensed to guests, however, were somewhat niggardly and had brought some shame upon him.

Shortly before the illness witnessed by Langness, the New Guinea government had levied a corvée on Abio's village. People were told to grow coffee and to work on the roads. They were forced to build new houses and give up some of their customs. Rumors were spread that a government counselor was going to seize their land. Villagers, including Abio, were making plans to kill this counselor, and it was on the way to a meeting of conspirators that Abio became *negi negi*.

Langness's portrait of Abio is of a man caught in a web of stifling social demands. Desperate to be *oropavoyave*, he was sinking under his various ritual obligations. His son was getting old for a *yapifana,* and he had been shamed by the cheapness of his funeral gifts. He was under enormous pressure to give up his second wife, which he could not decide to do, but he could not take his son from her and live with his first wife, either. His first wife, whom he loved, was disliked by his kinsmen. In the meantime, he was enmeshed in a dangerous plot. In spite of the fact that his wives and clansmen were blocking his moves, taboos prevented his voicing his frustration. The *negi negi* syndrome provided him a way of voicing his animosity in a stylized fashion for which he could not be blamed.

Some peripheral possession illnesses described by I. M. Lewis also permitted displays of otherwise taboo hostility.[15] As described earlier, these illnesses occur among women in male-dominated societies or among lower-class men in highly stratified groups. Among the Bena Bena, very young men are accorded considerable freedom; they encounter the kinds of pressures Langness enumerated only in their twenties, when they marry and settle down. At this stage of life they are subordinate to their elders, toward whom they must show deference. Hence, the men who become *negi negi* are the subordinate men in an age-graded society. But *negi negi* differs from illnesses described by Lewis in certain important respects. First, *negi negi* is understood to be transient. Langness gives no indication that specialized shamanic treatments are given to men with this syndrome, nor are there specialized cults these men are entitled to join. The illness, in other words, does not permanently mark a man or provide entrée into a counterculture. This difference may result from the fact that young Bena Bena men are subordinate only because of their age. Since they will one day rise to higher status positions, becoming themselves *oropavoyave* and men with names, they have no need to find alternative social groups in which they are better positioned. Langness specifically notes that, having been *negi negi*, Bena Bena men can still achieve high status. One man who was *negi negi* on three separate occasions later became a traditional leader of his clan. Second, the possession illnesses described by Lewis not only give victims permission to express hostility but also confer material rewards and special privileges. Langness gives no indication that comparable largesse or privileges accrue from an episode of *negi negi*. The Bena Bena, however, may implicitly understand that men who become *negi negi* must receive wider berth than men who more reliably suppress their aggressive impulses. In spite of its stylized quality, *negi negi* aggression is genuinely frightening, not only to women and children but also to Bena Bena men. Langness cites examples of men running off to hide from those who were *negi negi*. Consistent with this hypothesis, the cases cited by Langness show that *negi negi* is likely to recur. In spite of the fact that its cause is thought to be ghost attacks, men who become *negi negi* may become so again.

Abio himself suffered no further attacks in the time that Langness observed him, a period of 13 months after the night described. Whether or not his episode of *negi negi* contributed, Abio's social problems came to a climax and were resolved. After Abio abandoned his second wife, refusing to provide her with the minimal assistance customs required, she and his first wife fought, resulting in injuries to both. Family members and villagers took one side or the other, and Abio nearly came to blows with his father. For this he was severely chastised by clan elders. After a brief period during which Abio retreated from social activities, the second wife was forced to return to her native village. She left behind her son for Abio to raise. When Langness last observed him, Abio seemed well adjusted and was once again taking an active part in the clan.

Finally, Langness noted that, at the time of his writing, episodes of *negi negi* had become less common as areas in which the Bena Bena lived were increasingly controlled by the government. Under governmental control, young men subjected to intolerable family and clan pressures can leave the village for a while, or even permanently. Some young men, for instance, take jobs on the coast, while others move to town or visit neighboring clans. Also, the decline of interclan warfare has lowered the premium accorded group solidarity, so expressing hostility within clans has become more acceptable. Finally, greater safety while traveling and new gender mores make it easier for unhappy wives to return to their home villages, thus ameliorating the chronic marital feuds that previously contributed to the incidence of *negi negi*.

Latah

The *negi negi* syndrome provides an escape hatch for the expression of feelings that are normally taboo among the Bena Bena. In this respect, *negi negi* resembles certain possession illnesses cited by Lewis. Similar functions seem to be served by two disorders that have intrigued ethnologists studying Malay peoples, *latah* and *amok*. Since *amok* is quite complex, I address only *latah*.[16] However, before discussing *latah* and the purposes it might serve, I briefly describe certain pertinent features of Malay culture.

The Malays attach an extreme value to social propriety. According to Clifford Geertz, Malay life is governed by broad distinctions between what the Javanese call *allus* and *kasar* modes of behavior.[17] *Allus* behavior is courtly and aristocratic. A person is said to be *allus* insofar as he is stringently correct in his speech and behavior, is sensitive to the needs and desires of others, and avoids expressing differences of opinion. *Kasar* behavior violates rules of etiquette, is insensitive to others, or is crude or graphic. *Kasar* behavior also signifies lower-class status. A person is said to be *kasar* insofar as he is crude, fails to observe etiquette, is obtuse to the wishes of others, or openly disagrees. Children are taught at an early age to aspire to *allus* behavior. According to Geertz and others, the dominant theme in Malay socialization practices is to inhibit children's aggressive impulses.[18] Children are taught not to voice differences of opinion or negative feelings toward others. Independent action is overtly discouraged. Obedience, submissiveness, and dependence on social groups are highly rewarded, instead.

In socializing their children, Malays rely on a sense of induced shame and shyness, referred to as *mendapat malu*. Children learn that *kasar* behavior of any kind, and especially expressions of opinions or hostility, will be followed by feelings of shame. Several authors connect the Malay reliance on punishment (an induced sense of shame) for acculturation of children with the curious lack of initiative noted in Malay adults.[19] That is, not having been rewarded for virtuous social behavior but only punished for infringements of social codes, Malays see little hope for improving their social position through their own positive efforts. Of course, all cultures consider some behaviors appropriate and others inappropriate. But ethnographers see the Malays as being extreme in their emphasis on social propriety. These ethnographic impressions are confirmed by linguistic analyses. Osgood and colleagues, for instance, performed a semantic analysis of adjectives applied to 100 common nouns by speakers of 22 unrelated languages, one of which was Malay.[20] Consistent with the emphasis they place on appropriateness, the Malays alone applied a "proper-improper" dimension to these 100 nouns. Carr, who studied *amok*, notes that Malays are faced with "the constant task" of discriminating between proper and improper behaviors and interactions.[21]

Latah is a woman's disorder that occurs among the Malays and related peoples.[22] Though the Europeans who first saw it considered *latah* insanity, Malays themselves consider it less an illness than an amusing idiosyncracy. Children, for instance, sometimes entertain themselves by tickling or frightening *latah* victims, which elicits symptoms from them, or play at having symptoms of *latah* themselves. Ethnographic reports show that Malay hosts are willing to induce symptoms in victims of *latah* in order to show them to interested observers. No harm is seen resulting from *latah* behaviors.

However, in spite of their seeming complacence about it, the Malays explain *latah* in a way that suggests that they see it as less than healthy. The Malay theory of mind invokes a force or substance referred to as *semangat*, depletion of which in women can lead to *latah* symptoms. Plants, animals, and even inanimate objects are said to have *semangat*. *Semangat* makes people vital; its loss produces malaise and may even lead to death. *Semangat* is lowered by poor social relationships, by conflict, by lack of equanimity, or by sudden frights. Sudden frights, in particular, are considered responsible for cases of *latah*. Women and children are thought to have less *semangat* than men and hence to be more susceptible to becoming depleted.

Aspects of *latah* are also closely connected with Malay possession theories. Along with its other effects, depletion of *semangat* renders victims susceptible to hostile spirit intrusions. Hostile and amoral spirits are thought to be responsible for explicitly sexual dreams, which are an important symptom of *latah*, as well as for the repetitive use of obscene words and gestures. Thus, *latah* appears in part a possession illness similar to those described in the previous section.

Victims of *latah* are generally older women of middle to lower socioeconomic status. The symptoms include seemingly automatic imitative behaviors, obscene gestures and utterances, and automatic obedience to the commands of others. Victims typically repeat the Malay terms for male and female genitals, words no proper Malay woman would ever utter. Other victims publicly masturbate during their episodes. Symptoms are episodic; they are triggered by frightening or startling events, by emotional stimulation, or by being prodded or tickled. Flareups can last for seconds or a few hours. Some women claim to be unconscious during their episodes, but most simply claim to have no control over their actions. The episodes never occur when victims are alone. *Latah* victims also report vivid sexual dreams, both before their illness and after it has developed. Such dreams are thought to play a causative role in the illness, though sadness, shame, and worry are also credited.

Latah victims often are also depressed or anxious. For example, as part of a comprehensive survey of mental illness in Sarawak, one of the states located on the island of Borneo, Chiu and colleagues questioned *latah* victims concerning psychosomatic and psychiatric complaints.[23] Ethnic Malay victims reported poor appetite, weakness, shortness of breath, forgetfulness, stomach disorders, and feelings of lack of accomplishment. Ethnic Iban victims, members of a group that migrated to Sarawak some five hundred years ago, reported trembling hands, sweating and anxiety, and feelings of being hot or of being threatened or a sense that life is not worth living. Chiu and colleagues believed that these various symptoms point toward anxiety and depression. Consistent with the importance of general demoralization, personal difficulties, such as the death of a child, are known to contribute to onset of *latah*.

Yap described some cases of *latah* that illustrate both its features and its variability.[24] One 70-year-old poverty-stricken woman, for instance, had played at *latah* as a child but did not develop symptoms until she was 50 years old, after the death of her daughter. Both her maternal grandmother and her younger sister had experienced *latah* symptoms. Her attacks of *latah* could be triggered by poking her in the ribs. During an attack, she repeated words and phrases in Malay, Chinese, and English, the last of which she could not understand, and frequently interjected the Malay word for "vagina." She imitated movements, such as tapping a ruler, as well as facial expressions. She showed automatic obedience when she was told to dance, and she was ready to hand over her jewelry to Yap, except that her son intervened. Her symptoms and excitement seemed to tire her out. She reported that being worried worsened her attacks.

A second woman, age 50, was married to the village teacher, by whom she had three children. She differed from most cases in needing no stimulation to show symptoms, instead being more or less in a permanent *latah* state. When examined, she repeated Malay words spoken to her emphatically, and she echoed a sentence in English, which she did not understand. Her speech was interrupted by frequent interjections. When handed a cigarette, she uttered the Malay terms for male and female organs. She showed automatic obedience, going so far as to hit herself forcefully as instructed, but sometimes she did the opposite of what she was told to do. Her husband believed that if she were told to do so, she would quite readily attack someone with a knife. When the examiner tossed a matchbox at her, she immediately threw it back. When the examiner blew cigarette smoke from his mouth, she imitated the movements. She mimicked hand movements and movements of the tongue and face. Intense symptomatic periods were sometimes followed by faintness, or even apparent unconsciousness, from which she was revived by splashing her with water. Her family sheltered her from unwanted noise or excitement; her activities were limited to light household tasks.

The automatic obedience seen during *latah* episodes is reminiscent of the hypnotic role. Hypnotized subjects are expected to act on suggestions; their doing so leads some authors to claim they are particularly suggestible (see chapter 4). Having observed automatic obedience in Indonesia, Nathan Kline inferred that women with *latah* are also hypersuggestible.[25] In chapter 4, I note that the hypothesis as applied to hypnosis borders on circular thinking and that, insofar as it can be tested, it has proved inconsistent with empirical findings. Kline's hypothesis concerning *latah* obedience encounters at least the same logical difficulties.

Two aspects of *latah* suggest its possible functions in the setting of Malay society. First, according to some observers, *latah* derives from a Malay strategem for dealing with one's superiors that has been adapted by socially marginal women.[26] By imitating superiors, the Malay ostensibly opts out from the onerous burden of maintaining proper decorum. As we have seen, this burden is especially heavy in Malay society, which is exceedingly sensitive to matters of social propriety, and it is heaviest for social subordinates. The early ethnographic accounts of *latah* described its occurrence in servants of Europeans.[27] Europeans were more likely to notice those cases that occurred, so to speak, under their noses, but even those cases that occurred in native villages were observed by early colonists to develop in women in the lowest classes. The native aristocracy did not then and still does not manifest *latah* symptoms. As for obscenities, since *kasar* behavior is seen as a sign of lower-class status, those who are clearly subordinate have less to lose from showing it than those who maintain some pretensions. Therefore, uttering obscene words and making obscene gestures are ways of announcing a break with social pretense altogether.

As most children know, imitation and obscene language can be ways of expressing hostility. Lewis described a syndrome called *olon*, which occurs among Tungus tribesmen and which closely resembles *latah*, except that the hostile aspect is still less covert.[28] Like *latah*, *olon* is attributed to having been suddenly frightened; *olon* is a Tungus word that refers to fright. The victims are usually young women, but men are affected, as well. The affected individual compulsively utters obscenities, especially when custom requires restrained behavior, and also compulsively imitates words and actions in such a way as to ridicule the persons from whom they are copied. Lewis recounts the story of the Third (Tungus) Battalion of the TransBaikal Cossacks. While being berated by its Russian colonel, members of the battalion began to repeat all of his orders and gestures, and finally his obscene curses. Lewis did not report how this incident ended.

Second, Michael Kenny noted that *latah* behavior stakes a claim to childishness and dependency.[29] He cites the case of a woman who lived with her daughter and son-in-law after her husband's death. Being dependent and sexually inactive, she had become, in a sense, child to her own child. Her *latah* behaviors were treated in the same way as children's *faux pas*. The Malays explicitly draw a connection between *latah* and children who know no better than to violate social codes. In this respect, *latah* is one kind of false dementia, or second childhood, that is assumed by marginalized and dependent older women. Consistent with this notion, several of the cases described by Yap and Chiu suggest that typical symptoms occur in conjunction with others that suggest mental impairment.[30] The motives for feigning incompetence may be to enforce caretaking, to excuse oneself from onerous household tasks or from the demands of social propriety, or to express hostility and defiance without incurring blame. The Malays neglect of *latah*, and even their amusement by it, appears from this point of view to parallel Western folk attitudes toward the mild mental impairments commonly seen in the elderly. That is, both are seen as normal idiosyncracies at a late stage of life.

Acute Psychoses in Africa

Transient acute psychoses are more common in Africa than in most Western countries. E. A. Guinness, who served as a psychiatrist for the Swaziland Government Health Services between 1982 and 1987, published two studies and numerous case histories that illustrate the functions served by transient psychotic enactments in a modern African country.[31] Swaziland is a small, homogeneous country of fewer than one million persons. It is bordered by Mozambique and South Africa. The Swazis have long been a pastoral people, but, more recently, able-bodied workers have migrated to the towns in order to earn cash incomes. The old, the young, and the handicapped have been left behind. Swazis live in large extended family units. Women are usually subservient, and marriages can be polygamous. As in other African cultures, ancestors are revered, and their spirits are consulted concerning misfortunes or illness. Troubles are sometimes attributed to the actions of charms and witches. Traditional healers continue to play an important role, especially in mental disorders. Swazis who have moved to urban areas, where the old customs are weak and the comfort of family is missing, are likely to suffer from culture shock or alienation.

According to Guinness, adolescents and young adults have suffered the most from changes in Swazi society. Those attending Western-style schools in the late 1980s were the first in their families to obtain other than traditional educations. Many extended families in modern-day Swaziland have scrimped and sacrificed to educate their youngsters, and they have correspondingly high expectations of what the children will achieve. Yet, the schools, which offer instruction in English, mete out corporal punishments, and emphasize test performance, are difficult for most students. Although 80 percent of school-age children enter the primary system, only half enter secondary school, and fewer than a sixth achieve higher levels of education. A child who fails a class must repeat it later, thereby adding to the financial burden on his or her family. Perhaps because of the pressures and anxieties they face, students worry about evil charms or witches. They fear that spells may be cast on their books or food or that magical forces may lower their test scores. Epidemic hysterias occuring in student groups are attributed to bewitchment.

In his first paper, Guinness reported on the psychiatric diagnoses of 178 mentally ill Swazi adolescents and young adults who were still in school or had been in school less than a year before. These students were identified through community case-finding methods and by reviews of hospital admission records. Four syndromes were found to be common in students: depressive neurosis, the so-called brain fag syndrome, what Guinness called "hysteria" and panic, and brief reactive psychosis. "Brief reactive psychosis" is the former term for what the most recent Diagnostic and Statistical Manual (DSM-IV) calls "brief psychotic disorder."[32] Depression was diagnosed on the basis of sleep and appetite changes, social withdrawal, anhedonia, and suicidal thoughts. Subjective confusion was prominent. Like individuals in other non-Western societies, Swazi students generally denied mood symptoms per se. Some complained that their hearts were sore or that their souls were ebbing, and others reported feeling that bad things would happen soon. Many affected students thought they had been bewitched. Fewer than half the students diagnosed with depression had that disorder alone. Most of them also had brain fag, or at least some symptoms of it; one-third presented with symptoms of an acute psychosis; and one-sixth had hysterical symptoms as well as depression.

Brain fag, hysteria and panic, and brief reactive psychosis appear to be closely related.[33] These syndromes resemble one another in their symptom pictures; they occur in similar social settings; and, like depression, they are blamed on witches or charms. Brain fag, a disorder diagnosed in many African countries, resembles neurasthenia and chronic fatigue syndrome, which are discussed at length in chapter 4. Guinness's patients with brain fag reported headaches, abdominal and chest pains, fatigue, palpitations, tremulousness, and light-headedness. The latter symptoms, of course, suggest some degree of anxiety. Concentration was poor, and victims slept in class. Most victims complained of vision and hearing problems, which interfered with their work. Brain fag symptoms often developed before exams but in some cases lasted for years once they had developed. Brain fag also appeared following other stressors, such as family problems, illness, or disagreements. Once brain fag appeared, school performance suffered, and many victims eventually left school because of the disorder.

"Hysteria" and panic presented in two forms. The simplest form of the disorder, characterized by screaming or chanting while wildly running about in response to apparent auditory or visual hallucinations, occurred sporadically or in epidemics. Sporadic cases followed difficult situations. Victims often collapsed in exhaustion after attacks. The more complex form presented with pseudoseizures, which were sometimes difficult to distinguish from genuine seizures, confusion, frightening hallucinations, symbolic automatisms such as destruction of school books, fugue-like wandering, and conversion symptoms, such as paralysis or inability to swallow. Terror and shortness of breath suggested panic attacks, and the whole syndrome followed social precipitants. More than 80 percent of hysterical patients had longstanding symptoms of brain fag, and a third had depressive symptoms. Hysterical syndromes differed from brief reactive psychoses mainly in that they lasted just a few hours, while reactive psychoses lasted a week or more, and were of lesser intensity than the reactive psychoses.

Students diagnosed with brief reactive psychoses were violent or fright-ened. They stripped off their clothes, started fires, destroyed objects, or smeared feces. Their speech was often pressured, and they seemed confused. Some chanted nonsensically, while others expressed fears of magical influ-ences. Many seemed to be having frightening hallucinations. Psychoses de-veloped abruptly following stressful events and lasted on average two weeks, with only 12 percent lasting as long as three weeks. The stressful events were like those that led to brain fag or to the hysterical-panic syndromes. In fact, the incidence of psychosis showed significant peaks at times of school exams or when exam results were published. The symptoms waxed and waned in relation to social events; they waxed with visits by relatives or con-sequent on social pressures and waned when social pressures were alleviated. Three-quarters of victims of brief reactive psychosis reported longstanding symptoms of brain fag, and nearly half seemed to have been depressed for weeks or months before their psychosis began.

Consistent with the hypothesis that the syndromes described in students are rooted in Swazi culture, a comparison group of patients who were not in school showed similar syndromes to the student group. Nonstudents in gen-eral, however, seemed to be more depressed, and of course their illnesses were precipitated by somewhat different events. Among nonstudents, for in-stance, brief reactive psychoses were most frequent during the southern hemisphere winter, when agricultural work is at a low ebb.

Guinness provided case histories to illustrate various syndromes; I cite two cases of brief psychosis. The first, a 17-year-old son of a teacher, was at an elite boarding school. He became anxious when his books were stolen, fearing that spells would be placed on the pages. He believed these spells would enter his eyes as he read and cause him to fail at school. He had three brief psychotic episodes during a three-month period. During each of these, he ran away from school and cut himself superficially. Each episode cleared up after two weeks, but the illness came back when he returned to school or his brothers discussed school in his presence. His last episode was characterized by visual and audi-tory hallucinations. He believed that the radio carried information about him and that his brothers could be seen on TV. After spending a term at home, he was able to go back to school without relapsing again.

The second patient was a 19-year-old son of a bus driver. He was near to graduation, but he was not a good student and had had to repeat several classes. His family was expecting him to take his final exams, to pass them, and to start work to support his siblings. As his exams approached, he be-came progressively more anxious. He complained of memory loss, abdomi-nal pain, and a feeling that something was wrong with his chest. When a friend gave him a bun that caused him to vomit, he became convinced that he had been bewitched. His terror could not be allayed by a traditional healer. He became uncontrollably violent, saw visions, and heard voices. This lasted for five days, which he later claimed not to remember. After a brief remission, renewed pressure from his family caused him to relapse, but his symptoms abated this time as soon as he entered the hospital. His family, however, continued to focus on his exams, and he became increasingly depressed.

On the basis of his survey findings and case histories, Guinness suggested that brief reactive psychosis in Swaziland manifests illness behavior sanctioned by Swazi culture. According to Guinness, complaints of anxiety or depression per se are rare in Swaziland, and they are more likely to earn a scolding than sympathy and attention. Thus, depressed or demoralized Swazis convey their distress with brain fag or with hysterical symptoms, including apparent psychoses. While traditional healers treat the brief psychoses in the same way they treat other syndromes, that is, with curative rituals and social interventions, the apparent psychotic symptoms confuse the Western clinician, who is trained to view psychosis in a more serious light. For example, African students in the United Kingdom, where psychotic symptoms are not generally understood in illness role terms, are said to have an exceedingly high rate of schizophrenia.

Guinness's second paper, which included follow-up data, showed that most students with brief reactive psychoses either remained in good health following resolution of their acute illness or had recurrent episodes of reactive psychosis.[34] Brief reactive psychosis was generally not a prelude to either schizophrenia or bipolar disorder.

Transient psychotic disorders like those that Guinness described are sporadically seen in Europe and North America. In their most colorful forms, and in especially histrionic patients, such disorders have sometimes been called hysterical psychoses.[35] Hollender and Hirsch observed that patients who present with such psychoses are socially malleable and oriented to "affective truth" (i.e., it feels right, so it is right), rather than everyday facts.[36] Along the same lines, Spiegel and Fink presented two cases of hysterical psychosis that they attributed to stressful social situations.[37] Both patients were highly hypnotizable. These authors observe that such patients, being highly compliant, could "easily slip into a pattern of chronic psychological dysfunction" if treating clinicians misdiagnosed them and therefore expected them to do poorly. They suggested that hypnotizability can be used to distinguish patients with hysterical psychoses from those with more serious chronic psychotic disorders. From the point of view being developed here, the high hypnotizability of at least some patients with atypical brief psychoses is consistent with the hypothesis that some of these disorders manifest illness roles. The patient, that is, is playing the role of the mentally ill. (The social role view of hypnosis is outlined in chapter 4.) However, even those who believe that hypnosis is more than role playing agree that highly hypnotizable individuals are avid role players in their everyday lives.[38]

Bebainan

A curious Balinese illness, called *bebainan*, seems to occur in young women when they first encounter restrictions placed on adults of their sex. [39] The case of Anna O., cited in chapter 6, demonstrates how hysteria followed a similar time course in nineteenth-century Europe.

The Balinese themselves attribute *bebainan* to possession by *bebais*, which are evil spirits created by sorcerers from materials, such as placentas or stillborn fetuses, believed to have magical powers. Many Balinese think that women are especially prone to possession by *bebais* because they are mentally weaker than men. The victim possessed by a *bebai* experiences a sudden loss of volition, confusion and mental "blankness." Stomachaches, headaches, tinnitus, and loss of vision develop, and the subject feels chilled all over. The victim then abruptly loses self-control. She cries uncontrollably, shouts or screams, or talks angrily to herself. Some victims are also violent and difficult to restrain because of an accession of unusual strength. The victim recovers within an hour or two and remembers her behavior.

Suryani interviewed all of the 296 individuals living in *Puri Klungkung*, the residential compound of the royal family of Klungkung, in order to determine who had suffered *bebainan* and the circumstances of their attacks.[40] *Puri Klungkung* consisted of *Puri Agung*, or the compound where the king and his principal wives lived, *Puri Agung Semara Negara*, where the king's younger wives resided, *Puri Agung Saraswati*, where still younger royal wives lived, and three other *puri* where the royal siblings lived with their families. Twenty-seven of the 296 residents of the *puri* had experienced *bebainan* on at least one occasion. Subjects were given questionnaires, interviewed, and observed.

Most Balinese are Hindus and still recognize social obligations based on inherited caste. Although the last king of Klungkung died in 1965, the royal family of Klungkung is still widely venerated. Its members are thought to be able to intervene with the gods, and they are addressed with an honorific that means "elevated godly being." Within as without the *puri*, girls are less valued than boys. Though girls attend school when young, most adolescent girls are confined in the *puri*, where they are taught to weave, to prepare ritual offerings, and to behave according to intricate rules of etiquette. Once they have reached adolescence, their only contact with the outside world consists in what they view through the compound fence. Female adolescence begins with the first menstruation. At the time of Suryani's study, a few *puri* girls apparently had been allowed to continue their education, to graduate from the university, and even to seek employment in government and businesses, but most of the *puri* women were raised in traditional fashion. The older *puri* men generally were polygamous, while the younger men were mostly monogamous. Multiples wives lived in harmony in their husband's compound, supporting themselves and their children by weaving, dressmaking, or trade.

As expected, nearly 90 percent of *puri bebainan* victims were women. Episodes began suddenly, although not completely unexpectedly, and could not be attributed to poor physical health. Most victims had multiple episodes; more than 59 percent had had more than four, and 48 percent had had more than 10. Eighty percent of attacks lasted less than an hour, and nearly two-thirds were followed by a state of sleep. Nearly 60 percent of victims felt calm after their attacks, but the remainder reported feeling anxious. Victims felt out of control during their episodes, but they were fully cognizant of how they had behaved. Interviews with victims revealed no special risk for psychopathology. In particular, victims were not especially neurotic, depressed, or anxious in comparison with other *puri* residents, and there was no evidence that they suffered from psychotic disorders.

As I noted earlier, *bebainan* seems to strike women during the period after their elementary schooling and before their marriage, while they are serving apprenticeships for adult life in the *puri*. Only 7 percent of the subjects first experienced bebainan before they were 15 years old, 52 percent had their first attack between the ages of 16 and 20, 33 percent had their first attack between the ages of 20 and 30, and 7 percent had their first attack after the age of 30. Since Balinese women marry rather late, 70 percent of the victims were unmarried at the time of their first attack. Interestingly, all the married victims were young outside brides who had married into the *puri*. Socially and psychologically, their positions may have been similar to that of young native girls trying to adjust to their new confinement in the *puri* walls.

Suryani obtained information about family members' responses. Typically, at the first sign of attack, all available family members rush to restrain the victim, lest the *bebai* cause her to harm herself or others. In 93 percent of the cases Suryani heard about, family members rapidly sought help from traditional healers. The seriousness with which families viewed *bebainan* attacks is reflected in the fact that in 30 percent of these cases, the families consulted a Balinese-Hindu high priest, in addition to or instead of lesser traditional healers. In 11 percent of the cases, the victim was brought to a doctor, but this sometimes reflected a relative's belief that something other than *bebainan* was involved. Fewer than 4 percent of cases received no treatment.

Since most *bebainan* victims are young women confined within the *puri*, the traditional healers usually visit the victims' homes. In the cases observed by Suryani, the healers had sometimes arrived while the attack was in progress and had used the opportunity to interrogate the *bebais*. Speaking through his victim, a *bebai* will sometimes answer questions about his origin and the reasons for his attack. Holy water or ritual objects were used to exorcise *bebais*, but, in other cases, the healer just squeezed the victim's thumb until the *bebai* promised to leave the victim alone. Some *bebais* demanded food or gifts to leave, and these were usually granted if they were not excessive. Once the *bebai* had gone and the victim returned to normal, the healer left the family some holy water or oil, with instructions for regular administration. The family was very involved in the healer's curative efforts, both during the attack and in the subsequent days.

Suryani notes that girls from 16 to 20 years old, a period during which half of the *bebainan* victims experienced their first attack, are subject to substantial emotional distress. This is the time in which most of them are withdrawn from school and forced to begin a cloistered life inside *puri* walls. The Balinese spoil their children, whom they see as the incarnations of their ancestors, and high-caste children especially are free from any constraints. This makes it all the harder for young girls confined to the *puri* to adapt to the rigid regime to which they are suddenly subject. Suddenly, they are told that anger and other negative emotional displays are shameful. Suddenly, they are told they must bow to their elders' authority and spend their days learning skills appropriate to grown women. No longer free to play, they must learn to present a flawless persona to the world. The years from age 16 to age 30 are also the years in which women anticipate being married or learn to adjust to married life. *Puri* girls have little choice in their marriage partners, who are generally chosen by elders from among royal families. Girls who dare to marry outside the royal line at the least lose social status and may even be ostracized. Newly married women from outside the *puri* not only have to adjust to life in the royal compound but also have to cope with their inferior status. For example, when talking to *puri* natives, new-comers have to use a more refined form of language than these natives use when addressing them. Newcomers have to be especially deferential toward their husbands' kin.

Acute stressors play a part in the onset of *bebainan*. According to Suryani's informants, 70 percent of *bebainan* attacks occur in the setting of emotional stress and 40 percent in the setting of physical exhaustion. One-third were said to have started after a sleepless night. Native-born *puri* women reported that they were upset before *bebainan* attacks because they were refused money for sweets or cakes, because they could not see outsiders, because they could not go to school, because they were tired from weaving, or because they were forced to make offerings rather than visit their relatives. Women born outside the puri reported that they were upset before *bebainan* attacks because they could not adjust to life inside the *puri*, because of their low status, or because they were having trouble dealing with older wives or with their husband's family.

Nearly three-quarters of *bebainan* attacks occured on the Balinese religious day of *kajeng kliwon*, which occurs every 15 days. Evil spirits, including *bebais*, are thought to be especially active on this day, which is also an occasion of great stress for Balinese women, who are expected to prepare and execute elaborate ceremonies and ritual offerings. Being more complicated, the *kajeng kliwon* rituals expected of *puri* women are even more stressful than those for women from lesser families. Women also suffered attacks of *bebainan* on other holidays, when they may have been subject to similar pressures.

In light of these considerations, Suryani suggests that *bebainan* provides young women an opportunity to express anger and frustration that they would otherwise have to suppress. Though it does not change their prospects—for example, they are not even allowed to leave the *puri* for treatment—it gains them temporary respite from stifling social obligations and a measure of attention they would otherwise not receive. Because *bebainan* is viewed as an affliction or illness, victims are not stigmatized for expressing their feelings, as they would certainly be if they were not seen as ill. Insofar as Suryani is right, *bebainan* is an emotional safety valve for young Balinese women chafing under unaccustomed constraints during a difficult transitional period.

Suryani questioned the relatives of *bebainan* victims and others regarding the victims' personalities before they reached adolescence. Most personality measures failed to differentiate *bebainan* victims from others, but several significant differences did appear, and these differences are consistent with the view of the illness argued by Suryani. The *bebainan* victims were noted to have been more prone than others to tears, to despair, and to irritation. Compared with other children and adolescents, future *bebainan* victims were less likely to have lost their temper when punished and had shown better general control of their feelings of anger. A disproportionate share of *bebainan* victims had come from endogamous marriages. Both sides of their families, in other words, were royal. Being of higher status, children of such marriages were generally more spoiled, and perhaps less likely to learn to cope with frustration, than were children of exogamous pairings.

Ataques de Nervios

Many societies mandate ways of expressing strong feelings. Arab women, for instance, ululate at funerals. Such ululations are not heard at American funerals, in spite of the fact that feelings are presumably just as strong. Any culturally mandated "idiom of distress," to borrow a term,[41] can become an illness role if it is thought to be partially or wholly involuntary. In fact, in some societies certain affective expressions are either idioms or illness roles, depending upon the context in which they appear. Following losses, they serve to express feeling; in other settings, they may serve as illness roles. *Ataques de nervios*, which are seen among Latin Caribbeans, illustrate such ambiguous behaviors.[42]

Used as an idiom of distress, the typical *ataque de nervios*, or "attack of nerves," occurs at a moment of loss, such as during a funeral or at the scene of a death. The affected person experiences palpitations, a sense of warmth rising into his head, and numbness in his extremities. He begins to shake all over and then to shout, swear, or even attack other people. Soon he collapses. Some victims jerk all over as if in the throes of a seizure, while others lay unmoving as if they are comatose. Concerned family members respond by praying over the stricken victim and by rubbing his face with alcohol. The victim awakens quickly but cannot remember what happened during the later stages of the episode. This type of attack of nerves is considered perfectly normal and may even be expected. In some situations, failure to have an attack can be taken as evidence of a lack of feeling.

Used as an illness role, *ataques de nervios* frequently serve to vent anger. Rothenberg, for instance, described the case of a 16-year-old Puerto Rican boarding school student who suddenly began striking his classmates.[43] He was brought to the school dispensary and given a sedative, which calmed him down. A psychiatrist who interviewed him several days later found him to be histrionic, but there was no evidence of either an affective or a psychotic disorder. The young man told the psychiatrist that he had come to the boarding school only a month before and had been bothered by the teasing he had received. Other boys called him "sissy" or "queer" and suggested he perform sexual acts for them. He reported feeling embarrassed but not angered by this teasing. He also reported feeling confused before he attacked his tormentors. He could not remember the events leading up to his attack, nor could he remember what had happened once it started. Apparently, he had had a similar *ataque* nine months before, of which he also claimed to have no memory. Rothenberg made the point that this young man's attacks served to express the hostility he could not express more directly. Guarnaccia and colleagues also described a case of woman who had behaved angrily during *ataques de nervios*.[44] A patient that I observed had an *ataque de nervios* after he had been waiting for more than two hours to be seen by a clinic physician. During his *ataque*, he overturned waiting room furniture and threw objects at nurses and doctors. He later claimed not to remember his actions. He had had past *ataques* attributed to frustration.

Even when victims are not overtly aggressive toward others, *ataques* often emerge in the setting of conflicts with others. Guarnaccia and colleagues, for instance, described a Mrs. Orozco, a 26year-old Central American woman who had lived in the United States for about five months.[45] Her attacks consisted of sensations of heat that started in her feet and rose to her head, followed by cold sensations. She attributed these *ataques*, and her *nervios* in general, to problems she was having with her jealous husband. He had come to the United States some months before her. She felt better during his absence, but her attacks began again when he wrote her an angry letter. He claimed to have heard from friends that she was going to dances while he was away. At the same time, her sister became angry with her for another reason. She and her husband were reconciled, leading to another remission of her attacks, but, when he again became jealous and angry, her attacks recurred. Mrs. Orozco did not call her attacks *ataques de nervios*, since she believed that the latter involve aggressive behaviors. She nonetheless attributed her attacks to her nerves, which she traced to her marital problems.

Occasionally, *ataques de nervios* can be so prolonged and complex that they resemble hysterical psychoses like those seen in Africa. Oquendo and colleagues, for instance, reported the case of a 35-year-old divorced Dominican woman, resident in the United States, who complained of pain on the left side of her face after she learned that her former husband had remarried in the Dominican Republic.[46] She was brought to an emergency room, where she became agitated and began to scream. Alternately mute and mumbling unintelligibly, she was admitted to the hospital for evaluation. In the hospital, she developed stereotyped movements. She snatched another patient's purse and grabbed the gold chains around a male patient's neck. She ate plastic flowers and reported hearing her daughter's voice telling her to kill herself. There was little response to high-dose antipsychotic drugs.

At a family meeting, the patient was able to say that she was worried about her and her children's financial condition, now that her former husband had remarried. Following a meeting with the former husband himself, at which this issue was talked about and apparently resolved, the patient's condition improved. She showed no more psychotic symptoms or agitation, and her medication was rapidly decreased and then discontinued. Oquendo and colleagues note that the patient's *ataque*, as it was understood, mobilized family members. The symptoms abated rapidly once the perceived threat to her own and to her children's well-being had been ameliorated.

Another patient described by Oquendo and colleagues was an 18-year-old Dominican woman who was estranged from her family because they objected to her boyfriend.[47] Upset by this estrangement, she reported hearing her dead father's voice telling her to break off the relationship. When her boyfriend left her instead, she bought half a gram of cocaine, went to her sister's house, and ingested the cocaine together with vitamins, nail polish, dish detergent, and soda. She immediately told her sister what she had done, and then she fainted. In the emergency room, she was aroused with smelling salts but was verbally unresponsive. Admitted to the hospital, she denied that she could still hear her father's voice, but her affect and manner were inappropriate. When peace was made with her family and they offered to let her live with her sister again, she became more appropriate and was sent home without medications.

Because of their frequent connection with disavowed feelings of anger and interpersonal conflict, Rothenberg argued that *ataques de nervios* serve to express hostile feelings that Puerto Rican culture otherwise tries to suppress.[48] According to Rothenberg, Puerto Ricans hesitate to express disagreements directly, preferring instead to hide their differences behind a facade of politeness. In this respect, they resemble the Malays and other peoples described earlier. Women, especially, are forced to hide their anger toward abusive spouses and other family members.

On the basis of detailed interviews with victims and their families, Guarnaccia and colleagues argue that *ataques* are often used to express distress due to family problems.[49] Common problems involve conflicts between spouses and fear of abandonment by parents, siblings, or children. According to these authors, the key to understanding the function of an *ataque* is to understand the situation that triggered it. This model suggests that the high incidence of aggression in the course of *ataques* results from the fact that *ataques* occur in the setting of conflicts. Insofar as an *ataque* is used to express displeasure with another person's behavior, aggressive behavior is likely to appear as part of the syndrome.

Ataques de nervios can mimic panic attacks,[50] especially in its less complex forms. A number of studies conducted in the United States and in Puerto Rico using symptom checklists seem to show an extremely high incidence of anxiety disorders among Puerto Ricans, a group at high risk for *ataques de nervios*. The Midtown Manhattan Study, for instance, which was conducted during the 1950s, showed that nearly two-thirds of Puerto Ricans who completed the so-called 22-Item Scale reported having somatic and anxiety symptoms."[51] Guarnaccia, Rubio-Stipec, and Canino hypothesized that the 22-Item Scale and similar symptom checklists lead to overestimates of the prevalence of anxiety because they include symptoms of *ataques de nervios*, which are common among Puerto Ricans.[52] They report on data gathered in Puerto Rico using a Spanish-language version of the Diagnostic Interview Schedule (DIS), a structured interview designed to yield psychiatric diagnoses. Fifteen hundred and thirteen subjects between the ages of 18 and 64 were interviewed during the spring and fall of 1984. From questions on the DIS, the authors selected 12 items that corresponded to symptoms of *ataques de nervios*. Most of the subjects endorsed none or one of these items; they were considered to be free of *ataques*. Twenty-three percent of subjects endorsed between two and five of these items and were thought to have possibly had *ataques de nervios*. Only 2 percent of subjects endorsed more than six of these items, and they were found to suffer from severe psychopathology. In comparison with the group that was free of *ataques*, those who possibly had experienced *ataques* were more likely to be housewives, to be unemployed, to receive disability, or to have suffered losses, such as a death in the family. As a group, in other words, they were under more stress and less likely to be able to solve their problems independently and in straightforward ways. They were five times as likely to meet DIS criteria for depressive disorders and three to four times as likely to meet DIS criteria for an anxiety disorder. A panic disorder question on the DIS asks subjects whether they have ever "had a spell or attack when all of a sudden [they] felt frightened, anxious, or very uneasy in situations when the majority of people would not feel that way." Ten of the 55 subjects who answered yes to this question identified their episodes as *ataques de nervios*. This group included patients who had been placed in the possible *ataque* group on the basis of their answers to the *ataque* items. Interviews with these subjects supported the hypothesis that their episodes were *ataques de nervios*, rather than simple panic attacks; they tended to occur in the settings typical of *ataques de nervios*, rather than out of the blue, and they also featured symptoms, such as mutism or aggression, typical of *ataques de nervios*, rather than of panic attacks.

Medieval Illness Roles

Illness roles are part and parcel of the cultures in which they appear. They are maintained, that is, by particular cultural mores, by regnant beliefs about illness, the body, and human nature, and by current social and power relationships. Consequently, as cultures change and the mores, beliefs, and relationships that maintain illness roles shift, illness roles can die out or become less common. Lovesickness and tarantism, for instance, were widespread in medieval Europe, but lovesickness is now gone completely and tarantism is now seen only in backward regions of Italy and Sardinia. Demon possession survived into the Renaissance period, played a part in the Reformation, and then turned into hysteria and mesmerism.

Mary Wack reviewed classical and medieval texts on lovesickness.[53] The idea that frustrated passion could be a cause of illness originated with Galen, who described disappointed lovers who became depressed, sleepless, and feverish. Treatment consisted of frequent baths, drinking of wine, and activities intended to divert attention from the love object. One especially famous patient, the wife of Senator Justus, was apparently in love with an entertainer. This relationship was forbidden to her, both because she was married and because of the class difference between her and her lover, and she became melancholic. Galen detected the secret cause of her distress by noting irregularities in her pulse. Galen's work on the pathology of love, and the writings of his classical and Byzantine successors, was read by Arab physicians, who adopted and refined the notion of lovesickness and introduced new techniques for curing it. Therapeutic coitus, for example, was introduced as a treatment for lovesick male patients. From Africa, the concept of lovesickness was reintroduced to medieval Europe by Constantine the African, a Carthaginian who traveled throughout the Middle East before becoming a monk in the abbey of Montecasino in the eleventh-century. Constantine's *Viaticum Peregrinantis*, which was read in medical schools for several hundred years, was an adaptation of an Arabic medical text and featured a chapter on the subject of passionate love.

Constantine and his medieval successors believed that only the most refined temperaments were susceptible to lovesickness, which therefore afflicted only men of the noble classes. Women were no longer seen as sufficiently noble in character to suffer from excess passion. The lovesick man was insomniac, agitated or listless, and obsessed with thoughts of his beloved. He appeared pensive and inattentive, sighed continually, and wore a pitiable expression. His eyes grew hollow, and he cried upon hearing love songs. At other times, he laughed uncontrollably. He ignored all conversations except for those dealing with love; these he would not want to break off, exhausting his interlocutors. His pulse would race at mention or sight of the beloved, and taking the pulse provided medieval physicians with seemingly objective proof of the diagnosis. The disease was possibly fatal unless it was treated aggressively. Treatment included therapeutic sexual intercourse, which was believed to restore proper humoral balance, drinking wine among especially amusing or beautiful friends, and frequent baths, arranged so that the patient was shielded from the sight of ugly or repugnant people. Therapeutic intercourse was considered especially effective if performed with young, attractive sexual partners, who were hired especially for this medical purpose. Amusing conversations were considered of value, especially if they were held in flowering gardens or in rooms strewn with good-smelling herbs, and lively music was also thought beneficial. Hunting and games were desirable, and poetry recitations were recommended by some, but not all, physicians. The poetry, all agreed, should not dwell on themes of love. In especially desperate cases, old crones were sometimes brought in, in the hopes that the patient would see how his beloved might age. To cool the patient's passion, plasters were sometimes applied to his testicles.

It is impossible to know what was wrong, if anything, with men who were thought to be lovesick 600 to 800 years ago. Yet, the symptoms of lovesickness differed sufficiently from those of present-day illnesses, and the possible uses of those symptoms are sufficiently obvious, that many such patients must have been acting out illness roles. For young medieval men, lovesickness could have served to demonstrate courtliness and nobility, to gain concern and attention, and to procure diversions that were, to say the least, pleasant. It could also have been used to obtain favors from the beloved. Wack, for instance, cites a late twelfth-century story, the hero of which spends the night sleepless and sighing in anguish in hopes that his loved one will cure his all-too-obvious distress. Richard de Fournival, a thirteenth-century writer, urged women to recognize true lovers by signs of illness: "When he is before you humble, pensive, full of sighs and has a piteous and loving look, and it seems when he looks at you as though he will cry while laughing, know that it is one of the most beautiful and true proofs that one can find in one's friend, whether he loves from the heart or not."[54] Another medieval guide urged suitors to fake lovesickness in order to win their ladies: "It is worth much to be pale and discolored, for it seems that it is from the pangs of love, and then the women feel pity because of it."[55] One can imagine, too, the pressure felt by women not to let young noblemen die for the lack of their love, regardless of whether they themselves felt moved to pity.

Following epidemics of the Black Death in the fourteenth and fifteenth centuries, epidemic dancing manias swept through Germany, Holland, Belgium, and Italy.[56] In Northern Europe, this epidemic illness was called St. Vitus' Dance and was thought to manifest demoniacal possession, but in Italy it was called tarantism, after the spider whose bite was believed to have caused it. Victims experienced an irresistible urge to dance wildly until they collapsed, exhausted and temporarily cured. In the grip of the dancing mania, peasants abandoned their farms, tradesmen left their workshops, and housewives deserted their homes to dance together, foaming at the mouth and screaming and shouting furiously, in large public revels. Many victims reported religious visions and signs, while others had convulsions or appeared to be entranced. After the revels ended, victims remained sensitive to music, which readily triggered relapses or which could be used for therapeutic ends. Italians believed that the music of fifes, clarinets, and drums could disperse tarantula venom throughout the victim's body, leading to frenzied dancing and, ultimately, to the excretion of venom in the victim's sweat. As late as the seventeenth century, groups of musicians traveled from village to village in summer, treating the so-called *taranti* in large gatherings. For many years, physicians considered tarantism a bona fide toxic reaction, but I. M. Lewis reports that the tarantula spider thought to cause tarantism is actually harmless.[57]

Lewis also shows that, though material causes for the frenzies may be cited, the European dancing manias closely resemble the peripheral possession illnesses encountered in non-European societies. Most victims of medieval dancing manias were from the lower classes, and the preponderance of them were women. In Italy, the public catharses organized by musical groups were called "little carnivals of women," in recognition of the sex difference. Modern day *taranti* in Italy and Sardinia are likewise lower class and predominantly women. According to Lewis, modern-day *taranti* first experience their dancing mania at times of social stress or when embroiled in social conflicts. Many of them have *taranti* in their immediate families, on whose behavior their illness can be modeled, and, once the illness develops, relapses tend to occur on a more or less regular basis. Expensive musical rituals are needed to induce remissions, imposing a heavy burden on husbands and male kin and advertising victims' complaints about their families to the public at large.

A case described by Lewis illustrates the social uses of tarantism. Maria, as she was called, was raised by her poverty-stricken aunt and uncle following the death of her father when she was thirteen. At age 18 she fell in love, but the young man's parents would not approve of the match because Maria was poor, and the young man subsequently lost interest in Maria. Dejected by these events, Maria reported being bitten by a spider, which caused her to dance to exhaustion. About the same time, a neighborhood woman asked Maria to marry her son, but Maria felt no attraction to him and, to excuse herself, pleaded that she could not then afford a trousseau, because of the expenses incurred to hire musicians to treat her tarantism. St. Paul appeared to Maria and asked her to forgo human marriage in favor of a mystical union with himself, but the aggrieved neighbor and her son managed to lure Maria to a deserted farm, where they forced her to live in shame, or de facto marriage. Soon afterward, following a quarrel with her new common-law husband, Maria disappeared for several days. When she returned, she had the dancing craze, which lasted for nine days. St. Paul, she reported, had appeared to her again and, annoyed by the fact that she now had a human spouse, had caused her to be bitten by another spider. Her illness, which became recurrent, could be cured only by expensive visits to Pauline rites. In this way, Maria continued to protest her forced marriage, called public attention to her mistreatment, and imposed economic burdens on her husband's family, whom she did not like.

Demon possession was also known in medieval Europe and was cited to explain a wide range of symptoms, especially in women (see chapter 5). The *Malleus Maleficarum*, written in 1494, summarized late-medieval knowledge of demon possesion. Undoubtedly, many patients said to have demon possession had actual physical illnesses—convulsions, for instance, were cardinal symptoms of demon possession and some of those thought possessed were certainly epileptic. But, in some cases, demon posssession was also an illness role and was used for some of the purposes I. M. Lewis described in relation to other forms of peripheral possession. In late-medieval Europe, demon possession was also peculiarly linked with aggression. Since a demon could name the witch that had invoked him or in any event would betray her identity by convulsing in her presence, enactments of demon possession were powerful means for settling personal scores and grudges. The demon-possessed individual was in a position of power in relation to those her demons might choose to implicate. As described in chapter 5, Edward Jorden's tract, *A Briefe Discourse of a Disease Called the Suffocation of the Mother*, published in 1603, which helped create what later was called hysteria, concerned a case in which a certain Mary Glover, the 14-year old daughter of a London alderman, enacted demon possession to take her revenge on a neighbor with whom she had recently argued.

4

Playing the Hypnotic Game

Many patients who present with modern or premodern illness roles in Europe and North America have proven highly responsive to hypnotic commands (see chapters 5 through 7). Belief that hypnosis manifests a special state of mind has fostered the conclusion that these roles are real disorders. Charcot, for instance, thought that hypnotic responsiveness was proof of a brain disorder in his grand hysterics. Modern authors cite response to hypnotic commands as evidence that patients with ostensible multiple personality disorder (MPD) are prone to dissociation. In this chapter, by contrast, I cite evidence that hypnosis is just role playing. According to this view, hypnotist and subject collude to enact a drama in which something out of the ordinary only appears to happen. The reason that patients with illness roles respond to hypnotic commands is that role-playing talents and aptitudes predispose to both illness enactments and hypnotic responsiveness. By way of analogy, actors selected for skill in playing the part of Lear (producing illness enactments) are likely to do a passable job playing the part of Hamlet (responding to hypnotic cues).

Hypnosis as a Social Role

Franz Anton Mesmer, an eighteenth-century Viennese physician who relocated to Paris, is credited with the discovery of what we now call hypnosis.[1] Mesmer believed that he had harnessed a force, called animal magnetism, with which living beings could be controlled from a distance. In 1784, Mesmer's numerous critics persuaded Louis XVI to establish a commission to investigate his practice. The head of this commission was Benjamin Franklin, then in France representing the newly independent United States; its members included several elite scientists of the time. After investigating the matter for seven years, Franklin's commission reported that the phenomena of animal magnetism resulted from suggestion, not from any physical or physiological principal. Definitive though they appeared, Franklin's findings marked the beginning of a 200 year debate that is still very much alive: Does hypnosis, as we call it now, manifest a special state of mind or brain?

Although they quickly abandoned animal magnetism, many nineteenth-century theorists still thought that hypnotic "trance" corresponds to a novel state.[2] They described what they thought were the key special qualities of hypnosis, and they modified Mesmer's technique in ways that their theories suggested. Their hypotheses have endured in the work of some modern researchers. For example, James Braid, the mid-nineteenth-century surgeon who coined the word "hypnotism," believed that hypnosis resulted from a state of intense concentration on a single idea.[3] Consistent with this hypothesis, Braid introduced the practice of having his subjects stare at a candle or pendulum fob or into the mesmerist's eyes in order to enter a trance. Helen Crawford's work, which was cited in chapter 2, is in the line of thinking that derives from Braid. Bernheim, a French physician who was a contemporary of Charcot, believed that hypnosis manifests heightened suggestibility.[4] In the 1930s, Clark Hull revived this hypothesis, and, still more recently, Martin Orne further refined it.[5] Janet invented the concept of dissociation to account for the phenomena observed in the Salpêtrière.[6] Ernest Hilgard, who ran an experimental hypnosis laboratory at Stanford University from 1957 to 1979, rekindled interest in dissociation theory and applied it to several hypnotic phenomena.[7] Today, hypnotism is often referred to as one of a variety of possible "dissociated states." Mesmer's most important disciple, the Marquis de Puysegur, considered hypnosis a state of deep relaxation, a position since restated by William Edmonston.[8] In the early 1800s, Abbé Jose di Faria began to induce hypnosis by giving his subjects instructions to focus attention on sleep.

In contrast, most modern-day experimental and social psychologists believe that hypnosis is just the enactment of a social role, basically like any other.[9] According to Theodore Sarbin, who stated this view in the 1960s, hypnotist and subject stage an hypnotic scene.[10] The hypnotist sets the scene going by doing something understood to "hypnotize" the subject. He may have the patient gaze upward or at a swinging pendulum, or he may stroke the patient's arm while keeping up a patter of hypnotic "suggestions," many of which are really subtle stage directions. Modern-day studies show that virtually any technique will suffice for hypnotic "induction," as the opening scene is called, as long as both subject and hypnotist agree it induces hypnosis. Banyai and Hilgard, for instance, successfully hypnotized subjects by having them peddle a stationary bicycle, and Glass and Barber successfully hypnotized subjects by giving them inert pills.[11]

Following the induction, or opening scene, the hypnotist gives suggestions to the "hypnotized" subject. For instance, the hypnotist may tell the subject that his arm has turned to lead and thus cannot be raised or that the subject cannot remember his name. Hearing such suggestions, the subject defined as hypnotized is expected to follow the stage directions implicit in them. Hearing that his arm has turned to lead, he is expected to imagine a leaden arm and to make apparently futile efforts to raise it. Hearing that he cannot remember his name, the subject is expected to try to imagine a state of amnesia and to make apparently futile efforts to recall his identity.

After suggestions have been given and acted on, it is time for the closing scene. Using another ritual, which often symbolically reverses the induction procedure, the hypnotist must bring the subject back to normal. If, for example, the subject was hypnotized by slowly closing his eyes while counting to three, he might be woken up by slowly opening his eyes while counting down from three. As with induction procedures, the technique does not matter. Any procedure will work, as long as both subject and hypnotist agree that it results in the subject resuming his normal state.

Neither subject nor hypnotist, though, is entirely off the hook just because the subject has woken from his trance. The hypnotist must maintain that the subject was really hypnotized, and the subject must stand by his entranced behaviors. If the hypnotized subject was not able to raise his hand, he must later assert that he tried his hardest. If he was not able to recall his name, he must later claim his amnesia was real. Sometimes subjects are given "posthypnotic" suggestions, for example, to open a window at a particular time, which have to be honored to validate the performance. The subject must open the window at the appointed hour but deny that his doing so is related to having been hypnotized.

If the performance has gone well from beginning to end, the hypnotist will have persuaded himself that the subject was not acting normally and hence must have been in an altered state, and the subject will have persuaded himself that something special happened. If he was told that he could not raise his arm, for instance, he will have come to believe that real feelings of heaviness prevented his doing so. If he was told that he could not recall his name, he will have come to believe that he really suffered a transient loss of identity. Both subject and hypnotist are in situations resembling those studied by Janis and King, whose work in social role playing was discussed in chapter 2. Having acted a role that provides its own rationale, the hypnotist and the subject are under powerful pressures to express consistent beliefs. Successful staging of the full hypnotic performance leads to the subject being called "hypnotizable," or a "good hypnotic subject." As discussed later in this chapter, the subjects who actually cooperate with hypnosis are under the impression that such labels are desirable. The hypnotist, for his part, will take greater pride in his skill.

Sarbin's social role account of hypnotic events implies that hypnosis can be studied with research methods used to investigate other social transactions. Following Sarbin's lead, researchers such as T. X. Barber, at the Medfield State Hospital in Massachusetts, Nicholas Spanos, at Carleton University in Ontario, and John Chaves, at Southern Illinois University, conducted ingenious experiments to elucidate the factors that contribute to success in the hypnotic scenario.[12] These studies clearly confirm, as Sarbin's model suggests, that hypnotized subjects are better understood as active collaborators than as passive automatons and that, rather than being acted upon by the hypnotist, subjects act along with the hypnotist to create hypnotic scenarios. The results of some of these studies are described in this chapter.

If hypnosis, né mesmerism, is a social role without a particular correlate in either mind or brain, from whence did it come to Mesmer? Did Mesmer create it from thin air, or were elements of the role already known to him and to those who enacted it? The answer is the latter: Mesmerism was modeled on possession, which was still extant in England and Western Europe.[13] For example, though the agent and putative means differed in the two conditions, both possession and mesmerism were thought to be states in which persons were filled and controlled by others. While the possessed individual was filled and controlled by spirits, the mesmerized individual was filled with magnetic fluid and thereby controlled by the mesmerist. Possession and mesmerism were known by similar signs: uncontrolled weeping or laughing, posturing, trembling and falling, and dramatic convulsions. Possession and mesmerism utilized similar rituals: The early mesmerists, or so-called magnetisers, adopted stylized postures, modeled on those used by exorcists, to project and direct magnetic flux into their subjects. Group magnetic sessions, in which silent groups of patients in darkened, drape-lined rooms joined hands around oak tubs while eerie music played, resembled witches' Sabbaths. Wearing a lavendar robe and carrying a long iron wand, Mesmer himself played the part of the warlock or devil. Finally, possession and mesmerism were thought to be states in which persons enjoyed expanded powers: sight or hearing of distant events, communication with spirits, speaking in tongues, visions of past and future, and healing and curative knowledge.

Given their close resemblance, possession and mesmerism were bound to compete with each other or to spawn intermediate forms. The competition came early: As Mesmer was developing his theory of animal magnetism, a priest named Johan Gassner attracted royal attention by casting out devils from afflicted Bavarian peasants. After watching Gassner work, Mesmer opined that the priest was sincere but self-deluded: He was practising mesmerism while thinking that he was an exorcist!

During the nineteenth century, several sets of practices intermediate between mesmerism and possession emerged.[14] Phrenology, for instance, was a method for discerning the size of cerebral "organs" by feeling the shape of the skull. So-called phrenomesmerists combined phrenology with the practice of mesmerism. By directing magnetic flux to particular "organs" of mind, the phrenomesmerists could control their subjects' behavior. When the phrenomesmerist's fingers were placed on the scalp over the organ of veneration, the subject pantomined prayer. When his fingers were placed overlying the organ of destructiveness, the subject tore his clothes. "Magnetic evangelists" incorporated mesmerism into evangelical liturgy. Naturally, there was some debate about whether the magnetized worshippers were filled with the Holy Spirit or the Evil One. Early in the century, ostensibly "sensitive" invalids like Harriet Martineau were mesmerized to contact spirits of the departed. The theory was that invalids were halfway dead already. The magnetized ill were consulted on matters of health, love, and happiness. By the end of the century, healthier magnetized spirit guides were doing the heavy lifting at public and private seances.

Hypnotizability and Social Role Flexibility

Insofar as hypnosis is a social role, as opposed to a distinct physiological or mental state, hypnotizability must reflect ability and willingness to play that particular role. How can such ability and willingness be measured? In practice, the way it is done is to give subjects cues to act hypnotized and then to score them according to whether they actually do so.[15] Tests like these are called "work sample" tests, since they are based on the theory that the best way to assess performance is to obtain a sample of what is produced, in this case hypnotic behaviors. Work sample tests may be useful predictors of later behavior—someone who can sew a shirt well on one occasion is likelier than not to sew it well on another—but they cannot be understood as measuring anything other than the behavior itself, a fact oftenoverlooked by enthusiasts of hypnosis. As Gill and Brennan noted, work sample tests of hypnosis "lead to the less than remarkable finding that if you can hypnotize a person, he is probably a good hypnotic subject."[16]

By way of example, subjects taking one form of the Stanford Hypnotic Susceptibility Scale (SHSS), which is a typical test of hypnotizability, are asked to gaze upward at a small bright object.[17] While gazing upward, they listen to a lengthy discussion of hypnosis that includes many implicit instructions. They are told that gazing upward has tired their eyes, that they are becoming drowsy and sleepy, and that their eyes will close by themselves. Later, subjects are told that one arm is becoming too heavy to lift and, still later, that they cannot pry their interlaced fingers apart. Subjects are told that a fly is annoying them and that they cannot re-open their eyes. They are given a posthypnotic suggestion to change seats and to forget certain items. Subjects are scored according to whether they first close their eyes, whether they seem unable to lift their arms, whether they keep their hands together in spite of apparent struggles to separate them, whether they try to brush away the fly, whether they keep their eyes shut, whether they change chairs, and whether they claim not to remember the items they were told they would forget.

Although it is somewhat technical, there is an important point to make about the SHSS and similar tests of hypnosis: The items on these tests correlate well with each other.[18] A subject who brushes away a nonexistent fly is also likely to seem unable to lift his arm. A subject who seems unable to separate his hands is also likely to change chairs in response to posthypnotic cues. Similarly, a subject who lifts his arm will probably open his eyes when told he cannot do so. This type of correlation suggests that there is a tendency to respond to suggestions per se, regardless of what they involve, rather than separate tendencies to respond to separate suggestions. In terms of the social role model, there must be a tendency to respond to hypnotic role cues in general, at least within the range of cues used in the SHSS and related tests.

Subjects, of course, will not respond to role cues at all unless they perceive them as cues, which is no trivial matter. Studies by Barber and colleagues show that many subjects do not respond to hypnosis because they do not understand that the suggestions are role cues.[19] When the hypnotist tells them their arm is becoming heavy, for example, poor hypnotic subjects passively wait to see whether it is really the case. When the time comes to raise their arm, they make no particular effort to imagine that they cannot. When they are told they are numb, they wait to see whether that is true. They make no particular effort not to respond to pain. By contrast, good hypnotic subjects, who interpret suggestions as role cues, work to imagine their arm turning to lead or stone, which they cannot lift. They try to distract themselves from and therefore not respond to any pain they may feel. Unhypnotizable subjects begin to respond to suggestions and improve their scores on tests like the SHSS if they are coached to be active participants in hypnosis, not merely passive observers. The Carleton Skills Training Package, for instance, improves hypnotic responsiveness by teaching subjects to enact suggestions while making efforts to imagine a consistent situation.[20] A subject told that he cannot move his arm, for example, would be urged to enact a paralysis while imagining that his arm has been immobilized. As we might have expected on the basis of Janis and King's findings, subjects trained in this way to act a hypnotic role later report feeling that they were hypnotized. A subject who acted paralyzed is likely to report having felt paralyzed.

Even if they perceive them, subjects will respond to cues only if they are motivated to do so. In particular, subjects will respond to suggestions like those in the SHSS only if they really want to be hypnotized.[21] For example, some unhypnotizable subjects seem to fear loss of autonomy. These are people for whom autonomy is an important issue, and they believe, along with most of the general public, that hypnotized subjects cannot control their behavior. They are unwilling to play along with cues that they believe may lead to their being controlled by the hypnotist. Fear of losing control may also explain why some psychiatric patients—especially those who are anxious or fearful of others—cannot be hypnotized. Barber and colleagues have shown that normal subjects who fear loss of control in hypnosis become more hypnotizable once they are reassured that their fear is unfounded.[22] In a similar vein, some subjects believe that hypnosis connotes weak-mindedness. Not surprisingly, they are unwilling to take on a stigmatized role. Changing their beliefs about the hypnotic role increases their responsiveness to hypnotic suggestions. Similarly, subjects taught to equate hypnosis with gullibility are usually unresponsive to hypnotic commands.

Finally, subjects who perceive cues and are willing to act on them may nonetheless differ in their ability to act out the roles they demand. Hypnotic virtuosos, who respond to all or virtually all suggestions on tests like the SHSS, do indeed seem to have special skills that promote rapid role changes. I have already noted the theory that such subjects differ from other persons by virtue of a greater ability to concentrate their attention. It is easy to see how ability to focus attention exclusively on beliefs and perceptions consistent with new roles would make it easier to rapidly change personae. New roles would not be impeded by older beliefs and perceptions. Studies also suggest that highly hypnotizable individuals differ from those who are less hypnotizable by virtue of greater talent for what has been called imaginative involvement.[23] Imaginative involvement is the ability to forget oneself in the moment. Subjects who score high on tests of imaginative involvement report forgetting themselves while reading novels or watching plays or movies so that the novel or movie or play seems entirely real. Many such subjects report, for example, feeling terrified while watching frightening movies or crying uncontrollably while reading a sad novel. Imaginative involvement might result from highly focused attention. The moviegoer who concentrates his attention only on the screen, completely ignoring bodily sensations, distracting noises from the audience, the occasional opening and closing of the theater door, and other reminders that he is watching a movie might be more prone to feel absorbed by the movie than would the typical viewer. On a related theme, Wilson and Barber found that highly hypnotizable subjects were what they called "fantasy-prone."[24] Such subjects spend much of their time involved in daydreams they experience as extraordinarily vivid and real. Many of them, for example, are able to reach orgasm with sexual fantasies in the absence of physical stimulation. They report having trouble distinguishing some of their fantasies from reality, and they show extreme imaginative involvement in reading or watching dramas. Many of them report having had imaginary companions with whom they conversed as children or even as adults. Significantly, fantasy proneness appears to be fostered by early abuse, which may also be true for hypnotizability itself.[25]

André Weitzenhoffer, who worked with Hilgard on the SHSS, believes that hypnotic scales are tests of suggestibility, rather than of hypnosis per se.[26] Suggestibility, unfortunately, is as circular a concept as dissociation. Subjects are said to respond to suggestions because they are suggestible; they are said to be suggestible because they respond to suggestions. The concept of suggestibility, moreover, ignores the adaptive and cognitive aspect of role-cue responsiveness: The suggestible subject does something just because someone suggested it; the role-playing subject does something because it suits his purposes to respond to cues. A suggestible person acts more or less automatically; a role-playing person acts on more or less rational grounds. Putting all this aside, however, some researchers believe that hypnotic responsiveness is related only to so-called primary suggestibility, or responsiveness to cued motor acts, and not to other forms of suggestibility that involve beliefs or perceptions.[27] One common test, for example, of primary suggestibility is to have a subject stand with his feet together and eyes closed. While measuring body sway, the tester suggests to the subject that he is falling over. Highly suggestible subjects show more body sway than do others in response to suggestions of falling. In general, however, the theory that responsiveness to suggestions for motor acts differs from responsiveness to suggestions for beliefs has only weak empirical support. Studies have shown significant correlations between hypnotic responsiveness and tests of perceptual influence similar to those described in the previous chapter, and these in turn correlate highly with tests like the body-sway measure.[28]

Researchers who cannot agree on what hypnosis is nonetheless seem to concur that hypnotizable subjects are highly responsive to role cues and are avid role players. Nicolas Spanos, for instance, was a leading proponent of the view that hypnosis is just a role, while Herbert Spiegel and David Spiegel, the authors of a widely used textbook of hypnosis, are known for their view that it manifests a special state of mind. In his important book on hypnosis and MPD, published after his death, Nicolas Spanos observed that the most hypnotizable subjects are those who are most "responsiveness to social communications."[29] He cited studies showing that hypnotizability correlates with pantomime role-playing abilities and that people with backgrounds in drama tend to be hypnotizable. Spiegel and Spiegel observe that the most hypnotizable subjects are generally anxious to please, extremely sensitive to interpersonal cues, and eager to comply with the role demands of their immediate situation.[30] They unthinkingly take on ideas expressed by those they admire, and they are little discomfited by logical inconsistencies between these ideas and those they already hold. Spiegel and Spiegel caution those who deal with such subjects to avoid suggesting roles that the subjects might adopt.

The highly hypnotizable patient described by Spiegel and Spiegel resembles the patient with an "hysterical style" described by David Shapiro.[31] According to Shapiro, a psychoanalyst, patients with hysterical styles are highly responsive to social cues and little concerned with logical inconsistencies, either in their own behavior or in their beliefs. These are the patients, of course, who were once considered prone to hysterical illness, before the term "hysterical" was dropped from the psychiatric lexicon. Patients who would once have been said to have hysterical personalities now receive diagnoses in the so-called cluster B group of DSM-IV personality disorders, which are characterized by emotional instability, dependency, and histrionic behavior.[32] These disorders are now diagnosed in most patients with the syndromes described in chapters 5 through 7.

Hypnotic Feats

Many people believe that hypnosis must be a special state because they believe that hypnotized subjects can perform feats that would be impossible in the normal waking state. In this section I review some well-known hypnotic phenomena in order to show that they are explicable in social role terms. These phenomena include (1) age regression and recovery of lost memories, (2) pain control, (3) simultaneous mental activities, increased suggestibility, hallucinations, and trance logic, (4) feats of strength, healing, and physiologic effects, and (5) posthypnotic responses. In the late eighteenth and early nineteenth centuries, still more improbable claims—such as mental telepathy, sight at a distance, and the ability to foresee the future—were made for mesmerism and hypnosis, but these were residual aspects of the role of demon possession and have since dropped away.

Before discussing particular studies, I should clarify a point about methods. Many studies of hypnotic feats compare hypnotized and unhypnotized subjects on some physical or intellectual measure. If the measure, for instance, is grip strength, subjects may be hypnotized, told to imagine themselves as Arnold Schwarzenegger, and asked to squeeze a device that measures the strength of their grip. The control group may be the same subjects in a waking state, other subjects in a waking state who are pretending to be hypnotized, or unhypnotizable subjects exposed to an induction process, which is presumably ineffective for them. The social role view of hypnosis suggests that this type of design might lead to false positive findings. Being highly motivated to comply with expectations and to prove to themselves and to others that they are really hypnotized, hypnotizable subjects might try to squeeze harder when hypnotized than they would in the waking state, and they might try harder, too, when hypnotized than unhypnotizable subjects. A real control group, consequently, needs to be motivated as strongly as hypnotized subjects. For this reason, T. X. Barber began giving control subjects what he called "task motivational instructions," which make it clear to them that they are to try their hardest to picture the image they are given and to excel in the actual performance test.[33] Many positive findings in hypnosis research result from inadequate attention to motivational factors.

Age Regression and Recovery of Lost Memories

Hypermnesia, or memory enhancement, was ascribed to hypnosis very early on (see chapter 7) and remains a rationale for its use in clinical settings. It may be a surprise then, although not from a social role viewpoint, that hypnotic enhancement of memory has been shown to be ineffective. In a review on forensic use of hypnosis, the psychologist Graham Wagstaff notes that studies that test recall of known items show no increase in accurate recall under hypnosis.[34] Those studies that do show an increase in accurate item recall show even larger increases in false reports, as well. Hypnotized subjects apparently interpret suggestions for recall as giving permission to say things of which they would otherwise not feel sure. In doing so, they are likely to name some real items, but only at the cost of falsely reporting others.

Although they are not especially accurate, hypnotically recovered memories take on an aura of certainty simply because they are accessed through the hypnotic trance. Thus, hypnotized subjects express greater confidence in the accuracy of their recall than do unhypnotized subjects, even when their recall is objectively less accurate.[35] Subjects, furthermore, feel as certain about falsely reported as about correctly reported items. Insofar as clinicians, or juries, for that matter, are swayed by the confidence with which memories are recounted, they can easily be misled by this aspect of hypnotically recovered memories.

Age or time regression is frequently used in hypnosis as an aid to memory recovery. If, for example, the aim is to learn about childhood traumas, the patient might be told that he is a child again and asked to describe what is happening. Thus instructed, some hypnotized patients will not just recall events; they will use the present tense, speak in a childish voice, and express the feelings they supposedly experienced at the time. A classic study by True has often been cited in favor of age regression.[36] True's subjects were hypnotized and then age-regressed to 11, 7, and 4 years of age. At each age they were told that it was their birthday or Christmas, and they were asked to name the day of the week. Eighty-one percent of True's hypnotized subjects correctly named the day on which their birthday or Christmas fell at each of the three ages. However, at least eight subsequent efforts to replicate True's study have failed to show that subjects perform much better than chance.[37] One critical difference between True's and subsequent studies may have been that True knew the correct answer when he asked subjects the questions and thus inadvertently may have given them subtle cues. In another well-known study similar to True's, adults were "hypnotically regressed" to childhood and then presented with optical illusions that are typically perceived differently by adults and children.[38] The regressed adults perceived the illusions as children do, suggesting that regression had indeed reinstated early perceptual modes. However, four subsequent studies have failed to find such effects.[39]

A study by Laurence and Perry showed how memories obtained by age regression can be shaped by the demand characteristics of the hypnotic scenario.[40] Twenty-seven subjects were regressed to a night they had already described. While regressed, they were asked whether noises had awakened them from their sleep. Though none of the subjects had mentioned noises before hypnosis, thirteen "remembered" the noises in response to the question about them. These subjects, moreover, maintained that the noises were real even after learning that they had been suggested.

Studies of language and cognitive skills of age-regressed subjects show that their language and skills are not really age-appropriate.[41] Their behaviors are also inaccurate portrayals of children's behavior. O'Connell and colleagues, for instance, found that adults regressed to the age of three consumed mud-spattered lollipops with gusto, while real three-year-olds were more fastidious in their habits.[42] Furthermore, hypnotizable subjects can simulate childlike speech equally well in their normal state and when they are hypnotized, and control subjects who simulate regression report feeling that their state is real, just as do hypnotized subjects.[43] Whether or not other persons give cues for the childlike role—for instance, by speaking to the subject as if he is a child—appears to be more important than whether the subject is hypnotized. Consistent with the hypothesis that they are less skilled role players, unhypnotizable subjects give less convincing performances when simulating regression.

There are some impressive anecdotes involving age regression of adults who were raised speaking a different language. Hilgard, for instance, describes hypnotically regressing a Japanese-American graduate student who had spent his earliest years in a relocation camp where Japanese as well as

English was spoken.[44] Although he claimed to have no knowledge of the language beyond a few greetings, he broke into fluent Japanese when regressed to the age of three. Unfortunately, such cases are seldom thoroughly studied to ascertain, for example, whether the subjects really had lost conscious language skills. Also, there is no control group for anecdotal reports. Every hypnotic feat that has been studied using motivated controls (discussed earlier) has turned out to be achievable without an hypnotic induction.[45] Some subjects, like the one Hilgard cited, might likewise recover their language skills without being formally hypnotized.

Some of the processes at work during hypnotic regressions are illustrated by so-called past-life therapy, which is now widely practiced by fringe hypnotherapists. On the theory that unremembered traumas in past lives cause present-day distress, subjects are hypnotized and regressed to a previous life. Having been thus regressed, a patient with a fear of heights might recall falling to his death from a seventeenth-century rooftop. A patient with marital problems might learn that her feelings toward her present-day husband originated in a previous marrriage in medieval England. Perhaps the most famous case of past-life regression was that of Virginia Tighe, who was called Ruth Simmons in the best-selling book *The Search for Bridey Murphy*, written by Morey Bernstein in 1956.[46] When hypnotized by Bernstein, Tighe became Bridey Murphy, who lived in County Cork, Ireland, in the early 1800s. *The Search for Bridey Murphy* sold more than 170,000 hardcover copies alone and put hypnosis in vogue in the late 1950s. Because of the rich details recounted by Bridey Murphy, many readers accepted her story as proof of reincarnation and of hypnotic regression. Modern-day popular books recounting similar cases are direct descendants of the Bernstein book.

At the height of the Murphy craze, a reporter investigating Virginia Tighe's past discovered that she had once lived across the street from a woman named Bridey Murphy Corkell.[47] Many of Tighe's family had resided in Ireland and could have been the sources for some of her information. Also, much of the information provided by Bridey Murphy on nineteenth-century Irish life turned out to be incorrect.

Another famous case occured some 20 years later, when a 23-year-old English woman was hypnotically regressed to her previous life as a witch burned at the stake in Clemsford in 1556.[48] In her role as a witch, she spoke in archaic English and provided extensive details of life in the mid-sixteenth century, as well as of her trial. She seemed in tremendous pain from torture she had undergone. A book was discovered in which the Clemsford witch trial was cited, which seemed to corroborate the details of her story. She denied any conscious awareness of the trials, though, and had no apparent motive, financial or otherwise, for lying about the matter.

As it turned out, however, the woman was not speaking archaic English but rather a simulacrum of an archaic tongue frequently used in movies set in the Middle Ages. Moreover, obscure manuscripts proved that the Clemsford trials were held in 1566, rather than in 1556. The latter date resulted from an error in reprinted trial records, which had misled historians since the nineteenth century. The trials had been discussed at times on the radio. Like Virginia Tighe, this woman apparently pieced together her past life from scraps collected here and there, the sources of which she may have genuinely forgotten.

Robert Baker, a psychologist whose book on hypnosis should be required reading for therapists, reports having "regressed" to the past hundreds of individuals, many of them students in psychology courses.[49] According to Baker, all that is usually needed to have subjects "remember" past lives is to (1) discuss past life regression with them, (2) express a neutral or friendly attitude toward the concept, and (3) instruct them to relax, close their eyes, and imagine traveling backward through time. The first two steps essentially define the subject's role, and the third provides the "induction," or opening scene. Under these conditions, almost all subjects will produce some "past-life" material, and fantasy-prone individuals will provide richly detailed memories. Baker reports encountering several subjects whose "memories" of past lives, elicited in this manner, rival Tighe's or other reported cases. One subject, a Mr. R., reported having been hypnotized several years before for treatment of migraine headaches. He was cured when he learned that he had once been an Indian maiden killed by a blow to the head. He came to Baker wondering whether he could have once been his own grandmother. By suggesting relaxation, Baker had Mr. R. recount his previous lives as an Indian brave, a southern plantation slave, a cockney prostitute, and a Spanish conquistador, among other characters. As he relived his past lives, Mr. R. seemed to experience intensely powerful feelings. He provided a wealth of details, none of which could be confirmed.

Consistent with the hypothesis that subjects who report past lives are merely complying with role cues, Baker divided 60 students into three groups. The first heard a tape extolling past-life therapy. The second heard a more neutral description of past-life regression, and the third heard a tape ridiculing the notion. Then all the students were hypnotized and asked to regress to the past. Eighty-five percent of students in the first group, 60 percent of students in the second, and only 10 percent of students in the third reported past-life memories. Spanos and colleagues found that subjects who reported vivid memories in response to past-life regressions were more hypnotizable and had higher scores on tests of imaginative involvement than did other subjects.[50]

In general, the evidence on hypnotic memory recovery is sufficiently weak that even those who believe that hypnosis is a special state now doubt its reliability for recall of lost material. Martin Orne, for instance, believes that hypnosis is characterized by what he calls "trance logic" (discussed later in this chapter). Yet he condemns the careless use of hypnosis in legal settings.[51] He notes that there is no way to distinguish false memories, which may be stimulated by hypnosis, from those that might be real. Orne was a principal author of an American Medical Association report, published in 1985, that cautioned physicians against forensic use of hypnotically refreshed memories.[52]

Clinicians who use hypnosis sometimes encounter patients who seem to have lost some important memories and who recover them through hypnosis, thereby seemingly validating the belief that hypnosis enhances memory. A middle-aged woman, for instance, was admitted to a San Francisco Bay area hospital complaining of confusion. She could not remember her name or the names of her husband and children, the date, the town she lived in, or other important biographical information. Neurological evaluation was normal. She was readily hypnotized and, while in a trance, was told that a curtain was rising, revealing her memories to her. In this way, she quickly recovered her memory.

However, cases like this are not true cases of memory recovery, since the patients never really lose their memories. Just as a patient with conversion paralysis is not really paralyzed but merely acts that way, so the patient in this case merely acted amnesic. The amnestic behavior, in other words, was an illness role. Hypnosis provided a pretext for the patient to drop the role, which had already served its usefulness in terms of her social situation.[53] Providing a pretext for patients to drop their illness behavior is certainly a useful function, which otherwise is sometimes performed by religious healers, but it should not be confused with real memory enhancement.

Insofar as their memory lapses are part of their social role, posthypnotic amnesics are like the patients I have described. Spanos and colleagues showed that subjects claim amnesia for the events of hypnosis only if they believe that doing so is consistent with having been hypnotized.[54]

Pain Control

Hypnotic control of pain is important on two accounts. First, mesmerism survived its early debut in France because physicians used it for surgical anesthesia.[55] One early case occured in 1829. Jules Cloquet, a professor of surgery, removed the cancerous right breast of a mesmerized 64-year-old woman, who reportedly tolerated the procedure without discomfort. Shortly thereafter, John Elliotson, the first professor of medicine at the University of London, began to mesmerize patients for relief of surgical pain. Elliotson made elaborate passes over the patient for an hour or more before he considered the patient sufficiently deeply mesmerized that surgery could begin. Elliotson was criticized by his medical colleagues and had to resign his appointment to continue his mesmeric practices. James Esdaile used hypnosis to operate on native patients in India. His reports of successes influenced others to try the technique, but failures were reported in Austria, France, and the United States. A Bengal state commission observed Esdaile's procedures. Seven of ten preselected patients could be mesmerized. One of these tolerated the procedure, tapping a scrotal cyst, without apparent pain, but he also seemed to experience no pain when a cyst on the opposite side was tapped while he was awake. The six remaining patients testified that they felt no pain during surgery, but three of the six appeared to be in agony. The remaining three did not appear to be in pain, but two of them did show erratic pulse rates during the procedure. Pulse rate increases occur in response to pain. The commision reported that Esdaile's technique was not as effective as his reports had suggested.

Esdaile mesmerized patients by means of rhythmic passes over the patient's body and by breathing deeply over the patient's head. This procedure resembled a traditional Indian therapy called *Jar Phoonk*, meaning stroking and blowing. Thus, native patients not sufficiently impressed by Esdaile's credentials as an English surgeon might have nonetheless expected beneficial results.

James Braid, an Edinburgh surgeon, modified mesmerism to resemble today's hypnosis. In 1842, Braid coined the term "hypnotism." Observing a patient becoming entranced while staring at a lamp, Braid dropped the hand and arm gestures that had characterized mesmerism. Instead, he hypnotized patients by having them stare at a light and, later, by having them stare at a moving object. But the introduction of chloroform, ether, and nitrous oxide in the 1840s undermined surgical interest in Braid's work and in hypnotism. No careful studies were done until the turn of the century, when Bramwell reported successfully using hypnosis in place of chemical agents for minor surgical and for dental procedures. Moll, though, later reported rarely achieving complete analgesia.

Chaves reviewed more recent reports of the clinical use of hypnosis in surgical pain control.[56] Although some are cited as evidence for the efficacy of hypnosis, analysis of these reports shows that analgesia is usually incomplete and requires supplementation by chemical methods. In general, the level of analgesia achieved with hypnotic techniques is about the same as can be achieved with acupuncture or with nonhypnotic relaxation procedures. Two factors may be at work to make hypnosis appear more effective than it really is. First, although we assume that surgery must be intensely painful, the pain may be limited to certain critical steps.[57] Internal organs are sensitive to stretching or pulling motions but lack pain receptors responsive to incisions per se. Thus, the pain from many procedures may be limited to that resulting from cutting the skin, periosteum, or other sensitive membranes. The subjects in some surgical case reports that tout the use of hypnosis had been given local anesthetics for incisional pain. The hypnosis was utilized to mitigate that pain over and above pain due to incisions.

The second factor is that pain responses are amplified by anxiety or feelings of lack of control.[58] An extensive literature testifies to the beneficial effects of educational measures to relieve anxiety and to inculcate a sense of control during and after surgical procedures. It is easy to see how hypnosis, for those who believe themselves altered when they are playing the role, might relieve anxiety about pain control. Hypnosis, of course, is most often used in combination with standard analgesics, so much of the residual pain treated by hypnosis is actually the result of anticipation and fear.

Controlled studies are needed to answer the questions raised by cases and anecdotes. Spanos reports on 11 studies in which subjects were randomly assigned to be hypnotized or to receive nonhypnotic suggestions for pain relief and were then subjected to painful stimuli.[59] For studies of this kind, pain can be induced by applying pressure to fingers or submerging a hand in ice water. Four of these studies used subjects unselected for hypnotizability, while the remainder used only highly hypnotizable subjects or subjects selected to represent different levels of hypnotizability. Ten of these studies found nonhypnotic suggestions as effective as hypnosis in reducing perception of pain. The remaining study found hypnosis more effective, but hypnotized and control subjects were given different suggestions.

Several other studies comparing hypnotic and nonhypnotic suggestions for pain relief given to the same highly hypnotizable subjects seemed to show that hypnotic suggestions were more effective. However, these studies were done in such a way that subjects knew that nonhypnotic and hypnotic suggestions were to be compared. Some of the subjects were even warned not to "slip into hypnosis" while receiving waking suggestions, thereby implicitly cueing them not to respond too much. To test the hypothesis that highly hypnotizable subjects complained of more pain while unhypnotized in order to better present themselves as good hypnotic subjects, Stam and Spanos varied whether high hypnotizables who received waking suggestions knew that they would later be tested using hypnosis.[60] As predicted by this hypothesis, subjects who thought they would later have an hypnotic trial reported more pain while unhypnotized than subjects who expected no further testing. Subjects who expected no testing performed as well in response to nonhypnotic suggestions as did subjects who received hypnotic pain suggestions.

Another reason for interest in hypnotic pain control is that analgesia has been the focus of research on the so-called hidden-observer phenomenon, which some take as evidence for dissociation. Hilgard discovered this phenomenon by administering painful stimuli to highly hypnotizable subjects.[61] Subjects were hypnotized and told that a "hidden part" of them would remain aware of pain their "hypnotized part" could not feel. Their hidden part would speak when the hypnotist gave them a cue, such as placing his hand on their shoulder. Many of the subjects given these instructions reported low levels of pain in the usual hypnotic state but high levels of pain when their hidden parts were contacted. Hilgard believed these latter reports were of pain blocked from conscious awareness by the hypnotic instructions. The hidden observer, in other words, provided a channel for access to a part of the mind that was dissociated.

From the social role point of view, hidden-observer experiments merely require the subject to play a more complex role. Where the ordinary hypnotic role requires only that the subject deny feeling pain, the hidden-observer experiment requires that the subject drop the pretense at certain times. By admitting that he feels pain when instructed to do so, he "proves" that his previous claim of anesthesia was real. A number of studies conducted by Spanos and colleagues support the social role view of hidden-observer responding. Spanos and Hewitt, for instance, followed Hilgard's procedures with one group of highly hypnotizable subjects but varied these procedures with a second group.[62] The second group was told that their hidden parts were so deeply hidden that they would be even less aware of pain than their hypnotized parts. The hidden observers elicited from the two groups of subjects had opposite characteristics, reporting more pain in the first group and less pain in the second than in the "hypnotized" state. Spanos and Hewitt argued that hidden-observer reports are conditioned by expectations implicit in the instructions.

Spanos, Gwynn, and Stam told subjects that they had hidden-observers that could report pain intensity, but they gave subjects no cues as to the relative intensities of hidden-observer and other pain reports.[63] If hidden observers were really serving as channels for expression of otherwise dissociated information, as Hilgard hypothesized, then the hidden observers should have reported more pain than the subject in the "hypnotized" state. In fact, given no cues as to how pain reports should differ, subjects reported the same levels of pain directly and through their hidden observers. The subjects were then instructed that the hidden observer would be more or less aware of pain, as in the Spanos and Hewitt experiment. As expected, hidden observer responding shifted in the direction cued by the instructions.

Spanos and colleagues, moreover, showed that the hidden-observer phenomenon is not dependent on hypnosis at all.[64] Hypnotizable subjects were either hypnotized or given nonhypnotic suggestions for analgesia. All the subjects were told that they had hidden parts that would remain aware of pain they did not experience. Hypnotized or unhypnotized subjects were equally likely to report analgesia. They were also equally likely to give voice to a hidden part aware of higher pain levels.

A well-known study by Zamansky and Bartis used negative hallucinations (discussed later in this chapter), rather than analgesia, to study the hidden-observer phenomenon.[65] Before being shown a page on which was a printed number, hypnotized subjects were told that the page would be blank. Subjects who reported seeing nothing on the page were then told they had a hidden part that was aware of everything they had seen while in a hypnotic trance. When their hidden parts were contacted, all of these subjects correctly reported the printed number. Since the hidden-observer suggestion was given after the suggested negative hallucination occured, the authors claimed that the hidden parts must have been reporting unconsciously stored information.

Spanos, Flynn, and Gwynn repeated this experiment using highly hypnotizable subjects and a page with the number 18 printed on it.[66] Half the subjects were given instructions suggesting that their hidden part knew what had been seen. The other half were instructed that their hidden part reversed what had really been seen. As expected, the first half reported that their hidden observers had seen the number 18, and the second half reported that their hidden observers had seen the number 81. Those subjects who failed the negative hallucination suggestion, that is, those subjects who never denied seeing the number in the first place, were told they had hidden parts that were so deeply hypnotized they did not see the number. When these hidden parts were contacted, almost half of these subjects claimed that the page was blank. Thus, as is the case in studies of hypnotic analgesia, the hidden observer elicited with negative hallucinations gives reports congruent with the hypnotic role. It cannot be seen as a simple conduit to the unconscious.

Simultaneous Mental Activities, Increased Suggestibility, Hallucinations, and Trance Logic

Intriguing mental phenomena are reported during hypnosis. These are sometimes cited as proof that hypnotic and waking states really differ. In this section I review studies that show that these phenomena either are not what they appear or can be accounted for in terms of hypnotic roles.

Early experimenters believed that hypnotic suggestions could be used to establish mental subsystems that could function independently of each other and of consciousness.[67] Pierre Janet, who had worked with Charcot in the Salpêtrière, hypnotized a subject, Lucie, and instructed her to perform automatic posthypnotic acts whenever a cue was given. She was told she would not be aware of the acts thus performed. One such instruction, for instance, was to write a letter. The cue was given during a conversation. As she continued conversing, she wrote a brief note with one hand. She later denied she had written it. Another instruction required Lucie to multiply numbers, which she did while discussing her day's activities with Janet. Morton Prince, an American physician who reported some of the first cases of multiple personality, performed similar experiments. He concluded that hypnosis could create mental subsystems that operate independent of the conscious mind. Studies by Burnett in the 1920s led to the same conclusions: Hypnotized subjects could carry out activities without being aware of them and without interference with their ongoing activities. In the late 1920s, however, the experimental psychologist Clark Hull investigated hypnosis. His studies and those of his colleagues convinced him that interference does in fact occur between suggested acts and ongoing conscious activities. Ostensibly unconscious, suggested acts slow down conscious activities and make them less accurate. Hull found no evidence of parallel mental subsystems. Hull's conclusions, which were instrumental in the decline of the concept of dissociation, have stood the test of time.[68]

Hull considered hypnosis a hypersuggestible state.[69] Some 50 years later, Andre Weitzenhoffer, Hilgard's collaborator on the Stanford Hypnotic Susceptibility Scale, considered increased suggestibility during hypnosis "unquestionable."[70] Numerous studies seemed to show that hypnotized subjects are more likely than awake subjects to follow suggestions and to report doing so automatically. Martin Orne has argued that increased suggestibility in the hypnotic state results in part from suspension of critical faculties (discussed in this chapter). Other experiments, though, cast doubt on this whole line of argument. Barber and colleagues, for instance, assigned

186 college students to one of three experimental conditions.[71] One-third were given a standard "hypnotic induction procedure"; another third were exposed to "task motivational instructions," which urged them to try to imagine the things that would be suggested as vividly as possible and promised them a rewarding experience if they could do so; and the last third were simply told to imagine those things. Immediately afterward, subjects were tested with the eight items that make up the Barber Suggestibility Scale (BSS), which is similar in structure to the Stanford Hypnotic Susceptibility Scale and other tests of hypnotizability. One suggestion, for instance, is that one arm is getting lighter and rising into the air; another suggestion is that the patient is stuck to a chair and cannot get up from it. Fifty-three percent of the hypnotized subjects, 60 percent of the subjects given task motivational instructions, and 16 percent of the remaining subjects showed high-level responsiveness to the BSS. Instructions that motivated subjects to do their best to imagine along with suggestions were as effective as hypnosis per se.

Of course, responding to suggestions is part of the hypnotic role. Hence, subjects who believe that they have been hypnotized expect to respond to suggestions and might act accordingly. Barber and Calverley randomly assigned subjects to two conditions.[72] Subjects in the first group were told that they were subjects in an hypnosis experiment. Subjects in the second group were told that they were control subjects. Both groups were then administered the Barber Suggestibility Scale. Subjects told that they were involved in an hypnosis experiment were more responsive to the BSS items than were subjects told that they were controls. Related studies show that subjects made to believe that they are suggestible become more suggestible on objective tests. In one ingenious experiment, subjects were introduced to a tester as being either high or low in suggestibility. Those introduced as highly suggestible showed higher objective scores and those introduced as less suggestable showed lower objective scores.

Weitzenhoffer believed that involuntary responding to suggestions differentiates hypnosis from suggestibility in general.[73] In a review of this theory, though, Lynn, Rhue, and Weekes observed that the hypnotic role requires subjects to disavow agency or choice.[74] That is, hypnotized subjects are supposed to respond to suggestions because they are hypnotized, not because they choose to. Persons who acknowledge choice would not be playing the role of the hypnotized subject. Consistent with this point, hypnotic suggestions are phrased to convey the demand for subjects' denial of choice or agency. Hypnotists, for instance, tell subjects "your arm is rising," not "you are raising your arm." Or consider the following suggestion from the Stanford Hypnotic Susceptibility Scale: "Now I want you to imagine a force attracting your hands toward each other, pulling them together . . . closer and closer together as though a force were acting on them. . . ."[75] The suggestion tacitly requests that the arms be moved, but it also requests that the subject deny doing so voluntarily.

A study by Spanos, Cobb, and Gorassini showed that subjects report automaticity only if they believe it is consistent with having been hypnotized.[76] These authors assigned highly hypnotizable subjects to four different preparatory conditions. The first, or control group, received no preparation. The second group was told that deeply hypnotized subjects are incapable of resistance to suggestions, and the third group was told that deeply hypnotized subjects may or may not be capable of resistance. The fourth group was told that deeply hypnotized subjects can resist suggestions at will. All subjects were then hypnotized and given four motor suggestions. Subjects in the first three groups complied with most suggestions and rated themselves as having been unable to resist them. Having been told that resistance is consistent with deep hypnosis, subjects in the last group complied with only 5 percent of the suggestions received. They rated themselves as having been in control of their actions.

In the United States, hypnotizability test scores and self-reports of involuntary responding are closely correlated. Insofar as this correlation depends upon cultural knowledge of the hypnotic role, it might be less apparent with subjects from other cultures. Lynn and colleagues administered the Harvard Group Scale of Hypnotic Susceptibility and a measure of self-reported involuntary responding to English-speaking students at the University of Malaysia and to Malaysian students resident in the United States for at least six months.[77] Among Malaysian students outside the United States, hypnotizability was unrelated to reports of involuntary responding. Among Malaysian students in the United States, hypnotizability and reports of involuntary responding were correlated as they are for U.S. citizens. The average Malaysian students tested in the United States had lived here for 2.5 years. They may represent a more Westernized segment of their society than students who attend university in Malaysia.

Apparent hallucinations are among the most impressive of hypnotic phenomena. In response to hypnotic suggestions, subjects will converse with people who are not there or cower from wild animals only they can see. Hallucinations can also be negative; that is, subjects can be induced to apparently not see objects or people who should be clearly visible to them. A series of studies, however, casts doubt on the meaning of such hallucinations by showing that whether subjects report really seeing things or merely vividly imagining them is highly dependent on the wording of the questions they are asked.[78] In these studies, subjects were asked to rate the vividness and reality of suggested hallucinations. One type of rating scale permitted the subject to report that he "did not see" an object, "vaguely saw it," "clearly saw it," or "saw it and believed it was there." In studies that used such a scale, at least one-third of subjects reported that they "saw" the suggested object. Another type of rating scale permitted the subject to report that he had either "imagined" or "seen" the object. In studies that used this type of scale, the great majority of subjects reported only imagining suggested objects. Fewer than 10 percent reported that they had seen it.

Nonhypnotic task motivational instructions, moreover, produce these kinds of reports as effectively as do hypnotic suggestions. Spanos, Ham, and

Barber gave subjects suggestions to hallucinate an object both before and after either hypnotic inductions or task motivational instructions.[79] Using a scale that allowed them to distinguish between "imagining" and "seeing," the subjects rated the vividness and reality of the object. Before receiving either an hypnotic induction or task motivational instructions, only 2 percent of subjects reported seeing the object. Hypnosis or task motivational instructions raised this figure to 8 percent, but subjects were inconsistent in reporting whether they saw or imagined the object. Some of those who claimed to have seen the object reported in postexperimental interviews that they had only imagined it, and vice versa. Those few in both the hypnotic and nonhypnotic groups who reported really believing the object was present later indicated that they were concentrating so hard on the image suggested that they never thought of whether or not it was real.

Two studies have used evoked brain electrical responses to prove that hypnotic suggestions really can produce negative hallucinations. In the first, by Barbasz and Lonsdale, subjects were exposed to an odoriferous compound after receiving hypnotic suggestions for anosmia.[80] Highly hypnotizable subjects showed larger late evoked response components to the stimulus than did unhypnotizable subjects. The authors interpreted their finding to mean that hypnotized subjects screened out incoming odor signals. In the second, by Spiegel and colleagues, hypnotized subjects were told that their view of a video monitor was blocked by an hallucinated object.[81] Hypnotized subjects showed smaller late evoked responses to stimuli on the monitor than did simulators. Neither of these studies are at all straightforward. Late evoked responses are highly dependent upon the subjective probability of the stimuli that produced them and of their relevance to tasks the subject must perform. In the Spiegel study, for instance, the suggested-away stimuli were no longer task-relevant for highly hypnotizable subjects. Insofar as subjects were playing hypnotic roles, they had no need to respond to the stimuli they observed. In a review of methodological issues in hypnosis research, Jones and Flynn cast doubt on whether either the Barbasz and Lonsdale or the Spiegel study support their authors' conclusions.[82]

More straightforward studies cast doubt on the hypothesis that subjects really screen out negatively hallucinated perceptions. Barber and Calverly, for example, gave hypnotized and nonhypnotized subjects suggestions that they were deaf before testing them for their response to delayed auditory feedback.[83] Subjects exposed to the slightly delayed sound of their own voice have difficulty speaking. Both hypnotic and nonhypnotic subjects, including those who reported not hearing anything, showed slowing of speech, mispronunciations, and stammering in response to delayed auditory feedback. In spite of reports to the contrary, similar results are found when hypnotically color-blind subjects are given appropriate tests.[84]

In a recent but widely cited study, Kosslyn and coauthors claimed they found neural activity corresponding to hypnotically induced color hallucinations.[85] Eight highly hypnotizable subjects were shown a pattern composed of variably colored rectangles, resembling a Mondrian painting, along with the same pattern in varying shades of gray. After being hypnotized, subjects were instructed to perceive the colored pattern either veridically or in hallucinated shades of gray, and to perceive the gray pattern either veridically or in hallucinated colors. In another condition, the subjects were not hypnotized but were simply told to "visualize and remember" the colored pattern when viewing the gray one, or the gray pattern when viewing the colored one. While visualizing the patterns, subjects were given "PET" scans, which measure blood flow in various brain regions. Blood flow is known to correlate with local neural activity. Instructions to perceive the pattern as colored resulted in greater blood flow in a small region of the left hemisphere when the subjects were hypnotized than when they were unhypnotized. The enhanced blood flow was interpreted as a correlate of color hallucinations induced by hypnotic commands.

A number of flaws are evident in the design of this study, the most important being that the non-hypnotic instructions fell far short of being effectively "task motivational." Motivation, in fact, wasn't wanted: the authors expressed concern that stronger instructions to visualize could have induced hypnosis in these susceptible subjects. Insofar as subjects made stronger efforts to visualize colors (or their absence) when formally hypnotized, such efforts, not hypnosis, could account for the study findings. Oddly, data from a control group of unhypnotizable subjects is simply not reported.

The data shown, in any event, do not support the authors' conclusions. Although instructions to perceive color resulted in greater blood flow only when subjects were hypnotized, the effect was as pronounced when subjects viewed color patterns as when they viewed gray patterns. The increase in blood flow, in other words, was connected with color perception, real or imagined, in the hypnotic role, not with hallucinations. From the social role viewpoint, color was more salient to subjects when they were hypnotized, since color perception lay at the heart of the role they were playing. Subjects knew in advance how important color would be; they had been screened with the same task on which they were later tested.

Martin Orne has argued that hypnotized individuals exhibit what he calls "trance logic"; that is, they tolerate incongruities that they would ordinarily find disturbing.[86] For instance, hypnotized subjects told to hallucinate someone who is visible in the flesh may report that the person appears in two places at once. Other researchers, however, cast doubt on the claim that trance logic is really unique to hypnosis. Nonhypnotized subjects given task motivational instructions are equally likely to show seeming trance logic as are hypnotized subjects.[87]

Feats of Strength, Healing, and Physiologic Effects

When Charcot began to hypnotize grand hysterics, he discovered that they could perform apparently superhuman feats.[88] These patients, for instance, could readily be made cataleptic: For prolonged periods of time, their limbs would stay in whatever position Charcot had placed them. Conscious attempts to mimic these postures resulted in pain and fatigue. Under certain hypnotic conditions, muscle groups touched by Charcot contracted with maximal force and remained perfectly rigid. To the amazement of those who attended his clinical demonstrations, Charcot turned hysterics into human planks and then suspended them by their heads and their feet between chairs.

Since Charcot's day, demonstrations like these have become staples of stage hypnotists and have contributed greatly to public faith in hypnosis, even though most researchers now agree that all hypnotically induced motor feats can be replicated by motivated nonhypnotized subjects.[89] Most stage hypnotists screen volunteer subjects carefully before putting them on stage, using test suggestions like those on the Stanford Scale. Thus, at the very least, they are assured that their subjects will want to cooperate with them. They also are very careful to avoid testing the limits of their subjects' abilities.

Extraordinary healing and physiologic effects have also been claimed for hypnosis. Most of these, such as cancer cures, are no doubt apocryphal, but others are not and testify to the effects of imagination on health and bodily functions. The best-known healing experiments involve regression of skin warts due to hypnotic suggestion. Ullman and Dudek gave 62 patients with warts suggestions for relaxation, drowsiness, and hypnosis, followed by suggestions that their warts would disappear.[90] Of 47 patients rated relatively unhypnotizable, only two experienced remission of their warts within a four-week period. Of 15 patients rated highly hypnotizable, eight were cured of their warts, which in most cases were multiple, within a four-week period. Later studies confirmed Ullman and Dudek's finding.[91]

However, nonhypnotic suggestions and expectations of cure are equally efficacious treatments for common warts. Effective procedures include painting warts with an innocuous dye that the patient believes is medicinal, placing the warts under a machine that the patient believes emits x-rays, and placing the warts in a machine that the patient believes "electrocutes" them.[92] To test the relative efficacy of hypnotic and nonhypnotic suggestions, Spanos and colleagues divided 76 subjects with warts into four groups.[93] The first group was hypnotized and given suggestions for wart remission. The second group was given relaxation suggestions in combination with suggestions for wart remission. The third group received only suggestions for wart remission, and the fourth group received no suggestions at all. Hypnotic and nonhypnotic suggestions were equally effective. Success was predicted by patients' expectations and by the vividness of healing-related imagery they reported, regardless of which treatment group they were in.

How can warts, which are caused by a virus, be cured by suggestion, imagery, or expectation? A clue comes from a line of research initiated by Sinclair-Gieben and Chalmers, who hypnotized 14 patients with warts on both sides of their bodies and suggested to them that the warts on one side, but not the other, would disappear.[94] Although these authors reported achieving unilateral remissions, later studies show the effect to be all or none: Hypnotic suggestions result in remission of warts on both sides of the body or on neither side, but not on one side alone.[95] This pattern suggests that systemic or circulating factors, such as antibodies or white blood cells, are involved. A variety of suggestions and relaxation procedures have been shown to affect immune responses.[96]

Hypnosis has been reported to correct nearsightedness, but in fact nonhypnotic suggestions have the same effect on vision as hypnotic ones. Kelley, for example, categorized subjects according to their level of responses to hypnotic suggestions.[97] Only those deemed capable of hypnosis were given an hypnotic induction; the remainder served as controls. Three types of suggestions were used to correct nearsightedness. The most effective of these instructed each patient to imagine a series of pleasant scenes with his eyes closed. When he opened his eyes, he was told, he would continue to have the pleasant, relaxed feeling that had accompanied the visualized scenes. Dramatic improvements in acuity for distant objects were found in both hypnotic and nonhypnotic groups. Graham and Leibowitz hypnotized half their subjects and then suggested to all of them that they would relax the muscles around their eyes.[98] Subjects were instructed to practice relaxing at home. The hypnotic and nonhypnotic groups were equal in their degree of improvement of acuity. Harwood compared an hypnotic group with a control group trained in relaxation techniques.[99] Subjects were given suggestions that they would be relaxed and calm during visual testing. Both groups showed small enhancements of acuity. Increased acuity may result from decreased anxiety in the test situation.

Hypnosis is sometimes said to control allergic responses. However, in a well-known study, Ikemi and Nakagawa tested 13 subjects who were allergic to the leaves of two common trees in Japan.[100] Five of the subjects were hypnotized and told to keep their eyes shut; the remaining eight were blindfolded. All the subjects were then told that they were being touched with the leaves of a tree to which they were not allergic. In fact, they were touched with the leaves of the tree to which they were allergic. Four of five subjects who had been hypnotized and seven of eight control subjects failed to show the expected allergic reaction. Then the subjects were told that they were being touched with leaves of a tree to which they were allergic. In fact, they were touched on the opposite arm with leaves of a tree to which they were not allergic. All hypnotic and control subjects developed marked skin reactions where they thought they had been touched by the leaves to which they were allergic. These results suggest that allergic responses can be either triggered or inhibited by suggestions and expectations but that hypnosis itself is irrelevant to the phenomenon.

Like its healing effects, physiological effects attributed to hypnosis can be achieved without hypnotic inductions per se. Several studies, for instance, report electroencephalographic (EEG) changes during hypnosis consistent with preferential activation of the right hemisphere.[101] However, similar evidence of right-hemisphere activation is observed when subjects listen to stories or engage in activities that require imagination. The EEG obtained from hypnotized subjects changes with their activities as it does in the "waking" state.[102] Similar observations apply to autonomic nervous system changes during hypnosis. Hypnosis, nonhypnotic relaxation, and nonhypnotic imagery suggestions all alter sympathetic relative to parasympathetic nervous system activity.[103] Subjects capable of imaginative involvement are especially able to change autonomic nervous functioning using imagery.[104] Localized changes in skin temperatures have been reported due to hypnotic suggestions. Unhypnotized subjects, however, can produce the same effects by imagining feelings of warmth or cold in localized areas.[105]

Many modern-day hypnotherapists make a living helping patients to give up smoking or lose weight. Smoking cessation and weight loss are responsive to social support and to placebo effects. In a review of studies of the use of hypnosis for smoking cessation or weight loss, Spanos observed that the effects of hypnosis on these problems are usually small and transient.[106]

Posthypnotic Responses

Posthypnotic responses are sometimes cited as proof that hypnosis is real. A hypnotized subject is told that, after waking up, he or she will perform an act in response to a cue. The act may be scratching the head or changing seats, for instance, and the cue may be a sound, a movement, or a spoken word. Subjects are also instructed that they will not be aware of the connection between the act and cue. From a social role viewpoint, however, posthypnotic responses pose no special problem. The subject is seen as continuing with the hypnotic role even after the close of the trance scene itself.

Several studies support the view that subjects who follow posthypnotic suggestions are acting so as to safeguard the appearance of having been hypnotized. Fisher, for instance, gave 13 subjects the posthypnotic suggestion that they would scratch their ear whenever they heard the spoken word "psychology."[107] After posthypnotic testing for this response, Fisher gave subjects the impression that the experiment was finished. Although all 13 subjects had responded to the posthypnotic cue when they thought they were being tested, nine of the of the subjects failed to respond when they thought the experiment had ended. Seven of the nine began responding again when they were led to believe that the testing had resumed. St. Jean gave subjects suggestions to respond posthypnotically to a recorded stimulus.[108] Although subjects responded when the experimenter was present, almost all stopped responding when he left the room. Spanos and colleagues gave hypnotizable subjects suggestions to cough out loud whenever they heard the word "psychology."[109] Subjects showed posthypnotic responses when they were formally tested but not when they were approached by someone posing as a lost student looking for the psychology building or by someone pretending to be looking for a psychology experiment.[110]

5

Hysteria and Hysteria-like Disorders

The major modern-day illness roles in Europe and North America fall into three historically related types: disorders that resemble hysteria, multiple consciousness, and disorders ascribed to trauma. Hysteria and the modern-day illness roles that resemble it are described in this chapter; multiple consciousness is described in chapter 6, and disorders ascribed to trauma are the subject of chapter 7.

Textbook accounts of hysteria sometimes assert that it was first observed by physicians in ancient Greece and perhaps even Egypt.[1] Greek and Egyptian physicians supposedly thought this syndrome, which could only occur in women, resulted from the uterus's wandering through the body, causing symptoms wherever it went. If it lodged in the throat, for instance, the patient would feel something obstructing her swallowing, a symptom later referred to as *globus hystericus*. Consistent with this account, "hysteria" comes from *hystera*, the Greek word for womb.

Recent scholarship, though, has cast doubt on the antiquity of hysteria and suggests that hysteria, like hypnosis, was really an early-modern offshoot of demon possession. An extensive study of Greek and Roman medical writings conducted by Helen King, a British classicist, showed that, although Greek and Roman physicians attributed diverse female somatic complaints to the womb, they had no conception of anything akin to modern hysteria.[2] Convulsions, loss of sensation, paralyses, abnormal postures, or *globus hystericus*, the staples of hysteria in early-modern Europe, are not described as a syndrome in the classical texts. Some of the symptoms ascribed to uterine disorders, such as blackening of the skin, bear no connection at all to hysteria as we know it. Merskey and Potter have shown that ancient Egyptian texts also fail to mention a disease caused by uterine movements.[3]

Although the term "hysteria" in reference to an illness would not appear in France until 1731 or in England until 1801, the concept of the illness later called hysteria emerged at the beginning of the seventeenth century.[4] The way in which it emerged, and the symptoms thought to be typical, suggest that it represented a medicalization of the role of demon possession, as that was enacted during the Reformation.[5] A key early text, for instance, was Edward Jorden's discussion of Mary Glover, *A Briefe Discourse of a Disease Called the Suffocation of the Mother,* published in 1603. Fourteen-year-old

Glover, the daughter of a London alderman, developed convulsions and lost her sight and speech and all sensations on the left side of her body following a violent argument with an eccentric neighbour, Elizabeth Jackson. Jackson was accused of having practiced witchcraft, and, during the subsequent trial, Glover confirmed the charges by having hysterical fits and speaking in the voice of the demon Jackson was charged with conjuring. Aside from the prominence of Glover's father, this case was not unusual: In late medieval Europe, demon possession was often enacted to take revenge against a personal enemy, who would be charged with witchcraft. The demon confirmed the charge by naming the witch that had conjured him or sometimes by convulsing in the witch's presence. Eccentric women like Jackson were especially vulnerable to this type of revenge, since these were women against whom witchcraft charges seemed plausible. Jorden, a physician, testified for Jackson that Glover's fits and symptoms resulted from natural causes, but the jurors, who could see with their own eyes and hear with their own ears that Glover was possessed, convicted Jackson of witchcraft and sentenced her to prison. After the trial, Jorden wrote his famous discourse.

Written in the vernacular and distributed as a pamphlet to nonmedical readers, Jorden's *Discourse* was as much a political statement as the triumph of rational thinking that it is reputed to be. Possession had become an important sectarian weapon in late sixteenth-century England. Spanish Catholic priests smuggled into England during Elizabeth's reign held semipublic rituals to exorcise demons from the servants of wealthy Catholic families. Prior to being cast out, the demons that possessed these servants confirmed the Roman faith by praising the Anglican church while cringing in seeming terror from relics of Catholic saints. Demons that possessed Puritans praised both the Roman and the Anglican churches while cursing the name of Calvin and shrinking from Puritan prayer books. Similar events were also occuring in France: Demons that possessed Catholics claimed to admire the Huguenots but convulsed at the sight of the Host, while demons that possessed Huguenots heaped praise on the Roman Pope. Being the least adept at using possession this way, late-sixteenth-century Anglicans were eager to debunk it, a purpose quite well served by Jorden's published *Discourse*. Jorden, an Anglican clergyman as well as a physician, undoubtedly understood and thoroughly approved the sectarian implications of his approach to Glover.

However sectarian the motives for medicalizing possession, once the process was started, a new role began to evolve. With a medical explanation, the symptoms were no longer constrained by the need to demonstrate the presence of spirits or demons. Although the cardinal symptoms of what later was called hysteria initially coincided with those of Reformation-era possession—demonic enactments, convulsions, weakness, and sensory loss—by the mid-1800s the symptom picture had changed.[6] Demonic enactments vanished, and, with the exception of a small group of hysterics in the Salpêtrière hospital in Paris (discussed later), the incidence of dramatic convulsions diminished. The convulsions that still occurred were triggered by emotional distress or fatigue, not by witches or prayer books. Symptoms like *globus hystericus*, faintness, palpitations, loss of phonation, and weakness became prominent features.

Ironically, since the time of Charcot and his followers, who argued that the seventeenth-century witches of Loudon were suffering from hysteria, physicians have claimed that demoniacs are really just hysterics.[7] Descriptions of the possessed in the fifteenth-century guide to witchcraft *Malleus Maleficarum* are offered as proof that hysteria is really of more ancient provenance than the seventeenth century. This is but one instance of a common phenomenon: Insofar as current illness roles resemble the roles from which they evolved, proponents of the current roles try to redefine the older cases in the newer terms.

Several of the disorders described in the following sections have been widely discussed using concepts like "somatization,"[8] "alexithymia,"[9] "negative affectivity,"[10] "somatosensory amplification,"[11] and "psychophysiological concomitants" of dysphoric states.[12] Readers are referred to the references for explanations of these various concepts, which may be quite useful with respect to particular patients. Here I outline the case for applying the language and concepts of social roles to these disorders. Studies have shown that patients with unexplained medical symptoms are highly heterogeneous.[13] Among patients with similar lifetime unexplained medical symptoms, various causative factors may be active in some but not others. Also, reports of generalized symptoms and functional limitations don't always go hand in hand. Some patients with few unexplained symptoms are nonetheless chronically ill and disabled for work and activities.[14] Illness role concepts, especially, are more relevant to disability than to symptoms per se, since the function of illness roles is often to gain concessions and relief from one's obligations.

The syndromes described in this chapter differ from the illness roles described in chapter 3 with respect to the relationships formed between patient and therapist. As I described in chapter 3, those who treat culture-specific illness roles are generally on their patients' side; they validate diagnoses and help to negotiate settlements of the social problems that prompted the illness behavior. They are loathe to invalidate illness roles on which their own livelihoods and status depend. Modern physicians, by contrast, are often unhappy with and frustrated by patients with the syndromes I describe in this chapter. Such patients present with symptoms that physicians are forced to evaluate. The process of evaluating symptoms enmeshes physicians in their patients' illness behavior. If no definite cause is found and the physician tries to treat the patient's complaints symptomatically, the process of offering treatment may serve to validate illness, regardless of the physician's real appraisal of the situation. If the physician refuses to offer treatment or goes so far as to try to invalidate the illness behavior by attributing it to psychological causes, the patient can always start the process over again with another physician. Traditional communities may have only one shaman, whose judgments are thus final, but second opinions are readily obtained in modern societies. As I describe, some physicians support themselves by offering more sympathetic second opinions to patients with certain illness roles.

Grand Hysteria

Hysteria reached its full flowering by the late nineteenth century. Of the various forms it took, none was more dramatic than so-called grand hysteria. The designation "grand" distinguished this form of hysteria from garden-variety hysterical illness, which sometimes was called "petit." Although grand hysteria lacks direct descendants in modern-day illness roles, it played a critical part in the history of psychiatry and psychotherapy and hence is worth describing. Concepts like dissociation and the nineteenth-century revival of interest in hypnosis were in large part a result of the study of grand hysterics. Also, more than any other single illness role, grand hysteria shows how illness roles can be shaped by social reinforcement in closed institutions.

Grand hysteria was the creation of Jean-Martin Charcot, a pioneering French neurologist sometimes called "the Caesar of the Salpêtrière," the women's asylum in Paris.[15] In the 1860s and 1870s Charcot first described and named many of the illnesses he observed in the Salpêtrière. He was the first physician to describe multiple sclerosis and the illness now known as Lou Gehrig's disease. Joints destroyed by syphilis are still called Charcot joints, and a rare disorder of muscles is also named for Charcot, along with its codiscoverers. Gradually, Charcot became intrigued by hysterics and, in particular, by a small group of hysterics he later called "grand hysterics" because of their extreme symptoms. Until Charcot's death in 1893, he and his students, including several of the founders of modern neurology, carefully documented and photographed some of these patients and experimented with various forms of treatment. By studying grand hysteria, Charcot believed he could elucidate fundamental principles of nervous function. He came to see grand hysteria as his claim to immortality.

As it took shape in the Salpêtrière, grand hysteria was characterized by seizures and by so-called stigmata. The stigmata included chronic or fluctuating symptoms and disabilities, such as tunnel vision, gait disturbances, paralysis, loss of sensation, amnesia, or loss of speech. The seizures were stereotyped and consisted of four phases. During the first, or epileptoid, phase, the "seizing" grand hysteric would stiffen and jerk like patients with real epilepsy. The second phase, that of "grand movements," was manifested by sustained bizarre contortions, such as the *arc-en-cercle*; arching dramatically backward, the hysteric patient balanced on her feet and head. During the third, or "passionate attitude," phase, the contortions gave way to parodies of sexual intercourse, religious ecstasies, or dangerous adventures. The patient seemed to see snakes, monsters, or angelic beings. She cried out, shouted, or spoke to imagined companions. During the fourth, or delirious, phase the seizing grand hysteric wept or laughed insensibly or fell into a coma.

Grand hysteric seizures could be elicited or, in some cases, terminated by pressure on sensitive bodily areas, the so-called hysterogenic points. In a vain effort to treat what they saw as a reflex phenomenon, Charcot and his colleagues devised special corsets to apply constant pressure to such points.[16] Occasionally, grand hysterics pressed each other's sensitive points in order to induce seizures. Competing for Charcot's attention, the Salpêtrière grand hysterics were often at odds with each other.

In the 1870s, Charcot began hypnotizing his hysterical patients, with astonishing results. Patients who had been paralyzed or disabled for years could be made transiently well again in an hypnotic trance. Suggestions for longer cures were sometimes also effective, leading to longer-lasting improvements in chronic symptoms. Moreover, there were clear parallels between the signs and symptoms of grand hysteria and symptoms induced by hypnosis applied to normal subjects. Mesmer had earlier shown that bizarre contortions very much like those seen in the grand movement phase of seizures could be induced in normals subjected to "animal magnetism," as hypnosis was then called. Apparent hallucinations like those experienced by patients during the passionate attitude phase of their seizures could be induced in hypnotized normal subjects asked to relive past events. Hypnotized normal subjects could also be made to act paralyzed, anesthetic, or even blind.

Charcot's grand hysterics were easily hypnotized. When hypnotized, moreover, they achieved some remarkable feats, which Charcot and his followers characteristically called "grand hypnosis." These patients, for instance, could readily be made cataleptic: For prolonged periods of time, their limbs would stay in whatever position Charcot had placed them. They could be made lethargic: If the lights were dimmed or their eyes closed while they were cataleptic, hysterical patients went limp. If a muscle was touched, it contracted with incredible force. They showed sonnambulism: Given the proper signal, such as a touch to the head, the hypnotized grand hysteric entered a twilight state. She spoke and moved automatically and later claimed not to remember the events of the period.

Seeing that hypnosis could be used to modify or create hysterical symptoms and that hysterical patients were readily hypnotized, Charcot came to believe that hypnotizable subjects had something wrong with their brains. With the proper stimulus, he believed, this brain disorder could lead to hysterical illness. According to Charcot, highly hypnotizable but clinically normal subjects were potential hysterics in spite of their apparent good health.

While Charcot experimented with hypnosis in the Salpêtrière, others were using it with more normal subjects. In the 1860s, August Liébault, a country doctor near Nancy, began using hypnosis to treat various ailments of his peasant patients. His work caught the attention of Hippolyte Bernheim, professor of internal medicine at the University of Nancy and an established authority on pulmonary disease. After observing Liébault at work, Bernheim began experimenting with his own patients. On the basis of these experiments, he came to believe that hypnosis was a normal phenomenon and that highly hypnotizable subjects, rather than being afflicted with a morbid process, were simply more suggestible than average persons. In 1884, Bernheim argued that the grand hysteric phenomena Charcot had observed in the Salpêtrière resulted from suggestion on the part of Charcot and others.

Bernheim's critique of Charcot's theory of hypnosis and grand hysteria led to the so-called Battle of the Schools between Bernheim and his followers in Nancy and Charcot and his colleagues in the Salpêtrière. Until 1893, when Charcot died, hundreds of papers were published in professional journals and in the lay press arguing for one side or the other. In the end, the battle was settled in Bernheim's favor. While Charcot studied small numbers of patients in the Salpêtrière, Bernheim and his colleagues in Nancy conducted experiments on hundreds of normal subjects.[17] They showed conclusively that highly hypnotizable subjects could be as healthy and robust as those less readily hypnotized. They also showed that grand hypnosis as Charcot described it was, like grand hysteria, hardly ever seen outside the Salpêtrière, where patients were exposed to subtle role suggestions. With Charcot's death, grand hypnosis and grand hysteria, too, rapidly disappeared even from the precincts of the Salpêtrière.

The ambience of the Salpêtrière explains how an illness role like grand hysteria might have been created there. The Salpêtrière was a state women's asylum created, as the name implies, from an old saltpeter depot. In Charcot's time, nearly 5,000 women, many of whom had incurable neurological or psychiatric disorders, were crowded into its filthy, ill-lit wards. They came, for the most part, from the lowest classes, and many had no families to aid them.[18] Regardless of how wretched conditions were inside the Salpêtrière, they were still far better than those the women would have found on the streets. Today, a state-run asylum like the Salpêtrière might be staffed by doctors lacking the highest qualifications. But Charcot and his students were the cream of French physicians, and Charcot himself was well known in society circles. He and his students were hard working and ambitious, and they saw in the Salpêtrière patients the ore that they would mine for their reputations. When Charcot made hysteria his vehicle to immortality, the patients who could manifest dramatic symptom pictures found themselves suddenly a notch above the others. Being of interest to Charcot ensured that they would not be discharged. They were given privileges and better living conditions and enjoyed a measure of status with the hospital staff.

Louise, who was perhaps the most photographed of Charcot's grand hysterics, illustrates the handicaps common to these patients. Louise was the oldest of seven children of Parisian domestics; only two of the children survived infancy. At age six, she was sent to a Catholic boarding school, where she remained for seven years. Rebellious and temperamental, she was frequently beaten or locked in her cell. After finishing school, she lived with a family as an apprentice seamstress, but the head of the family, known only as

M.C., forcibly raped her. His wife then made her leave. Returning to her parents, Louise began to vomit to and complain of abdominal pain and, when these complaints were ignored, to hallucinate, and to have hysterical fits. She improved with bloodletting treatments and was sent to serve as a maid to a Parisian spinster, but her parents brought her back home after learning that she had become sexually involved with two adolescent boys. In the course of the ensuing quarrels, Louise learned that her mother had had a sexual liaison with M.C. and that her only surviving sibling was in fact M.C.'s son. Her hysterical fits grew worse, leading to her admission to the Salpêtrière. On admission, Louise was partially paralyzed, lacked sensation on one side of her body, and had diminished hearing, taste, and vision. She developed the four phase seizures typical of grand hysterics. Charcot studied her carefully for the next five years.

Grand hysteria could be called an idiom of distress within the Salpêtrière. But, rather than speaking a stable, culturally transmitted idiom, grand hysterics improvised a new role of their own. Rather than passively listening to patients expressing distress, Charcot and his staff helped stage-direct the improvised new illness. They rewarded the most convincing patients, coached others, and even punished some for poor performances. Charcot apparently banished many aspiring hysterics who failed to convince him. By giving them more attention, Charcot and his fellow physicians encouraged inventive patients to add dramatic new symptoms to their repertoires. The Salpêtrists were like a company in rehearsal: New roles were being refined and practiced by promising actresses under the guidance of their stage directors. Also, in the Salpêtrière, patients and doctors alike had goals above and beyond merely communicating. Grand hysterics, for instance, were using their illness behavior to secure their place in the hospital, to garner attention and privileges, and to raise their status in relation to that of other patients. Charcot and his colleagues were hoping to further their reputations. The more dramatic the symptoms, and the more sweeping the generalizations to which they led, the more they believed they would gain by studying grand hysterics. Their hope for dramatic findings, and the resulting competition between patients, led to more dramatic illness presentations. The drama was not needed just to express distress. The hysterics could have expressed their distress much more quietly if anyone had wanted to listen, but Charcot would be dead before Pierre Janet, a student of Charcot's and the founder of psychotherapy, discovered that listening served a useful purpose.

Somatization Disorder and Patients with Multiple Unexplained Somatic Complaints

During the nineteenth century, patients with multiple unexplained physical symptoms were common. Lacking the means to determine whether their internal organs were healthy, physicians confronted with such patients had little choice but to validate their complaints by ascribing them to occult,

and sometimes nonexistent, diseases. Such validation, of course, further enhanced the social uses of illness behavior for those who were not really ill. If
symptoms like weakness, paralysis, mutism, or *globus hystericus* were present,
and if the patient was female, the disease might be called hysteria or, in
France, petit hysteria, to distinguish it from the illness described by the
Salpêtrists. By the end of the century, simple or petit hysteria was widely
considered a brain disease to which women were most susceptible.

Most Victorian patients with unexplained complaints expressed their invalidism only at times of crisis. Charles Darwin, for example, led an active
scientific and social life except for occasional periods of unexplained somatic
illnesses.[19] At the very least, somatic complaints were the "idioms of distress" with which Darwin voiced his probable depression and anxiety, but
they also had specific effects on his social environment, which no doubt contributed to their recurrences and persistence. Some authors, for instance, attribute Darwin's illnesses to his wife's love of nursing, a case of the "perfect
nurse" meeting the "perfect patient." In 1959, Saul Adler, a parasitologist,
suggested that Darwin's symptoms were due to Chagas' disease, an infection
spread by beetles Darwin handled in South America during his famous
round-the-world voyage on the *Beagle*. As John Bowlby and others have
pointed out, however, some of Darwin's symptoms antedated this voyage,
and prolonged contact with beetles is usually necessary to contract Chagas'
disease. Other medical authors have argued that Darwin's symptoms cannot
be understood except as psychosomatic. Most telling in this regard is the
fact that Darwin spent the last 13 years of his life in apparent good health,
which was improbable if his earlier health problems had been caused by a
real disease. Bowlby himself agreed with Sir George Pickering, who argued
that Darwin's symptoms were due to hyperventilation syndrome brought on
by anxiety. Although hyperventilation can explain some of his symptoms,
though, others of Darwin's complaints differ from those seen in typical cases
today. Their constancy, moreover, contrasts with the episodic nature of such
symptoms in modern-day patients. Hyperventilation may have provided the
models for some of Darwin's complaints, which then took on lives of their
own and became the means by which he handled social crises.

Darwin's symptoms included headaches, palpitations, ringing in the ears,
weakness, and fatigue. His periods of invalidism, moreover, were marked by
severe gastrointestinal problems, such as abdominal pain and vomiting preceded by crying spells. These periods of invalidism coincided with major
emotional crises in Darwin's life, during which he was depressed and apparently wanted nurturance and attention from others. The first of these occurred, in 1839, one year after his marriage and shortly before his wife,
Emma, gave birth to their first child. The gastrointestinal problems that appeared at this time may have been modeled on Emma's symptoms of pregnancy or on symptoms Darwin had witnessed in his mother, who had died of
abdominal cancer or peritonitis when he was a child. Bowlby speculates that
Darwin linked Emma's symptoms to those he had seen in his mother and
therefore felt threatened with another bereavement. In her correspondence at

the time, Emma noted that Charles freely expressed his complaints and his desire not to be left alone. Darwin recovered his health after nearly two years of rest and nursing care.

A second period of invalidism occurred in 1848, at the time of his father's death, and a third occurred in 1863, after Charles Lyell, an eminent geologist and a crucial supporter of Darwin, disappointed him by failing to fully endorse his theory of evolution as it applied to man. In this third episode, Darwin's health collapsed immediately after he learned of Lyell's reservations. He again suffered from vomiting, which his physician attributed to excessive intellectual effort, and from weakness and fatigue. His son thought he was depressed and remarked on the part that Lyell's critique of his work had played, but his wife described him as cheerful when not acutely ill. His scientific colleagues feared he was mortally ill. He recovered only in 1865, after the famous London physician Henry Bence Jones placed him on a regimen of diet and exercise. Once again there were indications that his health collapse had gained him special cossetting from wife, family, and colleagues.

The case of Alice James, the sister of Henry and William James, shows how nineteenth-century patients could base their life adaptations on illness behavior so that illness became for them a kind of career or calling, rather than just an expedient used in times of crisis.[20] Born in 1848, Alice was the youngest of five children and the only daughter in the James household. Her father, Henry James, Sr., had inherited enough money from his own father that he did not need to work and, instead, devoted himself to religious, philosophical, and moral speculations, which he expressed in books, pamphlets, articles, and long disquisitions at the Jameses' dinner table. His notions of womanhood were typical of his age and undoubtedly played a role in Alice James's later problems. The elder James believed that women lacked mental abilities and that their proper role in life was as the self-sacrificing "household saint" common in late nineteenth-century portrayals of ideal women. Women were expected to think only of others' needs. In an article, published in 1853, the elder James claimed that the feminist movement would lead to muscular women and effeminate men.

Alice's problems began when she was 18 years of age, shortly after the James family moved to Cambridge, Massachusetts, in order to be near William, who had just entered Harvard. This was the time in her life when a transition was called for: From being the sheltered child, Alice, if she had stayed healthy, would have been called on to ready herself for a future marriage. In her father's terms, the time was coming close for Alice to be a mother and a saint in a home of her own. Instead, Alice developed fatigue and "excitability." Local doctors thought she had hysteria, but she was sent to New York City, where the eminent physician Charles Fayett Taylor diagnosed nervous exhaustion. Taylor was known for his belief that the female brain was easily overtaxed, especially by excessive reading or educational efforts. He treated nervous exhaustion with massages and inactivity, a sick role, in other words, to which Alice adapted too well. She spent the next 10 years living with family members, marriage and motherhood apparently out of the question. Relapses and nervous fits were followed by long convalescences. She had palpitations, headaches, stomach aches, leg pains, weakness, and fatigue. Sometimes she could not walk, and, even when she could, she was bedridden much of the time.

In 1884, after her parents' deaths, Alice moved to England with a friend, Katherine Peabody Loring, whom she had met through the Society to Encourage Studies at Home, a correspondence school for women students. Intense and devoted relationships, sometimes called "Boston marriages," were common between upper-class late-nineteenth-century New England spinsters. Some of these relationships were undoubtedly homosexual, but whether that was true in this case is not known. Alice had a better relationship with Henry James, Jr., than with her other brothers, and Henry had lived in England for many years. But, even with Katharine and Henry, life in England failed to help Alice's health. Several English doctors attributed her symptoms to "rheumatic gout," "spinal neurosis," "nervous hyperesthesia," and cardiac complications. Cared for by Katharine, Alice spent much of her time frequenting various spas.

Consistent with the hypothesis that Alice's illness served to keep her dependent and cared for, her relapses often occurred when she felt that others had turned their attention away from her. For example, one severe attack occurred during a trip in the Swiss Alps with her Aunt Kate and her brother Henry in 1872. The traveling party was joined by a young couple, the Bootts. Lizzie Boott, who later served as the model for Pansy Osmond in Henry's *Portrait of a Lady*, was just two years older than Alice, and the party apparently had begun to cater as much to her health as to Alice's. In 1878, another attack prevented her from attending her brother William's wedding to Alice Gibbens, who thereafter, rather symbolically, was also called Alice James. Alice James and Gibbens had not hit it off well at all, and James apparently resented the attention her future sister-in-law was receiving. In 1881, Alice and Katharine Loring detoured on a trip from Richmond to Kew, where the Royal Gardens were located, so that Katharine could visit with her aunt and uncle, the Asa Grays. Asa Gray was a well-known botanist whose support played a crucial role in gaining American scientists' acceptance of Darwin's ideas. Alice took to bed when they arrived at the Grays', forcing Katharine to nurse her until they departed two weeks later. Similar attacks occurred in later years whenever Alice had to share Katharine with her family. Katharine's tuberculous sister required occasional nursing, and Alice's breakdowns coincided with the times when Katharine was thus engaged. Hypnosis helped relieve some of Alice's symptoms, but Katharine Loring herself had to induce the trance, thereby ensuring her continued attention.

Alice James died of breast cancer in 1892. In her diary, which she kept for the last three years of her life, she wrote of her "relief" on learning she was terminally ill. Katharine preserved Alice's diary, which her family wanted destroyed, and it was eventually published in 1964. The diary reveals a powerful intellect that lacked an outlet in the real world. Handicapped by her upbringing and by the era in which she lived, and no doubt saddled with problems that we cannot fully discern, Alice was never able to find a "healthy" role that satisfied her needs. In lieu of such a role, she adapted to life through her illness behavior.

With so many patients like Darwin and many more like James, it is hardly surprising that the novel *Erewhon*, which gave voice to extreme skepticism about the moral status of the patient role, was written about this time (1872).[21] Samuel Butler, the author of this novel, had traveled to Italy, where he had noticed that peasants drew no distinctions between medical disabilities and unwillingness to work. Whoever did not work, for whatever reason, seemed to Butler's eyes to receive identical treatment. In Butler's dystopia, illnesses were treated as we treat intentional crimes. The sick were ostracized and subject to arrest. Families hushed up illnesses for fear of being disgraced. By contrast, crimes and criminal impulses were treated as we treat diseases. If someone reported, for instance, having murderous feelings, or even committing murder, he would be sent to a "straightener" who would attempt to cure him. Being free of blame, the would-be murderer would receive the gentlest care.

Between 1849 and 1859, Pierre Briquet studied more than 400 hysterical patients treated at the Pitié Hospital in Paris.[22] His work provided the largest single data base for the study of *petit* hysteria in nineteenth-century Europe. Most of Briquet's patients were lower-class women with severe family and social problems. The onset of illness was most often gradual, and loss of apetite, epigastric pain, and headaches were prominent. Other symptoms included spasms, hysterical fits and seizures, pain in the spine or legs, fatigue and generalized weakness, and various conversion, or pseudoneurological, symptoms (discussed later in this chapter). In general, the picture drawn by Paul Briquet resembled Alice James, in spite of the social class difference between her and his patients. The outcomes Briquet recorded were highly variable: Sometimes the symptoms would persist unabated for years, but in other cases they would disappear for no apparent reason. Briquet also observed that symptoms waxed and waned according to their utility. In describing, for example, a treatment-resistant case of hysterical paraplegia, he noted that the victim suddenly regained the ability to walk when she anticipated meeting a visitor outside the hospital. Her improvement lasted a week until, after hearing bad news, she again became paraplegic. Although he saw hysteria as a brain disease, affecting that part of the brain that controlled emotions and feelings, Briquet nonetheless believed that it was psychogenic. He described cases, for instance, precipitated by frights or emotional shocks, by physical abuse, and by feelings of sadness. Five percent of his patients had become ill themselves after seeing others with hysteria or epilepsy. In many cases, other family members were ill, raising the question of whether the problem was inherited.

Little additional progress was made in describing hysteria until, in 1951, a group of psychiatrists at Washington University in St. Louis rediscovered Briquet's research.[23] They found that 50 women hospitalized for "hysteria" in the St. Louis area were similar in some respects to those Briquet described, and they suggested that the disorder be known as "Briquet's Syndrome."[24] They proposed criteria for diagnosing the syndrome and showed that it presented a stable clinical picture, even on long-term follow-up.[25] In 1980, the third edition of the American Psychiatric Association's Diagnostic and Statistical Manual (DSM-III) defined a new illness, somatization disorder, modeled on Briquet's syndrome.[26] In order to be diagnosed with somatization disorder, male patients had to report having been distressed by and seeking care for at least 12 of 37 possible symptoms. The number for women was 14, both because the symptom list included some gynecological complaints and because studies showed that normal women reported more medical complaints than did normal men. The onset of these symptoms had to occur before age 30, and the symptoms could not be explained by medical diagnoses. The DSM-III listed no emotional symptoms, consistent with the notion, as Slavney has observed, that the DSM-III version of "hysteria" was to be based on unexplained medical symptoms.[27] The revised edition of the the DSM-III, the DSMIII-R, required that 13 of 35 symptoms be present for both men and women, and the fourth edition of the Diagnostic and Statistical manual (DSM-IV) further modified the criteria by requiring a minimal number of symptoms in each of several categories.[28] Thus, to meet DSM-IV criteria for somatization disorder, patients must have histories, beginning before age 30, of pain complaints related to four different bodily sites. They must also report at least two gastrointestinal symptoms, one sexual symptom, and one pseudoneurological, or conversion symptom. Each of these symptoms, of course, must be medically inexplicable and have been the cause of distress or care-seeking behavior.

While the St. Louis group and the authors of the Diagnostic and Statistical Manuals have rightly emphasized the importance of specific diagnostic criteria, the number and groupings of symptoms are at best imperfect guides for identifying illness-role behavior. One patient may play a role with numerous protean symptoms, while an otherwise similar patient may play a role with fewer, more chronic somatic complaints. If nothing else, since it takes time for patients to accumulate a large number of lifetime unexplained complaints, some patients who do meet the given criteria for somatization disorder must at some time have had too few somatic symptoms to be counted as definitely ill. Research by Javier Escobar and colleagues using the Diagnostic Interview Schedule (DIS), which elicits information on each of the 37 symptoms needed to diagnose somatization disorder according to the DSM-III, confirms that individuals fall on a continuum with respect to the number of unexplained somatic complaints and that some subjects with many fewer lifetime unexplained somatic complaints than required by the DSM-III or DSM-IV nonetheless resemble patients with outright somatization disorder in their care-seeking behavior and disability.[29]

A case described in some detail by Phillip Slavney shows how medical symptoms are used by some modern-day patients to adapt to often difficult lives and illustrates some of the research findings described later in this chapter.[30] The patient, whom Slavney called "Mrs. V," was a 42-year-old woman admitted to a psychiatric ward after telling her neurologist that she was depressed and having suicidal thoughts. She appeared sad and anxious, and she claimed to hear a voice as she was falling asleep telling her that "bleeding to death would be a peaceful way to die." However, she did not appear severely depressed, and there were none of the more usual signs of psychosis. Initially, she appeared to have some memory problems, but subsequent observation and testing showed that her memory was normal. Her medical history was remarkable for numerous unexplained somatic complaints, including chronic nausea and vomiting, chest pain and palpitations, migraine headaches, periods of amnesia, extremity numbness and weakness, and numerous pains, including chronic back pain for which she received monthly disability payments. She had been hospitalized nine times for medical evaluations and had also had several surgeries, including a tubal ligation, a spinal operation, an "emergency abortion," an intestinal bypass for obesity, a subsequent revision of the bypass necessitated by weakness, and a gastric stapling procedure. Because of complaints of leg weakness following her spinal surgery four years before Slavney saw her, Mrs. V. had had a lumbar puncture, the results of which were interpreted as indicative of multiple sclerosis. After receiving this diagnosis, Mrs. V. became wheelchair bound. Repeat lumbar punctures were normal, however, and the earlier, abnormal finding was later considered anomalous. Moreover, electroencephalographic tests and a brain scan showed no abnormalities consistent with multiple sclerosis. In spite of these normal tests, and the reassurances given her by her neurologist, Mrs. V. continued to believe she had multiple sclerosis. Mrs. V. also suffered from chronic depression, for which she had been treated for some 15 years, following an attempted overdose immediately after the death of her foster father. Ten years before her admission, she had impulsively driven her car into a wall. On occasion, too, she had abused alcohol.

Mrs. V. had been abandoned at nine months of age. Her mother, whom she never met, killed herself at age 42. She never knew her father. She was raised by a neighbor couple, whom she called her foster parents. Her foster mother, who had only a fourth-grade education, apparently resented her presence in the house and repeatedly reminded her that she had no mother. She was not allowed to play with other children. Her foster father, who had only a seventh-grade education, was apparently kinder, but he had died 15 years before, precipitating the suicide attempt mentioned earlier. When she was eight years old, Mrs. V. developed eczema, asthma, and respiratory infections. There is some evidence (given later) that patients with somatization disorder tend to have received attention for illnesses incurred when they were children. Mrs. V., by contrast, stated she never remembered her foster mother ever taking her to a doctor, although a neighbor apparently did take her once to a doctor and to a dentist as well. Her foster mother failed to prepare her at all for the onset of menstrual periods, which frightened and surprised her when they first occurred. Later, her periods were accompanied by such severe cramps that she sometimes missed school and work.

When Mrs. V. was raped at age 12 by a neighborhood boy, her foster mother responded by punishing her. She was not allowed to date as an adolescent, but, knowing nothing about sex or contraception, she became pregnant at age 17 and had to drop out of school in the eleventh grade when she delivered a baby boy. The father, who was only 17 himself, married her and lived with her in her foster parents' house, but this arrangement lasted only three months. Her young husband moved out and, although they remained legally married for 10 years, they rarely saw each other. She then entered a common-law marriage with the father of her second son, an alcoholic gambler who verbally and physically abused her for 10 years before she finally threw him out of the house they shared. Shortly afterward, she met her current husband, a high school graduate who was working as a plumber.

Mrs. V. had started working shortly after the birth of her first child. Not having finished high school, she could obtain only manual jobs, the last of which was as a school cafeteria aide. While holding this position, she frequently missed work due to numerous illnesses, which apparently were never worked up. She began having back pain at home, but she later claimed that she had injured her back on the job, and she had been on job-related disability for four years at the time Slavney met her.

The immediate social problem facing Mrs. V., which precipitated her depression and suicidality, was a conflict involving her second son, Kevin, who was then 17, and her current husband. Kevin was hyperactive, set fires, and was often in trouble at school before dropping out at age 15. Currently, he was living with his parents or with a friend. He was not working and supported himself in part by stealing from his mother and stepfather. He was said to be lazy and untidy, and it was hard for his mother to keep the house neat when he was present. Mr. V. wanted to punish Kevin's behavior, but Mrs. V. could not assert herself with her son. The resulting family conflict was too much for her to handle. Therapy largely consisted of helping Mrs. V. deal with her family.

Like other patients who take on illness roles, patients with Briquet's syndrome or somatization disorder are responsive to social cues and prone to playing roles. For example, Purtell, Robins, and Cohen noted that more than 90 percent of the patients with Briquet's syndrome they studied presented themselves and their problems in an "exaggerated and dramatic manner."[31] Kaminsky and Slavney found that patients with Briquet's syndrome resembled patients with hysterical personality disorder,[32] which implies that they are self-dramatizing and that they simulate affects and attitudes.[33] In the DSM-III and later diagnostic manuals, hysterical personality disorder is supplanted by histrionic personality disorder, which is characterized by excessive attention seeking, theatricality, and suggestibility.[34] Morrison found that more than two-thirds of patients with somatization disorder met DSM-III criteria for histrionic personality disorder as well.[35] Lilienfeld and colleagues reported a similar figure.[36] Bliss gave the Stanford Hypnotic Susceptibility Scale, form C, to 17 patients with Briquet's syndrome.[37] Their average score of 9.5 (on a 12-point scale) placed them in the top 10 percent of the population. In the previous chapter, I presented evidence that hypno-tizability reflects role-playing tendencies. Ross found that 35 percent of the patients with multiple personality disorder he studied met diagnostic crite-ria for somatization disorder.[38] As I show in chapter 6, patients with multi-ple personality disorder are role players par excellence.

In chapter 3, I cited data from I. M. Lewis showing that illness roles are often adopted by persons who are handicapped in otherwise meeting their needs. This general rule applies to Briquet's syndrome and somatization dis-order. Mrs. V., for instance, was handicapped by her lack of education and by her poor social skills. In the study cited earlier, Kaminsky and Slavney found that patients with Briquet's syndrome belonged to a low social class, had on average less than a high school education, and were often unhappily married. Their spouses were often alcoholic or violent, and more than a fourth of them had been deserted by their spouses. Tomasson reported that nearly three-quarters of patients with somatization disorder had less than 12 years of schooling and that less than a third of them were gainfully employed.[39] Pribor reported similar findings in a group of patients with multiple unex-plained symptoms.[40] Smith and Brown found that more than a quarter of their patients with somatization disorder belonged to the lowest social class defined by the well-known Hollingshead index, and half belonged to the next lowest social class.[41]

Like patients with other modern-day illness roles (see chapters 6 and 7), patients with somatization disorder or multiple unexplained symtoms re-port that they were victims of sexual abuse. One-quarter of subjects with unexplained medical symptoms studied by Pribor and colleagues reported childhood incest.[42] Morrison reported similar findings from a group of patients with somatization disorder,[43] and unexplained medical symptoms are also common in patients with multiple personality disorder, which is generally attributed to childhood sexual abuse.[44] Widespread claims of sexual abuse in patients with several disorders have raised important ques-tions that also pertain to somatization disorder. First, many patients with somatization disorder wish to appear distressed. When asked about sexual trauma, they may well be biased to answer in the affirmative. Also, such patients are responsive to social cues. Asked about abuse, they may try to please their therapists and interlocutors by "recalling" events that never ac-tually happened. Finally, even in cases where sexual abuse occurred, it is un-clear that sexual abuse, per se, has played a specific pathogenic role. Sexual abuse most often occurs in families that are otherwise abusive and neglect-ful, and what appear to be the results of sexual abuse may be caused, in fact, by abuse or neglect in general. For example, in the study by Pribor, in which 25 percent of subjects with unexplained medical symptoms reported having been sexually abused, 60 percent of subjects reported having been emotion-ally abused, and 25 percent reported having been subject to nonsexual physical abuse.[45] A study by Craig and colleagues suggests that parental neglect may be the decisive factor with respect to physical symptoms.[46] Pa-tients with unexplained medical symptoms were distinguished from other patients by their lack of parental care, in combination with childhood physical illnesses. Childhood physical illnesses may have led to expressions of parental concern that were otherwise lacking in neglectful families. Mrs. V., Slavney's patient, had been neglected and also physically ill as a child. Although her foster mother paid little heed to her illnesses, a neighbor was suffciently concerned to take her to a physician. Her foster father, with whom she had a better relationship, may also have expressed more concern for her when she was ill. Reports of childhood sexual abuse in relation to modern-day illness roles are discussed more fully in chapters 6 and 7.

Depression is common in patients with illness roles in general and in patients with Briquet's syndrome or somatization disorder in particular. Kaminsky and Slavney, for instance, found that 65 percent of the patients with Briquet's syndrome they studied were currently depressed or anxious.[47] All but one had had a history of depression, and the typical subject had made at least one prior suicide attempt. Sixty percent of the patients with somatization disorder studied by Tomasson and colleagues had a history of depression.[48] Mood disorders may be caused by the same life problems that promote illness behavior, or they may cause such behavior, if only by blocking adaptive responses to problems. Some indication of a casual role is found in studies that show a high genetic risk for mood disorders in patients with unexplained symptoms.[49]

Unexplained somatic complaints run in families, suggesting that patients learn to make such complaints by observing how others use them or that genetic factors play a role in causing such complaints. Routh and Ernst found that half of the children and adolescents they studied with unexplained complaints of abdominal pain had a relative with somatization disorder.[50] Golding and colleagues found that 10 percent of the children of adult patients with somatization disorder or multiple unexplained somatic symptoms also had multiple unexplained medical symptoms.[51] Again, Slavney's patient illustrates this phenomenon: Although Mrs. V.'s older son was married and working at the time Mrs. V. was treated by Slavney, as a child he had experienced unexplained blindness and seizures. In Golding's study, 23 percent of the subjects who met DSM-III-R criteria for somatization disorder also had a parent with multiple unexplained symptoms, and many of these may have met DSM-III-R criteria for somatization disorder themselves. More than 14 percent of subjects with somatization disorder also had siblings with multiple unexplained symptoms. Hotopf and colleagues found that adults with multiple unexplained physical symptoms were likely to have witnessed parental ill health at a young age.[52] The effects of parental ill health were probably due to parental illness behavior, rather than illness per se, since early parental death did not predict later symptoms.

Researchers at Washington University confirmed the familial aggregation of Briquet's syndrome and, later, somatization disorder, and found that these disorders also run in families with antisocial personality disorder. In one representative study, for example, Guze and colleagues reported that nearly 7 percent of female relatives of subjects with Briquet's syndrome had Briquet's syndrome themselves, and 8 percent of these female relatives had antisocial personality disorder.[53] By contrast, less than 3 percent of female relatives of subjects without Briquet's syndrome had this disorder, and less than 3 percent of them had antisocial personality disorder. Over 18 percent of male relatives of subjects with Briquet's syndrome had antisocial personality disorder, compared with about 10 percent of male relatives of subjects without Briquet's syndrome, but none of the male relatives of women with Briquet's syndrome had Briquet's syndrome themselves.

Based on findings like these, Guze and other researchers hypothesize the existence of genetic factors that cause Briquet's syndrome or somatization disorder in women and antisocial personality disorder in men.[54] Briquet's syndrome, or somatization disorder, possibly manifest antisocial traits in women patients. Consistent with his hypothesis, Lilienfeld and colleagues found that somatization disorder and antisocial personality disorder tend to co-occur, both in patients with these dosorders and in their relatives.[55] As I noted earlier, patients with somatization disorder are likely to meet criteria for histrionic personality disorder. Antisocial and histrionic personality disorders are both cluster B personality disorders, as defined by the DSM-IV.[56] All cluster B disorders are characterized by dramatic, overly emotional, and erratic behavior, while antisocial and histrionic personality types in particular tend to be manipulative, irresponsible, and unwilling or unable to delay gratification. A group of subjects with characteristics like these would likely be called antisocial, histrionic, or both. Draper and Harpending argued that antisocial personalities and patients with somatization disorder "cheat" persons of the opposite sex.[57] According to these authors, antisocial men cheat women with whom they are or might be sexually involved, while women with somatization disorder use their illness behavior to obtain more assistance from men. However, as I have argued elsewhere, antisocial types and patients with somatization disorder can be seen as "cheating" in relationships of all kinds.[58] The former tend to seek their goals aggressively, while the latter control those around them by acting ill. Passive-dependent behavior is more consistent with feminine social roles and is probably safer for women, thereby accounting for the excess number of female patients who present with somatization as opposed to antisocial personality disorder.

Of some note, patients with multiple unexplained somatic complaints are sometimes "healed" by faith, in which case they may become religious healers themselves. The progression from illness role to the role of healer is already familiar to us from study of possession illnesses (see chapter 3). Two well-known cases illustrate this phenomenon.[59] The first involves Rosa Quattrini, who for 16 years before her death in 1981 reported apparitions of the Virgin Mary in San Damiano, Italy. Born in north central Italy in 1909, Quattrini attended school only to the third grade before dropping out to work on her family's farm. At age 28, she married a brickyard worker, with whom she had three children. She and her husband had little financial security and apparently moved about a great deal before settling down in San Damiano. Quatrini's poor health began with the Caesarean births of her children, which apparently caused an abdominal hernia. She was given a corset to wear but nonetheless suffered from chronic abdominal pain, nausea, vomiting, and loss of appetite. Although she had previously maintained a normal routine, Quattrini's condition deteriorated early in 1961. After 24 hours of severe abdominal pain, she was hospitalized on March 6 and discharged without specific treatment recommendations on March 14. On June 30, she was hospitalized again for the same complaints, and she stayed in the hospital until July 8. Once again, there apparently were no specific treatment recommendations given. At home, she remained bedridden until September 29, the feast of St. Michael the Archangel, when a young woman came to her house seeking a contribution for candles for Padre Pio, a well-known Italian stigmatic and religious healer. Accounts differ as to what transpired, but all of them recount that, amid portentous signs, the visitor miraculously healed Rosa's hernia and instructed her to seek out Padre Pio. The local Padre Pio group denied knowledge of Quattrini's mysterious visitor, but, in any event, Quattrini was suddenly free of pain and resumed her normal activities.

Quattrini joined a Padre Pio group and, in May 1962, made her first pilgrimage to San Giovanni Rotondo, where Pio himself resided. Pio told her that Mary had visited her and instructed her to care for the sick and dying. He predicted a "great event," which transpired two years later, in October 1964, when the Virgin Mary reappeared to Quattrini. She gave Quattrini a message for the general public and, as a sign of its authenticity, caused a pear tree to flower. On a later visit, the Virgin told Quattrini where to find healing waters, which eventually became a pilgrimage site for thousands. By 1967, a public subscription was raised to build a "City of Roses," including a hospital and medical center, a youth village, accommodations for pilgrimages, and foundations for youth and the elderly, on the site of Quattrini's visions. Ten years later, however, Rosa and her children were charged with criminal fraud in connection with money raised for this worthy purpose. The charges had not been settled when Quattrini died in 1981.

The second case is that of Mary Ann Van Hoof, a 41-year-old Necedah, Wisconsin, housewife. Raised in a violent family and subjected to physical abuse, Van Hoof spent her adult life in a struggle with poverty and suffering from a series of inexplicable somatic complaints, for which she was hospitalized on several occasions. She was apparently greatly affected by the care and attention she received in the hospital, and she later observed that one nurse, a Catholic sister, had been kind to her in a way she had never before experienced. In November 1949, Van Hoof was lying in bed with "heart pain" and a kidney ailment when the Virgin Mary first appeared to her. On Good Friday in 1950, she was lying awake with heart pain when the Virgin Mary gave her instructions that she was to pass on to the Parish Priest. Apparently, these instructions were not entirely heeded, for the next month the Virgin appeared to her and told her she must do penance for the community. Her symptoms from this point on became more ritualized and symbolic, and she understood them as a form of penance for others' sins. She could feel the wounds of Christ and the crown of thorns. Her body convulsed and assumed a posture of crucifixion. She could not retain any food and ostensibly lived on liquids for 24 days in a row.

When, in 1950, Van Hoof announced that the Virgin would appear at religious festivities, 100,000 people flocked to Necedah to witness the apparition. According to one observer, this was the largest gathering in the history of rural Wisconsin. In the next few years, Van Hoof fell under the sway of a man named Henry Swan, one of her earliest advocates and the editor of her revelations, who convinced her that "Elders of Zion," Freemasons, and communists were trying to gain control of the world for Satan. By the mid-1950s, Van Hoof's revelations from the Virgin Mary were openly anti-Semitic. She touted Joseph McCarthy and criticized liberal elements in the Catholic Church. Challenged by the local bishop, Van Hoof admitted herself to Marquette University hospital, where, under close observation, she proved unable to manifest the stigmata she claimed at home, nor could she stay healthy on a liquid diet. In 1955, the Church condemned Van Hoof's apparitions as false, but Van Hoof continued to report revelations on topics as diverse as Russian submarines, food and water poisoning, and even livestock feed. Van Hoof and her followers were formally interdicted twice in the 1970s, but she continued to report visions until her death in 1984. An organization headquartered in Necedah, called "For My God and My Country," continues to spread her message.

Conversion Disorder

As it is defined by DSM-IV, conversion disorder is characterized by movement or sensory deficits suggestive of neurological or general medical disorders in the absence of pathology able to cause such deficits.[60] Typical conversion symptoms, which are sometimes referred to as "pseudoneurological," include impaired balance or coordination, paralysis or spasms, loss of voice, *globus hystericus*, loss of touch or pain sensation, double vision, blindness, deafness, and seizures. Such symptoms were among the most prominent aspects of eighteenth- and nineteenth-century hysteria and are often observed today in somatization disorder, the descendant of petit hysteria. In conversion disorder, however, they occur alone, or at least without manifold other unexplained bodily symptoms. Because they correspond to lay ideas of illness, conversion symptoms frequently fail to jibe with deficits that result from real disorders. Conversion patients, for instance, sometimes complain of loss of sensation in an entire hand, to the wrist. The neurological innervation of the hand is such that no nerve lesion can produce this pattern of deficits. Other conversion patients report loss of sensation on one side of the body, with a sharp division at the midline. Sensory skin innervation is such that sensory deficits caused by nervous lesions diminish gradually at the midline, rather than abruptly. Conversion seizures frequently vary from seizure to seizure; seizures resulting from nervous system disease are typically stereotyped. Of course, better educated patients with conversion are able to avoid making such telltale errors, in which case extensive evaluations may be needed to rule out, if possible, a physiological cause for their symptoms. For historical and clinical reasons, the DSM-IV assigns patients with only unexplained pain complaints to another category, in spite of the fact that pain is clearly a sensory symptom.[61]

In his case history of a young woman he called "Dora," published in 1905, Freud argued that hysterics choose their conversion symptoms to symbolize unconscious wishes and defenses against them.[62] According to Freud, moreover, certain parts of the body are more "compliant" than others, when it comes to expressing unconscious wishes. Dora's real name was Ida Bauer. The only daughter of a wealthy Bohemian Jewish family, Ida was only 18 years old when her father brought her to Freud in the year 1900. Her symptoms included headaches, a persistent cough, whispering speech, a mysterious limp, what was thought to be irrational hostility, depression, and suicidal thoughts. Of her various symptoms, Ida's cough most clearly illustrates Freud's theories.

Ida complained to Freud that her father had a lover, a Frau K., whose husband had made sexual advances toward her, which she claimed to find repugnant. The K.s were friends of the family, and Ida believed that her father countenanced Herr K.s behavior to secure Herr K.'s complicity in his own affair with Frau K. Ida's mother was said to suffer from "housewive's psychosis," which apparently meant she spent her time obsessively cleaning the house. Ida's father denied that Herr K. had misbehaved, and, along with Herr and Frau K., he attributed Ida's charges to an overwrought imagination, stirred up by excessive reading on the topic of love. Sometime after Freud and Ida had parted, however, Frau K. admitted that she and Ida's father had had an affair, and Herr K. admitted having tried to seduce Ida. Freud himself took it for granted that Ida was telling the truth, and he seemed to admire her insight into her father's motives, but he thought that she had repressed her own love for Herr K., incestuous love for her father, and even a homosexual attraction to Frau K.

Ida's father had developed tuberculosis when she was six years old. His illness forced the family to move to a provincial health resort, where the climate was more favorable and where the family lived for the next 10 years. Later, the family moved to a town where the father owned a factory and, later still, to Vienna. The father still suffered occasional relapses of coughing and illness, which forced him to return alone to the resort. Ida suspected that these relapses were excuses for assignations her father planned with Frau K., but, regardless of whether Ida's suspicions were justified, her father did in fact remain sick from his disease, to which he succumbed in 1913. Her mother also died from tuberculosis, but Freud did not mention the history of her illness.

Ida began to suffer shortness of breath at age eight. Enforced rest for six months apparently cured her condition, which the family doctor put down to nervous causes. When she was 12, Ida developed intermittent spells of "nervous coughing," which continued until Freud saw her. These spells generally lasted three to five weeks, although one had gone on for two months, were associated with loss of voice, and had failed to respond to the hy-drotherapeutic and electrical treatments then in vogue.

Attributing Ida's coughing spells to conversion, Freud had several hy-potheses concerning the wishes expressed. First, Freud believed that cough-ing expressed Ida's desire to take her father's place *vis-à-vis* Frau K. Believ-ing that her father's coughing spells were excuses for assignations with Frau K., Ida could symbolize her own wish for such assignations by having her own spells. Second, Freud believed that coughing expressed Ida's longing for Herr K. as well. Herr K., who traveled frequently, often found his wife ill when he was home. Knowing that she had been well only the day before, Ida surmised that Frau K. was using poor health in order to avoid "conjugal du-ties." Believing that Herr K.'s absences coincided with Ida's spells, Freud surmised that these served to express her affection. While Frau K. became ill when Herr K. was present, Ida became ill when Herr K. was gone. Her loss of voice, moreover, served to express the idea that speech had lost its mean-ing when Herr K. was gone. Finally, Freud believed that coughing expressed Ida's sexual longing for her father and her rivalry with Frau K. Ida believed that her father was currently impotent. Though she never stated it clearly, she hinted that Frau K. performed fellatio on him. Freud hypothesized that Ida's throat irritation, and her consequent cough, symbolized her desire to take Frau K.'s place in this respect.

Freud was aware of the various social functions served by illness behavior. According to Freud, however, these functions are after the fact; rather than cause conversion, as an illness-role model would postulate, they merely com-plicate its treatment. In a well-known passage, Freud explained that once a conversion symptom had been set in motion by unconscious conflicts,

> Some psychical current or other finds it convenient to make use of it, and in that way the symptom manages to obtain a *secondary function*. . . . And so it happens that any one who tries to make [the patient] well is to his aston-ishment brought up against a powerful resistance, which teaches him that the patient's intention of getting rid of his complaint is not so entirely and completely serious as it seemed. Let us imagine a workman, a bricklayer, let us say, who has fallen off a house and been crippled, and now earns his livelihood by begging at the street-corner. Let us then suppose that a miracle-worker comes along and promises to make his crooked leg straight and capable of walking. It would be unwise, I think, to look forward to see-ing an expression of peculiar bliss upon the man's features. No doubt at the time of the accident he felt he was extremely unlucky, when he realized that he would never be able to do any more work and would have to starve or live upon charity. But since then the very thing which in the first instance threw him out of employment has become his source of income: he lives by his disablement. If that is taken from him he may become totally helpless. He has in the meantime forgotten his trade and lost his habits of industry; he has grown accustomed to idleness and perhaps to drink as well.[63] (italics in original)

Freud believed that the secondary function of Dora's illness was to get her father's attention and to break up his relationship with Frau K.

As this passage suggests, Freud assumed that conversion symptoms are real symptoms: The blind conversion hysteric was thought to really be blind; the paralyzed hysteric was thought to really be paralyzed. But Freud could never account for what he called the "mysterious leap from the mind to the body" required by this assumption, and this "leap" continued to puzzle those who came after him. How do repressed wishes seeking expression cause physiological systems to stop functioning? How can these systems dysfunction in ways that fail to jibe with known anatomic pathways? The problem is further compounded by more recent studies, which fail to find physiological concommitants of conversion.[64] Using sophisticated techniques, for example, researchers have shown that patients with conversion blindness actually use visual information in the same way as normal persons. Patients with conversion deafness likewise use information presented to them in sounds. Patients with conversion paralyses show perfectly normal functioning of their peripheral nerves, as shown by electrical studies, and, during conversion seizures, nervous system activity appears to be perfectly normal, as judged by the EEG.

To avoid the problem of the "mysterious leap," some later psychoanalysts viewed conversion symptoms as communicative behaviors, rather than as symptoms in the usual sense of the term.[65] According to this view, the patient who acts blind is not really unable to see; he is communicating something by acting blind. Likewise, the patient who acts paralyzed is not really unable to move; he is making a point by acting paralyzed. Dora coughed in order to send a message; there was nothing wrong with her throat. The "mysterious leap" remains, but, as in other areas of psychology, it is from mind to behavior, not between mind and body.

In shifting to a communicative model, some later psychoanalysts also admitted that wishes of all kinds, and not just sexual ones, can be expressed via conversion symptoms. For example, referring to illness more generally, Balint observed that people who "find it difficult to cope with the problems of their lives resort to becoming ill."[66] According to Balint, such patients "offer or propose various illnesses" until they reach an agreement with their physicians "resulting in the acceptance by both of them of one of the illnesses as justified." Balint, in other words, postulates the existence of illness roles. Rabkin applied this idea to conversion symptoms specifically.[67] Reporting on conversion symptoms in the army, he notes that the conditions that face enlisted men are such that even in peacetime many of them are distressed. Some of them have the "happy thought," as Rabkin describes it, that to be medically ill would allow them to escape the situation in which they find themselves. Some of them, moreover, are able to preserve their self-esteem by convincing themselves they are ill. Their complaints range from those typically seen in somatization disorder to simple conversion symptoms. Army physicians negotiate with such patients, in the sense Balint described, and, depending on the specific symptoms adopted and on how the negotiations go, some of these patients succeed in leaving the service entirely. Others receive breaks or special benefits, and others are sent back to duty with no relief at all. The process becomes more complex when more than one physician is involved. For example, Rabkin notes that, because of the structure of army medical care, some patients reach a mutually satisfactory agreement with one physician, only to encounter another physician who is unwilling to accept the terms offered by the first. Such cases are likely to pose especially difficult problems for the second physician. Negotiation processes like those described by Rabkin have been described by Kleinman for Chinese neurasthenics (discussed later). The problems Rabkin cites when patients see two or more doctors also are apparent in cases of chronic fatigue and multiple chemical sensitivity (also discussed later). None of these problems, of course, can occur in traditional cultures, in which patients know in advance which illness behaviors will work.

By attributing etiologic significance to what Freud thought were merely secondary functions of conversion symptoms, the illness-role approach stresses their functionality and downplays their symbolic meaning. As long as conversion symptoms succeed in affecting the social milieu in the way patients desire, their form may be arbitrary, or at least not symbolic of unconscious wishes or attitudes. Assuming that conversion symptoms symbolize wishes and attitudes may lead clinicians to overinterpret some symptoms. Not every patient with hysterical blindness, for instance, is unconsciously trying to avoid seeing something, denying having seen something, or punishing himself for having seen something.

On the other hand, sometimes conversion symptoms that are most functional are also the most symbolic, since they hint at the situation the patient would like to change. A case described by McCue and McCue illustrates such a symptom.[68] The patient, a 44-year-old woman, was alert but unresponsive to verbal commands when she was admitted to the hospital. She quickly became more responsive but remained unable to speak. She had no previous psychiatric history, no current symptoms indicative of psychosis or depression, and no physical disorder that could account for her speechlessness. She had been married for 25 years, but five years earlier her husband had started drinking heavily. When drunk, he was threatening and violent, and the police had recently been called after he assaulted the patient and a neighbor. At the time she lost her voice, the patient was scheduled to testify at a criminal court hearing against him. He had threatened to harm her if she testified, and she was apprehensive about what would befall her if she took the stand as expected. The hearing was postponed because of her loss of voice.

With hypnosis and supportive therapy, which initially had to be conducted in writing and with gestures, the patient recovered rapidly. She initiated divorce proceedings against her husband and, with the help of a tranquilizer, was able to testify at the postponed court hearing. A follow-up conversation two and a half years later revealed that she had separated from her husband and had had no further episodes of loss of voice or conversion.

Her illness had apparently galvanized social supports sufficient to make her husband back down from his threats.

From a functional point of view, loss of voice served to excuse the patient from testifying. One can imagine her ruminating on her husband's threats and having the "happy thought," to borrow Rabkin's phrase, that if she could not speak, she could not testify. But precisely because it was so functionally to the point, loss of voice symbolized her wish to not speak up. In losing her voice—as opposed to other possible deficits she could have developed—she hinted to those who would treat her the nature of her problem.

Patients sometimes learn which conversion symptoms are effective in gaining the ends they desire only by trial and error or by paying careful attention to the responses of those around them. In such cases, the symptom pattern may change as symptoms are reshaped or discarded for better ones. Changing symptom patterns are hard to understand if symptoms are chosen for their symbolic meaning. Walker and colleagues described five patients with recurrent psychogenic respiratory distress, which led in most cases to intubation and mechanical ventilation and in one case to a tracheostomy.[69] All of these patients initially presented with symptoms suggestive of serious neurological diseases, which in some cases lead to respiratory distress or failure. The patients were questioned closely about their respiratory symptoms and gradually learned that such symptoms galvanized the interest of medical personnel, led to special attention and observation, and convinced those around them that they were gravely ill. As the symptoms progressed, the level of attention and interest increased concommitantly, until some of the patients appeared not to be breathing at all. According to the authors, of the variety of conversion symptoms presented by these patients, including paralyses, tremors, mutism, and blindness, respiratory complaints dominated the picture because they were most reliably rewarded with prompt attention. The authors argued that the patients were overresponsive to the attention they received from medical personnel, but they did not present sufficient information on the patients to determine whether they also had reason to appear gravely ill to family, friends, employers, or social service workers.

One of Walker's patients, a 32-year-old man, was admitted to the hospital with acute weakness in his lower extremities. He did not seem fully cooperative with strength testing, and his reflexes and sensory examination were normal, but his physicians thought he might have Guillain-Barré syndrome, a peripheral nerve disorder. Guillain-Barré syndrome can cause ascending weakness, so the patient was carefully observed for loss of upper extremity strength or respiratory difficulty. With frequent checks, arm weakness soon appeared, followed by decreases in his vital capacity. Vital capacity is a measure of breathing strength that depends upon the patient making a maximal effort. He began to speak in a whisper and to make gasping noises. He nodded when asked whether he was short of breath. Measurements of oxygen in his arterial blood remained normal, but when his apparent vital capacity dropped to a critical level, the patient was rushed to the intensive care unit, intubated, and mechanically ventilated. He was treated for Guillain-Barré syndrome and allowed to breathe on his own again after several days. He recovered completely after two weeks of treatment.

Four months later, the patient reappeared with weakness in all four extremities and with apparent respiratory distress. Although his blood oxygen levels were normal, he was immediately intubated and placed on a mechanical ventilator in the intensive care unit, and treatment for a peripheral nerve disorder was started again. He was extubated and allowed to breathe on his own after just four days, but his weakness remained and he developed tunnel vision, a symptom widely considered to be due to conversion and not to organic disease. In any event, tunnel vision should not appear in the course of Guillain-Barré syndrome. His weakness and tunnel vision improved within two weeks, and he was discharged from the hospital. Ten hours later, however, the patient was brought back paralyzed in all four extremities and in apparent need of respiratory assistance. His spontaneous breathing efforts were interrupted by gasping. He made gagging and choking noises, rolled his eyes, and contorted his head and trunk as if straining to breathe. His blood oxygen was normal despite his apparent distress. The nursing staff and others were told not to interfere but merely to discreetly observe the patient's breathing. His choking and gagging diminished, and orderly breathing resumed. By the next day the patient was once again speaking normally and having no trouble breathing. Once it was neglected, his extremity weakness resolved. When psychiatric treatment was suggested to him, the patient signed out of the hospital and never returned.

Another of Walker's cases, a 31-year-old woman, came to the hospital complaining of neck rigidity and trouble swallowing. In light of her symptom picture, she was treated for possible tetanus, which can lead to general rigidity and respiratory distress. After two days of observation, she developed rigid spells during which she seemed to be suffocating. She was intubated and mechanically ventilated, and she eventually received a tracheostomy. She recovered completely after a month in the hospital. Two weeks later she reappeared with rigidity and respiratory distress. She was intubated again and mechanically ventilated and recovered within two days. When her illness reccured a third time, she was referred to Walker and colleagues for evaluation. Although no abnormalities were found on physical examination, she was noted to be having 20- to 30-minute spells of rigidity several times each day, during which she arched her back, closed her eyes, and forcefully clenched her teeth. During these spells, she held her breath intermittently, but never for longer than 20 seconds and never long enough to become cyanotic (blue). She never bit her tongue, lost bowel or bladder control, or showed jerking movements. Her rigid spells occurred only when she was awake. Infectious disease consultants found no evidence of current or previous tetanus, and a psychiatric consultant found that she was disturbed by severe marital and family problems. Nursing staff were instructed not to intervene in her rigid spells or when she held her breath, and, as a result, these symptoms quickly subsided. They stopped completely by the time she was discharged and did not recur during the follow-up period.

Intubation and mechanical ventilation is extremely uncomfortable for alert patients. The patients described by Walker and colleagues were given sedatives while they were intubated, which may have helped them cope with the discomfort entailed by their particular symptom.

Sometimes conversion symptoms are modeled on symptoms patients have observed in others. Someone whose brother was paralyzed due to physical illness might develop conversion paralysis, if paralysis would serve some social end. Someone whose mother was blind might develop conversion blindness, if blindness would solve a pressing problem. Thorpe and colleagues described a 22-year-old woman whose loss of voice apparently was modeled on her father's postsurgical voice dysfunction several years earlier.[70] She was said to have been especially close to her father. The evening proceeding her illness, Miss A., as these authors called her, had argued with her boyfriend about his continued involvement with his previous girlfriend. After this argument, Miss A. claimed to have driven about town in a dreamlike state. A number of men had looked at her in a threatening way, and one, she believed, had cut her left breast with a knife while unsuccessfully trying to rape her. The police, however, were not notified, and she could not state where the attack had occurred. She awoke in her bed the next morning, found blood on her breast, and was unable to make any sound.

Miss A. was not too concerned about her loss of voice. In this respect she was like other conversion patients, who are said to show *la belle indifférence*. Conversion patients with symptoms that would frighten most patients, such as sudden blindness or paralysis, appear remarkably undisturbed by their illness. This is, of course, understandable insofar as their symptoms manifest illness roles. In any event, Miss A.'s roommate was more alarmed by her loss of voice than she was and persuaded her to visit her family physician. On examination, she was able to move her lips normally but could not make a sound, a finding inconsistent with real voice disorders. She wrote out the story of the attempted rape. Although she described findings "lots of blood," no laceration was found on her breast. Over the next four weeks, with psychotherapy, Miss A. gradually recovered the use of her voice. Miss A.'s loss of voice apparently gained attention and sympathy from her boyfriend.

In the case report by McCue and McCue, loss of voice hinted at its function: the patient did not want to testify. By contrast, Miss A.'s loss of voice provided no hint to its function or to the situation which had triggered it. The symptom, apparently, had been chosen because it was known, not for its expressive value. Hints, however, appeared in the near-rape story, which Miss A.'s inconsistencies and the physical evidence suggested was untrue. Superficially, this story served to account for the loss of voice; Miss A. must have thought that loss of voice could be explained by traumatic events. Symbolically, however, the story made a statement that Miss A.'s loss of voice was due to mistreatment by men. Miss A. may have been feeling victimized by her boyfriend or believed that he had exploited her for sexual reasons.

Thorpe and colleagues provide little relevant data. Alternatively, the story may have been Miss A.'s way of reminding her boyfriend that other men found her attractive.

Conversion symptoms can also be modeled on real symptoms the patient himself has experienced. Many patients with conversion seizures also have real seizures, for example.[71] Since seizure disorders are often not completely controlled and can sometimes be exacerbated by emotional factors, patients with such disorders who are looking for illness behaviors can always produce more seizures without being questioned too closely. Unlike Miss A. they generally won't be called upon for a cover story. Also, patients with chronic disorders learn that they get attention from family and medical staff to the degree that their illness is out of control. Like the patients described by Walker and colleagues, they can learn to produce the symptoms people are looking for, which in these particular cases are those of an illness that they really have.

Ziegler and Schlemmer described a 43-year-old man who at age 13 had suffered a penetrating wound to the right eye that had left him with the ability to perceive only light with that eye.[72] He had been well until one week prior to his presentation, when he awoke with a headache and discovered that he could perceive only light through his left eye, as well. Opthalmological examination revealed the long-standing damage to his right eye, with no abnormalities of his left eye, which the patient then claimed was blind even to light. Neurological and general medical evaluations were normal, and the patient failed to respond to several treatment regimens for optic nerve disorders. After three weeks had elapsed, a nurse encouraged the patient to take off the dark glasses he had taken to wearing and to count fingers held up six feet away. The next day the patient's acuity was once again 20/20, and his headache had disappeared. For five years thereafter, the patient remained well except for occasional headaches.

When he was 49, though, the patient began to experience recurrent episodes of abrupt loss of vision. These were triggered by bright lights, music, or emotional upset, occurred together with headaches on one side or the other, and lasted a matter of days. Six years later he had a more sustained loss of vision, except for light perception, in his uninjured eye. Ophthalmological and neurological workups were again unremarkable. In the hospital, he was noted to be frequently angry and irritable. At the time Ziegler and Schlemmer described this remarkable patient, he was living the life of the totally blind. His chores were limited to those he could do by touch, and he had to be led by his wife when he left the house. His wife continued to keep a detailed daily record of his headache severity and times when he "sees more light." Neither the patient nor his wife had accepted referrals to a psychiatrist.

Ziegler and Schlemmer also described the vicissitudes of two of this patient's children, who also developed conversion blindness, which in their cases was modeled after their father's illness. A 25-year-old son had developed a left-sided headache and noted that one eye was red. Two days later he woke up with 20/400 vision in both eyes, with restricted visual fields.

An ophthalmological examination and a test for so-called optokinetic nystagmus, the presence of which betrays more intact visual functioning, were both normal, however. An extensive neurological workup was also normal. With coaxing, his vision improved to nearly normal before he suffered a relapse and could not see again. In subsequent months, he reported occasional vision, which would always disappear when the headaches relapsed. On one occasion, he was treated with an intravenous sedative, which apparently relaxed him to the point that he admitted seeing again, but the blindness returned just a few days later. The syndrome disappeared for no apparent reason after seven months. This young man believed that his illness was the same as his father's but not quite as severe. As in his father's case, the functions served by blindness were never entirely clear but seemed to involve a desire to be cared for by others. Indicative of the family environment, even his four-year-old son was said to be proud of the services he rendered his blind father.

The patient's 15-year-old daughter also suffered transient loss of vision in one eye. When she was 25 years old, she suddenly lost visual acuity in her left eye but recovered the next day. Six months later, she lost acuity in both eyes. Ophthalmological examination was normal, and she recovered quickly, but recurrent attacks like this one occurred for several years. One such episode lasted more than three months. She was said to be totally blind for three weeks during this time. As in her brother's case, repeated neurological and ophthalmological examinations and tests were normal.

Unlike her father and brother, this particular patient also had nonvisual symptoms suggestive of conversion disorder. These included recurrent fainting spells followed by 30 to 40 minutes of flaccid unresponsiveness, which were thought inconsistent with a seizure disorder; an occasion on which she could not wake from sleep; and a three-day period of loss of memory. Eventually, the visual symptoms did remit, an improvement she attributed to her discovery that she was "allergic" to monosodium glutamate, a flavor enhancer found in Chinese and some prepared foods. In following pages, I discuss patients who attribute their illness behavior to what they call "allergies" to chemicals not known to have such effects.

Particular conversion symptoms can also be epidemic. Epidemics of conversion symptoms, which often occur in wartime and sometimes in prison settings, not only model the symptoms, but also impress future patients with their potential utility. For example, soldiers who observe their fellows being removed from the front lines because of paralyses in their trigger fingers may readily conclude that paralyzed trigger fingers are given some medical credence and that this disorder might be useful to them as well. This is the same process, albeit on a larger scale, that must have occurred in the family reported by Ziegler and Schlemmer. Symptom epidemics were especially common during the terrible trench slaughters of World War I, when the only way to survive was to be wounded or ill (see later discussion). Some soldiers wounded themselves; others developed conversion symptoms. For example, one particular epidemic conversion symptom, called camptocormia, from the Greek words for "curved" and "trunk," was described among French soldiers in World War I, reappeared briefly in World War II, and has since been seen in only a few scattered cases.[73] Many patients reported family histories of this symptom. Patients with camptocormia present with a flexed spinal column. The curvature is so severe that the patient can hardly look up. The arms, typically, droop by the sides like an ape's and sometimes swing widely in the process of walking. Although polite most of the time, soldiers with camptocormia can become explosively angry. In World War I, physicians forcefully straightened such patients and then, to keep them straight, either fastened them to boards or placed them in plaster casts. Physicians in World War II found that discharging the patients from military service often led to later improvements in the syndrome.

In the family members described by Ziegler and Schlemmer, visual symptoms sometimes cleared up transiently in response to coaxing or other interventions. These symptoms, however, returned, either immediately or following a variable period of remission. The problem of recurring conversion symptoms, and occasional cases in which new symptoms develop when an old one has been cleared up, was emphasized by early psychoanalysts, who considered it evidence for the superiority of their own treatment approach.[74] According to these writers, only therapy aimed at resolving the unconscious conflicts that had produced the conversion symptoms could succeed in permanently eradicating them. It should be evident, though, that the tendency for conversion symptoms to recur is predicted as well by an illness-role model as by Freudian theory. Insofar as patients develop such symptoms to meet social needs, needs that have not been resolved may continue to lead to new symptoms. While a patient may be coaxed to give up a particular symptom, he may choose to use it again or to invent a new one, as long the motives for illness have not been addressed more directly.

Anton Mesmer, the charismatic eighteenth-century discoverer of "animal magnetism," was forced to leave Vienna in 1778 after his cure of a young pianist protegé of the Empress Maria Theresa proved to be temporary. The patient, Maria Theresa von Paradis, had awakened without sight one morning in 1762, when she was three years old.[75] Her parents, however, provided her the finest education and, when she proved to have great musical talent, presented her to her namesake, who granted her a lifetime pension. The Empress also arranged for Maria's first concert and for her first tour of Europe, both of which were successes. As Fraulein Paradis's fame spread, the Imperial physician, Anton von Stoerck, tried to restore her sight with leaches, cauterizations, purgatives, and diuretics, to which she responded with headaches and with delirium. She had painful ocular spasms, during which only the whites of her eyes could be seen. Von Stoerck resorted to newly invented electrical treatments, but more than 3,000 shocks to the skin around her eyes increased her irritability without relieving her symptoms. To save face for Von Stoerck, consultants pronounced her incurable.

Mesmer was an estranged student of Von Stoerck's and a friend of the Paradis family. By 1777, when Herr Paradis asked him to treat his daughter,

Mesmer was well known for his magnetic treatments. In fact, he had already given up the use of actual magnets and iron filings and had taken to using his body to direct "magnetic fluxes." No account has survived of Mesmer's actual treatment of Fraulein Paradis, but other accounts give a sense of his method of working with patients. Typically, he pressed the patient's knees between his own, pressed her hands together, gazed deeply into her eyes, and made "magnetic passes" with his hands or wand over her bodily "poles." Mesmer's was an intimate method of working with patients. By her second treatment, Fraulein Paradis, who had been blind for 15 years, was able to follow movements of Mesmer's wand with her eyes. By the fourth treatment, her ocular spasms had ceased, and her eyes had resumed their normal positions. She reported being able to distinguish light and dark areas and colors. Her eyes, however, had become extremely sensitive to light; the slightest illumination could cause her to fall to the ground. Mesmer had her move into a wing of his house so that he could treat her on a daily basis. After slightly more than a month of treatment, Fraulein Paradis had completely recovered her sight. Mesmer's was the first face she had seen since her childhood.

Overjoyed at his daughter's recovery, Herr Paradis published an account of her cure, as the result of which a commission from the University of Vienna medical faculty was appointed to investigate Mesmer's seeming success. That the commission was headed by Von Stoerck, who had failed to cure Fraulein Paradis and considered himself Mesmer's enemy, suggests that the commission was set up to get rid of Mesmer. In fact, while the commission acknowledged that Fraulein Paradis, who still lived in Mesmer's house, could see, at least when Mesmer himself was in the room, they declared that her illness had been in her mind all along. They prevailed on Herr Paradis to remove his daughter from Mesmer's unwholesome influence. The Paradis family, alarmed by the fact that the sighted Fraulein Paradis could not play the piano and perhaps, too, by their concern that the Empress would cut off her pension, accepted this recommendation.

Herr Paradis traveled to Mesmer's house and demanded his daughter back. When Mesmer refused, Paradis drew his sword, threw his shrieking daughter headfirst into a wall, and attempted to drag her, still clinging to Mesmer, from the premises. For the time being, Paradis left without his daughter, who had lost her sight again and on top of that was delirious. Two weeks of intensive treatment with Mesmer restored her sight, but in the end Fraulein Paradis was forced to return to her parents. One day after arriving home, she was blind again, and she remained blind for the rest of her life. She never met Mesmer again, although he was in the audience in 1784, when she gave a harpsichord concert for the French court in Paris.

Following these incidents, Mesmer was expelled from the Vienna medical faculty. He was also ordered to stop practicing magnetic therapy. Rather than comply, Mesmer went to Paris, where he prospered until 1784, when Benjamin Franklin's commission reported its adverse findings.

The events that transpired between Mesmer and Fraulein Paradis show how conversion symptoms wax and wane with changes in social motives. For whatever reasons, before meeting Mesmer, Fraulein Paradis had apparently developed a social adjustment based on her being blind. With his well-known seductive charm and his intimate method of treatment, and by removing Fraulein Paradis from her home, Mesmer destabilized this existing social adjustment. Fraulein Paradis must have felt that the key to her happiness now lay in pleasing Mesmer, who wanted her to see. Her sight was conditional, though, on Mesmer's continued attention: It functioned only when Mesmer himself was in the room, and it disappeared for a while when she was threatened with removal from his house. When Mesmer was defeated and Fraulein Paradis taken back to her parents, she returned to her previous mode of social adjustment.

Finally, the illness-role viewpoint suggests that patients with conversion symptoms are likely to be skilled at playing social roles, motivated to play them, and sensitive to role cues. In a classic article, published in 1958, Paul Chodoff and Henry Lyons noted that the concept of the hysterical personality grew out of attempts to describe social behavior of patients who presented with conversion symptoms.[76] Rather than being seen as a separate diagnostic entity, hysterical personality was seen as a facet of conversion hysteria, the diagnostic forerunner of today's conversion disorder. Characteristics of hysterical personality types cited by Chodoff and Lyons include, among others, dramatization, play-acting, histrionic behavior, simulation of attitudes and affects, and a demanding, dependent approach to social relationships. Chodoff and Lyons conducted a study of 17 patients with conversion symptoms and found that only three of them fulfilled their criteria for hysterical personality disorder. Conversion symptoms, they argued, could appear in the setting of various personality disturbances. However, Chodoff and Lyons's criteria for hysterical personality included characteristics, such as emotional lability and sexual frigidity, that are unrelated to role playing tendencies. Many of their patients could have been histrionic without meeting the other criteria required by Chodoff and Lyons for diagnosis of hysterical personality. Also, six of the 17 patients were said to have passive-dependent personality disorders, suggesting that dependency was a common finding.

The DSM-IV has no listing for "hysterical personality," but it does say that conversion disorders tend to occur in patients with histrionic, antisocial, or dependent personality disorders.[77] Histrionic personalities are characterized by excessive emotionality and attention seeking, along with theatricality and heightened suggestibility. Antisocial personalities are said to be deceitful and to manipulate others for their own ends. Dependent personalities, among their other features, will go to any lengths to obtain assistance and support from others.

As for motivation, conversion patients are generally depressed or demoralized. In one representative study, for example, Kinzl and colleagues found that only four of 22 women with conversion loss of voice met their criteria for hysterical personality but that 10 of the 22 patients had depressive disorders.[78] Many patients experienced their social supports as inadequate and resorted to conversion to obtain help and attention. The DSM-IV notes an association between conversion and depression and between conversion and stressful life events.

Van Dyck and Hoogduin summarized the relationship between conversion and hypnotizability, which, according to the argument made in chapter 4, measures subjects' willingness to respond to cues.[79] As I noted earlier, Charcot, whose grand hysterics showed mostly conversion symptoms, believed that extreme hypnotic susceptibility—as evidenced by catalepsy, lethargy, and somnambulism—indicated predisposition to hysteria. While later clinical experience supported Charcot's thesis that hysterics were highly hypnotizable, Bernheim's studies suggested that normal persons, too, could be hypnotized and that catalepsy, lethargy, and somnambulism in particular resulted from suggestions given to Salpêtrière patients.[80] Hypnosis, in any event, could not be taken as proof of psychopathology. It was almost a hundred years before a controlled study, by Bendefelt and colleagues, was carried out to prove that conversion patients are more hypnotizable than other psychiatric patients; although the results were positive, experimental flaws vitiated the finding.[81] In this study, a clinical impression of heightened suggestibility was used as a criterion for diagnosing conversion. Later, Bliss administered the Stanford Hypnotic Susceptibility Scale, form C, to 18 patients with conversion disorder and found that the average patient scored highly enough on this scale to be in the top 10 percent of the general population.[82] As one might expect if both hypnosis and conversion are social roles, the phenomena of the latter are readily reproduced in response to hypnotic instructions. In one well-known study, for instance, patients with narrowed visual fields resulting from conversion or hypnotic suggestions gave fewer correct answers than would be expected by chance when asked to name objects presented in the area in which they were ostensibly blind.[83] In both cases, apparently, subjects who wished to appear blind avoided revealing what they had seen, thereby inadvertently giving away the game.

Chronic Fatigue Syndrome and Some Related Disorders

During the 1980s, a syndrome whose major characteristic is chronic, disabling fatigue was widely discussed in both professional and lay publications and in the mass media. In 1988, the Centers for Disease Control adopted defining criteria for this puzzling disorder, which henceforth would officially be known as chronic fatigue syndrome (CFS).[84] According to these criteria, patients with CFS must manifest new-onset fatigue sufficiently severe to produce at least a 50 percent impairment in daily activities for at least six months. Patients must not have any other physical disorder known to produce fatigue, such as heart, lung, renal, gastrointestinal, hematologic, or malignant illness, must not be using medications known to cause fatigue, and must not have psychiatric disorders, such as depression, known to be associated with persistent fatigue. In addition to their fatigue, patients must have unexplained symptoms, such as sore throat, lymph node tenderness, weakness, muscle aches, headaches, joint pain, forgetfulness, irritability, or confusion, and unexplained physical findings, such as low-grade fever, throat irritation, or swollen lymph nodes in the neck and under the arms. At least eight of a list of 11 symptoms, or six such symptoms in combination with two of the three unexplained physical findings, were needed to make a definite diagnosis of CFS. When studies showed that few patients with chronic fatigue satisfied these criteria because most of them had mood disorders, the criteria were modified to allow for mood disorders as long as they begin after fatigue has started.[85] The relation of mood disorders to chronic fatigue is discussed later. The obvious difficulty of quantifying impairment has received less comment than it may deserve.

The fact that physical findings are part of the diagnosis suggests that CFS is more than an illness role. Illness roles, after all, should not cause low-grade fevers, inflame the throat, or cause lymph nodes to swell. However, the significance of these physical signs is unclear. Healthy subjects, for instance, can have one or more of these signs during the course of transient infectious illnesses. Also, in different studies, the proportion of CFS patients reported to have them varies. Lane, Manu, and Matthews studied 200 patients evaluated at the Chronic Fatigue Clinic at the University of Connecticut Health Center between March 1988 and September 1989.[86] The 60 of these patients who met modified CDC criteria for chronic fatigue syndrome were compared with 60 controls chosen at random from the remaining 140 patients seen. Only 12 of the CFS patients and eight of the controls had a single physical sign when examined at the University clinic, and only four of the CFS patients and two of the controls had two or more such signs. Neither any one physical sign nor the overall number of signs differed significantly between the CFS and control subjects. A higher proportion of CFS patients than controls had been reported to have had physical signs in the past, but these were no longer evident at the time of the study. What reliably distinguished CFS from control subjects was the greater number of subjective symptoms reported by the former. Thus, CFS patients more often reported fevers or chills, sore throat, painful lymph nodes, muscle aches and weakness, fatigue after exercise, headaches, joint pains, and a sudden illness onset. Physical signs played a role in meeting diagnostic criteria for only two of the 60 CFS patients.

Buchwald and colleagues reported on 348 patients consecutively diagnosed as having CFS by the modified CDC criteria at the University of Washington Chronic Fatigue Clinic.[87] They found more physical signs than did Lane and colleagues, but methodological problems render their findings suspect. Sixty percent of the female and 33 percent of the male subjects reportedly had enlarged or tender lymph nodes, and 22 percent of the female and 42 percent of the male subjects had throat inflammation on physical examination. It is unclear, however, what proportion of subjects had objectively enlarged, as opposed to subjectively tender, lymph nodes or how enlarged the lymph nodes actually were. Patients with CFS are rarely subjected to lymph node biopsies, in spite of the fact that malignancies and other disorders that cause lymph node enlargement can cause fatigue. Therefore, it seems unlikely that the degree of lymph node enlargement is often substantial. In the Buchwald study, there was no normal control group, so it is not clear how often enlarged lymph nodes might have been found according to Buchwald's criteria in subjects without CFS. Buchwald and colleagues note that fever is the most objective of the physical signs associated with chronic fatigue syndrome. Twenty-five percent of the female and 22 percent of the male subjects had measured temperatures greater than 99.5 degrees Fahrenheit. Again, however, there was no control group, nor is there any indication of the conditions under which these measurements were taken or of whether these temperature elevations were constant or intermittent. No data are presented concerning the distribution of bodily temperatures. Healthy individuals can maintain body temperatures slightly above or below 98.6 degrees, and they also show circadian variations of about one degree.

Various theories concerning organic causes of CFS have been popular, and some have limited empirical support. One of the earliest theories was that CFS results from chronic infections with Epstein-Barr virus, the agent responsible for mononucleosis.[88] Early immunologic studies of CFS patients seemed to support this theory; patients had higher than normal levels of antibodies directed at Epstein-Barr, and these antibodies were of the type usually seen during active infections. More recent studies, however, have seemed to discredit this theory. Some results were not reproducible, and others were nonspecific. Some physicians have claimed that CFS is caused by diffuse yeast infections, but this theory has never had sufficient research support to be taken seriously in the medical community at large.[89] Most recently, attention has shifted to immune system abnormalities thought to be found in patients with CFS.[90] These include impairment of types of white blood cell activity and impairments in responses to mitogens, or agents that normally cause certain white cells to proliferate. Although these abnormalities are thought to reflect the effects of chronic viral infections, no evidence of infection with a wide range of viruses has been found in CFS patients thus far. Claims have been made for treatments aimed at enhancing immune system function, but clinical studies in this area have been flawed and are presently inconclusive.[91] Similar immunological abnormalities have also been found in depression.[92] A large proportion of patients with chronic fatigue are depressed (see later discussion), and some reports indicate that the immunological abnormalities found in CFS normalize following treatment with antidepressant medications.[93]

Certainly, in an age of "new" diseases, the most notable being AIDS, no one can state with confidence that there isn't a physical illness, albeit not yet understood, that is responsible for many or even most CFS cases.[94] However, even if that is so, a theatrical model may account for some "copycat" cases that currently can't be distinguished. I review here the evidence that suggests that chronic fatigue is an illness role for at least some patients.

First, like patients who present with other illness roles, most patients who present with unexplained chronic fatigue, whether or not they have the other symptoms needed to meet the CDC criteria, are depressed or demoralized. For example, Buchwald and colleagues found that 22 percent of 287 CFS patients they evaluated met DSM-III criteria for current major depression.[95] One-third of the female and more than 40 percent of the male patients met DSM-III criteria for some current mental disorder. Almost three-quarters had had a major depressive episode sometime in their lives. Lane and colleagues reported that more than three-quarters of 120 fatigued patients they studied had current mood disorders.[96] About half of the mood disorders preceded the patients' complaints of fatigue. Kreusi, Dale, and Straus studied 28 CFS patients and found that nearly half of them met DSM-III criteria for major depressive disorder.[97] Another 25 percent met DSM-III criteria for dysthymia, a milder form of depression. Only two patients became psychiatrically ill after they were fatigued, while 10 patients clearly were psychiatrically ill before their fatigue developed. The remaining nine patients who had DSM-III diagnoses became psychiatrically ill about the time their fatigue began. Manu, Matthews, and Lane reported that 84 of a group of 100 patients with unexplained chronic fatigue had been psychiatrically ill, mostly with mood disorders, at some point in their lives.[98] Sixty-six of the patients met DSM-III-R criteria for psychiatric disorders during the time they were studied. Skapinakis and others studied 10,000 subjects in Britain.[99] Nine percent of subjects complained of chronic fatigue for which no medical explanation was evident. In this population, chronic fatigue was predicted by psychopathology, perceived lack of social support, age, and female sex. Psychopathology raised the chance of reporting fatigue by a factor of five. Functional impairments in subjects with chronic fatigue were largely explained by co-morbid psychiatric disorders.

Not only does depression often antedate chronic fatigue; fatigue patients' current depression also cannot be wholly accounted for by their physical limitations. Katon and colleagues, for example, compared 98 patients with unexplained chronic fatigue to 31 patients with severe rheumatoid arthritis.[100] In spite of the fact that the arthritic patients had been ill longer, were more severely disabled, and had more severe pain than the patients with chronic fatigue, the patients with chronic fatigue were more likely to be depressed. Forty-five percent of the fatigued patients had some current DSM-III-R diagnosis, compared to only 6.4 percent of the arthritis controls. Most current diagnoses were of mood disorders. Eighty-five percent of the fatigued patients had met criteria for a DSM-III-R diagnosis at some point in their lives, compared to 48 percent of the arthritis patients. Once again, the majority of these were mood disorders. The differences in the rate of mood disorders between fatigue patients and controls persisted even when fatigue was not counted as a symptom of a mood disorder. Fifty-three percent of the fatigued patients, but only 12.5 percent of the arthritics, scored above a critical cutoff indicative of illness on a well-known measure of general psychopathology.

Second, complaints of chronic fatigue are often part of a larger pattern of illness behavior. The CDC criteria require that other complaints be present in cases of CFS, but in fact the other complaints are sometimes so varied and protean that patients meet the criteria for somatization disorder. Returning, for example, to the studies cited earlier, Lane, Manu, and Matthews found that 17 of the 60 CFS patients they studied met DSM-III criteria for somatization disorder at the time they were studied.[101] Fifteen of these 17 patients had somatization disorder before they began to complain of chronic fatigue. Buchwald and colleagues found an overall rate of DSM-III-R somatization disorder of about 30 percent in their CFS patients.[102] Manu and colleagues found only 15 cases of DSM-III somatization disorder in the 100 patients with chronic fatigue they studied, but nearly half their subjects reported at least six symptoms of somatization disorder.[103] Katon and colleagues found that 46 percent of their subjects with chronic fatigue met DSM-III-R criteria for somatization disorder, compared to none of the control subjects with disabling rheumatoid arthritis.[104] To show that this high rate was not explained by symptoms of CFS per se, Katon and colleagues rediagnosed their subjects without counting symptoms common to both CFS and somatization disorder. Even without these symptoms, more than 20 percent of the fatigued subjects still met DSM-III-R criteria for somatization disorder.

Buchwald and Garrity compared 30 patients with CFS to an equal number of patients with multiple chemical sensitivity (MCS).[105] Patients with multiple chemical sensitivity complain of diffuse symptoms that they attribute to exposure to common chemicals at levels far below those believed to have toxic effects. (Multiple chemical sensitivity is discussed as an illness role in a later section.) Eighty percent of the MCS patients complained of disabling fatigue, and 30 percent of them met CDC criteria for CFS. All of the MCS patients complained of adverse effects following exposures to pollution, gas, perfumes, smoke, paint fumes, or other common chemicals, but more than half the subjects with CFS also reported having had such adverse effects.

Along the same lines, Manu, Matthews, and Lane found that 27 of the 200 patients with chronic fatigue they studied reported multiple food intolerances (MFI).[106] Patients were asked to identify foods that made them ill. The MFI subjects were those who identified foods from at least three food groups that predictably made them feel ill but who had no confirmed food allergies or gastrointestinal problems that could be responsible for their subjective distress. The symptoms the patients reported following food ingestion were varied and difficult to explain in physiological terms. One patient, for instance, reported abdominal pain after eating tomatoes, severe fatigue from red meat, a persistent bad taste in the mouth after eating eggs, and shortness of breath from chocolate. Another patient reported chills from eating fish and nasal congestion from peas. A third reported headaches from tomatoes, nasal congestion from milk, and fatigue and aches from crabmeat. The authors cite previous research that showed that patients who report adverse food reactions without demonstrable food allergies often claim to be disabled by their symptoms. They are generally hypochondriacal and show signs of distress on psychological testing.

Stricklin and colleagues administered the Minnesota Multiphasic Psychological Inventory (MMPI) to female patients with "epidemic neuromyasthenia," a form of chronic fatigue that appears in clusters in communities and is therefore often attributed to unknown viral infections.[107] Compared to control subjects, neuromyasthenics showed striking elevations on the "hypochondriasis," "depression," "hysteria," "psychasthenia," and "schizophrenia" scales of the MMPI. High scores on these scales are typical of patients with Briquet's syndrome, with multiple personality disorder, and with borderline personality disorder.[108] (Briquet's syndrome was discussed earlier; multiple personality disorder is discussed as an illness role in the following chapter.) The reader will recall that more than a third of the patients with multiple personality disorder studied by Ross met DSM-III-R criteria for somatization disorder.[109] Most patients with multiple personality disorder, and a significant number of patients with somatization disorder, also meet criteria for borderline personality, the manifestations of which include emotional instability, impulsivity, and poor social and occupational functioning (see chapter 6).[110] Borderline personality is part of the same personality cluster as histrionic personality disorder. In fact, Millon and colleagues administered the Millon Clinical Multiaxial Inventory to a group of CFS patients and found that fully a third of them had severe histrionic personality features.[111]

Abbey and Garfinkel discussed the similarity between CFS and a nineteenth-century syndrome called neurasthenia.[112] Although the term "neurasthenia," or, literally, "nervous weakness," was in use for decades before his work appeared, neurasthenia as a syndrome was introduced by George Beard, a prominent New York physician, in 1869, when he described 30 typical cases. A book, *Neurasthenia*, published by Beard in 1880, and two sequels, *American Nervousness* (1881) and *Sexual Neurasthenia* (1884), further brought neurasthenia to the public's attention. By the end of the nineteenth century, neurasthenia came to be known as "the American illness." In his 1869 paper, Beard elaborated on more than 75 symptoms of neurasthenia, a list that expanded still further in later monographs. Fatigue, however, was the cardinal feature. Patients described by Beard felt "absolute exhaustion," felt they might die of fatigue, and could not count on having the energy to complete their scheduled activities. Neurasthenics reported that their limbs felt heavy and ached, especially after exertion but often out of the blue. Headaches, head pressure, or heaviness and migratory joint pains were also prominent, along with a variety of more purely mental symptoms, such as irritability, excessive forgetfulness, trouble concentrating, trouble finding words, and depressed mood. Patients' sleep was disturbed; they woke up in the morning as tired as when they had gone to bed and felt drowsy during the day. Like patients with CFS, some patients with neurasthenia were said to have sore throats and intermittent fevers. Beard, however, did not describe lymph node enlargement.

Beard, who worked for a time with Thomas Edison and was familiar with experiments that showed the electrical nature of nervous impulses, believed that neurasthenia was caused by depletion of electrical energy in the nervous system. In addition to enforced rest, Beard recommended the application of electrical currents, in the hope of replenishing electrical energy stores. Beard speculated that energy could be depleted in several different ways. For men, the most important cause of depletion of nervous energy was immersion in the hubbub of modern life, which the telegraph, railroad, and modern marketplace had rendered too strenuous for mortal nervous systems. Most neurasthenic men were businessmen and professionals (Beard himself claimed to be a sufferer) exposed to the full effects of modernization. According to Beard, four-fifths of his male patients were "brain workers" and belonged to the "higher orders" of American life. Lower-class or manual workers were believed to be safe from the illness, as were Negroes and "savages" in general. George Frederick Drinka, a psychiatric historian, referred to Beard's theory as a "Prometheus myth."[113] Just as the titan Prometheus suffered for stealing fire from the Olympian gods, so Beard's patients suffered for reaching too high. If neurasthenia was the American illness, it must be because Americans were more ambitious than others.

While men were falling ill by imitating titans, women, according to Beard, fell ill by imitating men. Lacking men's endowments of nervous energy, women depleted their stores through excess education or intellectual efforts. Thus, when Charlotte Perkins Gilman had symptoms of neurasthenia, Silas Weir Mitchell, an eminent Philadelphia doctor, advised her to live as domestic a life as possible and by all means to give up her efforts to write. Gilman responded by writing a story about a woman who became psychotically depressed due to Mitchell's "rest cure." Jane Addams, the social worker and founder of Hull House, was also told by Mitchell to give up her life's work. Dr. Margaret Cleaves, herself a neurasthenic, felt called upon to argue that women's neurasthenia resulted from thwarted ambition, not from ambition itself.

As Drinka's term implies, one of the obvious functions served by Beard's "neurasthenia" was to provide an illness-role equivalent to hysteria but for upper- and middle-class men. No self-respecting man could enact hysterical illness, since to do so would imply nervous defects, but he could enact an illness attributed to hectic life in what was then the fast lane. This particular social function of neurasthenia was evident during World War I, when conversion and "nervous" disorders were rampant among the troops exposed to the brutal trench warfare. While psychologically disabled enlisted men were typically labeled hysterics, implying that they had inner defects, officers with the same symptoms were usually called neurasthenics, implying that they were exhausted by their heroic efforts.[114] The distinction between neurasthenia and hysteria is akin to the distinction between central and peripheral possession illnesses as defined by I. M. Lewis (see chapter 3), which are also characteristic of particular "classes" in traditional societies. The reader will recall that possession by malign spirits indicates vulnerability, or victimization by witchcraft, while possession by central spirits suggests that one is chosen. Likewise, just as central and peripheral possession illnesses have many features in common, so also was there a broad symptom overlap between neurasthenia and hysteria, as the World War I data show.

According to Abbey and Garfinkel, the themes of overwork and conflicts related to work that were evident in nineteenth-century discussions of neurasthenia continue to play a role in modern-day chronic fatigue. As in the late nineteenth century, the present cultural climate overemphasizes financial success, status, and power and calls on men and women to make great sacrifices to achieve those ends. Businesspeople and professionals are expected to work extraordinary hours to get ahead, and women in particular are often caught between the conflicting demands of work and home life, with the latter most often having to give way. "Burnout" and work stress have become everyday matters for the upwardly mobile, a part of the population prone to chronic fatigue, which was once called the "yuppie flu." Abbey and Garfinkel argue that, by providing a face-saving and even, insofar as it is seen as resulting from overwork, praiseworthy reason for retreat from the demands of the workplace, chronic fatigue is a safety valve for those who are tired of battle. The choice of fatigue complaints to press work-related concerns is an intuitive one, since fatigue is a normal experience after working long hours or under severe stress.

By the 1950s, neurasthenia per se had largely disappeared in the United States, but it remained in the World Health Organization's International Classification of Disease, and it is still diagnosed in some countries, such as China, where it seemingly corresponds to indigenous diagnoses. Traditional Chinese medical practitioners, for example, diagnose several disorders that they believe are caused by depletion of energies, with symptoms that resemble neurasthenic symptoms. The latter, of course, are so broad that it is easy to find corollary symptoms in other diagnoses. Arthur Kleinman's studies of Chinese neurasthenics illustrate possible functions of somatic complaints, some of which may be important for American patients said to have CFS or other illness roles.[115] I describe Kleinman's findings at some length, as they are the best descriptions of illness-role functions to be found in the literature.

Many of the functions served by neurasthenia and described by Kleinman related to the rules then governing work in China, but others related to family or living situations. Qin Zijun, for example, was a 40-year-old mother of three children with a two-year history of headaches, dizziness, weakness, and loss of energy. Two and half years before, her husband had been ordered to another city to work and Qin Zijun was distressed by the enforced separation. She also disliked her job as a machine operator, but, because her husband had come from the landlord class, she had been denied bonuses and promotions. For 18 months preceding her interview with Kleinman, Qin Zijun had been requesting a change in assignment because of her illness, which several physicians had diagnosed as neurasthenia, and had asked that her husband be allowed to return home to care for her. For three months she had not been to work, but she was still receiving her full salary. She felt that returning to work would worsen her health problems. She had symptoms of major depression and agoraphobia, which responded in part to an antidepressant, but the antidepressant failed to alleviate her physical symptoms. At the time of a follow-up visit, Qin Zijun was still negotiating with cadres at her factory for transfer to lighter, part-time work and for her husband's return in order to care for her.

Lin Hung was a 24-year-old factory worker who reported headaches, dizziness, weakness and lack of energy, among other symptoms. He had been ill for six months at the time Kleinman met him. His mother had been neurasthenic, and he believed he was, too. Although Lin Hung hated his current job, employment rules dictated that he would have to stay in it for the rest of his life. His parents had moved away from the city in which he worked, so Lin Hung had been forced to move to a dormitory. He wanted his sister to join him in the city, but she could not get permission to leave the countryside, and he could not see his girlfriend because their work shifts did not coincide. He had been criticized by others in his work unit for shoddy work and for wanting to get married at too young an age. He thought his poor health would improve if he could change his job, rejoin his parents, and marry, but he saw little hope that any of that would happen. Depressed and anxious, he was thinking of suicide. He pleaded with Kleinman to write a letter to the factory clinic, recommending rest at his parent's home. In commenting on this case, Kleinman noted that social control in China was currently so tight that only physical illness provided a ground for exercise of personal control, if only temporarily and to a limited degree.

Wu Baihua was a 42-year-old woman who had complained of headaches, dizziness, palpitations, tension, and other symptoms of neurasthenia since the death of an elder sister five years before. Previously a science teacher, she had reluctantly served as a middle school principal for the past two years, a position in which she was highly successful but that left her feeling overwhelmed by work. She went to work early in the morning, returned home late in the evening, and brought work home with her. She felt guilty that she had no time to spend with her children and feared that her long hours were ruining her marriage. She was also involved in a conflict with the Communist Party secretary assigned to her school. He countermanded her orders, changed faculty assignments without consulting her, and reversed her decisions concerning curricular reforms. Wu's faculty, moreover, blamed her for his directives. Wu Baihua had several times requested permission to resign as principal and to once again teach science, which she had enjoyed, but the local authorities refused her requests. Wu Baihua responded by telling them that she was ill and needed to rest and recuperate for the sake of her health. Kleinman saw her symptoms as part and parcel of her work negotiations.

Li Xiangu was a 40-year-old neurasthenic bus driver who had complained of neck pain, insomnia, and constricted feelings in the neck and throat for the past six years. When Li was first seen, Kleinman diagnosed depression and panic disorder. Three years later, Kleinman found that these disorders had remitted, but Li Xiangu still reported residual physical symptoms. Li Xiangu's symptoms developed after an accident he had while driving his bus, but the larger context in which they occurred was that of a family conflict. Shortly before the accident, Li's mother, whom he called "difficult," had left his older brother's house and moved in with Li and his family. She and Li's wife quarreled daily about the children and about household chores. His mother threatened to leave and live on her own, which would bring shame on Li, while his wife complained that Li failed to take her side. She threatened suicide if he could not control his mother. The block committee was called in to mediate between the parties, but these efforts, as well as appeals to Li's elder brother to intervene, were unsuccessful. Li took to visiting clinics, but this did not solve the problem. His mother blamed Li's wife for not taking care of her son, while his wife told his mother to care for Li herself.

Eventually, Li's work unit took charge of the matter. On the grounds that the family conflict was worsening Li's health and interfering with his job, as evidenced by his accident, they arranged for Li's mother to move to a nearby apartment where Li could visit her daily but where she would not be in contact with Li's wife. Both women agreed to this settlement, which had lasted more than a year at the time of Kleinman's follow-up visit. Li and his wife were once again getting along, Li's mother was less contentious, and Li's brother had even agreed to help pay her living expenses. Li's symptoms had greatly improved, but, referring to the family conflict that had eased, he warned Kleinman that "if this is a big stress again in the future, my neurasthenia will again get worse." Kleinman notes how illness had served in this case to force others to intervene for the patient in a difficult impasse.

All of these patients and others cited by Kleinman were depressed, anxious, or demoralized. Qin Zijun, for instance was depressed and agoraphobic, Lin Hung was thinking of suicide, Wu Baihua felt tension and guilt, and Li Xiangu was depressed and had panic attacks. Kleinman reported that patients, like Qin Zijun, who received antidepressant medications experienced improvement in their depression and anxiety symptoms but not in the physical symptoms that had led to their being diagnosed as neurasthenics. These improved, as they did for Li Xiangu, only when the social impasse that was causing them was resolved. Li Xiangu explicitly cited physical symptoms as likely to return should his situation return to what it had been.

Gulf War syndrome, the mysterious ailment or family of ailments reported among American veterans of the 1991 Persian Gulf War, sometimes resembles CFS. Milner and colleagues studied 166 Persian Gulf War veterans who sought treatment at a Department of Veterans Affairs medical center and found that their complaints resembled those I have described in relation to CFS;[116] 59 percent of the patients reported joint pain, 38 percent reported shortness of breath or chest pain, 35 percent reported neuropsychiatric problems (decreased attention or concentration, irritability), and 33 percent reported persistent fatigue. Other common symptoms included rashes, insomnia, diarrhea, nightmares, hair loss, cold symptoms, and bleeding gums.

As is the case with CSF, it seems probable that some and perhaps most patients with Gulf War syndrome are suffering from a disease or exposure to toxic agents that has not yet been fully characterized.[117] However, it also seems likely that some of them are playing an illness role. I have had the opportunity to examine a number of patients with Gulf War–related complaints seeking medical care at the Veterans Affairs Medical Center in Palo Alto, California. The most common symptoms reported by these patients were fatigue, muscle and joint pains, headaches, decreased concentration, decreased memory, insomnia and irritability. Some patients reported rashes, but these were not observed during their examinations. Patients were given medical evaluations to rule out illnesses known to cause symptoms like theirs, and, if these were normal, were referred for psychiatric evaluations. The psychiatric evaluations consisted of standardized measures of anxiety, depression, and cognitive functions, together with clinical interviews. Although most of the patients complained of decreased attention, concentration, or memory functions, cognitive tests revealed no objective impairments. Virtually all the patients had significant social problems, ranging from unemployment to severe marital discord, and the majority of them were depressed. In several cases, treatment for depression improved mood, but it had only an equivocal effect on somatic complaints. Like Kleinman's neurasthenics, these patients' subjective symptoms seemed to be maintained by their social problems, in relation to which they served a strategic function. For one patient, in particular, Gulf War syndrome had become his *raison d'être*. He had started a lobbying organization and spent all his time seeking publicity for the plight of Gulf War syndrome victims. He was successful enough in this way to interest news organizations in his own medical problems. All his social contacts were with other Gulf War veterans who also complained of physical symptoms. Like the victims of peripheral possession described by Lewis, his illness had become a key to a new life.

Multiple Chemical Sensitivities

In the 1950s, case reports appeared of patients with multiple symptoms ostensibly due to food allergies. Other reports soon followed, in which protean symptoms were attributed to allergies to chemicals in the environment, rather than just in food. Those who react adversely to multiple chemicals present in low concentrations have been said to have "multiple chemical sensitivity (MCS) syndrome," "indoor air syndrome," "environmental illness," "ecological illness," "twentieth-century disease," or "total allergy syndrome." Here I refer to the syndrome as MCS, since this term is now the most widely used. Though some patients with MCS may have a disease that is not yet understood, many if not most are probably acting out illness roles.

One widely known definition of MCS requires that patients have symptoms referable to more than one organ system, that recur in response to chemical exposures at levels below those known to cause human toxicity.[118] The symptoms must be elicited by diverse chemicals that have no common structural or toxicological property, and they cannot be attributable to any demonstrable abnormality on physical or laboratory examinations. The syndrome can develop insidiously, without any known precipitants, it can follow varied illnesses, or it can occur following verified high-level toxin exposures. In the last case, for instance, the syndrome has been described in factory workers who were first made ill by high-level exposures to industrial chemicals. Once the syndrome begins, the symptoms recur in response to putative low-level exposures to diverse chemicals, usually including the one to which the patients were first exposed.

Interest in MCS has been fueled by social concerns with pollution of the environment. As concern with pollution grows, it seems inevitable that some individuals will claim to have suffered harm from ambient chemicals. However, the growth of MCS has also been fueled by those who specialize in its treatment.[119] During the 1960s, clinicians who specialized in diagnosis and treatment of MCS called themselves clinical ecologists. During the 1980s, they began to refer to themselves as environmental medicine specialists. The American Board of Environmental Medicine was established to certify specialists in treatment of MCS and to organize conferences for other clinicians. The board claims to have trained thousands of physicians.

Although they are as varied as any other large group of clinicians, those who call themselves clinical ecologists or environmental specialists share certain theories and diagnostic and treatment practices. First, specialists in this field believe that low-level chemicals derange immune responses in a way that causes diffuse sensitivities and sometimes disabling symptoms. Like patients with chronic fatigue, patients with MCS are said to have abnormalities in several immune measures.[120] One subgroup of MCS specialists believes that chemicals act on the olfactory system and on its limbic nervous system connections in a way that deranges patients' immune, autonomic, and endocrine systems.[121] The limbic system, of course, is also responsible for emotional experiences—depression, for example, is widely thought to reflect limbic system dysfunction—so this hypothesis also accounts for the emotional problems commonly observed in MCS patients (discussed later). Bell and colleagues, for instance, surveyed undergraduate students enrolled in introductory psychology courses at the University of Arizona.[122] Among other questions, students were asked to rate how ill they felt after smelling pesticides, automobile exhaust, paint, new carpets, or perfumes. Clinical ecologists claim that fresh paint and new carpets, drapes, and furnishings give off toxic chemicals. "Sick building syndrome" refers to an epidemic MCS-like illness that is known to occur among workers in new office buildings. No definable cause is usually found. Ninety-seven (15 percent) of 643 subjects queried by Bell reported feeling moderately to markedly ill after exposure to odors in four of these five categories. Highly sensitive subjects reported being more shy than subjects who reported lesser responses to odors. Bell and colleagues suggest that olfactory-limbic "kindling" could account for this finding, since social avoidance is known to be a limbic phenomenon in some animal models. "Kindling" refers to the sensitization of neural structures, in this case by chemical odors, so that their activity becomes unregulated.

Clinical ecologists believe they can verify their diagnoses by exposing patients to chemicals suspected of causing their symptoms.[123] These are most
often injected or administered orally as aqueous extracts, but at some specialized centers patients are placed in booths and exposed to airborne substances. Patients report their subjective sensations after exposure, and any
reported symptoms are taken as proof of their sensitivity. If the patient reports no symptoms, progressively more concentrated solutions are administered until an exposure is reached at which symptoms are reported. The patients are told what they are being given, and no attempt is made to control
for placebo effects (see later discussion). In 1989, Terr reported that 71 of 90
patients he studied who had been diagnosed by clinical ecologists as suffering from environmental illness had been tested in this fashion.[124] Some of
the 90 had also been subject to "hair analyses," to "cytotoxic tests," or to so-
called elimination diets, among other procedures. Patients given elimination diets are placed on restrictive diets until they report feeling better. The
foods left out of the diet on which they report improvement are blamed
for their previous symptoms. Once again, there are no controls for placebo
effects.

Once a substance is identified as pathogenic, an extract is prepared that is
sufficiently dilute that the subject reports no symptoms. This is then prescribed to be taken sublingually. Repeated administrations of "neutralizing
doses," as these dilute extracts are called, are thought to reduce sensitivities,
or at least to keep them in check. Patients are also advised to avoid exposures
to chemicals, to adopt restrictive diets, to use special enemas and douches,
and to take vitamins and pure oxygen. Avoiding exposure often entails quit-
ting one's job or building a special "environmentally safe" addition to one's
house, at a cost of tens of thousands of dollars. Patients wear charcoal breathing filters when outside their houses, and they are sometimes admitted to
special hospital units that are said to be "environmentally controlled." One
quarter of 26 patients, 88 percent of whom were women, studied by Black
and colleagues had been advised to move (e.g., to the mountains or shore)
because of their MCS.[125] Half of Black's subjects also attended an MCS support group, and 92 percent reported having friends with MCS, most of
whom they had met while attending support groups. Some MCS patients
are housebound; on the advice of clinicians, they leave their homes, if at all,
only to go to support groups, dragging their oxygen cylinders and wearing
their charcoal masks.

There is little empirical support for clinical ecologists' theories and methods or for their concept of MCS. Simon and colleagues recruited 41 patients
diagnosed as "chemically sensitive" from a local allergy practice and compared them to 34 control patients with back and musculoskeletal problems.[126] The chemically sensitive patients had been ill for at least three
months and reported sensitivities to at least four of 14 common chemical
sources, including fresh paint, newspapers, perfume, hair spray, and solvent
fumes. Eighty-five percent of the chemically sensitive subjects and 82 percent of the controls were women, and the mean ages of subjects in the two

groups were 46 and 42 years, respectively. Subjects received comprehensive tests of immune function, including leukocyte counts, cell-surface marker studies, antibody screens and measures of interleukin-1 generation. On only one of these multiple measures was there a difference in the expected direction between subject groups. To detect abnormalities of the nervous system, subjects also were given tests of memory functions, of visuomotor speed, of cognitive flexibility, of auditory and verbal learning, and of attention and concentration. None of these measures differed significantly between the chemically sensitive and the control subjects.

In 1986, Terr reported immunologic findings from 50 patients diagnosed with environmental illness by clinical ecologists.[127] Forty of these patients were included in the 1989 report by Terr cited earlier. Chart reviews were performed for laboratory tests and physical findings, and patients were given physical examinations. Thirty-nine of the subjects were women, and the mean age was 38 years. The majority of patients were thought to be sensitive to chemicals present at work, and 43 of them had filed Workers' Compensation claims for their illness. The patients were divided into three groups: (1) Eight had no symptoms at all but believed that they had been harmed by exposure to chemical toxins, (2) 11 complained of symptoms referable to a single organ system, which could be explained by a known disease process, such as asthma, or neurodermatitis, and (3) 31 had symptoms that involved multiple organ systems, which had been present for years and could not be accounted for by a known disease. Only minor differences were found between these subgroups on immunologic measures; the asymptomatic subgroup had fewer "null cells," and the subgroup with physical illness had higher immunoglobulin A levels. There were no notable abnormalities on other cell-type measures, on antibody testing, or on other measures of immunologic activity. Physical examinations revealed that nine patients were obese, three had scarred ear drums, two had hypertension, and one each had asthma, eczema, and conjunctivitis. One patient had a murmur suggestive of a leaking heart valve, and another had scars from self-inflicted wounds.

In his 1989 report, Terr noted a similar lack of physical findings in the larger study group of 90 patients, 70 percent of whom were women.[128] This study, too, shows how fashions change regarding alleged sensitivities. Thirty-two of the 90 patients described in 1989 were diagnosed as having "*Candida* sensitivity." *Candida Albicans* is the micro-organism that causes "yeast" infections. In the mid-1980s, clinical ecologists were claiming that their patients had subclinical *Candida* infections, which evoked an immune response and thereby caused protean symptoms. They verified this diagnosis by giving *Candida* extracts to the patients and having them report on their subjective symptoms. Regardless of whether normal microbiological methods showed the presence of *Candida,* patients were chronically treated with anti-*Candida* medicines. None of the patients who presented to Terr in 1979 or 1980 were diagnosed as having *Candida* sentivity. By 1983, 37 percent of the patients presenting to Terr received that diagnosis. In 1985 and 1986, more than 60 percent of the patients presenting to Terr had been told they were allergic to *Candida*, and many had been given antibiotic treatments. A similar fad belief regarding dental amalgam had MCS patients running to have their fillings removed.[129]

A number of studies have shown that provocation tests using subjective endpoints are unreliable.[130] Subjects with proven allergies are as likely to report subjective complaints with placebo as with active extracts, as long as they are not informed of what they are receiving. Likewise, subjects without proven allergies who are said to have MCS are as likely to report subjective responses to salt water or to dilute extracts as to concentrated extracts of putative allergens, as long are they are not informed of what they are receiving. Similar results have been reported with airborne chemical antigens. Putative food allergies diagnosed on the basis of subjective symptoms after provocative testing often cannot be confirmed by subsequent feedings.

Finally, the evidence strongly suggests that patients do not get better as the result of treatments offered them by clinical ecologists. Of the 90 patients Terr described in his 1989 report, 75 believed that they had become allergic to one or more new substances after beginning treatment.[131] Thirty-four patients had also developed new symptoms posttreatment. If anything, patients treated by clinical ecologists become more obsessed with their symptoms, more socially isolated, and more firmly entrenched in an illness role. For example, a 29-year-old former store clerk described by Black and colleagues was well until age 26, when he developed weakness, fatigue, difficulty walking, subjective confusion, speech problems, and even loss of consciousness.[132] Diagnosed with environmental illness, he believed his symptoms resulted from exposures to numerous chemicals, including products like deodorants and perfumes. His treatment included hypoallergenic vitamin treatments, a restrictive diet, and sublingual drops to "build immunity." He carried an oxygen mask to use around pollutants. After being told that he was sensitive to humid air and unstable barometric pressure, he moved to Phoenix, Arizona, where he lived in a "safe" trailer with only ceramic and wood surfaces and without carpeting or drapes. He was on disability when seen by Black and colleagues, and he believed he needed a wheelchair because of his multiple symptoms. His only social contacts were other patients with environmental illness, whom he had met in support groups.

Terr described a 30-year-old hairdresser who had suffered a skin irritation from a permanent wave solution.[133] A clinical ecologist told her she had immune deficiency and advised her to quit work, move, and adopt a restrictive diet. Subsequently, she developed itching and fatigue from gasoline, exhaust fumes, and groceries, which led to a diagnosis of "universal allergy." She was placed on sublingual drops of alcohol and hormones and, at the time Terr saw her, was unable to work because of her fear of exposure to various chemicals.

A 50-year-old woman described by Brodsky entered his office carrying an oxygen mask and container.[134] She warned him that he should ask his questions quickly, since hydrocarbons seeping from his books and journals might soon incapacitate her. She was working as a statistician when she first noticed memory problems, some seven years before her interview with Brodsky. A physician told her she was reacting to chemical fumes and prescribed restrictive diets, which did not help. Two years later, she was treated in a "chemical-free" ward in a Chicago hospital for two weeks. She was told that she was sensitive to common chemicals and that she might not be able to continue working. She tried to work with a gas mask, which helped her symptoms but seemed unacceptable to her coworkers. Soon, however, she began passing out four or five times daily and complained of stupor and lethargy. She took an early retirement and became an "outdoor person." At the time Brodsky met her, she spent virtually all day outdoors, coming inside only to cook and sleep and keeping the windows wide open. When she was indoors for too long a time, she experienced memory problems and hearing and visual loss. She became so weak that she could not stand or even sit up without help.

The American Academy of Allergy and Immunology, the American College of Physicians, the American Medical Association, the American College of Occupational and Environmental Medicine, the California Medical Association, and the National Research Council have all issued statements critical of the practice of clinical ecology.[135] These statements all cast doubt on the existence of multiple chemical sensitivity or environmental illness and note the paucity of objective evidence to support the theories and treatments advocated by clinical ecologists.

Like patients with other illness roles, patients with MCS are often depressed and anxious. Of the 90 patients evaluated by Terr, 12 had been diagnosed with an anxiety disorder, and 10 had been diagnosed with depression.[136] Simon and colleagues administered the Diagnostic Interview Schedule (DIS) and the Hopkins Symptom Checklist-90 (SCL-90) to the 41 MCS patients and 34 controls whom they studied immunologically.[137] Patients' scores on the SCL-90 revealed higher levels of anxiety and depression than did those of control subjects. Twenty-four percent of the MCS patients met the DSM-III-R criteria for panic disorder, 10 percent met the criteria for generalized anxiety disorder, and 29 percent met the criteria for major depression. Comparable figures for the controls were 3, 0, and 12 percent, respectively. The psychiatric disorders appeared to predate the diagnosis of MCS.

Simon, Katon, and Sparks studied 37 workers who filed compensation claims following an outbreak of illness at an aerospace factory.[138] No cause for the outbreak was ever determined, nor were there definite medical or immune system findings. Thirty-six subjects completed a four-item symptom survey that asked them whether they (1) followed a special diet, (2) took special precautions in their home or in choosing their home furnishings, (3) wore particular clothes, or (4) had trouble shopping in stores or eating in restaurants due to chemical or food sensitivities consequent to their illness. Responses on this survey were markedly bimodal: Most subjects either answered "no" to all of these questions or answered "yes" to at least three questions. The 13 subjects who answered at least three questions affirmatively were said to have "environmental illness," and their SCL-90 and DIS scores were compared to those of the remaining 23 subjects.

Although the environment illness group had higher average depression and anxiety scale scores on the SCL-90 than the comparison group, these differences did not reach a significant level. This is not surprising in light of the small number of subjects in the environmental illness group. However, seven of 13 subjects in the environmental illness group met the DSM-III-R criteria for anxiety or depression antedating their current illness, in comparison with only one of the remaining 23 subjects. This difference was highly significant.

Black and colleagues administered the DIS to 23 of their 26 subjects with environmental illness and to 46 age- and sex-matched controls.[139] The lifetime risks of DSM-III-R mood and anxiety disorders were significantly higher in the environmental illness subjects than in the controls; 30 percent of the environmental illness subjects met criteria for major depression, compared to just 7 percent of controls. Thirty-nine percent of the environmental illness subjects met the DSM-III-R criteria for some mood disorder, compared to just 13 percent of the controls. Thirteen percent of the environmental illness subjects met the DSM-III-R criteria for panic disorder, compared to just 2 percent of the controls, and the comparable figures for all anxiety disorders were 43 and 17 percent for the two groups, respectively.

Panic attacks in particular may be attributed to chemical sensitivities, and the avoidant behavior commonly associated with such attacks may consequently be reinforced by treatment regimens designed to avoid chemical exposure. An illustrative case of this sort was described by Stewart and Raskin.[140] The patient, a 42-year-old single woman, had complained of shortness of breath, palpitations, headaches, hoarseness, loss of voice, unsteady gait, fatigue, muscle aches, twitching, faintness, and some flu-like symptoms, which she attributed to exposure to fumes from floor cleaning at work. Several physicians had been unable to diagnose her, but a clinical ecologist told her she had "twentieth-century disease." The patient, a Canadian, traveled to a clinic in the United States, where she was given neutralizing solutions and a restricted diet and told to construct an "environmentally safe haven" in her home. At the time Stewart and Raskin interviewed this patient, she had not worked in seven months, she seldom left her house, and she never left her house without a companion, an oxygen tank, and a vial of neutralizing solutions for use in an allergic emergency. She had few social contacts other than with people she had met in a social support group for patients like herself.

Stewart and Raskin established that this patient had a long history of phobic anxieties and consequently restricted social interactions. They found her acutely anxious, and they observed her hyperventilating while complaining of faintness and tingling in her fingers. They diagnosed her as having panic disorder and treated her with a sedative commonly used in such cases. Her attacks improved, she stopped hyperventilating, and she resumed eating a normal diet. She was beginning to leave her house again when she stopped coming for treatment.

The prominence, in some cases of MCS, of symptoms suggestive of panic attacks has led some authors to argue that MCS is anxiety triggered by fumes or odors. According to Kurt, for instance, anxiety symptoms often begin after exposures to toxins severe enough to cause respiratory symptoms.[141] The patient fears further exposures and begins to restrict his activities. Further anxiety symptoms are interpreted as sensitivity, reinforcing his fear that poisons cannot be avoided. Toxic exposures, in fact, do appear to cause later anxiety. Schottenfeld and Cullen studied 21 patients, treated at the occupational medicine clinic at Yale-New Haven Hospital between June 1981 and November 1982, who were severely disabled due to unexplained symptoms.[142] Ten of the patients were men, and 19 were factory workers. Twelve were on medical leave or disabled when they were seen, and the remainder were frequently absent from work. Symptoms had persisted an average of 24 months. Three patients met the DSM-III criteria for posttraumatic stress disorder (PTSD), which is classified as an anxiety disorder, and two of these had had life-threatening exposures to toxic agents. Both of these patients had intrusive dreams and memories of their toxic exposures. Both patients also met DSM-III criteria for major depressive disorder. An additional seven patients seemed to have atypical forms of PTSD, which differed from typical PTSD only in that recollections were less salient. One of these patients had had a toxic exposure at work, and the remaining six had had repeated exposures to organic solvents or other volatile liquids. Five of these patients reported episodes of lightheadedness, chest pain, and feelings of being "spaced out" at work, accompanied by anxiety, which Schottenfeld and Cullen argued were consistent with solvent intoxication. These episodes generalized, though, and could later be triggered by diverse and otherwise harmless pollutants.

In a related vein, Spyker viewed MCS as a generalized conditioned anxiety response to odors, subsequent to an initial, unconditioned toxic response.[143] He reported on several patients who were successfully treated using exposure techniques in combination with relaxation and biofeedback, similar to the treatment regimens used for simple phobias, such as of snakes or heights. One patient, for instance, was a 40-year-old woman who had been exposed to chlorine gas four months prior to her evaluation. Her exposure to this highly toxic substance apparently was serious; she was disabled for three weeks. Subsequently, she complained of feeling "drunk" and of headaches, chest congestion, chest pain, nausea, and blurring of vision due to fumes and odors. These symptoms were so severe that she could not work. She was taught general relaxation and successfully desensitized to varied odors in four treatment sessions.

Simon, Katon, and Sparks reported that although none of the 37 aerospace workers they studied attributed their symptoms to a single toxic exposure, many patients described symptoms of physiologic arousal that first occured on exposure to solvent or irritant fumes and later occured more generally, in response to diverse odors.[144] They agree with other authors that, in such cases, phobic avoidance of odors helps to maintain the illness.

The hypothesis that MCS is an anxiety syndrome triggered by fumes and odors seems to relate MCS to a theory of panic disorder presented by Klein and his colleagues.[145] According to these authors, panic attacks are triggered by real or imagined sensations of suffocation. Panic disorder patients may have overly sensitive brain receptors, which trigger false suffocation alarms in response to minor fluctuations in blood oxygen or carbon dioxide levels. Toxic exposures, of course, can initially cause real sensations of suffocation, which are then re-imagined in response to conditioned cues. The hypothesis also relates MCS to certain mass hysterias, or "mass sociogenic illnesses," as these are now called, triggered by obnoxious, but otherwise harmless, odors. In one such episode, which occured in 1989 and was extensively documented by Small and others from the University of California, Los Angeles, 247 junior high and high school choir singers performing at a recital in Santa Monica, California suddenly developed headaches, dizziness, weakness, abdominal pain, and nausea after smelling what some thought was fresh paint.[146] Sixteen students fainted, and 19 students were taken to hospitals by ambulance. No toxic exposure or other cause of illness could be demonstrated, and the pattern of symptom spread documented by Small strongly suggests that anxiety played a major role. Students, for instance, were more likely to fall ill if they had first seen a friend fall ill, as opposed to a stranger. In a similar well-known 1994 incident, the emergency room staff treating a dying patient in a Riverside, California, hospital suddenly sickened after inhaling fumes they believed were emanating from the patient's body.[147] Twenty-nine percent of the 37 staff members present in the emergency room reported smelling an unusual odor, which some described as ammonia-like but which others said was fruity, garlicky, musty, or sweet. Forty-two percent of the staff members developed headaches, 32 percent became dizzy, 24 percent became nauseated, and 14 percent passed out. Shortness of breath, confusion, and actually passing out were observed only in staff who had actually treated the patient. Five staff members were hospitalized, but laboratory studies failed to document definite toxic exposures or diagnosable illnesses. Within two hours of the incident, a Hazardous Materials Team sampled air in the emergency room for toxic chemicals, but no detectable amounts were detected, nor were toxic materials found in the patient's body bag or body (the cause of death was cancer). The paramedics who had brought the patient to the hospital had not noticed any odor, nor did they suffer unusual symptoms, in spite of the fact that they had been confined in the ambulance with the patient for 14 minutes, had had skin-to-skin contact with her, and had started an intravenous line, with some small spillage of blood. Interestingly, at least one staff member apparently was disabled for some months after this incident.

The anxiety-syndrome hypothesis of chemical sensitivity does not explain certain aspects of the syndrome, however. First, most patients with MCS have never been subject to a real toxic exposure that aroused some initial anxiety. Instead, clinicians have told them their symptoms were caused by chemicals. Nor are their symptoms consistent with phobic anxiety states. Persistent headaches, weakness, muteness, and loss of hearing and vision, among other symptoms reported in MCS, are not seen as part of anxiety states in other phobias, such as of heights or snakes, or even in agoraphobia, in which symptoms may be more diffuse.

Also, many patients with MCS, like those with other syndromes I have argued are illness roles, report illness behaviors that antedate their current disorder. Illness behaviors, in other words, antedated their phobic avoidance of putative chemical toxins. In Terr's 1989 report, he notes that 75 of the 90 environmental illness patients he studied had extensive medical histories long before the reported onset of chemical sensitivity.[148] Seventeen patients had previously been diagnosed with somatoform psychiatric disorders, such as somatization or conversion disorders, by physicians other than clinical ecologists. Simon and colleagues reported that their 41 MCS patients had significantly higher somatization scale scores on the SCL-90 than had the 34 controls with musculoskeletal problems.[149] On the Diagnostic Interview Schedule (DIS), MCS patients reported an average of 15.5 physical symptoms, compared to just 3.5 for control patients. The DSM-III-R, of course, required just 13 unexplained medical symptoms for the diagnosis of somatization disorder, while other research has shown that many fewer such symptoms indicate likely problems.[150] Most of the symptoms reported on the DIS antedated the MCS. MCS patients reported an average of 7.9 earlier somatic symptoms, whereas control subjects reported only 2.4 such problems. Nine patients with MCS met DSM-III-R criteria for somatization disorder purely on the basis of pre-existing symptoms; none of the controls did.

In their study of 36 aerospace workers who filed compensation claims for a mysterious illness at work, Simon, Katon, and Sparks found that the 13 subjects who appeared to have developed subsequent environmental illness reported an average of 6.2 prior somatic complaints, compared to 2.9 for the remaining subjects.[151] This difference was highly significant. The number of prior unexplained medical symptoms was the strongest predictor of which workers would claim to have become chemically sensitive following their acute illness; a patient with eight prior unexplained symptoms was more than seven times more likely to develop environmental illness than a subject with only three such symptoms.

Stewart and Raskin studied 18 patients referred to a University of Toronto clinic with "twentieth century disease" or "total allergy syndrome."[152] Symptoms had been present for from three to 60 months, with a mean duration of two years at the time patients were seen. Stewart and Raskin observed that seven of these 18 patients appeared to have longstanding somatoform disorders, antedating their belief in their own chemical sensitivity. A representative case was that of a 41-year-old mother of two teenage children, referred by a neurologist for a psychiatric consultation. She believed that she had developed a total allergy syndrome after breathing polluted air three years before. She complained of dizziness, faintness, insomnia, bone aches and backaches, vaginal itching, menstrual abnormalities, weakness, fatigue, bloating, disorientation, muscle twitching, occasional muteness and paralysis, and recurrent respiratory infections, among other manifestations of her allergies. She had moved to the country, where she had isolated herself in an "ecologically safe oasis," free from synthetic materials, sprays, shampoos, or perfume. A line piped oxygen directly into her room. Her few visitors were required to wear clothes made of natural fibers that had never been dry cleaned and to wear surgical caps, masks, and gowns. An "ecological insult" of any kind led to "coma," which could be terminated only by neutralizing solutions. Her husband believed she could die suddenly at any time. He had taken over the shopping, cleaning, and household chores to mimimize his wife's exposure to chemicals.

Although the patient dated the onset of her illness to age 38, in fact she had ostensibly been sick her entire life. As a child, she frequently missed school due to respiratory infections and vomiting, headache, and abdominal pain for which no medical causes were ever found. After puberty, she was disabled by severe menstrual pain, leading to a surgical procedure by age 15. By age 30, she had sought treatment from numerous physicians for 90 different somatic complaints in 15 organ systems; none of these visits led to definite medical diagnoses. During one particularly active 12-month period, she had seen 19 specialists and several general practititioners and had also sought treatment in several emergency rooms. Like many other patients with somatization disorder (discussed earlier), this patient had been exposed at an early age to illness behavior in others. Her mother reportedly had had symptoms much like hers since age 25, and her older sister also had had health problems and required a special diet in order to calm her nerves.

Like other syndromes that may be illness roles, environmental illness has been linked to child abuse. Staudenmayer and colleagues compared 63 patients with undiagnosable multiple somatic complaints that they attributed to environmental chemicals with 64 controls with chronic medical problems and psychiatric disorders that were not attributed to chemical sensitivities.[153] The environmental illness patients presented with pulmonary, cardiovascular, genitourinary, musculoskeletal, cutaneous, neurologic, or psychiatric symptoms. Twenty of these subjects had been blindly exposed to agents to which they were thought to be sensitive, and none had responded to these differently than to placebos. The control patients had headaches, asthma, allergies, bronchitis, and other medical illnesses, along with either anxiety or affective disorders. All subjects were interviewed and filled out a questionnaire concerning their families of origin; 30 of the subjects with environmental illness, 20 of whom were women, and 36 controls, 25 of whom were women, also received psychotherapy. Of the 20 women with environmental illness who received psychotherapy, 10 eventually reported having been subjected to physical abuse, 12 eventually reported having been subjected to sexual abuse, eight eventually reported having been subjected both both physical and sexual abuse, and 10 eventually reported having been victims of incest. Only three of the 25 women control patients who received psychotherapy reported physical abuse, six reported sexual abuse, two reported combined physical and sexual abuse, and four reported incest. These differences between the environmental illness patients and the controls were statistically significant. No significant differences in reported abuse were found between male patients with environmental illness and male controls.

Staudenmayer's patients, though, may have reported false memories created by psychotherapy (see chapter 7). Six of the 20 women with environmental illness who received psychotherapy and reported sexual abuse were said to have had repressed memories. Their recall, in other words, occurred only in the setting of psychotherapy, presumably with therapists who encouraged recovered memories. The same was true for three of the control women subjects who received psychotherapy and reported sexual abuse. Significantly, only four of the 25 women with environmental illness who did not receive psychotherapy reported physical abuse during their initial evaluations, only two of these 25 women reported having been sexually abused and only one reported having been the victim of incest. There were no significant differences in frequency of reports of abuse between the environmental illness patients and the controls who received only an initial evaluation.

Where recovered memories are spotted, multiple personality disorder (MPD) cannot be far behind. In the following chapter, I argue that MPD is an illness role created by psychotherapists who believe in recovered memories. Staudenmayer and colleagues reported that five of the 30 environmental illness patients who received long-term psychotherapy were eventually diagnosed with MPD, along with one control subject who also received such treatment. All of the MPD patients reported having been sexually abused. A case described by these authors illustrates how one illness role (environmental illness) can be replaced by another (MPD), as a result of the efforts of therapists who believe in the latter. The patient, a 45-year-old woman, had been told by a clinical ecologist that chemical sensitivities were responsible for her weakness, flushing, tremulousness, chattering teeth, stammering, nausea, vomiting, abdominal pain, insomnia, depression, and cognitive problems. She was receiving sublingual neutralization drops, vitamins, amino acids, and "glandular supplement" therapy. As part of her initial evaluation by Staudenmayer and colleagues, a blind, randomized challenge showed that she could not distinguish sublingual drops that contained chemicals to which she was said to be sensitive from drops that contained only a salt solution. When exposed to peppermint-scented air that contained none of the chemicals to which she was thought to be sensitive, the patient developed tremors, weakness, and speech impairments. In light of her dramatic response to an inactive scent, she was not exposed to an actual airborne challenge. When these results were explained to her, the patient agreed to stop therapy with her sublingual drops and to enter long-term psychotherapy.

Over the next two years, the patient recovered memories of childhood physical and sexual abuse that seemed to explain her various physical symptoms. Her flushing and tremors, for instance, were said to embody a memory of an incident in which her father dipped an electrical cord into the water, while she and her brother were taking a bath together. Her gastrointestional symptoms following exposure to chemical odors were traced to her father's habit of forcing her to ingest chemicals used to process photographic film. MPD was established in just a few months of therapy. After two years of therapy, the patient was able to "laugh" at her previous fears of chemicals, but she remained disabled by "sequelae" of her abuse. The authors opined that longer-term therapy would be required before she was once again functional.

Insofar as MCS is an illness role, it must serve some functions for those who take it on. In many cases, clinical ecologists seem to provide a haven for patients with longstanding illness behaviors who have encountered resistance from traditional practitioners. Clinical ecologists not only validate such patients' symptoms but also encourage them to leave their work and to break off problematical social ties, and they help them force family members to cater to their needs. Some of these functions are evident in the cases cited. The 29-year-old store clerk described by Black and colleagues was able to get disability for illness behavior that otherwise would have engendered skepticism.[154] His move to Arizona was financed by several service organizations, the members of which were moved by his apparent plight in being allergic to everything in their community. The 50-year-old woman described by Brodsky also received disability for her MCS, in spite of the fact that she spent much of her time playing tennis.[155] She supposedly was well as long as she stayed outdoors. Her husband had retired so that they could live in the mountains. She said her current life was "like a vacation." Like the store clerk described by Black, she was also relieved completely of social obligations. The 41-year-old woman described by Stewart and Raskin had also moved to the country.[156] Stewart and Raskin felt this patient was relieved not to have to work or socialize too much with others or to have sex with her husband. Her husband, as I noted, believed she could die any moment and did all the household shopping and most of the housework and child care.

Gots reviewed some data on disabiity claims related to MCS.[157] Data on such claims are difficult to gather, since many are filed under terms such as "chemical allergy" and "immune dysfunction," that obscure their real nature or according to alleged causes, such as "pesticide poisoning" or "solvent toxicity." However, between 1985 and 1994, court cases in California, Louisiana, Minnesota, New Hampshire, Ohio, Oregon, and Pennsylvania established MCS as a compensable illness under workers' compensation statutes. New Jersey, too, has recognized MCS. "Sick building syndrome" claims are also on the rise and are likely to gain recognition by courts and state legislatures.

Patients with MCS are considered disabled under the Americans with Disabilities Act (ADA) and the Department of Veterans Affairs Compensation Act. Since the ADA requires employers to make "reasonable accommodations" for disabled employees, patients with MCS have argued that perfumes, fragrances, and most cleaning products should be banned from their work-places. One state university created a "chemically safe" building for MCS sufferers, in which fragrances and many personal hygiene products are banned. A housing discrimination suit led to the establishment of a pesticide-free zone around one patient's house, and MCS sufferers have argued in court for the establishment of safe zones around highways on which they have to travel. These claims have been bolstered by rulings from the Department of Housing and Urban Development, the Department of Education, the Environmental Protection Agency, the Food and Drug Administration, and the Occupational Safety and Health Administration, among other agencies.

Finally, Brodsky and other authors note that MCS provides a sense of distinction and community membership.[158] Like the fairy tale princess whose sleep is disrupted by a pea, the patient who believes himself more sensitive than others to pollution or other toxins can feel perversely superior to those who are more robust. He can see himself as a figure, much like Paul Revere, who warns other people of dangers they cannot perceive. MCS patients socialize mainly with other such patients, whom they meet in support groups or through MCS organizations, and they often eschew the company of those without MCS, who they feel cannot understand the problems that they face. Like some of the culture-bound syndromes described in chapter 3, MCS confers membership in an exclusive group.

6

Multiple Personality Disorder

In the previous chapter, I noted that the major modern-day illness roles in Europe and North America are of three types, and I discussed the first: disorders that resemble hysteria. The second type is multiple personality or, in DSM-IV terminology, "dissociative identity disorder."[1] Multiple personality disorder is conceptually linked to the recovered memory movement and to ostensible satanic ritual abuse; these are the subjects of the following chapter.

The patient with multiple personality disorder ostensibly has more than one discrete personality, and sometimes many discrete personalities—or "personality states" or "personality fragments"—that take turns controlling the body. One of these personalities, which usually first seeks treatment, is said to be the "host," and the rest are said to be "alters." Typically, the host personality claims to be unaware of the alters, but the alters usually claim awareness of the host personality and often of one another. Changes in body control between the host and alters, or between various alters, is sometimes presaged by a headache, by rolling of the eyes, or by other behaviors visible to others. When they are in control, alter personalities can be recognized by their distinctive memories, intellectual skills, emotional tendencies, interpersonal styles, linguistic habits, morals, accents, voices, and manners. They claim to have different names from each other and from the host and even to be different ages. Some claim to be of the opposite sex. Some make animal noises and act as if they were animals, and a few even claim to be demons, dragons, or heavenly spirits.

Two well-known studies paint a clinical picture of typical MPD. Between May and December 1982 Putnam and colleagues distributed a 386-item questionnaire to 400 clinicians with an interest in MPD.[2] Each clinician was asked to fill out a questionnaire regarding a single patient with MPD whom they recently had had in treatment. About 40 percent of the questionnaires were returned completed, from which Putnam and colleagues extracted data on 100 patients. Ninety-two of the patients were women, and the mean age at diagnosis was about 31 years. Patients had received psychiatric treatment for about seven years before being diagnosed with multiple personality, and in fact they complained of varied presenting symptoms, discussed later, that are suggestive of disorders other than multiple personality. Three patients were dual personalities, that is, they had only one alter, and the rest were true multiples, with up to 60 alters. The mean number of personalities, including the host, was 13.3, the median number of personalities was nine, and the modal number of personalities, found in 16 patients, was three. Five clinicians reported patients with so many alters that they could not be counted, a phenomenon sometimes called "polyfragmentation."

Respondents characterized the alter personalities and their interactions. Eighty-five percent of patients had alter personalities that claimed to be age 12 or younger, and 30 percent had alters that claimed to be older than the patient's actual age. Fifty-three percent had at least one alter who claimed to be of the opposite sex to the host individual. Eighty-six percent had at least one alter who claimed to be aware of all the other alters. Assaultive or aggressive alters occured in 70 percent of patients. Twenty-nine percent of patients were said to have been homicidal at one time or another, and six patients had actually murdered others. So-called internal homicides, or suicide attempts made by one alter in order to kill the host or other alters, had occurred in 53 percent of the patients, and 34 percent reported self-mutilation by one alter trying to punish another. Fifty-three percent of the patients had at least one alter personality who abused drugs or alcohol, and 52 percent had a personality who was considered promiscuous or hypersexual.

There were said to be various clues to the diagnosis of multiple personality. For example, 98 percent of patients reported experiencing periods of amnesia. These were presumably times when alter personalities, outside the host's awareness, had taken control of the body. In more than a third of the cases, the clinicians reported noticing changes in patients' behavior or appearance that led them to suspect the existence of more than one personality. In all cases, the diagnosis of multiple personality was said to have been "confirmed" when the therapist met the alters, which sometimes occurred spontaneously and in other cases occurred during hypnosis or in response to therapists' requests.

Ross and colleagues sent 36-item questionnaires to more than 2,000 clinicians who belonged to the Canadian Psychiatric Association and/or the International Society for the Study of Multiple Personality and Dissociation.[3] Two hundred and twenty-seven clinicians responded, of whom all but 44 belonged to the latter group. The respondents returned questionnaires describing 236 patients who appeared to meet the DSM-III-R criteria for multiple personality. Two hundred and seven (87.7 percent) of these patients were women, a proportion about the same as in Putnam's study. The average age of patients was about 31 years, and patients had been treated about seven years before the MPD diagnosis was made. Patients had an average of 3.5 personalities at the time they were diagnosed, and an average of 15.7 when the questionnaires were completed. Eighty-six percent of patients had a child alter, 84 percent had a so-called persecutor alter, or an alter hostile to the host or to other alters, and 62 percent had at least one alter of the opposite sex. Interestingly, more than 28 percent of the patients reported by

Ross's respondents had a personality that claimed to be a demon, 28 percent had a personality that claimed to be the spirit of a living person, 21 percent had alters that claimed to belong to a different racial group than the host, and 20 percent had alters that claimed to be spirits of deceased relatives. Approximately 12 percent of patients had been convicted of crimes, and nearly 20 percent had worked as prostitutes.

Ross gives no data concerning possible clues to occult MPD, except to note the high incidence of reported "Schneiderian-first rank" symptoms, or certain types of delusions and hallucinations that most clinicians consider to be indicative of schizophrenia. A patient with Schneiderian symptoms believes that others can magically read his mind, put thoughts in his mind, remove thoughts from his mind, control his bodily movements, or cause him to experience bodily sensations, desires, or impulses. He may also report hearing voices arguing about him or a voice repeating his thoughts or describing what he is doing. It is easy to see how such symptoms might be considered consistent with multiple personality, concretely understood: The influences and voices might simply arise from the alters struggling for control and letting their thoughts be known to the host personality. Ross and colleagues found that the average MPD patient, according to their informants, experienced 4.5 Schneiderian first-rank symptoms. Seventy-one percent of the patients reported hearing voices arguing, and 66 percent reported hearing voices commenting on their behavior. Forty percent of the patients studied by Ross had at one time been diagnosed as schizophrenic, although it is not clear whether these diagnoses had been based on Schneiderian symptoms or whether they reflected other symptoms then salient. Since they are susceptible to symptoms they see or read about (see later discussion), patients with MPD may present at various times with symptoms of several disorders.

Colin Ross, the principal author of this study, published a casebook in 1994 in which he describes the varied presentations of multiple personality disorder.[4] "Jenny," for example, was a 32-year-old mother of two children when Ross first met her in Winnipeg. Her childen lived with their father in Vancouver, from which she had just returned following a three-day visit for which she claimed to be amnesic. According to Jenny, she also could not remember how she had spent four weeks, apparently also in Vancouver, just prior to the recent three-day visit, and she claimed to have memory lapses dating back 10 years. She could not remember how she had recently spent several thousand dollars of her boyfriend's money, nor could she recall buying expensive items she found in her house. She reported feeling depressed much of the past 10 years and had twice taken overdoses in the context of family conflicts. She consumed as much as 52 ounces of whiskey each week. Her boyfriend reported two "fits." On one instance, Jenny had lain in a fetal position on the bathroom floor, clutching her stomach and moaning. Taken by ambulance to an emergency room, she was thrown out for making noise and later claimed to be amnesic for the whole episode. On another occasion, she was found sitting on a bench, hunched over and shaking. On the way to the hospital, she appeared to stop breathing at times. The hospital staff apparently were not too concerned about this, since they gave her only something to help calm her down.

Concluding that the woman's memory lapses were psychologically caused, Ross tried using hypnosis to uncover the missing events. Like other patients said to have MPD, Jenny was easily hypnotized. She revealed the details of her trip to Vancouver and remembered depositing her boyfriend's money to accounts in her name. The money, as it turned out, had already been spent. Learning that Jenny and her boyfriend sometimes joked about her having two personalities, the second of which they dubbed Sally, Ross hypnotized Jenny and asked Sally how she was doing. He reported feeling surprised to find himself speaking with Sally, an opinionated, sarcastic, impulsive, and hostile alter that Jenny knew nothing about and who claimed responsibility for the missing money. Sally had been in charge during the trips to Vancouver, which is why Jenny had no memory of them.

No sooner had Ross established three-way communication among himself, Jenny, and Sally, than a 10-year-old alter appeared, who called herself Barbara Anne. Later, another alter, 15-year-old Margaret, and two other adolescents, Sheila and Liz, were discovered. When Sheila was in control, she acted as if she were drunk. Roseanne and Samantha were additional, prostitute, alters. When she came to treatment, Jenny told Ross that, at age 12, she had been beaten and raped by her father, which sent her to the hospital with a concussion. In the course of hypnotic regression to the age of 12, Jenny seemed to relive this particular trauma. Later, however, the alters revealed additional traumas of which Jenny was ignorant. Margaret, for instance, had been in control of Jenny's body during additional sexual assaults by her father, and Liz had been assaulted by her father's friends. Sheila had been raped on a date at age 17. She was drunk at the time of the rape, which effectively "froze" her in time, in a permanently intoxicated and traumatized state.

Margaret, a woman in her early twenties with chronic anxiety, depression, dissociative symptoms, and substance abuse, was referred to Ross by another therapist, who had inadvertently triggered the emergence of a child alter by touching her on the arm. The therapist had been trying to talk to the child alter, and, although the child alter no longer seemed to fear her, no progress had been made in communicating. In her first meeting with Ross, Margaret allowed him to touch her to bring out the child alter, whose name turned out to be Maggie. Ross took over Margaret's treatment and over a six-month-period was able to piece together a map to her complex system of alter personalities. These were organized into two communities, each with some internal organization, with Observer and Guide personalities mediating between them. Observer and Guide personalities are frequent in MPD patients and serve the functions for which they are named.

Margaret had several remarkable alter states. One, called Tonie, had been asleep for six years at the time Ross woke her up. A "party girl" who liked to dance and flirt, she was amazed to find herself in Winnipeg, rather than Vancouver, where she had gone to sleep. Tonie had several conversion symptoms, such as intermittent paralysis of her left arm, for which she claimed to have sought medical attention. Another alter, called Tonie-Adu, was a 12-year-old mute with a frightened expression. Tonie had rendered her mute to stop her from audibly screaming. This had not stopped her "internal screaming," however, which had gone on continuously for 10 years. Tonie-Adu started screaming when she was raped by two bikers and witnessed her boyfriend, Andrew, being shot to death. She screamed "Andrew" repeatedly, until it sounded like "Adu," thus giving rise to her name. Two angry alters were called "the Destroyer" and "Flash." Flash was named for the flashbulbs used in pornography filmings made when Margaret was three years old. During these filmings, Margaret was given drugs and alcohol to keep Flash from coming out and creating a disturbance. Violet, another alter involved in child pornography, was locked in a room inside Margaret, which, the other alters reported, always smelled of Pine-Sol. Using hypnosis, Ross opened the door to Violet's room and asked her to come out. He learned that, inside the room, boys and girls of various ages were making pornography films, and Pine-Sol was being used to clean up their vomit. Other alters seemed psychotic to Ross, and some led double lives of which Margaret was unaware. The psychotic alters had accompanied Margaret's father on drug-dealing trips in British Columbia. They had witnessed murders and buried bodies and had had intercourse with her father and his friends. One alter claimed to have been abducted by aliens, while other alters described abuse by satanic cults. On one occasion, a fight between alters caused all the alters to be "called in." Without anyone in charge of it, Margaret's body collapsed like a doll on the sidewalk. An ambulance was called, and Margaret was taken to the hospital.

Ross reported that Margaret did not improve with three and a half years of therapy. She continued to abuse drugs and remained involved in self-destructive activities, including, possibly, ongoing satanic rituals. Additional alters may have remained uncovered.

Another of Ross's patients, a 26-year-old woman dubbed Pam, illustrates so-called polyfragmentation. Pam had been hospitalized 13 times in the previous six years for borderline personality disorder and cocaine abuse, and she was a patient at Charter Hospital in Dallas, where Ross ran an MPD unit. At their first encounter, Pam was crouching in a corner of a room, screaming, "Don't hurt me!" to an invisible assailant. Suddenly, she stopped and asked Ross who he was and how she had gotten into the room. It was immediately evident to Ross that Pam had MPD and that he had just witnessed a frightened child alter in transient control of her body. Aside from this child alter, who did nothing but relive episodes of abuse and could not be engaged in conversation, Pam was found to have two other alter states, a so-called helper personality who called itself "the Friend" and an abusive, growling, violent persecutor alter who apparently had no name. The persecutor alter yelled "Die" over and over and rammed Pam's head so forcefully into the wall that she required emergency medical treatment. Helper personalities are opposites to persecutors; instead of harming the host or other alters, they dedicate themselves to solving the others' problems.

Ross gave Pam sodium amytal, which is sometimes thought to be a kind of "truth serum" but which is actually just a relaxant, and discovered an adolescent alter who called herself Midge. It was Midge, as it turned out, who had decorated Pam's hospital room. She knew of the four personalities identified to that point and told Ross that numerous others were still in hiding. In fact, Pam eventually proved to have more than 300 alters, each with its own name and properties, which she listed on a large chart on the wall of her room. Since Ross could obviously not deal with each of these "fragments" individually, he asked Pam to group them into "teams." One team, for instance, comprised alters with paranormal powers, such as astral projection, or alters who claimed to represent past lives. Other groups comprised rebellious teenagers, frightened child alters, or alters with access to certain types of memories. Each team appointed a leader, who by taking control of Pam's body would serve as the team's spokesperson and take part in therapy sessions.

Some alters, however, were less cooperative. One baby alter repeatedly took control of Pam's body in the day room or hallway, curled up on the floor in a fetal position, sucked its thumb, and demanded a bottle. Other personalities informed Ross that this baby had been neglected and urged him to meet its demands. Fearing that actual milk might be too "regressive," Ross asked some of the alters to provide the infant with "internal milk." Another alter, called Bob, was belligerent and sarcastic. Perhaps to get sympathy from those treating her, Pam had falsely claimed that her mother had recently hanged herself. Bob acknowledged being responsible for this "delusion." Through a process of thought interference, he had made Pam believe that her mother had died and that the woman who called herself her mother, whom she visited frequently, was someone to whom she was actually unrelated.

Pam also claimed that she had developed inoperable lung cancer. Although she named the type of malignancy she had been told she had and the type of chemotherapy she was receiving, and although she lost her hair and eyebrows, a social worker found that she had not been seen by the doctor she claimed was treating her. Another mischievous alter had told Pam she had cancer and had shaved her hair and eyebrows. Another alter threatened to kill Pam's therapist, prompting Ross and his treatment team to terminate therapy. Pam and her 300 alters were lost to follow-up.

Until recently, writers on MPD have clearly believed that alters are like separate people, albeit often unidimensional or underdeveloped. According to the DSM-III, for instance, patients with multiple personality have "two or more distinct personalities, each of which is dominant at a particular time," and "each individual personality is complex and integrated with its own unique behavior patterns and social relationships."[5] The DSM-III-R employed different criteria for MPD, but one of these was still "the existence within the person of two or more distinct personalities or personality states (each with its own relatively enduring pattern of perceiving, relating to, and thinking about the environment and self)."[6] Consistent with the notion that MPD patients manifest separate "persons," writers on MPD sometimes cite evidence of physiological differences between personality states; for example, alter personalities have been said to respond differentially to medications, to have different allergic sensitivities, to show differences in electroencephalographic (EEG) activity, and even to have different bodily diseases. I discuss such claims later.

Although it retained as a diagnostic criterion "the presence of two or more distinct identities or personality states (each with its own relatively enduring pattern of perceiving, relating to, and thinking about the environment and the self)" and stated that "at least two of these identities or personality states [must] recurrently take control of the person's behavior," the DSM-IV renamed MPD dissociative identity disorder (DID).[7] Apparently, the new name was needed for cosmetic reasons: to distance psychiatrists from the increasingly embarrassing claim that alters are separate persons. David Spiegel, who chaired the committee on dissociative disorders for DSM-IV and who is credited with taking the lead in changing MPD's name, has argued that the fundamental problem in DID, reflected in the new name, resides in the patient's inability to experience himself or herself as whole, rather than in the proliferation of personalities per se. According to Spiegel, "Acknowledging that a patient with DID feels herself to be fragmented and unable to integrate various aspects of her past and present experience does not mean agreeing that there really are 12 people inside that body. As psychiatrists, we have an obligation to carefully understand, describe, and treat the subjective experience of the patients who seek our help without giving their belief systems objective validation."[8] Spiegel's sentiments are to the good, but critics of MPD are unlikely to be assuaged. First, the diagnostic criteria for DID still mention personalities with enduring traits who take control of the body. Second, from the critics' point of view, psychiatrists such as Spiegel have fostered the widespread belief in multiplicity and have thereby encouraged patients to present themselves as "12 people." Those who have encouraged patients are hardly in the position to claim now that these patients are wrong. Paul McHugh, a prominent figure in the anti-DID camp, aptly noted in a companion piece to Spiegel's that "even [DID's] champions are wavering in their enthusiasm, shifting their definitions of the condition as the force of counter-arguments is felt and their reputations are threatened. As they shift, they often claim that they were misunderstood . . . or that critics need to understand just how subtle the actual concepts of multiplicity and personality are."[9]

Colin Ross, from whose casebook the examples presented here are drawn, shows how the new name, DID, is used for cosmetic purposes, even while practitioners do what they've always done. In the introduction to his casebook, Ross took the same line as David Spiegel:

> Although MPD patients are, by definition, diagnosed as having more than one personality, they in fact don't. The different "personalities" are fragmented components of a single personality that are abnormally personified, dissociated from each other, and amnesic for each other. We call these fragmented components "personalities" by historical convention. . . .
>
> In order to correct misconceptions from use of the term "personality" . . . the official name of the disorder has been changed to Dissociative Identity Disorder. . . .[10]

Even from these few sentences, an alert reader might guess that Ross does not mean what he says; for example, "amnesic" is an adjective applied to cognizant beings, not to "fragmented components," whatever that noun phrase signifies. Ross's case histories confirm this reader's impression: In describing his DID patients, Ross recounts meeting, cajoling, comforting, restraining, assisting, and treating his patients' alters as if they were real people. He describes them as if they are active when they are out of sight—for example, alters are said to join groups, select representatives, and help or threaten each other—and he even seems to worry about their rights, which apparently may conflict with those of the host personality. Whatever he says about the significance of the name change, personification of alters is intrinsic to Ross's way of thinking about DID and to his clinical approach to affected patients.

Ross's emphasis on Schneiderian first-rank symptoms as clues to the presence of alters is also incomprehensible unless he believes that the alters can act outside conscious awareness, that is, that they are real.

Not surprisingly, not all patients and MPD clinicians welcomed the new name, DID, with open arms; some of them understood that even cosmetic changes can be dangerous if they are allowed to impinge on vital "cult" ideologies.[11] If the MPD patient's self-presentation as multiple becomes a matter of permissible doubt so that other than literal acceptance is allowed, then what might become of other claims of MPD patients, such as their recovered memories of childhood sexual abuse (discussed later)? Will theoreticians like Spiegel soon question these as well or withhold their "objective validation" from the patients who report them? How will doubt be circumscribed, once it has begun? In spite of objections, however, the largest professional group devoted to MPD, the International Society for the Study of Multiple Personality and Dissociation, did change its name in 1994 to leave out the reference to multiple personality. The Society's name now refers only to the "Study of Dissociation."

The reader undoubtedly noticed that the three patients of Ross's that I have described each reported being sexually abused as a child. Jenny reported being raped by her father at age 12. Margaret, one of Jenny's alters, also claimed to have been assaulted by Jenny's father, and Liz, another alter, claimed to have been sexually assaulted by his friends. Sheila, a fourth alter, had been date-raped when Jenny was 17. The second patient, Margaret, had ostensibly been exploited for pornographic films when she was just three years old. An alter, Tony-Adu, had been raped by bikers, and other psychotic alters had witnessed killings and drug dealing and had had intercourse with Margaret's father and his friends. The third patient, Pam, had a child alter whose sole activity was to relive episodes of abuse.

In reporting abuse, Ross's patients are typical. Putnam and colleagues, for instance, included questions pertaining to childhood abuse in the question-naire they distributed to clinicians.[12] Eighty-three percent of the MPD pa-tients described by Putnam's respondents were believed to have suffered childhood sexual abuse, 75 percent were believed to have suffered repeated nonsexual childhood physical abuse, and about 70 percent were thought to have suffered both. About 60 percent were thought to have suffered extreme neglect, and 45 percent were believed to have witnessed violent deaths. Only three patients seemed to have suffered no trauma. Ross and colleagues also inquired about abuse.[13] Of the 236 patients about whom they had in-formation, 79 percent were thought to have been victims of childhood sexual abuse, 75 percent were thought to have suffered childhood physical abuse, and 88 percent were thought to have suffered one or the other form of abuse. Clinician respondents suggested that most of the remaining patients had been abused, but definite memories had not yet been obtained. Abuse was thought unlikely in fewer than 5 percent of the cases reported.

According to the regnant theory of its causation, MPD is really a defensive response to abuse: To deal with otherwise overwhelming feelings of fear and betrayal, the abused or assaulted child denies that it was she who was vic-timized and creates an alter personality, which retains sole access to memo-ries of the inciting events.[14] Once established as a psychic defense, fragmen-tation of the personality becomes easier and easier to accomplish, leading to multiple alters with disparate traumatic memories. According to this theory, memories of abuse have been "dissociated" from the rest of the mind. It follows that MPD is a "dissociative" disorder, akin to conversion disorder, and that it is linked to hypnosis (see chapter 4). Most clinicians today are so confident of this theory that they would assume that patients who seem to have MPD but who deny abuse, like the 5 percent of patients reported in Putnam's survey, are simply repressing the memories of the abuse they suf-fered. In other words, the alters who carry these memories haven't yet made an appearance. On the basis of this supposition, therapy is directed toward contacting such alters, usually with hypnosis.

Is There a Physiological Foundation for MPD?

Before proceeding to study MPD as a role, we should discuss some physio-logical observations that are sometimes cited as evidence that MPD is real. First, some MPD researchers claim to observe physiological differences be-tween alter and host personalities, such as would normally occur between different people.[15] Alter personalties have been said to respond differently to medications, to have different allergic sensitivities, to show differences in cerebral blood flow patterns and in electroencephalographic (EEG) activity, both spontaneous and in response to stimuli, and even to have different serious bodily illnesses! If they could be proven, claims like these would undermine an illness-role account of MPD, as well as the notion, embodied in the term "dissociative identity disorder," that the alters are not real people.

Some of the claimed somatic differences are absurd; even if alters exist, they simply cannot have radically different somatic disorders, such as cancer or diabetes, as long as they share the same body. As for the plausible claims, several researchers have studied them and found the evidence lacking. Most objective findings are mixed and inconclusive, and those that are more certain are readily explained by transient changes in the patients' overt behavior and mood. For example, a patient expressing anger while enacting a hostile alter may have a more rapid heartbeat and higher blood pressure than the same patient when he or she is enacting the calm host personality, but the changes in heart rate and pressure are readily explained by angry behavior per se without a change in identity. When people allow themselves to express anger, their heart rate and blood pressure rise. Transient changes in these and other physiological measures can be evoked in normal subjects instructed to act out a role.

Second, some authors suggest that multiple personality is caused by brain dysfunction, especially in the temporal lobes, manifested by abnormal EEGs and epileptic seizures.[16] These authors are cited later. The temporal lobes play an important role in memory; conceivably, temporal lobe dysfunction might produce deficits in memory integration of the kind seen in MPD. From the earliest days, MPD patients were known to be prone to seizures, but most of these seizures appear to have been hysterical, or what neurologists now call "nonepileptic," or "psychogenic" seizures. The classic four-phase seizures of Charcot's grand hysterics, several of whom were later called multiple personalities, differ dramatically from seizures seen today that are caused by brain dysfunction.

However, in an article, published in 1981, that is widely cited as evidence for a link between MPD and brain dysfunction, Mesulam described 12 patients with temporal lobe abnormalities, evident on EEGs, who also exhibited seemingly dissociative behaviors, which in seven cases resembled MPD.[17] Patient 1, for instance, was a 19-year-old woman with possible absence attacks and EEG abnormalities in the left temporal leads. Three different personalities were said to be present at times. The host personality, "Edna," was conscientious, dependent, and suggestible. "Linda" was hostile and had tortured animals, and "Hanna" was gullible, immature, and "sexually vulnerable." Linda was said to be conscious when Edna was in control but unable to influence her behavior, while Edna was aware of Linda only indirectly, through written notes they exchanged. In one series of notes, reported verbatim by Mesulam, Edna and Linda traded jibes and insults. It is not clear why this patient was seen by Mesulam, but there is a clear implication she had had psychiatric treatment. Patient 2 was a 21-year-old woman with a long psychiatric and criminal history and abnormal EEG activity over both temporal lobes. On one occasion she found herself in a new city where people called her by a different name, and on another occasion she found herself holding a bloody stick next to an unconscious man she did not know. She held her psychiatrist at knife-point for several hours and later reported amnesia for the event. A former roommate reported observing a tough, angry alter and a frightened alter child spontaneously emerge. Patient 3 was a 27-year-old woman with EEG abnormalities in the left temporal lobe who was reported to show alters representing herself at earlier ages. The alters acted their stated ages but sometimes knew more than they should have if these ages were accurate. The alters were apparently aware of the environment, since they could be called forth by the patient's husband, but the host herself denied awareness of her behavior when the alters emerged. The patient referred to the alters as her "little people." Patient 4 was a 37-year-old woman with a long psychiatric history and right temporal EEG abnormalities who claimed to have MPD when she was first seen. Her three personalities were fully aware of one another, and the patient provided detailed descriptions of her mood and perceptions in each of her three states. In one state, for example, she claimed to feel more pain, to be more sensitive to others' emotions, and to see all colors as brown or of brownish hue. In a second state, she reported feeling smarter and lacking a sense of mortality. Patient 5 was a 27-year-old woman who showed epileptiform EEG spikes over the temporal lobes and who reported having once believed that she was more than one person. She knew of her alter personae and had even dubbed them "Susan-1," "Susan-2," and so on. Patient 6 was a 30-year-old woman with a long psychiatric history who had abnormal EEG activity over the temporal lobes. She reported feeling that there were two alters inside her, one a black girl named Mary, who was aggressive and combative, and the second a two-year-old boy. Mary was apparently modeled after a black china doll the patient had owned as a child. There was no amnesia between the various states. Patient 7 was a 33-year-old woman with a long psychiatric history and predominantly left temporal EEG abnormalities. She felt as if she were two different people, one good and religious and the other not. On further questioning, she acknowledged that these were just two aspects of her personality.

No definite conclusions can be drawn from Mesulam's article. First, most of the seven women Mesulam thought were multiples had syndromes very different from what is called MPD. Patient 7, for instance, acknowledged she was not multiple. Patients 4 through 6 were not amnesic for their alter selves, and one of them, patient 4, even claimed to be aware of the alters' subjective experience. All four of these patients may have been describing changing emotional states, rather than alter personae. Two more patients also were quite atypical: Patient 1 traded written jibes with her alter self, and Patient 3 had alters who simply embodied herself at various ages. No mention is made of abuse or of resistance to the diagnosis, which are said to be pathognomonic of true MPD. The last case, Patient 2, claimed amnesia mostly for her criminal activities. Although Mesulam does not tell us previous diagnoses, at least four of his seven patients had long psychiatric histories and could have been exposed to models of multiplicity or have been encouraged to speak of themselves in these terms (see later discussion). There is also no mention of base rates: None of the seven patients had had definite seizures, and EEG abnormalities are common in the psychiatric patient population, from which patients with apparent MPD will also likely emerge. Mesulam notes that his clinic receives a disproportionately large number of referrals of severely disturbed psychiatric patients.

Shortly after Mesulam's paper appeared, Schenk and Bear published another paper with data on what appeared to be three more patients with MPD and temporal lobe dysfunction.[18] Although this paper is often cited along with Mesulam's as evidence for the connection of MPD and brain dysfunction, Schenk and Bear's three patients appear to be among those presented by Mesulam but with pseudonyms, rather than numbers, and with different names for the alters.[19] Thus, the patient called Rebeccah by Schenk and Bear appears to be Mesulam's Patient 2, and the patient they call Hilda appears to be Patient 3. The patient Schenk and Bear call Dinah, with alters named Kildra and Jean, appears to be the patient Mesulam dubbed Edna (Patient 1), with alters Linda and Hanna. Schenk and Bear, who worked with Mesulam at Boston's Beth Israel Hospital, cited Mesulam's article but failed to mention that their cases had been reported in a previous paper.

Although their cases are not new, Schenk and Bear do present a possibly useful conjecture, which may explain why some patients with temporal lesions would wish to present themselves as having alter personæ. Temporal lobe epileptics are known to experience powerful emotional states and impulses, which are often discordant with their ordinary temperament and personality and which are thought to reflect temporal lobe activation. Schenk and Bear suggest that patients who experience powerful affects and drives of which they disapprove might be relieved by attributing these affects and drives to another, over whom they have no control and for whom they are not responsible. Later, I show that this type of denial is evident even in patients without neurological illness.

Benson, Miller, and Signer described two patients said to have dual personalities and seizure disorders.[20] Case 1, a 22-year-old woman, had had seizures since age six. Her IQ was subnormal, but she did well until she received valproic acid (an anticonvulsant) at age 16. The valproic acid controlled her seizures, but she became sullen and hostile. She insisted that she was a member of the Cassidy family (stars of a TV show). At age 18, she was admitted to a psychiatric hospital after attacking her mother, whom she thought was an imposter who had kidnapped her. She insisted that her real name was Michelle Cassidy. Her seizure medications were stopped, and, after having several seizures, the patient acknowledged her own and her mother's correct identities. She had only vague memories of her disturbed behavior, about which she felt remorseful. She was pleasant and cooperative and not at all aggressive. There was clearly an inverse relationship between this patient's seizures and her behavior disorder: When the medicines were restarted, the seizures again disappeared and she once again believed she was Michelle Cassidy. A subsequent decrease in dosage was followed by more seizures and a return of her normal behavior.

Case 2 was a 19-year-old woman who had been having seizures for a year and a half. Initially an average student with good interpersonal relationships, she now had periods of anger and hostility and had even struck her mother. When hostile, she called her mother by another name and insisted that she was adopted. She also denied a relationship with her father and twin brother and claimed that they, too, were impostors. Her hostile periods lasted from hours to a few days and were terminated by seizures. After a seizure, her personality returned to normal. She denied any memory for events in her altered state.

In both of these cases, unlike in MPD, there were only two separate states, and these did not rapidly alternate. Instead, like some other psychotic states that occur in patients with seizures, the delusional states of identity exhibited by these patients flared up during seizure-free periods and cleared up when seizures recurred. In both of these cases, unlike in MPD, the patient, when psychotic, misidentified family members. Misidentification of friends and family members is a well-known sign of psychosis with brain disorders. Family members, especially, are sometimes perceived as impostors. The most that can be said of these particular patients is that they showed psychoses that waxed and waned with seizures, with delusional themes of identity and misidentification.

A few other scattered reports of patients with seizure disorders, personality changes, and possible MPD also offer no conclusive evidence.[21] In short, with respect to ostensible physiological differences between alters, or with respect to ostensible brain causes of MPD, there are as yet no physiological findings that cannot be explained if multiple personality is an illness role.

MPD as an Illness Role

Several lines of evidence contribute to the impression that MPD is an illness role, in this case one fostered by specialists and serving the interests of both patients and therapists. First, until rather recently, most patients with MPD required a great deal of coaching to overtly display the disorder. In fact, most patients with MPD initially entered treatment seeking relief from depression, emotional instability, or work or relationship problems and not with complaints related to MPD at all. Therapists with a special interest in MPD, however, are quick to suspect that the disorder is present, and the practice among such therapists has been to aggressively seek confirmation that this is the case, coaching patients in the process. For example, Frank Putnam, a leading authority on multiple personality, advocates repeatedly questioning patients for evidence of the disorder.[22] Patients may be repeatedly asked these and similar questions: Are there any time periods for which you have no memory? Have you ever found clothes in your drawers or closets that you do not remember purchasing? Have you ever been greeted by people you do not remember meeting? Have you ever awakened in a strange place, or with someone you do not know? Have you ever gotten in trouble for something you do not remember doing? Have people ever been angry with you for reasons you do not know? Do people ever tell you that you seem to have two personalities or that you seem to be different every time they meet you? Patients are asked to consent to be interviewed using hypnosis. They are told that hypnosis can help contact parts of their personality of which they may be unaware. During hypnosis, the therapist calls on these parts to show themselves. He asks to speak to such parts. Repeated hypnotic sessions are used if there is no response. If the patient takes the bait and complies with the call for "parts," the therapist suggests that the part be given a name. The part is then asked whether its "host" knows that it exists or whether it has knowledge of parts still more deeply hidden.

This type of repetitive inquiry, which so clearly suggests to the patient what the therapist has in mind, is justified on the basis of the patient's supposed resistance. Ostensibly, the typical host personality is so reluctant to admit that she is not in sole control, and the alters are so reluctant to admit their existence, that negative first responses are only to be expected. Insufficient interrogation, taking "no" at face value, is seen as a clinical error, typical of the novice. Perseverance is seen as the hallmark of an expert in MPD. According to Putnam, for instance, no one without MPD could possibly want to have it, so there can be no real danger in suggesting its symptoms to patients. The worst that can happen, he claims, is that the probing will not prove relevant to the patient.

Patients, of course, are aware that, to hold their therapist's interest and possibly even regard, they have to comply with their therapist by giving at least some positive responses to the questions so insistently asked. Observing the signs of approval and heightened attention and interest that follow some responses, and the signs of disapproval and diminished attention and interest that follow other responses, they draw their own conclusions as to what the therapist wants. The compliance motive is heightened by the fact that most MPD patients are chronically mentally ill. According to several surveys, for example, the typical MPD patient receives about seven years of treatment, with little relief of symptoms, before MPD is discovered.[23] Therapists, being human, tend to lose interest in patients who have been treated a long time without much sign of improvement. At the same time, such patients, having become dependent on their psychotherapists for meeting the emotional needs normally met by friends and family, are often exquisitely sensitive to any sign of disinterest on the therapist's part. As a result, desires to please the therapist and to hold his or her attention are even more salient factors than they might be for healthier patients.

In any event, enough patients are willing to concede something to the therapist—a little missing time, a purchase not remembered, a stab at being

different when hypnotized—that the MPD diagnosis can frequently be confirmed, one step at a time. Initial small concessions, an unrecalled purchase,
for instance, lead to later larger ones, such as missing time, by a process social psychologists call incremental commitment. In the case of MPD, the
process isn't fast. Most patients, it seems, are reluctant to climb on the MPD
wagon. According to Putnam, the median length of time it takes to diagnose multiple personality, from the time of the first loaded enquiry, is six
months.[24] Some cases take several years. The diagnosis is finalized when the
patient speaks to the therapist in an alter's voice.

Kohlenberg did an experiment with an MPD patient that showed how attention by therapists can shape the expression of symptoms.[25] The patient
was a 51-year-old man who had resided in a large state mental hospital for
16 years. Although the patient was originally admitted with a diagnosis of
"schizophrenia," the diagnosis was later changed to multiple personality disorder. The patient had three personalities that denied knowledge of one another. The first personality was characterized by extremely rapid speech and
movements. The patient in this state claimed to be a spiritualist and to be
chaneling spirits of the dead. In this state, the patient sometimes broke windows and glasses and threatened staff and patients. In his second personality,
the patient spoke normally, read the newspaper, watched television, and was
socially appropriate. In his third personality, the patient spoke slowly in a
low-pitched voice, appeared depressed, and predicted world destruction.
These personality states rapidly alternated but could be distinguished reliably. Kohlenberg gave the patient 30 structured interviews, consisting of
banal questions concerning the patient's activities. After each of the first 10
interviews, without regard to which personalities had appeared, Kohlenberg
gave the patient some tokens that could be exchanged for privileges or sup-
plies. During each of the second 10 interviews, Kohlenberg gave the patient
a token and touched his hand each time the patient answered a question in
his second, most normal state. The last 10 interviews were treated the same
as the first 10; the patient received some tokens after the interview finished,
regardless of the "voices" in which he had answered the questions. In comparison with the first and third sets of interviews, during the middle 10 interviews the percentage of the time the patient spent in the second, rewarded state increased, while the number of questions answered in the other
voices declined. Kohlenberg noted that this patient had been receiving attention from other staff members for enacting his alters and that this regime
was reversed during the middle 10 interviews.

Consistent with the notion that therapist cues are important, Spanos estimated that two-thirds of patients said to have MPD are diagnosed by less
than 1 percent of therapists.[26] A paper by Allan Seltzer, from Ontario,
Canada, shows how even a single therapist with a special interest in MPD
can create many cases.[27] In his paper, Seltzer described five patients who
came to him after they had been evaluated by a local psychotherapist trained
in MPD techniques. All five patients had been told they had MPD, on the
basis of signs and symptoms evoked by the therapist's methods. In an adden-

dum, Seltzer noted that, since writing his article, he had seen three other patients from the same psychotherapist, each of whom had also been wrongly diagnosed as having MPD. Seltzer's first case, for instance, was a 31-year-old divorced mother of two who had had severe bulimia and poor self-esteem since she was 16. Along with a social worker, Seltzer treated the patient with antidepressants and cognitive therapy between 1986 and 1988, with some improvement in her self-esteem but with little improvement in her eating disorder. She began supportive therapy with the local psychotherapist, called D., in March 1990. In February 1991, D. brought up the question of dissociation. The patient agreed to enter a "relaxed state" to explore memories that were otherwise unavailable to her. In such a state, she recalled having intercourse with her father when she was seven years old. Upset, she took an overdose. In further sessions, 15 alters appeared. One embodied the patient's anger and was blamed for her bulimia. Two others were sexually promiscuous and used drugs. The patient told her father, who had staunchly denied abuse, that he too had alters and that some of these had abused her. Two years later, though, the patient began to doubt that her memories and alters were real. She realized that she had been "infatuated" with D. and felt that she had responded to his suggestions to please him. She felt ashamed of her behavior with D.

Another of Seltzer's patients, a 36-year-old woman, consulted D. to deal with her excessive drinking. Although her parents had been alcoholics, she did not recall either physical or sexual abuse. She quickly developed eight alters, all of them children, and thought she had recovered memories of abuse. She confronted her parents, who denied that they had abused her. When she expressed doubt about her memories, D. told the patient that there was no other explanation for her MPD. He urged her to file legal charges against her father. She began to mutilate herself. Eventually, she stopped therapy and improved on her own.

Another of Seltzer's cases, a 33-year-old man, was the separated spouse of the previous patient. His father, an alcoholic, had physically abused him. When he was hypnotized by D., in early 1992, an eight-year-old alter, Billy, emerged, who reported having had an incestuous relationship with the patient's mother. When the patient refused to converse with Billy, D. told him he was in denial. Anxious and confused, the patient stopped seeing D. He considered the alter, Billy, merely a thought experiment.

The other two cases included a woman with six alters who came to believe she had had intercourse with her father and a patient with 58 alters, who reported paternal rape. In the latter case, sessions with D. lasted up to five hours and were followed by periods of catatonia, amnesia, and self-mutilation. Both patients later concluded that they were responding to pressure in acting out alter personae and had not been sexually abused by their fathers.

Actually, a significant number of therapists treating MPD claim to have had MPD themselves.[28] Such therapists have a personal stake in MPD and in this way resemble the peripheral healing cult shamans described by I. M. Lewis (see chapter 3).

As the features of MPD have become better known to the public and the disorder has increased in incidence (see later discussion), patients are less dependent on therapists' role directions. Some patients now come to their therapists with symptoms of MPD, or at least with enough basic knowledge of what will be expected that they need fewer hints to develop the full-blown syndrome. North and colleagues, for instance, reviewed accounts of MPD published during the twentieth century from which patients might gain information.[29] The first of these, *The Dissociation of a Personality*, was published by Morton Prince in 1906. (Prince's patient, Christine Beauchamp, is discussed later.) In the 1950s, two popular books, *The Three Faces of Eve* and *The Final Face of Eve*, were written about a subdued and shy young woman from Augusta, Georgia, dubbed Eve White, whose real name was Christine Sizemore. Initially, Sizemore was thought to have two alter personalities. The first, Eve Black, was fun-loving and flirtatious, in contrast to Eve White.[30] The second, called Jane, was calmer and more mature. A popular movie was made that was based on the first book. No further accounts appeared in the 1960s, but several popular books were published during the 1970s. One of these, *I'm Eve*, was a biographical account of her illness by Christine Sizemore. After her alters had fused, Sizemore had gone on to show 19 additional alters before achieving a cure. By the mid-1970s, Sizemore had gone on the road to spread the MPD gospel. Another well-known book told the story of Sybil, who had 16 personalities, including an aggressive alter called Peggy Lou, a child alter named Vicky, two carpenters called Mike and Sid, and a pianist named Vanessa. Sybil turned out to play an especially critical part in the evolution of the MPD illness role (see later discussion). During the 1980s, two popular books appeared on the subject of criminal alters: Billy Milligan, a serial rapist, claimed that his crimes were committed by an alter outside his awareness, and Kenneth Bianchi, the notorious "Hillside Strangler," a Los Angeles serial killer, claimed that an alter named Steve had committed the murders. Another successful book published during the 1980s concerned a woman called Trudi Chase, who was said to be host to more than 90 personalities, some of whom coauthored her book. One of the personalities, who must not have helped with the writing, was a creature named Rabbit, who could only howl. In case Chase's story alone provided too little guidance, an introduction, written by the psychologist who had treated Chase, explained MPD to lay readers, with particular stress on the role played by child abuse. A television drama based on Chase's story appeared on a national network.

A case brought to my attention showed how movies and books can prompt susceptible patients to adopt the MPD role. P., a 45-year-old married mother of two, had a long history of undiagnosable somatic complaints, but these had never reached the level of somatization disorder, and she had never before been treated for psychological problems. Neither her children, who were 15 and 18 years old, nor her husband of 25 years had ever noticed signs of multiple personality. One month before seeking treatment, P. had watched a television movie about a woman with MPD. The movie had made her aware that she had memory gaps and that she could not remember making important decisions. She claimed, for example, not to remember her wedding or her children's births. She claimed to have clothes in her closet she did not remember buying. After watching the movie, she began to have daily headaches and periods of amnesia. On one occasion, she woke up in a motel room with a stranger, with whom she had apparently spent an afternoon. Fearful of what else her alters might be up to, she sought psychological counseling.

P. was found to be highly hypnotizable. Under hypnosis, two alters quickly emerged. One was a teenage "vixen" who claimed responsibility for P.'s infidelity. She claimed to have had numerous lovers in the past, but she had never before allowed P. to know what was going on. She wanted to scare P., though, so P. would "mind her business." She was thinking of killing P. if P. did not get the message. The second alter was devoutly religious. She knew of the first alter's liaisons, and she prayed that God would forgive her. She worried about P.'s soul. When the second alter was out, she tried to be nice to people, to make up for P.'s shortcomings. An additional 21 alters were identified in short order. After some months of therapy, some alters began to admit that they had been molested by P.'s alcoholic and abusive father.

From an illness-role perspective, P.'s sudden development of multiple personality disorder after watching a television movie suggests that she had problems from which she hoped to gain relief by being ill. Her history of undiagnosed somatic complaints suggests that she had used illness behavior before, and her responsiveness to hypnotic suggestions suggests that she was skilled at adopting roles in general. The fact that her primary alter claimed to have had affairs, and that in fact she had an illicit relationship before she came to the clinic, suggests that P.'s problem in life somehow involved her husband. However, the clinicians who treated P. did not take an illness-role view. Instead, they believed that P. had always had MPD, which she had hidden from herself and her family. The TV movie, they argued, had shifted the balance of power between P. and her alters and destabilized their internal relationships. Destabilized, P. could no longer avoid knowledge of her multiplicity or keep it from coming to light. Working with these assumptions, and with the belief that MPD is caused by childhood abuse, these clinicians concentrated their efforts on uncovering memories of abuse and never really tried to fully understand P.'s present relationships.

Until the 1980s, so few patients had MPD that there was little opportunity for other patients to observe the role firsthand. However, during the 1980s, the disorder became sufficiently common that other hospital and public clinic patients, especially the chronically ill, were likely to be exposed to it.[31] Seeing the attention devoted to MPD patients, and having models at hand, some patients without MPD emulated its symptoms. In this respect, they resembled the unfortunate Salpêtrière patients who copied the grand hysterics, thereby gaining a measure of Charcot's attention. In comparison with an earlier generation of patients who had never seen MPD modeled, patients who were exposed to MPD in the clinic or the hospital setting were less dependent on coaching provided by MPD specialists.

A study by Bennet Braun, a well-known MPD advocate (see chapter 7), shows just how contagious the MPD role can be, even outside the setting of a mental hospital.[32] In a misguided effort to prove that MPD has a genetic component, Braun presented data from the families of 18 patients to show "transgenerational" transmission of their disorder. Many of the patients did have parents, children, uncles, or cousins with MPD, but others had nominal kin or employees with the disorder. Braun's case number three, for instance, had parents and a daughter with MPD, but her husband, too, was considered to have probable MPD. Cases 4, 7, 12 and 17 also had husbands affected with MPD. Cases 9 and 11 had former husbands with the disorder, and case 10 had two former husbands who Braun thought were multiples. Case 11 had a stepdaughter with probable MPD, and case 5 had a live-in babysitter who was affected. The babysitter's daughter also had MPD, according to Braun. Case 16 had two adoptive parents with MPD and two adopted siblings with probable MPD. Since no genetic disorder can affect spouses, stepchildren, stepparents, foster kin or the live-in help, there are only two factors that can account for Braun's finding: Either everyone Braun examines ends up having MPD or those who observe MPD, and the benefits it confers, want to climb on the bandwagon. Both factors may be at work. Children, especially, may be influenced by adults. When children observe adults successfully laying off their poor behavior on alters and thereby escaping blame, the temptation to do so themselves may be irresistible. In fact, most if not all the children Braun reported had MPD had observed family members playing this illness role.

Further Evidence That MPD Is a Role

Several epidemiologic and clinical features of MPD point to its being an illness role. First, in the past 20 years, the efforts of MPD therapists, books and films about MPD, and the increased availability of MPD models have combined to produce a veritable MPD epidemic.[33] From the 1870s until the 1970s, no more than 20 cases of MPD were reported in published form in any given decade. In most decades, fewer than 10 case reports were published. A review of published reports in 1944 found just 76 reported MPD cases that the authors considered to be genuine. Between 1944 and 1969, only a handful of MPD cases were reported. By about 1960, MPD was considered "extinct."[34] In the 1970s, however, there were 80 reported cases of MPD; then, in the 1980s, more than 600 such cases were reported. In 1986, Putnam and colleagues observed that "more cases of MPD have been reported in the last 5 years than in the preceding two centuries."[35] The diagnostic pace continued to accelerate, at least through the mid-1990s.

MPD specialists, of course, attribute the increased incidence to enhanced diagnostic acumen. According to these authors, cases of MPD were missed in earlier decades.[36] Now that more is known about what to look for and about how to examine possible MPD patients, they assert, more cases are being picked up. In fact, however, MPD and dissociation were fashionable topics for discussion among professionals around the turn of the century. The account that MPD specialists give of the recent increase in the incidence of the disorder implies that knowledge was somehow lost in earlier decades, only to be rediscovered late in the twentieth century. If MPD is as ubiquitous as some of these authors maintain—some claim to find MPD in 5 to 20 percent of patients with serious mental disorders[37]—it is hard to see how knowledge of MPD could have been lost, unless previous generations of psychiatrists were complete incompetents.

Second, until very recently, MPD was largely a North American phenomenon, suggesting that it is a culture-bound syndrome, much like *latah*, *negi negi,* or others of the syndromes described in chapter 3. As of 1944, for example, 57 percent of the reported cases came from the United States.[38] Since then, that proportion has increased. Between 1960 and 1989, when the incidence of MPD took off in the United States, only two cases of MPD were reported in Britain. In 1987, Aldridge-Morris, a British psychologist, was able to find few cases of MPD in the United Kingdom.[39] Similar low rates of diagnosed MPD occurred throughout Europe.

This is not to say that MPD is strictly limited to North America. Many foreign physicians receive training in North America, and North American publications, like the *American Journal of Psychiatry*, which prominently feature MPD, are widely read by professionals throughout the world. Hence, it was only a matter of time before MPD spread abroad, at least on a limited basis. In 1991, for instance, Boon and Draijer published a relevant study from the Netherlands in the *American Journal of Psychiatry*.[40] These authors gave 44 patients, most of whom had been referred to them for evaluation of dissociative disorders, a translated version of the Structured Clinical Interview for DSM-III-R dissociative disorders (SCID-D) and concluded that 12 of them met the DSM-III-R criteria for MPD. In terms of previous history, reported abuse, and associated symptoms, these 12 patients resembled North American patients with MPD. In 1993, the same authors published another study, in the same journal, of 71 patients with MPD diagnosed by the SCID-D.[41] Like those in the earlier cohort, these patients had been referred to the authors for suspected MPD or for other dissociative disorders and resembled typical MPD patients in the United States.

In a report published in 1989 in the *American Journal of Psychiatry*, Adityanjee and colleagues report three cases of apparent multiple personality disorder in New Delhi.[42] According to the authors, these were among only five cases reported from India as of the late 1980s. These cases are worth describing in some detail here. The first, a Mr. A., was a 15-year-old student from a remote, rural tribe who was then living in Delhi. A month before his admission, he woke from sleep claiming that he was a Mr. B., a business executive who lived with his mother at a different address in Delhi. He denied knowledge of his real family and accused them of detaining him against his will. He spoke in an authoritative manner and claimed to play the guitar and chess and to ride a motorbike. He gave a detailed description of an imaginary girlfriend. After five days of this behavior, he awoke from another sleep in his normal state. He denied knowledge of the previous five days. In the ensuing weeks, he made several such switches. Each switch occurred on awakening and was accompanied by amnesia for his alter state. After a brief stay in the hospital, Mr. A. was treated with supportive therapy and remained well for a two-year period of follow-up. The only identified precipitants for his disorder was a love affair he had been having with a neighborhood girl, for which he had been severely criticized, and difficulties in school.

Another patient, Ms. D., was a 16-year-old student, the youngest of eight siblings. For three days, she had claimed to be Ms. E., a student who lived with her mother at a different address in Delhi. She, too, accused her family of detaining her against her will. As Ms. E., she behaved and spoke quite formally, complained about the food, and expressed a desire for jeans and a game of badminton. Following admission to the hospital, she awoke from sleep in her normal state. She claimed to be amnesic for the preceding days. The only apparent precipitant had been her involvement with a neighborhood boy of whom her sisters disapproved. Like Mr. A., she had been scolded severely. She had also been bothered by some neighborhood boys, who had made crude advances to her. Her sisters blamed her for this, too, claiming that it resulted from her "love affair." The patient remained well with supportive psychotherapy.

Finally, Ms. E. was a 15-year-old student in Delhi, the youngest of five children, who claimed to be Ms. F., an illiterate girl who had never attended school. She, too, denied knowing her family, claimed that she lived with her mother at a different address, and demanded to be released. When released, she went to a girlfriend's house and claimed that her friend's mother was really her own. Her girlfriend, she claimed, was a servant. After admission to the hospital, she reverted to her normal self and denied knowledge of her time as Ms. F. She did, however, insist that she was still illiterate, and she made a show of learning the alphabet from nurses. She had a previous history of conversion blindness related to school difficulty, and the current episode occurred at the time of her final examinations.

In an issue of the *American Journal of Psychiatry* published in 1996, Sar and coworkers described 35 patients in the University of Istanbul medical center who met the DSM-IV criteria for dissociative identity disorder.[43] In an issue of the same journal published in 1998, these authors reported results from 166 psychiatric inpatients in Istanbul who were given the Dissociative Disorders Interview Schedule (DDIS), which yields DSM-III-R diagnoses of dissociative disorders.[44] On the basis of their findings and of clinical interviews, the authors estimated that 5.4 percent of psychiatric inpatients in their facility had dissociative identity disorder.

In an article published in 1998 in *Psychiatry and Clinical Neurosciences*, Fujii and colleagues reported finding only 12 cases of MPD, including two they had treated, described in Japanese medical journals prior to 1997.[45] After excluding two of these cases on methodological grounds, these authors analyzed the remaining 10 cases. The patients, all of whom were women, had an average of 4.9 personalities, with the maximum number being eight, including the host. All but one case showed an alter who was aggressive and "unreservedly did or said anything," characteristics "opposite" to those of the host personality.[46]

From the illness-role viewpoint, two aspects of these reports from other countries are notable. First, all but one of them were published in the *American Journal of Psychiatry*, which has devoted considerable space over the years to MPD, and all of them used diagnostic criteria and even diagnostic instruments, like the SCID-D, from the DSM-III and -IV. Hence, the authors were clearly aware of American diagnostic practices and thinking about MPD. They were not discovering the syndrome afresh, so to speak, but were simply extending the geographical range of the MPD paradigm. Boon and Draijer, moreover, were sufficiently known in the Netherlands for their interest in dissociation and MPD that essentially all of their patients had been referred for this reason. Second, in the reports from India and Turkey, hints emerge that the disorders called MPD may be more closely related to local beliefs and illness roles than to MPD as seen in North America. Sar and coworkers, for instance, failed to give information on the numbers and types of alters shown by their MPD patients, so readers cannot ascertain whether they really resembled American patients with MPD. The single strongest predictor of reported dissociation in these authors' first study was a measure of "extrasensory" experiences, such as mental telepathy, contact with spirits, possession by the dead, or visions of the future in dreams. This finding suggests that the patients were steeped in traditional culture. In Turkey, as in other Islamic countries, *jinns*, or demon-like creatures, are thought to cause diseases, especially possession disorders. *Jinns* were among the spirits that caused the possession disorders discussed by I. M. Lewis (see chapter 3). Sixteen of the 35 patients with dissociative identity disorder described in the first publication from the Istanbul group reported possession by *jinns*.

None of the Indian patients described by Adityanjee had disorders resembling North American MPD. Instead, as Adityanjee and his colleagues observed, these patients may have been following Indian cultural models for expression of their frustration. Two had been reprimanded for an adolescent love affair. All three developed a single alternate personality that was in some sense a rejection of their usual, family identity. In two cases, for instance, the alternate personality spoke in English, rather than the usual Hindi. In each case, the alternate personality rejected the family and gave voice to the patient's feeling that he or she was "detained." In each case, too, the alternate personality laid claim to an alternate family, at a different address. The popular Hindi cinema, according to these authors, has glamorized dramatic changes in personality brought about by sudden events or occurring on wakening from sleep. In each of the three reported cases, personality changes occurred on arousal from sleep.

Although eight of the 10 Japanese patients reported by Fujii and coworkers had suffered from emotional abuse and neglect in childhood, only one reported sexual abuse, and only two reported physical abuse. The authors suggest that the link of MPD with sexual abuse may be specific to North American cases. Some of the Japanese cases may also have been influenced by the concept of Fox or Badger possession, cases of which are still reported in modern Japan.[47] At the very least, the concept of unwilled behavior is endemic to Japan, as it is to other societies.

To counter the claim that MPD is culture bound, and hence suspect, some MPD specialists argue that possession illnesses as seen in other cultures are forms of divided identity related to MPD.[48] According to this argument, faulty identity processes can produce MPD or possession, depending upon the culture in which they are expressed. At least divided identity, if not MPD per se, is then in fact universal.

The problem with this argument is that it ignores the wealth of data, like that cited by I. M. Lewis, that suggest that possession disorders and related culture-bound syndromes are best understood as strategic maneuvers.[49] As described in chapter 3, individuals in traditional societies who lack social power are possessed by peripheral spirits when concessions are thereby gained. The cures for possession by peripheral spirits typically involve concessions to the host or changes in family relationships that could not otherwise have been achieved. Other individuals in such societies, who have more social power, are possessed by central spirits as part of the process of bidding to become a shaman. In both cases, advantages ensue from repudiating one's speech and actions, borrowing spirit authority, and appearing to be another person. If MPD specialists want to claim possession disorders as examples of MPD, then they must surrender their claim that MPD is an enduring state of being, outside the host's control, with alters who don't necessarily work to promote the host's interests.

A patient brought to my attention at a large southern medical center illustrates the naiveté shown by some MPD specialists in their thinking about possession. The patient, a woman in her thirties who had been raised in a charismatic Christian sect, had a long history of depression, anxiety, and emotional instability. She had relationship and work problems and inadequate social support. Recently, she had acted in church as if possessed by a demon. Among other things, she had spoken in tongues, but outside of the usual setting in which such speech is encouraged, made lewd and suggestive remarks, blasphemed, and referred to herself in the third person. She was sent to an out-of-state pastor known for his success in casting out demons, but, before the pastor could act, her demon assaulted and injured him. Since no real demon would have dared to attack this man, who was known to have holy powers, the assault constituted a faux pas in the role of demonic possession. The church authorities realized she was not really possessed but that she had MPD, with an alter personality that was pretending to be a demon. The patient was sent to a hospital for psychiatric treatment. The hospital staff concurred with the church authorities. In fact, they elicited additional alters and made progress uncovering the repressed memories of abuse that were responsible for her disorder. An earnest trainee expressed her sense of relief that the alter personality that was pretending to be a demon had given itself away by making a serious error, without which the patient's illness might never have received proper medical attention.

A third aspect of MPD that points to its being an illness role is that its features have changed since it was first described. An illness role, of course, is more likely to change its features than a real disorder. In MPD, the number of alters has increased, new types of alters have appeared, and child abuse, which was not mentioned in the early reports, has emerged as a causative factor.[50] With regard to the number of alters, most nineteenth-century cases had only dual personalities (see later discussion). Only one case reported prior to 1944 had more than eight separate alters. In a series of 54 cases reported in 1982, by contrast, 24 patients had more than 10 personalities, and seven had more than 20. Another large series of patients reported in 1990 averaged 24.1 alternate personalities. In 1986, a case was reported with 300 putative alternates, and, a few years later, another case was reported with more than 400 alters. MPD specialists argue that the increase in numbers of alters is a result of improved diagnosis; alters that might have escaped detection in earlier decades are now routinely uncovered.[51] On the other hand, gradual escalation in the number of alters is only to be expected as patients and therapists try to enact more dramatic disorders.

With regard to the types of alters, modern-day MPD patients typically manifest alters who are said to be children or animals or artistic or specially-talented, or who are so-called persecutor or helper personalities.[52] Persecutor personalities are angry and self-destructive and may try to kill the patient; helper personalities appear at difficult moments and get the host out of a jam and may try to comfort alters, especially the child alters, who are suffering from abuse. None of these personalities appeared in the early reports. As with the number of alters, the change can be due to improved diagnostic practices but is also readily explained if MPD is a role subject to fads and fashions.

Before 1973, when the story of Sybil was published, MPD had not been linked with child abuse.[53] Sybil, who had as many as 16 alternate personalities, reported severe sexual and physical abuse inflicted by her ostensibly schizophrenic mother. According to Sybil's account, when she was a child she had been kicked, beaten with objects, administered cold-water enemas, locked in a trunk in the attic, burned with an iron, and choked. Her mother, according to Sybil, sometimes hung her upside down from the ceiling with her legs apart, for the purpose of inserting a catheter into her bladder, which was then filled with cold water. The mother reportedly forced flashlights, bottles, boxes, knives, and other objects into Sybil's vagina. Although some of Sybil's reports were doubtful—she claimed, among other things, to remember incidents from the first year of her life—they nonetheless changed theories and treatment of MPD. Some authors suggest that the link between MPD and abuse contributed to the rise of MPD in the 1980s since sexual abuse was a topic of interest to feminist authors.[54] In any event, abuse is now so closely linked to MPD that modern-day therapists make it a goal to recover memories of abuse. As is made clear in the following chapter, reported abuse today is even more graphic than Sybil's. Once again, the usual contrasting accounts can be given for the change in the clinical picture.

In light of her role in the history of the MPD movement, it is especially worth noting that Sybil may have been coached both to report abuse and to act out her alters. Herbert Spiegel, whose work on hypnosis was cited in chapter 2, was asked by Cornelia Wilbur, Sybil's psychiatrist, to assess Sybil and to give his opinion.[55] In a television interview, Spiegel described what happened when he interviewed Sybil:

> She [Sybil] would ask . . . when she wanted to go to a certain period of life, well shall I become Flora, or can I just say it? I didn't know what she meant at first. Well, she said, well, when I'm with Dr. Wilbur, she wants me to be that person. And I said, well, if you want, you can, but you don't have to if you don't want to. So, with me, she didn't have to be these personalities.

As Spiegel saw it, Sybil's MPD was created by her psychiatrist. He also expressed his opinion that Sybil had not been abused.

Who Has MPD, and Why Do They Have It?

If MPD is a role, then patients with MPD are likely to be habitual role players, and there must be ways in which they benefit from having MPD. With regard to the first of these points, all observers agree that many, if not most, MPD patients are hypnotic virtuosos, in the sense that they are readily hypnotized and exquisitely responsive to hypnotic cues.[56] Hypnosis, in fact, is a mainstay of treatment for MPD. It is used to meet and later to draw out the alters and to recover memories of childhood abuse. Insofar as hypnotic ability manifests role-cue responsiveness, the extreme hypnotic ability of patients with MPD suggests that they are skilled role players.

Patients with MPD often have other complaints that are attributable to role playing. Studies have shown that between 19 and 80 percent of patients with MPD meet diagnostic criteria for somatization disorder.[57] The reader will recall that, to meet DSM-III criteria for somatization disorder, men had to have at least 12 and women at least 14 of 37 bodily symptoms referable to different organ systems, each of which was a cause of significant distress or disability. To meet DSM-III-R criteria, both men and women had to have at least 13 of 35 such bodily symptoms; to meet DSM-IV criteria, patients must have at least 10 such symptoms, in specific categories. Ross and colleagues administered the Dissociative Disorders Interview Schedule (DDIS) to 20 patients with multiple personality disorder and to equal numbers of patients with schizophrenia, panic disorder and eating disorders.[58] The DDIS includes questions regarding the 35 symptoms that contribute to a

DSM-IIIR diagnosis of somatization disorder. Subjects with MPD reported an average of 13.5 unexplained medical symptoms, compared to 5.2 for eating disorder subjects, 8.7 for panic disorder subjects, and 3.4 for schizophrenics. In chapter 5, I noted that patients with enough undiagnosable somatic complaints to reach or be near the diagnostic criteria for somatization disorder may be playing an illness role.

Studies have also shown that between 10 and 93 percent of patients with MPD have conversion symptoms.[59] The reader will recall that conversion is characterized by movement or sensory deficits suggestive of neurological or general medical disorders but that occur without pathology able to cause such deficits. Conversion symptoms were typical of the petit hysterics observed in the nineteenth century. In chapter 5, I argued that patients with conversion symptoms are playing an illness role.

Consistent with the hypothesis that they are playing an illness role, MPD patients are likely to have cluster B or self-dramatizing personality disorders and to be depressed (see chapter 1). With regard to personality disorders, several observers have noted that patients with MPD tend to be self-dramatizing, egocentric, demanding, dependent, deceitful, untrustworthy, and manipulative.[60] More than half of patients said to have MPD meet the diagnostic criteria for borderline personality disorder, and more than a fifth of patients said to have MPD meet the diagnostic criteria for histrionic personality disorder. Several authors have noted prominent narcissistic features of MPD patients. About a third of patients said to have MPD meet the diagnostic criteria for antisocial personality disorder. Pseudologia, or the invention of fantastic stories, forgeries, and impersonations have also been noted in published cases of MPD.[61]

The overwhelming majority of MPD patients have episodes of depression.[62] The depressions these patients experience are triggered, if not caused, by their difficult situations. One cannot overstate the problems faced by some MPD patients. Most of them have poor relationships, both with their families of origin and with their spouses and children. Many are simply alone, without even friends to turn to. They lack education or job skills, and they often have money problems. Some have trouble meeting even their basic needs, such as a place to live.

On psychological tests, MPD patients show a response pattern similar to that seen in Briquet's syndrome or somatization disorder.[63] They seek to present their distress in the strongest possible form, and they endorse symptoms more or less indiscriminately. This response pattern is consistent with the observation that MPD patients are histrionic and attention seeking, but it is wholly at odds with the notion, advanced by some MPD therapists, that the MPD host personality is trying its best to seem normal.

How do MPD patients benefit from their role? In some cases, patients appear to gain permission to act out their normally forbidden fantasies. Ms. P., for example, had an illicit sexual relationship after learning from a TV movie that alters could engage in behaviors for which the host was not responsible. MPD patients frequently blame their current misdeeds on their alters; some of them go so far as to claim they are helpless bystanders. In many other cases, having MPD provides an excuse for past blameworthy behaviors. As described earlier, MPD case descriptions feature accounts of patients whose past misbehavior is attributed to alters of which they had no knowledge at the time they misbehaved. Several criminal defendants have tested in court the theory that the host cannot be legally punished for alters' crimes,[64] Not surprisingly, the courts are generally loathe to establish this type of precedent.

An even more powerful benefit of developing MPD is that it pleases the therapist. The therapist-patient relationship is so unequal, both with respect to authority and with respect to needs, that even well-functioning patients have a hard time perceiving their therapists as mere human beings. They attribute more knowledge to therapists than therapists really possess, and they are eager to please them. The typical MPD patient is even more in thrall. Most of these patients have been treated for years for depression or for personality problems, their social situations are bad, and they lack friends and family with whom they are on good terms. The therapist may be the only person in their lives who is willing to listen to them with any degree of sympathy. When they hear their therapists asking repetitive questions—"Are there time periods for which you have no memory?," "Have you ever found clothes in your drawers or closets which you do not remember purchasing?," and so on—and observe the heightened degree of interest their therapists take in affirmative answers, they can readily draw conclusions about what their therapists want, and they take steps accordingly. Kohlenberg's study showed how one MPD patient tracked the rewarded behavior.[65]

The therapist, of course, is expected to repay the patient for responding to MPD role cues by showing heightened concern, attention, and sympathy, once the MPD symptoms and recovered memories appear (see chapter 7). A therapist who suddenly lost interest in the patient once the alters appeared would either extinguish the alters she had previously, cultivated or she would lose her patient, who would feel betrayed by her. In fact, well-known biographical accounts of MPD, which have no doubt played a large part in its recent spread, suggest that therapists do gratify MPD patients, especially if they are colorful and tell dramatic stories.[66] Some therapists, for example, were apparently so intrigued by their patients with MPD that they had lengthier than normal sessions with them, some sessions lasting up to eight hours, saw them outside their offices, and helped them with problems of living. One therapist went with his patient on a publicity tour.

There is another aspect to the therapist-patient relationship in many MPD cases that is seldom discussed in the literature but that may be quite important in promoting role-cue responses. When patients are treated for years for depression and mood instability, like most patients about to be labeled multiples, their therapists—and, more generally, others who try to help them—get tired of them, and angry. This is especially the case for patients with cluster B features, whose histrionic behavior and repeated suicide gestures wear out their therapists. In adopting the MPD role, the long-term unimproved patient receives a kind of forgiveness for not having gotten bet-ter. The onus shifts from the patient—who might have remained unim-proved for lack of motivation—to the therapist—who acknowledges having failed to make the correct diagnosis or who in any event acknowledges that someone else, such as the previous therapist, failed to make the correct diag-nosis. With the slate wiped clean in this way, the therapist treats the patient as if she were really a fresh case, without the built-up resentments that fol-low on failed treatments.

The element of forgiveness and starting afresh is especially evident in pub-lic or teaching hospitals, where many patients are diagnosed with MPD. Chronically ill, emotionally unstable, and sometimes misbehaving patients who fail to improve over a period of many years become persona non grata in such institutional settings. Harried staff members lose interest in their in-tractable problems. They get tired of their patients' misbehavior and view it in punitive terms. The patients notice that their welcome has worn thin. However, once the patient becomes a multiple, the staff's attitude changes remarkably. Though everyone blamed the patient for her earlier problems, the lack of improvement is now put off on misdiagnosis. Though no one wanted to talk to the patient, everyone suddenly wants to meet and converse with her alters. Insofar as MPD is believed to be due to abuse, the patient is now a victim and perhaps an heroic survivor. The net result, for the patient, of accepting the MPD label may be a complete change in attitude on the part of the hospital staff. I have seen staff and trainees who have grumbled at having to treat a chronically ill, unimproved, or misbehaving patient dis-cover reserves of interest when the patient is labeled a multiple. Kohlenberg also observed that his MPD patient had received much attention from the hospital staff for enacting his alters. According to Kohlenberg, the patient was considered sufficiently interesting that he "was always one of the first one or two to be presented to visiting professionals and students."[67]

The reader may recall that Charcot's patients in the Salpêtrière used grand hysteric behavior to obtain interest and privileges. The same social processes at work in the Salpêtrière can be observed in modern clinic and hospital set-tings, if we think to look for them.

The Earliest MPD Cases

To show that MPD is not an illness role, MPD specialists sometimes point to the first cases of split personality, from the nineteenth and early twentieth centuries.[68] Supposedly, neither these patients nor their physicians had heard of the concept of multiples, so these illnesses must have been real, and therefore today's MPD must be real. This argument, however, rests on two misconceptions: First, split personality was in fact a very familiar notion for nineteenth- and early-twentieth-century physicians and laypersons. Second, the earliest split personalities were quite unlike today's MPD patients.

With regard to the first misconception, multiplicity, or at least duality,

was a familiar theme in nineteenth-century literature. According to Ellenberger, the prototypical story in this particular genre was *The Devil's Elixir,*
written by E. T. A. Hoffmann (1776–1822).[69] In *The Devil's Elixir*, a monk
drinks a magic elixir that makes him a criminal. In his criminal state, he
meets his double, who mirrors him in every respect. The double drinks the
rest of the elixir, goes mad, and is committed to an asylum before being sentenced to death for the crimes that the monk committed. The monk con-
fesses before the double can be executed, both of them escape, and the double disappears. The monk is saved and returns to his normal self.

Edgar Allan Poe took up the theme of the double in 1839, in his story
"William Wilson."[70] The protagonist, William Wilson, meets another boy
at his school who shares his name and date of birth and looks like him.
Frightened, Wilson runs away, only to be confronted again and again by his
double. In the end he murders his double, whose dying words inform him
that he has killed himself. Also in 1839, *La Médecin du Pecq*, by Léon Gozlan,
was a best-selling novel in France. In a somnambulistic state, a rich neurotic
young man, who resides in a sanatarium, impregnates an innocent woman.
He is not aware of his crime. A physician helps him discover what he has
done by interpreting his dreams. This novel marked the appearance of the
physician as an investigator of the double's activities.

Six years later, Dostoevski published a short novel called *The Double*. In
Dostoevski's novella, Golyatkin, a petty clerk, begins to behave erratically.
Soon thereafter, a double, who looks like Golyatkin and shares his birthdate,
joins Golyatkin's office as a new employee. Initially diffident with Golyatkin, the double eventually takes over his post, spends his money, and woos
away his friends. Unable to fend him off, Golyatkin allows his double to
send him to an asylum.

In the 1880s, several widely read novels appeared that had as their theme
the double. The authors of these novels, as well as their avid readers, were no
doubt affected by the then current Battle of the Schools (see chapter 5),
which had made hypnotism and somnambulism matters of public interest.
The most famous of the 1880s novels was Robert Louis Stevenson's *The
Strange Case of Dr. Jekyll and Mr. Hyde*, which became an instant success after
its publication in 1886.[71] Both because of its success, and because it was
written in English, Stevenson's novel served to disseminate widely key ideas
that later reemerged as seeming clinical facts. These ideas included the
host's lack of control over the alter's emergence and subsequent behavior, the
multiplication of alters, and the division of alters according to their moral
development. In Stevenson's novel, Dr. Jekyll, a physician and scientist,
takes a potion of his own invention, which has the effect of releasing his base
and primitive alter, Mr. Hyde. Being a gentleman, Dr. Jekyll is horrified by
Mr. Hyde's actions, which soon include murder, but he cannot suppress Mr.
Hyde, once Mr. Hyde has emerged. Jekyll's only remedy proves to be self-
destruction.

Actually, although Stevenson seemingly wrote about dual personality, *Dr.
Jekyll and Mr. Hyde* is less about "multiplicity," in today's sense of the word,

than about the dual nature of humankind, as this was conceived after Darwin. The split between Jekyll and Hyde embodied the gulf between civilized humans and animals that so disturbed late-nineteenth-century scientists and intellectuals. On the one hand, man was a being created in God's own image; on the other hand, man was a being descended from the apes. Jekyll, of course, also represents Charles Darwin, the scientist who really let the genie escape from its bottle.

Other great literary works, among many in the double tradition, include Oscar Wilde's *The Picture of Dorian Gray*, which was published in 1891, and Joseph Conrad's *The Secret Sharer*, which was published in 1909.[72] In *The Picture of Dorian Gray*, the double, of course, is a portrait, able to take on the moral stains incurred by its subject. In *The Secret Sharer*, a sea captain anchored in the Gulf of Siam meets a mysterious boarder, his double, who is fleeing a nearby ship on which he killed a man. At great risk to his ship, the captain helps his double escape from his pursuers. Wilde's and Conrad's treatments are more psychologically nuanced than previous works on the double, showing an advance among turn-of-the-century authors, if not among physicians.

Regarding the second misconception, the earliest split personalities were not at all like patients with MPD today. They differed from patients today in the number and types of alters, in the nature and timing of switches from one alter to another, and in associated symptoms and behaviors. If they demonstrate anything, nineteenth- and early-twentieth-century cases of split personality show a slow evolution of an MPD illness role, not an early discovery of an unchanging disorder.

The first widely known case of split personality was that of Mary Reynolds, which was reported by John Kearsley Mitchell, the father of the famous physician S. Weir Mitchell, in the *Medical Repository of New York* in 1816.[73] Mitchell's report was the first detailed medical account of a case of split personality. The case was described again, by Macnish, in a popular book, *The Philosophy of Sleep*, in 1836, and by the Reverend William S. Plumer in *Harper's* in 1859 and 1860. Some readers failed to realize that these various accounts described the same patient, and they quoted them as separate instances of duality. S. Weir Mitchell himself published a thorough account of Mary Reynolds's case in 1889. Mary Reynolds was born in 1785, the second child and the first daughter of William and Lydia Reynolds of Birmingham, England. Mary's parents, who were Baptist dissenters, were forced to emigrate to America in 1794. After a stay with their maternal grandfather, Mary and her older brother followed their parents to New York in 1795. By 1797, the 12-year-old Mary, her parents, and her seven siblings had moved to wilderness land in western Pennsylvania, close by Oil Creek of mid-nineteenth-century fame. There they lived in primitive, harsh conditions, trying to eke out a living by farming their few acres.

Prior to her illness, Mary was described as sedate and thoughtful. Her spirits were often low, and she was not known for laughter. She did not enjoy company but preferred to read her Bible alone and uninterrupted. At 18 years of age, Mary began to have "fits," concerning which little is known. In 1811, she was found unresponsive in a field near her house. On awakening, she was blind and deaf. She continued in this state before gradually recovering her senses. Within a few months, on awakening one morning she appeared to have lost her identity and knowledge of her family. After five weeks in this "second" state, she suddenly returned to her normal, or "first," state, claiming not to remember the events of the past five weeks. Thereafter, Mary frequently cycled between her two states, spending more time in her second than in her normal first. In contrast with Mary's normally dour disposition, Mary in her second state was cheerful and gay, fond of company, and given to writing poetry.[74] She wandered freely about the countryside and moved to a nearby town, where she was known as a wit and a sharp-tongued satirist. She rejected her parents' authority and, indeed, all conventional wisdom. When a physician opined that marriage would cure her ills—at the time, sexual deprivation was thought to cause hysteria—Mary responded by insulting and rejecting her suitors, whom she called "matrimonial pills."

Michael G. Kenney, a social anthropologist who studied early American cases of MPD, showed how Mary's illness reflected the religious and social milieu in which Mary was raised, how—like possessed women elsewhere—she used her second state to give voice to demands and comments that were otherwise unspeakable, and how certain others encouraged her in her performance.[75] Mary's second state conferred a freedom of action, for example to live in town, that her family would not have allowed had she been seen as well. It is especially significant that Mary's illness began when she came of age to marry, that she used the freedom conferred by her second state to resist the pressure to marry, and that once Mary had passed marriageable age, in her late thirties, her alternation of personalities ceased.

Another early case, "Estelle," described by Despine, apparently inspired later French physicians.[76] Despine, a general practitioner in Aix-en-Savoie, practiced magnetic treatment. In 1834, nine-year-old Estelle, who lived in Neuchâtel, fell to the ground after being pushed by another child. Thereafter, she became paralyzed and complained of excruciating pains, which her doctors believed to be caused by a spinal cord lesion. In 1836, after all other treatments had failed, she was placed in a large willow basket padded with eiderdown and taken by coach to Aix-en-Savoie, drawing large crowds en route. If anyone other than Estelle's mother or aunt touched her, she screamed in pain. She had visions and hallucinations and could not remember what was happening from one moment to the next. In Aix-en-Savoie, Despine began treating Estelle with hydrotherapeutic and electric treatments, but, when he learned from Estelle's mother that Estelle heard a choir of angels singing for her each evening, he realized that animal magnetism was the treatment of choice. Although she was reluctant at first to be magnetized and insisted that every word she spoke when magnetized be repeated to her later, Estelle was readily put into a trance. During her magnetic sessions, Estelle prescribed her own diet and treatment regimens. Following each of these sessions, when Estelle was in a state of magnetic sleep, an angel, Angeline, appeared and conversed with her. Soon Angeline directed Estelle's treatment. Unsurprisingly, Angeline proscribed foods Estelle disliked and insisted that Estelle be given whatever she wanted and allowed to act on her whims.

In January 1837, Estelle developed a double. Normally paralyzed, pain ridden, and deferential, in her second state she could walk and even run, she despised her mother, and she addressed Despine with the familiar *tu*. Normally abstemious and picky, in her second state Estelle had a hearty appetite. Curiously, the sight of cats and certain other objects in her second state induced catalepsy, but this could be relieved by rubbing her body with gold objects. Estelle's states came and went on a 12-hour schedule. At the end of March, Estelle predicted she would have a vision of a big ball that would burst, which would herald the onset of her recovery. Sure enough, the vision appeared to her in April, and for the first time in more than two years, she was able to take a few steps in her normal state. Soon thereafter, she could swim and take walks in the mountains. By the middle of June, Estelle's two personalities had largely fused, and she was discharged from treatment. Returning to Neuchâtel, Estelle was called *la petite ressuscitée*, or "the little resurrected one." Estelle eventually married and died in Le Havre in 1862.

Another important European case, presented in medical forums and published in France by Azam in 1887, was known as Felida X.[77] Born in 1843, Felida was the daughter of a merchant marine captain who died when she was a baby. Her childhood was impoverished, and she had to work as a seamstress. She developed hysterical symptoms when she was only 13. Along with headaches and numerous other symptoms, she had daily "crises." After a brief state of lethargy, she would become a different person, gay instead of dour, vivacious instead of dull, and free of physical symptoms. Of average intelligence in her normal state, in her second state Felida was brighter. After a few hours, a brief period of lethargy would herald her return to her normal self. In her normal state, Felida claimed to know nothing of her second state, but, in her second state, she could give a full account of her life. When Felida became pregnant, her first state denied any knowledge of how this had happened. Her second state, however, laughingly acknowledged having had sexual intercourse and claimed to have known she was pregnant. Felida married the man with whom her double had slept. By 1876, Felida's second, more cheerful, and healthier state had become her usual state; her primary state returned only for brief periods. Curiously, Felida was in her first, unhealthy state when she delivered each of her 11 children.

Regardless of her state, Felida also had an unusual bleeding disorder, reminiscent of religious stigmata. When Felida slept, but not when she was awake, a slow continuous flow of blood seeped from her mouth. Yet, she had no lesions of the nose or mouth. As Felida aged, this symptom worsened and involved other mucosae.

Ansel Bourne, another American case of split personality, was immortalized in William James's *Principles of Psychology*, published in 1890.[78] In late October 1857, Bourne, then a 31-year-old carpenter, had been walking to nearby Westerly, Rhode Island, when he lost his sight, hearing, speech, and power of movement. Although the local doctor reported that Bourne was "insensible," Bourne in fact was conscious of the events around him. He concluded that God had condemned him. When his sight was suddenly restored, he took to communicating by writing. Following other epiphanies, his hearing and speech were restored by mid-November. At the end of November, however, during another attack, a Being appeared to him and instructed him to give up his worldly affairs, leave his friends and family, and become a preacher. Bourne's friends and Bourne himself attributed the events of October and November 1857 to divine intervention, his doctor attributed them to a "cerebral disturbance," and the local paper, the *Providence Daily Journal*, suggested that fraud was involved. In any event, Bourne did as his vision suggested and became an itinerant preacher.

Thirty years later, Bourne was changed again. In January 1887, he was living in Greene, Rhode Island, where he had moved after remarrying, following the death of his first wife in 1881. He had resumed carpentry and had money in the bank. On January 17, Bourne traveled to Providence, withdrew his savings, and disappeared. Calling himself Albert Brown, of Newton, New Hampshire, he traveled to Norristown, Pennsylvania, where he rented a vacant store on February 1 and established a small variety store. In March, however, he approached his landlord in a state of confusion and asked him where he was. He denied being Mr. Brown and had no memories at all for the period since January 17. Learning of these events through the Society for Psychical Research, William James suggested that Bourne's memories of Albert Brown might be recovered hypnotically. Bourne, who had had some exposure to hypnosis previously, was willing to come to Boston for this purpose and proved readily hypnotizable. Under hypnosis, the character of Albert Brown reappeared. He gave his date of birth as that of Bourne himself, but he claimed to have been born in New Hampshire, rather than in New York. He claimed that his wife had died in 1881, as had Bourne's first wife, and he cited financial and family problems that roughly corresponded to those faced by Ansel Bourne at the time Albert Brown appeared, but he denied any knowledge of Ansel Bourne. He recalled that, after leaving Provincetown, he had visited New York and later Philadelphia before settling in Norristown. James established that Brown's account of his travels was plausible, but there was no indication than an Albert Brown had existed prior to his appearance in Provincetown.

After his stint with James, Ansel Bourne apparently lived out his life without further dramas. In his history of early cases of MPD, Michael G. Kenney shows how Ansel Bourne's transformations, to divinely inspired preacher and later to Albert Brown, seemingly promised relief from the problems of living he was facing when these transformations occurred.[79]

Ian Hacking described a brief epidemic of fugue, or "dissociated" travel, that occurred mainly in France in the 1880s and 1890s, which was appar-

ently sparked by publication of a case discovered in Bordeaux in 1886.[80]
Philippe Tissié, the physician whose case report began the French epidemic,
considered Bourne a fugueur and cited his case to prove that fugue personalities, in this case Albert Brown, showed signs of self-awareness.[81] Essentially, fugueurs were split personalities whose alters liked to travel. Nearly
all the French fugueurs were men, and, in many if not most cases, fugue was
offered as a medical explanation for military desertions or absences without
leave. Deserters diagnosed by sympathetic doctors avoided the harsh punishments that were then the norm. Although some cases of fugue were described in Germany, where conscription was also practiced, the fugue epidemic never really caught on in England or in America. James attended a
conference at which Tissié spoke in 1889.[82]

Louis Vivet, who was treated by Jules Voisin in the Bicêtre, the men's asylum in Paris, between 1883 and 1885, and later by Bourru and Burot in the
military hospital in Rochefort, is sometimes considered the first patient
with MPD, as opposed to mere dual personality.[83] In 1889, he was also described as a fugueur.[84] Born in Paris in 1863, Vivet was raised by an alcoholic prostitute who beat and neglected him and from whom he ran away at
age eight. In 1871, he was sent to a reformatory for stealing clothes and then
two years later to a prison farm in northwest France, where he remained for
nine years before becoming disabled by hysterical symptoms. In 1880, he
was sent to an insane asylum south of Chartres, where he learned to be a
tailor. However, after prolonged convulsions, he stole money and clothes
and escaped. He was captured en route to Paris and returned to the asylum.
The physician-in-charge, Camuset, considered him to have two personalities, one gentle and paraplegic, the other violent and fit, and wrote him up
as a case of dual personality. After Camuset released him, Vivet was briefly
reunited with his mother before going to Burgundy to work on a large es-
tate. This arrangement lasted only a short time, however, before his hysterical crises led to his being sent to another asylum. There followed a period
during which he resided in several asylums and had several arrests for theft
before he was judged retarded and consigned to the Bicêtre and to the care of
Voison.

In the Bicêtre, Vivet displayed the following symptoms, among others:
pain, paralyses, anesthesias, spasms, mutism, rashes, bleeding, coughing,
vomiting, seizures, somnambulism, *arc de cercle*, mimicking a dog, mimicking a steam locomotive, loss of sight, loss of taste, loss of smell, visual hallucinations, auditory hallucinations, constipation, anorexia, and bulimia. At
first, magnets had little effect on his various symptoms, but later he realized
that Voisin believed in magnetic treatments, and he began to respond. The
sight of a nearby magnet was sufficient to change his condition. Gold coins
applied to his body made him scream in pain. Reminiscent of grand hysterics observed in the Salpêtrière, he was cured temporarily of his hysterical fits
by pressure applied on his heel. Apparently learning from Voisin that Camuset had described his two personality states, Vivet began to show these in
the Bicêtre. In his docile state he was paralyzed from the waist down. In his

violent, aggressive state, he was able to walk about. When hypnotized, he showed what Voisin considered a third state, in which he was still 16.

Late in January 1885, Vivet was released from the Bicêtre and enlisted in the French Navy. Posted to Rochefort, a naval base on the Bay of Biscay, he was once again caught stealing clothing. He was found not to be responsible for this crime, however, and was sent to the military hospital, where he was treated by Bourru and his assistant, Burot. Bourru and Burot were intrigued by drug effects over distance. They published studies showing that drugs held behind Vivet's head affected him just as if he had ingested them. Metals and magnets applied to Vivet's bodily parts produced instant paralyses or anesthesias, along with a change of character and memories of life segments. Where Camuset and Voisin had discovered just two states, moreover, Bourru and Burot reported many more. In their 1888 book on Vivet, they reported six distinct, fully developed personalities, as well as a larger number of un- developed ones. Photographs of Vivet show him posing in 10 of his states, each of which was characterized by specific physical symptoms, dispositions, and general and biographical knowledge and which corresponded with him- self at various ages.

To give a sense of how Vivet's alters appeared, on one occasion, when pre- sented a flask containing gold bromide, Vivet slept and woke five times in rapid successsion, entering a different state on each arousal. On the first arousal, he was five years old, with childish speech, and trailed his right leg when he walked. He believed he was still living with his mother in Chartres. On the second arousal, he was six and a half years old, with spasms of his left side and an extended left leg. He believed he was living in Lève, near Chartres. On the third arousal, he was 16, with spasms of his face and leg and slurred speech. In this state, he begged for bread. He believed he was living in Luysan, near Chartres. On the fourth arousal, he was eight years old, with a contracted left arm and an extended right leg. He believed he was living in Chartres. On the fifth arousal, he was 13 and believed he was on the prison farm to which he was sent as a youth. Age regression was a common trick used by stage mesmerists during the nineteenth century. Ian Hacking, from whom this account of Vivet is taken, states that he has "no doubt" that Bourru and Burot, and perhaps Vivet as well, knew of the tech- nique before these events at Rochefort.[85]

Perhaps the most famous nineteenth-century case of split personality was Christine Beauchamp, who came to Morton Prince in 1898 and was the sub- ject of his famous 1906 book, *The Dissociation of a Personality*.[86] Beauchamp's real name was Clara Norton Fowler. Born in 1873, to Mary Norton and John Conway Fowler of Beverly, Massachusetts, she was a student at Bradford Academy when she first went to Prince. Her father, John Fowler, was a violent-tempered bricklayer and her mother, who rejected her, had died when Clara was 13. Clara ran away from home at age 16 and enrolled in a nurse's training program in Fall River, Massachusetts at age 20. In Fall River, she had a sexual relationship with an older man, called Jones, which ended trauma- cally; it was to this failed relationship that Prince attributed her illness.

Fowler consulted Prince for headaches, fatigue, and neurasthenic symptoms. According to Prince's account, by using hypnosis with her, he was able to give her transient relief of her physical symptoms. One day, however, Prince was surprised to hear Fowler deny some statements she had made during her previous hypnotic trance. Shortly thereafter, when hypnotized, she spoke of herself in the third person. Prince soon established that he had contacted an alter state, "Sally." In contrast to Clara, who was overly scrupulous and inhibited, Sally was playful, adventurous, and possessed of a sense of humor. She described herself as amoral. She claimed to be conscious even when Clara was in control. Although she emerged in the setting of an hypnotic trance, within a matter of months she was able to emerge and converse with Prince whenever she wanted to, regardless of whether Clara was hypnotized. A third personality showed up but stayed just a minor player.

A remarkable fact about Fowler is that her friends and family were ignorant of her alters. Furthermore, during a trip to Europe she took while in treatment with Prince, she was able to stay herself except for a very few hours. Prince believed that Fowler's personality had shattered into component parts—the neurasthenic, overly scrupulous Christine and the hedonistic Sally—as the result of the trauma she had suffered in love while living in Fall River. To explain away the discrepancy between what he saw in his clinic and what others observed of Clara, Prince first proposed the argument, now applied to all patients with MPD, that Clara's alters wished to hide from others' view. Clara's personalities, he wrote, "have endeavored by every artifice to conceal the knowledge of their trouble from friends, and have done so with a success that is astonishing."[87]

Harold Merskey, a well-known Canadian psychiatric historian and expert on somatization, noted that Prince encouraged Fowler to name the mood states she showed during hypnosis.[88] In this way, according to Merskey, Prince encouraged Fowler to present herself as a multiple, a role this avid reader might have been prepared for in any event. In exchange for following leads, Clara enjoyed special favors. Prince never disguised the fact that he was fond of his patient. According to a biography written by Prince's daughter, Clara could come to see Prince at any time, day or night, and be assured of attention.[89] Eventually, Clara's various personalities fused into one, more balanced character type; she married a colleague of Prince's and became a society hostess.

Recovered memories of childhood abuse are a major component of modern-day MPD. Such memories are discussed in the following chapter.

7

Recovered Memory Roles

In the past two decades, increasing numbers of patients have reported recovering memories of severe abuse or trauma that no one else, except, presumably, the perpetrators, had known about previously. In most cases, the trauma recalled was child sexual abuse, but in some cases the trauma was ritual abuse by satanic covens. Therapists who treat such patients theorize that memories of extremely traumatic events, especially of early sexual molestation, are so painful that they are barred from awareness by repression or dissociation.[1] "Repressed" memories are those that are strictly forbidden to surface, while "dissociated" memories are allowed expression only when the patient is in an alternate state of mind, as in MPD. Whether in the context of MPD or another disorder, repressed or dissociated memories are thought to cause various symptoms, both mental and physical. Patients with repressed memories of childhood rape, for example, may fear intimacy with others or have undiagnosable pelvic pain. Such symptoms are thought to be relieved by the patient's recovering memories and "working them through." Recovering memories entails certain steps or procedures that I will outline later and that provide the resulting memories with a certain legitimation. A patient who is working through memories endures the initial shock of encountering the memories, grieves the events they reveal, and comprehends how her symptoms result from past mistreatment. I use the feminine pronoun here because, consistent with the emphasis recovered memory therapists place on childhood sexual abuse, the vast majority of recovered memory patients are women.

As the reader no doubt knows, this conceptual formulation is controversial, to say the least. First, although there is evidence that early child abuse is associated with later psychopathology, the association has not been proven to be a causal one. Abuse in general, and sexual abuse in particular, may be less a direct cause of injury than a marker of family dysfunction.[2] Second, many researchers doubt that repression really occurs and hence that early traumas are more likely to be forgotten than other early events.[3] Third, many researchers doubt that memories recovered by the means advocated by recovered memory therapists are likely to be accurate.[4]

On the one hand, if recovered memories are false, the patients who invent them and subsequently work them through can be said to be playing an illness role. The role in this case consists less in developing symptoms, which are often present to start with, than in inventing memories and appropriate "working through" reactions—shock, grief, and comprehension—in order to prove correct the theory about the cause of the disorder, that is, repressed or dissociated memories of abuse. I describe later the rewards contingent on providing proof of this theory. On the other hand, if the recovered memories and the subsequent "working through" reactions are genuine, then the patients are doing something more than just playing a role. Insofar as some recovered memories and subsequent reactions are genuine and others are false, then only some patients are playing a role or some patients are playing a role only part of the time. I therefore also review the evidence for and against the validity of such memories.

As discussed in chapter 1, illness roles are generally deeply rooted in the cultures in which they appear and have progenitors in earlier illness roles. Eighteenth- and nineteenth-century hysteria appears to have evolved from early-modern European possession illness (see chapter 5). Multiple personality disorder appears to have roots in nineteenth-century literature, in mesmerism, and in cases of dual personality (see chapter 6). Consistent with the hypothesis that recovered memories manifest illness behaviors, recovered memory therapy has deep roots, as well. In fact, recovered memory therapy represents the wholesale return of older clinical practices once considered outmoded.

Interest in trauma as a cause of illness was sparked by the poor saftey records of early railways, which were plagued by disastrous collisions.[5] Until the late nineteenth century, when signaling systems improved, hundreds of passengers were killed or maimed in such accidents each year. Some passengers even showed symptoms following railroad accidents—paralyses, seizures, or loss of sensation or strength—although they had no obvious injuries at the time of the collision. Puzzled by how symptoms could occur in the absence of obvious inuries, a British surgeon, John Erichsen, argued that shocks and concussions due to railroad accidents could damage the nervous system without demonstrable lesions. He coined the term "railway spine" to describe such cases. Within just a few years of Erichsen's publication, however, Charcot and the Salpêtrists found that railway spine could be treated hypnotically. Charcot concluded that symptoms that arise after accidents were caused not by physical shocks but by traumatic ideas. To show that ideas alone could produce disorders in brains predisposed to illness, Charcot and his colleagues caused symptoms of railway spine to appear in hysterical patients by means of hypnotic suggestions.

Noting the similarity of symptoms of railway spine and idiopathic hysteria, Janet applied Charcot's theory of railway spine to ordinary hysterics.[6] Assuming that such hysterics differed from patients in accidents only in being unable to report the relevant traumas, he hypnotized them to uncover the past traumatic events responsible for their illness. It is important to note that the memories Janet uncovered were far removed from the kinds of memories therapists find today. For example, one patient, called Marie, was hypnotized to recall her first menstrual period, which, being unexpected, caused an embarrassing accident. Another patient, Lucy, had been frightened at age nine by a practical joke.

In *Studies on Hysteria*, published in German in 1895 and in English in 1909, Josef Breuer and Sigmund Freud discussed the case of Anna O.[7] Since Breuer had treated Anna in 1880, he would seem to have priority over Janet and the Salpêtrists in treating hysterical memories, but in fact it appears that the case was retrospectively crafted to establish this claim artificially.[8] In 1880, Breuer had yet to conceive the idea that memories could cause hysteria. Anna, who was 21 years old at the time of her treatment, was partially paralyzed, often spoke nonsense, saw snakes that were not there, threw tantrums, and threatened to kill herself.[9] Each of her symptoms was cleared up as, in a trancelike state, she recalled the inciting events responsible for their occurrence. The story of Anna O.'s treatment, along with other cases in *Studies in Hysteria*, played a critical role in spreading outside France the notion that traumas could cause hysterical illness.

On the basis of documents not previously available, Mikkel Borch-Jacobsen argued that Anna 0.'s symptoms not only were not caused by trauma but were actually iatrogenic and started with Breuer's involvement.[10] Also, although Freud and Breuer described Anna O. as greatly improved by Breuer's memory therapy, Borch-Jacobsen showed that in fact she wasn't improved at all. Anna O., who later in life helped found the social work movement in Germany, never had positive words for Freud or his methods of treatment.

Freud later recanted his early traumatic theory of the origin of hysteria and instead evolved the theories and methods of psychoanalysis. However, as traditional psychoanalysis has lost intellectual clout, some modern-day psychotherapists have looked back to early Freud and to Janet's work from the 1880s, according to which unremembered traumas cause psychopathology. They dusted off hypnosis, long marginalized in psychiatry, and started using it pretty much as did Janet and Freud. In helping to trigger this flight of therapists to the past, the well-known former analyst Jeffrey Masson claimed that Freud abandoned his early, trauma-based theory of illness because it was too controversial.[11] According to Masson, Freud lost the courage to document the high rate of child abuse reported by his patients. A careful reading of Freud's early cases, however, shows that Freud suggested traumas to his patients and pressured them to acknowledge these. There is little reason to think the reports Freud was hearing were real.

The widespread appearance of shell shock in soldiers who had endured trench warfare during World War I further strengthened the seeming link between trauma and illness.[12] While the term "shell shock"—like "railway spine"—implied a physical cause, the concussion of falling shells, for neurological symptoms, physicians in World War I increasingly came to view the syndrome as caused by traumatic memories. Patients suffering shell shock had paralyses, gait disorders, and symptoms, like camptocormia (see chapter 5), indicative of hysteria, for which a traumatic memory account already existed. W. H. R. Rivers, a British army physician specializing in shell shock, advocated treating patients with shell shock with a method that resembled

Janet's method for treating hysterical illness. Like Janet and Freud, Rivers is sometimes hailed as an early recovered memory therapist, but, as with Janet and Freud, the truth is less clearcut.[13] Rivers thought that soldiers cited remembered traumas as a way of explaining their symptoms, not that the traumas really had caused their disorders.[14] Since the 1970s, posttraumatic stress disorder (PTSD), a successor to shell shock, has been widely diagnosed, especially in veterans of the Vietnam War. The extent to which present-day patients said to have PTSD are enacting illness behavior is not dealt with here. A study by Allan Young, a medical anthropologist, provides essential background reading on this question.[15] As Harold Merskey observed, even if traumas do cause some mental disorders, disorders due to trauma little resemble the illnesses described by recovered memory therapists.[16] Anxiety and depression are the dominant symptoms, not "dissociation" or somatic symptoms.

Evidence in Favor of the Recovered Memory Model

Studies that do not rely on recovered memory procedures suggest that parental neglect and abuse or early sexual abuse are in fact associated with later psychopathology and especially with borderline personality disorder. Patients with borderline personality disorder are emotionally unstable and prone to self-injurious behaviors, to drug abuse, to alcoholism, and sometimes to criminal acts. They have particular problems modulating their anger and maintaining relationships. The reader will recall that patients with MPD are often borderlines. With respect to early abuse, Bryer and colleagues administered questionnaires to 66 female patients admitted to a private psychiatric hospital.[17] Fifty-nine percent of the subjects reported physical and/or sexual abuse prior to age 16. The degree of abuse predicted the women's psychopathology scores, and severe abuse was common among the borderline patients. Bryer and colleagues suggested that childhood physical and sexual abuse are major factors that affect illness severity ratings in adult mental patients.

Zanarini and colleagues administered a standardized interview concerning early experiences to 467 psychiatric inpatients with personality disorders.[18] The patients were hospitalized at McLean Hospital in Belmont, Massachusetts, between March 1991 and December 1995. Ninety-one percent of the 358 patients who met the DSM-IIIR diagnostic criteria for borderline personality disorder reported having suffered abuse as children. Seventy-two percent reported having been subject to emotional abuse, 76 percent to verbal abuse, 59 percent to physical abuse, and 27 percent to sexual abuse by their caretakers. Fifty-six percent reported having experienced sexual abuse by someone other than the caretaker. The 109 subjects with other personality disorders also had high rates of abuse, but these were significantly lower than the rates for the borderline subjects in all categories.

Brodsky and colleagues administered standardized tests and interviews to

60 consecutively admitted borderline female inpatients at the New York Hospital-Payne Whitney Psychiatric Clinic in 1992.[19] Sixty percent of the patients reported having been physically and/or sexually abused. Consistent with the results obtained by Bryer and colleagues, high scores on abuse severity predicted more severe illness.

Figueroa and coworkers administered standardized tests to 47 patients with borderline personality disorder and to 16 patients with major depressive disorder hospitalized on a general psychiatry unit at the University of Michigan at Ann Arbor and to 15 normal controls.[20] Seventy-nine percent of the borderline patients, 31 percent of the depressed patients, and 20 percent of the controls reported having experienced some form of childhood sexual abuse. Within the sample as a whole, reported abuse predicted higher severity scores on two measures of general psychopathology.

However, these studies do not prove that there is a causal relationship between specific incidents of abuse and later psychopathology, as the recovered memory model requires. Abuse in general, and sexual abuse in particular, may be a marker of a chaotic environment in which children's needs for nurturance and security go unmet or of parental dysfunction due to alcoholism or mental illness. If so, the seeming effects of abuse on later psychopathology may really be the result of growing up in a chaotic environment or even of carrying genes inherited from disturbed parents. In line with the first suggestion, Nash and colleagues administered standardized tests to 56 women who reported having been sexually abused and to 49 women controls.[21] One of the tests given was the Family Functioning Scale, which is designed to elicit ratings of subjects' families of origin on such variables as cohesion, sociability, democratic style, authoritarian style, and conflict. Reported childhood sexual abuse was associated with more severe psychopathology as revealed by standard tests, but this effect was mediated by the perceived environment in the family of origin. That is, a typical subject who reported sexual abuse had no more psychopathology than one who did not report sexual abuse as long as their family environments were more or less alike. Rather than being the cause of the problem itself, the authors note, sexual abuse "may be a signal variable that the home environment is profoundly and broadly pathogenic."[22] Subsequent impairment may be less an effect of abuse than of the broader context in which such abuse occurs. A similar finding was reported by Fallon and colleagues, who studied bulimic women,[23] and by Mullen and colleagues, who studied sexual abuse in a community sample of women.[24] Other studies have only deepened this controversy.[25] The second, genetic hypothesis is more difficult to test, but it should be given some credence in light of recent research showing that unstable affect is strongly determined by genes.

Also, if repression and dissociation are responsible for illness, as the recovered memory model requires, then the most severely ill patients should tend not to report abuse. Yet, in four of the studies I have described, reported abuse predicted more severe psychopathology.[26]

Consistent with the recovered memory model, some women abused as children are not aware that they were abused. This has been demonstrated in case reports, several of which are discussed later, and in one especially well-known study conducted by Linda Meyer Williams, of the University of New Hampshire.[27] In 1990 and 1991, Williams located and interviewed 129 women, ages 18 to 31 years, resident in a large northeastern city. From city hospital records, all of these women were known to have been sexually abused between April 1973 and June 1975, at an average age of 8 years and 3 months. In 60 percent of the cases, the abuse had involved sexual penetration, and, in 62 percent, some type of force had been used. In slightly more than half the cases, the abuser had been a family member. Subjects were asked to participate in a "follow-up study of women who during childhood received medical care at the city hospital."[28] In the course of wide-ranging interviews, during which they developed good rapport with the researchers, the subjects were asked to detail each specific incident of abuse they had suffered as children.

Thirty-eight percent of the interviewed subjects neither recalled the index incident, for which they had been examined at the hospital, nor any episode of abuse by the same perpetrator. One subject, for instance, repeatedly and calmly denied abuse. When she was asked if anyone in her family had been in trouble as the result of sexual behavior, she at first answered "no," and then recalled her uncle. In the subject's words, "I never met my uncle (my mother's brother). He died before I was born. You see, he molested a little boy. When the little boy's mother found out that her son was molested, she took a butcher knife and stabbed my uncle in the heart, killing him."[29] In fact, according to records from 1974, the subject, then four years old, had been molested by the uncle she later could not recall knowing. The uncle was killed by the mother of the subject's four-year-old playmate, after she learned (from the subject) that he had also molested her son. The subject had forgotten her own role in this family disaster, which she then placed before her birth.

Williams's subjects were not simply too shy to talk about an embarrassing matter. More than two-thirds of the women who could not recall the index events nonetheless reported unrelated episodes of childhood sexual abuse. Only 16 (12 percent) of Williams's subjects recalled no abuse at all. They also divulged embarrassing aspects of their adult sexual histories. Also, although many of the subjects, like the subject described earlier, were very young at the time of the index episode, most were old enough that their lack of recall cannot be attributed simply to infantile amnesia. There is general agreement among memory researchers that events that occur before four to five years of age are seldom recalled in adulthood. Seeming exceptions are likely to be due to later discussions of family events, rather than to direct recall. Yet 28 percent of the 87 subjects who were at least seven years of age when the abuse occurred did not recall the abuse. The maximum age of subjects at the time of abuse was 12. Twenty-six percent of the 51 subjects who were 11 or 12 years old when they were abused did not recall being abused.

Critics of recovered memories, though, argue that William's data are at best inconclusive with respect to the model used by recovered memory therapists. In a comment on William's paper, Loftus, Garry, and Feldman note that even adults forget moderately unpleasant events, presumably for reasons other than repression or dissociation.[30] They cite studies, for instance, that show that large proportions of adults fail to recall serious motor vehicle accidents in which they were involved nine to 12 months previously, having been hospitalized nine months previously, or HMO visits made for serious or very serious illnesses within the previous year. If 15 to 25 percent of adults forget serious incidents that occurred less than one year before, these authors argue, then it is not surprising that some of William's subjects forgot events that had occurred 17 years earlier. Loftus, Garry, and Feldman criticize Williams for making forgetting "appear exotic."

Normal recall, especially of early events, is strongly influenced by later conversations with others. Events not discussed at all are more likely to be forgotten, while false versions heard from others may replace true recollections.[31] Among Williams's subjects, women with close relationships to the abuse perpetrators were somewhat more likely to have forgotten that they were abused. Possibly, families found it easier to talk about strangers' misdeeds than about similar crimes committed by family members. Williams' provided no data regarding such family patterns. With respect to the subject quoted earlier it would be useful to know whether her parents had fostered the false version she later repeated. If so, one would view her own report in a different light.

The recovered memory model suggests that subjects able to repress or dissociate memories of the index episode may also repress or dissociate other traumatic memories. However, in Williams's study, whether or not subjects recalled the index episode had no effect at all on reports of other abuse. Also, since the model attributes pathology to repression or dissociation, it suggests that nonrecallers should be more disturbed than those who remember their abuse. In her paper, Williams provided no data on psychological problems other than substance abuse, in respect to which no difference was found between those who did and did not recall the index episode. However, since substance abuse is a major feature of borderline personality disorder and is commonly cited as a manifestation of repressed or dissociated memories, the negative finding suggests that the two groups do not differ with respect to psychopathology.

Finally, as Loftus and colleagues observe, Williams's study does not show that missing memories can be accurately restored through procedures like those used by so many therapists. Williams did note than one-sixth of the subjects who recalled the index episode claimed that they had forgotten it at some earlier time. However, since ordinary forgetting can be reversed by reminders, while repression or dissociation are supposed to be more robust, spontaneous memory renewal like that Williams's subjects report is actually most consistent with ordinary forgetting.

A study by Della Femina and coworkers of young adults who had been incarcerated during adolescence also revealed subjects who denied having been

victims of documented abuse.[32] However, all of those who agreed to be rein-
terviewed later acknowledged memories of having been abused. Neither the
subjects nor the procedures were comparable to Williams's, so the implications of Femina's study for Williams's work are uncertain.

Briere and Conte obtained questionnaire data from 450 patients, 420
of whom were women, who reported having been sexually molested as
children.[33] Two hundred and sixty-seven (59 percent) of these subjects reported having had a period, sometime before age 18, during which they had
not had any memories of being abused. This figure is strikingly higher than
that obtained in Williams's study and suggests that something more than
simple forgetting may have been at work in Briere and Conte's sample.
However, Briere and Conte's subjects were recruited through therapists who
belonged to an "informal, nationwide sexual abuse treatment referral network" and were probably mostly patients who had undergone some form of
recovered memory therapy or who were self-selected for belief in recovered
memories. Briere and Conte noted that "misrepresented" memories may
have confounded their findings, but they dismissed such concerns on the
basis of their own "clinical experience." Similar remarks apply to a study by
Herman and Schatzow of a group of 53 women in "incest survivor" group
treatment.[34]

A number of case reports describing individuals who forgot seemingly
proven early abuse and later recovered their memories of it have been offered
in support of the recovered memory model. A 52-year-old woman described
by Nagy had suffered from panic attacks for 27 years.[35] The patient was the
younger of two sisters and the mother of three grown children, and she had
formerly acted in commercials. After she failed to benefit from cognitive-
behavioral therapy, she was offered hypnotic treatments for the purpose of
symptom relief. In the eighth hypnotic session, the patient recalled feeling
trapped when she was four or five. She remembered an odd, frightening figure and a shed near a lake where her family once took summer vacations.
During a later session, she pictured her father undressing and raping her in
the shed. As she described this occurrence, she wept, cried out in fear, and
experienced pain and nausea. Several sessions later, she described an episode
of forced oral copulation, which occurred when she was three. Later hypnotic
sessions produced more accounts of rape.

Significantly, when the patient's own daughters had been six and seven
years old, the patient's father had displayed himself to them in the bathroom
of her house on the pretext that they should be knowledgeable about male
anatomy. Her daughters, in their mid-30s at the time the patient was
treated, both acknowledged continual recall of this event.

After eight months had passed, during which the patient was said to have
"processed" her recovered memories, she confronted her father about the
memories she had recovered as well as about the episode involving her two
young daughters. Her father had had several strokes, but he understood her
charges and vehemently denied them. Three months later he died. In a cigar
box on his nightstand were found a dozen sexually oriented photographs, in-

cluding nude pictures of the patient's mother and of the patient, taken when she was as young as three years old. The backdrop for some of these photos strongly resembled the shed she had recalled in hypnosis. The patient continued in treatment for about two years longer, during which time her panic attacks greatly improved, though with periodic relapses.

Martínez-Taboas described two patients whose recovered memories seemingly were confirmed.[36] "Madeline" was a 28-year-old woman with a 10-year history of suicide attempts, blackouts, self-mutilation, "dissociative crises," and other symptoms thought to be consistent with multiple personality disorder. Before being treated by Martínez-Taboas, she had recalled several episodes of childhood abuse. A written account of these episodes contained several handwritings, suggesting that the memories were carried by separate alters. The patient had been referred to Martínez-Taboas, a specialist in dissociative disorders.

In her first session with Martínez-Taboas, Madeline showed him some drawings, based on "flashbacks" she had experienced during the previous week, that showed a figure tied to a bed in a room with chimes by the door. Martínez-Taboas was allowed to speak with a male alter who called himself Andrés. Andrés was also the name of a cousin of Madeline's, nine or 10 years older, who had lived nearby when she was a child. In subsequent sessions, the alter calling himself Andrés claimed to have repeatedly raped Madeline as a child. Sometimes, he claimed, he had tied her to her bed. He stated that he lived nearby and had the trust of her mother. He admitted having threatened to kill Madeline if she revealed the truth.

Madeline's parents confirmed that Andrés had been a frequent visitor to their house when Madeline was between five and ten years old. They also recalled chimes near her bedroom door. Madeline and her mother took an overnight trip to New York, where Andrés then resided, in order to confront him, but in New York, fearing that Andrés would be less forthcoming in her mother's presence, Madeline decided to visit Andrés alone. In a private meeting with Madeline, Andrés admitted abusing her and tying her to her bed. He told her she had seemed to be in a trance at these times. Back in Puerto Rico, a cousin revealed that she, too, had been molested by Andrés.

A second patient, Evelyn, was a 32-year-old woman with a long history of suicidality, depression, psychogenic seizures, memory lapses, and command auditory hallucinations. Martínez-Taboas was consulted after Evelyn spontaneously seemed to enter a trance in her psychiatrist's office. In her first interview with Martínez-Taboas, Evelyn was replaced by a hostile alter called Rongal, who claimed to be responsible for her suicide gestures. Since Evelyn had MPD, Martínez-Taboas suspected she had been abused as a child, but, in subsequent interviews, Evelyn had no memories of having suffered abuse.

Shortly after a family meeting in which she participated, Evelyn's older sister requested a private meeting with Martínez-Taboas. She told him she had suspected her sister had MPD. She told Martínez-Taboas, "I know why my sister has multiple personality disorder. My father is a very sick man. When I was about 13 years old he raped me at night; after finishing with me he entered Evelyn's room to do the same. That went on and on for many months. I had never talked about that with Evelyn. I always supposed that she knows." Evelyn's older sister had told her mother about the sexual molestation, but the mother did nothing about it. The older sister left the family home at age 16.

Martínez-Taboas did not give this information to Evelyn. Five months later, Evelyn, who by then had shown several alters, reported that she sensed another alter emerging. The alter, a seven-year-old girl, was crying and trembling. She reported being molested by her father. In response to Martínez-Taboas's question about where she was being touched, she pointed to her genitals. The child alter said she didn't want to talk about it. When the child alter had "left," Martínez-Taboas told Evelyn what her sister had told him. In a later session, the child alter confirmed the sister's story, and, later, "co-conscious" with Evelyn, it showed Evelyn images of how she had been molested.

A case described by Duggal and Sroufe is especially interesting, since the subject was not in therapy at all, and the abuse and amnesia came to light incidentally.[37] "Laura," as the authors call her, was enrolled in a prospective study of child development from the age of six months. Laura's parents separated when she was two years old, and they divorced when she was three years, nine months old. Laura spent equal time each week with both parents. Shortly after her fourth birthday, Laura's preschool teacher observed what appeared to be sexualized behaviors indicative of abuse. When Laura was four and a half years old, her mother informed the researchers that Child Protection Services had been involved with Laura; Laura had reported that her father had fondled her. Although Laura's father, an alcoholic and drug abuser, denied abusing Laura, he agreed to see her only for one-hour periods three times per week with a third party present. There was insufficient evidence to completely stop visitation. Laura was seen by a therapist, whose notes documented that Laura had indeed made these reports. She continued seeing this therapist for at least ten months. Collateral evidence strongly supported the belief that some abuse had occurred.

At an assessment conducted at the end of the first-grade, the researchers learned that Laura had told her first-grade teacher that her parents had divorced because her father was abusing her. She was once again spending some nights with her father, and, although her mother was concerned for her safety, Laura reported that her father no longer abused her. In the third grade, Laura again was seen in psychotherapy. Therapy notes confirmed that Laura recalled the abuse.

When Laura was reassessed at ages 12 and 13, no information about abuse was obtained. At age 16, however, Laura was interviewed and asked the following question: "Have you ever been sexually abused? Sexual abuse is when someone in your family or someone else touches you in a place you did not want to be touched, or does something to you sexually which they shouldn't have done." Laura responded "no." Similar questions were asked at an interview one year later. Again, she denied abuse. On both these occasions, she answered without hesitation and seemed to be quite sincere.

During an interview when Laura was 18 years, 10 months old, she responded to a question on sexual abuse by telling the interviewer that within the previous few months she had remembered being abused by her father. During a conversation with her boyfriend about first memories of parents, Laura had recalled her father kissing her on the cheek in a way that seemed highly sexual. Although she couldn't remember anything after the kiss, she felt that her father was naked and that something had happened between them. A week or two later, Laura discussed her memory and her feeling she had been abused with a female teacher with whom she had a good relationship. Later, her mother was told. Her mother asked Laura whether she recalled being in therapy as a child. Laura did recall the therapy, but not the reason for it. She remembered the changes in visits with her father, but she thought that these had occurred because an uncle who smoked marijuana was living at her father's house. Laura's mother was taken aback that Laura did not recall being abused by her father. Although they had never discussed it, she assumed Laura remembered.

These cases and others support the recovered memory model, but their significance is open to some doubt. Nagy's patient, for instance, recovered memories for events involving herself and her father, in the course of which she was undressed. In this she was aided by what had happened with her daughters—knowing that her father had exposed himself to her daughters, it must have occured to her that he might have done so with her—and by the effects of hypnosis on accurate (as well as inaccurate) recall (see chapter 4). Yet, we do not know from Nagy's account whether her memories were correct in detail. Did the father rape her and coerce her to have oral sex, or did he simply take photographs, which is all the hard evidence proves? The memories of rape and fellatio may be the inaccurate fantasies that so often accompany accurate recall during hypnosis. The fact that her panic attacks improved after treatment with Nagy can be taken as evidence for the ill effects of repression, but panic attacks can improve with nonspecific treatments. The patient's recovered memories, whether wholly accurate or correct only in parts, gave her reason to think that she now could understand her attacks, which in itself could have produced some degree of symptom improvement. The cure, in any event, wasn't complete or definitive; the patient suffered relapses. Finally, Nagy's case doesn't speak to the validity of recovered memory therapy, in which patients are urged to recall presumed instances of abuse. Nagy specifically noted that incest had not been discussed prior to her recalling the incidents with her father.

Regarding Martínez-Taboas's cases, the only direct confirmation of Andrés's abuse of Madeline is Madeline's word that Andrés confessed. Deceitfulness and lying are common problems among borderline patients, and Madeline was thought to have borderline personality disorder before she was diagnosed with MPD. A skeptic might wonder why, after flying to New York with her mother, Madeline decided to confront Andrés alone. Her cousin's report of having been abused by Andrés lends credence to Madeline's memories, but raises additional questions: How was the cousin abused? Was there any family lore about Andrés? How close were the cousin and Madeline? Unless the fact of an alter's reporting abuse by her father after five months of treatment is interpreted as a memory, Evelyn never really recalled being abused. The story obtained from her sister was later "confirmed" by the alter, but only after the story had been told to Evelyn. In neither case, moreover, is there strong support for the notion that repressed memories per se cause illness or that memory recovery dramatically improves subsequent health.

As for Duggal and Sroufe's report, there is no doubt that, sometime between the third grade and age 16 Laura forgot being abused as a child. But, although she later remembered that she had been abused, she never really recovered the memory of what happened. There is no evidence that she repressed or dissociated, rather than simply forgot, the fact that she was abused, nor did she suffer apparent ill effects of forgetting, as the recovered memory model predicts.

False Memories

The evidence in favor of the recovered memory model is equivocal, at best. Without benefit of recovered memory therapy, many patients recall being abused as children. Some people who have been abused do not recall it later, but there is no evidence that they have repressed it or that unremembered abuse causes mental illness. In a few cases, people who had forgotten that they were abused may have recalled their abuse. However, the evidence of their recall is sketchy and uncertain and fails to fully conform to the predictions of the recovered memory model.

Arguing against the recovered memory model, numerous highly detailed but implausible allegations have been lodged against well-meaning parents. Criminal and legal charges emanating from patients in recovered memory therapy have for the most part been found by courts and other authorities to be without merit. Loftus and Ketcham and Ofshe and Watters review this material admirably for interested readers.[38] In a growing number of cases, the patients themselves have retracted charges against their parents once they managed to free themselves from the influence of the treatment and thus from its role demands and rewards. The number of cases in which implausible charges have been made or in which charges have been retracted greatly outnumber the few ostensibly verified cases reported in medical journals. Whether this reflects the relative difficulty of proving that abuse occurred or whether it reflects a relatively large number of role-playing patients isn't entirely clear, but the problem has been severe enough to have attracted wide interest. Some parents dismayed by false charges have banded together to form the False Memory Syndrome Foundation, the aim of which is to provide legal and psychological assistance to others who have been falsely accused, only to find their foundation attacked by the memory therapists as a front for child abusers. Although it was initially limited to the

United States, the False Memory Syndrome Foundation has also opened branches in the United Kingdom and in Europe, following the spread of recovered memory therapy.

In many cases, the memories recovered by patients are implausible on their face. This is the case, for example, with ostensible memories of satanic ritual abuse, which began to supplant recovered memories of simple child abuse in the late 1980s.[39] Patients who recover memories of satanic ritual abuse claim to remember being forced by their parents to take part in organized satanic rituals with robed and masked participants, held in secret locations late at night, with many others present. Since satanic worship supposedly runs in families, grandparents are often also alleged to be involved. The patients recall chanting, sexual molestation, kidnapping, the murder of infants and children, ritual sexual intercourse, cannibilizing of babies, and human and animal sacrifice. Women are forced to be "breeders," to produce infants to eat. The patients claim to be "programmed" to have forgotten these rituals, rather than to have repressed them because they were so traumatic. They claim to be victims of mind control by satanists trying to kill them for having betrayed the cult. Some of them claim to be programmed to kill themselves or others if they hear or read a certain word or if they see an object with ritual significance. Their self-destructive and hostile acts are therefore not their fault.

There isn't a shred of evidence that satanic abuse like that reported by patients in recovered memory therapy actually occurs.[40] In spite of the fact that large numbers of patients report serious criminal activity, including kidnapping and murder, no physical signs can be found at any of the numerous sites identified by these patients. Nor are there large enough numbers of kidnapped or missing children in the United States to account for the numbers of victims whose killings have been reported. A conspiracy large enough to account for the patient reports would involve tens, if not hundreds, of thousands of coconspirators. As Kenneth Lanning, an FBI specialist in child abduction cases, observed, no conspiracy even approaching this size has ever managed to stay hidden from law enforcement or to avoid betrayal.[41] Investigators in the United Kingdom, where such allegations have spread, have reached the same conclusion: No supporting evidence exists.[42]

The folly of such allegations, and of the role of psychiatrists and psychologists in promoting them, is tragically shown by the well-known case of Patricia Burgus, a patient of Bennet Braun, a leader in the recovered memory field.[43] In the late 1980s, Burgus, a happily married, observant Catholic mother in Des Moines, Iowa, delivered her second child. The birth was traumatic, and the child, her second boy, was born with a broken and paralyzed arm. Although she had no previous history of psychological problems, Burgus developed a serious postpartum depression, which led to her seeing a therapist in Des Moines. She developed pseudocyesis, or hysterical pregnancy, and, before it was clear that she wasn't really pregnant, she referred to herself and her fetus using the plural pronoun. Although it had been Burgus's practice during her two pregnancies to refer to herself as "we," her therapist told her she thought she wasn't referring to herself and the fetus but to herself and alters. She asked Burgus and her husband what they knew about MPD and whether they had seen signs that she had the disorder. They had both seen the movie *Sybil*, and they agreed there had been no sign she had the disorder.

The therapy nonetheless centered on contacting alters. By Burgus's later account, the therapy sessions began by defining her current mood. Burgus would then be hypnotized and her mood state ascribed an identity, which she was then asked to role-play. Within a short while, as many as 30 alters had been given names such as "The Evil One," "The Religious One," and "Just Fine." Burgus lost track of the fact that she was playing roles and began to believe she had alters. Feeling hopeless and out of control, she stopped working and tried to kill herself. Six psychiatrists who evaluated Burgus in Des Moines doubted she had MPD, but her therapist convinced her and her husband that she needed specialized care. Burgus called the National Institute of Mental Health and was referred to Bennet Braun, who ran the Dissociative Disorders Unit at Rush-Presbyterian-St. Luke's Medical Center in Chicago, popularly known as Rush. Rush is one the best-known hospitals in the country. Braun, a well-known "expert" on MPD and recovered memories, had published a book on the subject and had been listed by *Good Housekeeping* magazine as one of America's outstanding psychiatrists. Burgus went to Chicago and was admitted to Rush. According to later court records, the then 29-year-old Burgus was distraught and agitated when she entered the hospital.

As a patient with MPD, Burgus presented a problem. Braun was deeply committed to his belief that MPD was caused by sexual abuse. When Burgus was admitted, Braun told her and her husband that 99 percent of multiples were abused. But Burgus denied abuse. She thought she had loving parents. Her response to Braun was, "I'm the 1 percent!" In the terms I have used in this book, she was willing to play the MPD role, which her therapist in Des Moines had suggested to her, but not the abuse survivor role that Braun seemed to think she should play.

Surrounded day and night by patients who had reported abuse and by staff who believed that she, too, had been abused, pressured in subtle ways to stop "denying" the abuse, and taking massive doses of medications that further confused her thinking, Burgus took less than a month to start recovering images of physical and sexual abuse she had suffered at her parents' hands. As it happened, however, this was only the start of the process. One month into treatment, Braun came to her room one evening and abruptly asked her if she had eaten people. She impulsively answered "yes" and then wondered why she had said that. Braun hit his fist on the door, which Burgus took to mean that he had suspected it all along. Over the next few months, Burgus recovered memories of satanic abuse dating back to her childhood. She described participating in hundreds of murders, rapes, and cannibalistic orgies. Moreover, she still was a satanist. In a "dissociated state," she herself was a high priestess in a satanic cult and had sexually abused her own children, then three and five years old, who had also taken part in murderous rituals. At Braun's urging, Burgus's sons were admitted to the locked children's psychiatric ward at Rush.

For the next two years, Burgus and her sons remained in Rush, she on Braun's dissociative disorders unit and her sons on the locked children's ward. She developed more than 300 alters. As each of these alters told stories of rape, murder, torture, and cannibalism, Burgus and Braun rushed to the children's ward to help her two sons recover memories of their involvement in the events thus recounted. Among other crimes they recalled, the two young boys confessed to killing and eating babies and to eating babies alive. In 1988, as her hospital bill was approaching the $1 million cap on her health insurance policy, Burgus was deemed to be fit for outpatient therapy. She was discharged, leaving her two children in the hospital.

Since Burgus's story sounds ludicrous, it is surprising how seriously Braun and others at Rush took it. Taking stories like Burgus's at face value, and oblivious to his own role in creating them, Braun is convinced that there is an international, transgenerational satanic conspiracy that he claims involves "pimps, pushers, prostitutes, physicians, psychiatrists, psychotherapists, principals and teachers, public workers, police, politicians and judges, and priests and clergy of all religions." Many other recovered memory therapists share Braun's delusion. Since Burgus had reported that her father and mother used the flesh of human victims to make meatloaf, Braun sent Burgus's husband to a barbecue at his in-laws' home. The meat he managed to steal was tested for human content in the hospital lab. The results, of course, were negative. The FBI was called, but they were unimpressed by Burgus's own confessions or by the reports she gave of her parents' involvement. According to Burgus, Braun concluded from this that the FBI had been corrupted. Burgus, a devout Catholic, had taken her first son to Rome to receive the Pope's blessing. According to Burgus, Braun thought the photograph of the Pope holding the infant boy proved that the Pope had molested him. The Pope, Braun suggested, was the head of the international satanic conspiracy. During Burgus's stay at Rush, items and presents sent to her were carefully screened by the staff. On several occasions, flowers sent to Burgus by her parents were confiscated. In a taped deposition, Braun testified that red roses with white baby's breath are satanic messages instructing the receiver to commit a bloody suicide. Pink roses or pink carnations with baby's breath instruct the receiver to commit suicide bloodlessly, perhaps by hanging. He told Burgus that her parents had sent her these flowers because she was exposing the cult's activity.

Just as religious cult members may lose faith in the cult ideology if they are sent away (see chapter 2), so Burgus began to doubt the reality of her memories after she left the hospital. She and her husband searched exhaustively near Des Moines for evidence of the murders she believed she had witnessed. Yet, in spite of the fact that they visited what she thought were the sites involved, no evidence could be found. She stopped taking the medicines Braun had prescribed, and her thinking seemed clearer. She realized she had no alters and that she was neither the victim nor the perpetrator of abuse. It had all been fantasy. She retrieved her children from Rush. Their benefits too, $1 million apiece, had nearly been exhausted by their two and half years in the hospital. It took Burgus nearly eight years to repair her relationship with her parents. The long-term effect on the two boys of spending more than two developmentally critical years on a locked psychiatric ward while confessing to horrendous crimes remains a question mark.

Burgus and her husband eventually sued Braun and Rush, winning an out-of court settlement of $10.6 million. At the time of the settlement, 10 other similar cases were pending against Braun and Rush. The Dissociative Disorders Unit was closed, and Braun became the object of an Illinois state probe, as the result of which he lost his medical license. While the action against Braun was justified, Braun himself was only the tip of an iceberg. Overenthusiastic recovered memory therapists are numerous, and cases as extreme as Burgus's are more common than anyone cares to admit.

Learning the Role of Survivor

Insofar as "abuse survivor" is a illness role, how is it acquired? One way, as the case of Pat Burgus illustrates, is to learn the role from a therapist committed to uncovering memories. Many therapists, like Braun, directly tell patients what they are expected to recall. However, role cues are also embedded in various treatment techniques. Patients, for instance, are given long lists of possible symptoms caused by child abuse, to see whether they have any. These symptoms are common and general, so every patient can claim some. Patients are urged to imagine or draw scenes of child abuse. When they produce such scenes, the scenes are called possible memories. Patients are told to keep journals of their thoughts on the theme of abuse. Dreams may be plumbed for concrete or symbolic themes of abuse, and bodily feelings and symptoms are treated as clues, as well. A pain in the wrist, for instance, may mean that one's hands were bound, while pelvic pain means rape. Hypnotic age regression is employed with suggestive instructions. Group therapy sessions with others who have recovered their memories put pressure on patients, as well. Those who persist in doubting that they were in fact abused may be told they are in denial.

From the very beginning, individuals who seek to learn the recovered memory role have had access to information in the popular media. The impetus for the spread of this particular role has not been completely dependent on the activities of professionals. One remarkable book, *The Courage to Heal: A Guide for Women Survivors of Child Sexual Abuse,* by Ellen Bass and Laura Davis, from Santa Cruz, California, has been especially important.[44] First printed in 1988, this book, with an accompanying workbook, has become a virtual bible in the incest survivor movement. Hundreds of thousands of copies of *The Courage to Heal* have sold, making it among the best-selling self-help books ever. Bass and Davis give workshops and sell audiotapes. The third edition of *Courage to Heal*, printed in 1994, includes a frontispiece with fervid quotes from "survivors." These capture the genuine feeling patients express for this book. One writer states, for instance, that the book was a "miracle" to her. Another observes that the book helped "reconstruct" her life. A third writer thanks the authors for saving her life and her sanity.

Like many therapists, Bass and Davis begin by informing their readers of symptoms caused by child sexual abuse, whether remembered or not. Among many other symptoms, for instance, survivors may feel bad, dirty or ashamed, powerless ("like a victim"), different from other people, or self-destructive or suicidal as the result of their abuse. They may hate themselves, be unable to trust their intuition, be afraid to succeed, or feel they have to be perfect. They may have trouble recognizing or expressing their feelings, be uncomfortable with anger or sadness, or be prone to depression or panic attacks. They may misuse drugs or alcohol or have eating disorders. They may have a hard time loving their bodies or "feeling at home" in their bodies. They may have physical illnesses "connected to" abuse, or they may intentionally hurt or abuse their bodies. Survivors may have trouble trusting others or making close friends or giving or receiving nurturing. They may get involved with people who remind them of their abusers, have trouble making commitments, and have multiple failed relationships. They may "cling" to people, live in fear of rejection, or have trouble saying "no." They may not enjoy making love, find sex disgusting, or have violent sexual fantasies. Survivors may feel uncomfortable around children, not feel close to children, abuse children, or be overprotective with children. They may have strained relationships with their families, feel "crazy, invalidated, or depressed" after seeing their families, or expect their families to change. There is hardly a problem in life that can't be explained by abuse, and there probably are few people who could not recognize themselves in some of Bass and Davis's symptoms.

Also, like many therapists, Bass and Davis provide instructions and cues for recovering memories of abuse. Bass and Davis, for instance, advise readers to be attuned to images, daydreams, slips of the tongue, bodily sensations, and emotional responses that might be clues to memories. By speculating on and fantasizing about the meanings of such events, readers can recover memories. Feelings of tension or anger may herald the emergence of memories; images and ideas that emerge at such times may have to be given more weight. True memories may be accompanied by feelings of shame or anger, guilt, shock, horror, terror, suicidality, or uncontrollable rage. Readers are advised not to doubt possible memories; to do so is a sign of continued denial. A written record of fragments, developed over months or years, helps shape as coherent a narrative of child abuse as is possible. To increase their commitment, readers are also advised to tell others what they've recovered. Survivor support groups and counseling also are recommended.

Bass and Davis also clue their readers in to the rewards of role playing. First, the survivor role, like possession, explains away poor behavior. Bass and Davis's readers, for example, are advised not to be ashamed of past drug or alcohol abuse, of promiscuity, of stealing, of lying, of gambling, of eating disorders, of having created chaos for themselves and for others, or of failures at work or in relationships. Each of these is seen as a consequence of abuse or as something the victim of child abuse had to do to ensure psychic survival. Like patients with MPD, those who have "survived" abuse may be excused by clinicians for past lack of improvement. Second, survivors are portrayed as honest and courageous. Their courage is manifest in their having survived their abuse and in their being willing to face and talk about their recovered memories; that is, in making what Bass and Davis call a "decision to heal." Finally, survivors are entitled to special consideration from others. In a chapter addressed to those who live with abuse survivors, Bass and Davis urge partners of survivors to listen compassionately to them, to cook hot meals for them, to do more child care, to do more of the housekeeping, to offer them extra comfort, and to be patient with them. Partners are advised that survivors may need to make even minor decisions, such as when and where to go out to eat, which movie to see, or where to hang a picture, in order to feel safe. Partners should see the survivor as "courageous and determined," rather than as sick or weak, and they should concentrate on the survivor's "strength and . . . spirit." Bass and Davis also promote survivor support groups, which may be especially appealing to isolated readers. Such groups are open to those who define themselves as survivors, but not to those who won't.

Two books, *Michelle Remembers*, by Michelle Smith and Lawrence Pazder, and *Satan's Underground*, by Lauren Stratford, have been widely credited with starting the epidemic of satanic abuse allegations.[45] *Michelle Remembers*, first published in 1980, is still widely thought to be truthful by recovered memory therapists, though their interpretations of it vary according to their beliefs. Michelle Smith was a young Canadian woman living in British Columbia who was treated by Lawrence Pazder, a psychiatrist in Victoria. A "Note from the Publisher" lists Pazder's qualifications, for the purpose of showing that he is more than a marginal figure. Aside from being a Fellow of Canada's Royal College of Physicians and Surgeons and a member of the American Psychiatric Association, Pazder served as chairman of the Mental Health Commission of the Health Planning Council for British Columbia and practiced on the staffs of two Victoria hospitals.

Smith was first treated by Pazder in 1973 for problems "rooted in her family background and upbringing."[46] At that time, she was in her early twenties. Her father, an alcoholic, had had violent fights with her mother, who died of cancer when Michelle was 14. Her father disappeared, never to be seen again, and Michelle, an only child, became a ward of her maternal grandparents. She was sent to a Roman Catholic boarding school, where, not being Catholic herself, she felt like an outsider. Her grandparents soon died, however, and she was effectively on her own. She attended a university in Victoria and began to see Dr. Pazder when she was still a student. Her specific complaints included fears of airplanes, spiders, and being left alone and unresolved grief for her mother, whom she still idealized. It appears from *Michelle Remembers* that Smith and Pazder considered her therapy completed by 1976, by which time Michelle had married and become pregnant, but the chronology is confusing.

In any event, in the summer of 1976, Michelle became distraught after she had a miscarriage. In discussing her grief with Pazder, she developed the strong feeling that she needed to tell him something, but she did not know what it was. A lengthy impasse ensued, during which Pazder thought Michelle was like "a pressure cooker with a blocked valve," in danger of exploding.[47] After several months, Michelle developed a rash, which seemed to confirm Pazder's judgment: Her body was trying to speak and thereby release the pressure. He began seeing her after hours in lengthy marathon sessions. Over the next 14 months, in hundreds of hours of sessions, Michelle repeatedly regressed to the age of five and described events in her life some 22 years earlier as if they were just occurring.

Smith recalled being held prisoner by a satanic cult for about 14 months when she was five years old. During this time she was sexually assaulted and tortured, observed and took part in murders, including the killing of babies, was nearly killed herself, was caged and confined in a satanic ritual effigy, had her teeth pulled, had horns and a tail surgically attached to her, witnessed the creation and re-animation of a Frankenstein-like monster, saw hell, and met Satan himself, whose attempted return to Earth was stymied by her resistance. According to Smith and Pazder, the five-year-old Michelle had been the pivotal figure in a battle of heaven and hell. The rash was a "body memory" of having been touched by Satan.

Why did Smith make up these stories? From *Michelle Remembers*, it seems obvious that these stories kept Pazder's attention and that Smith wanted to keep his attention at a time when therapy would otherwise have been ending, if it had not already ended. Her assertion that she had something important to tell him but could not remember what served to prolong their engagement for several additional months after Smith had miscarried. According to *Michelle Remembers*, Smith started recovering memories in the fall of 1976 only after Pazder consciously broke his usual rules with patients by agreeing to see her outside his office hours. During subsequent marathon sessions, sometimes held late at night, there was physical contact between them of an unusual kind. When she was frightened, for instance, Pazder held Smith's hand, sat close to her, or let her rest her head on his shoulder. Although both Smith and Pazder were married in 1976, when she miscarried, somehow they were later married to each other. They also, of course, authored *Michelle Remembers* together.

Smith and Pazder literally believed she had met Satan in the act of his coming to Earth at the behest of a coven. They consulted Roman Catholic priests and even went to the Vatican to alert Church authorities. Recovered memory therapists who are not religious accept Smith's memories as real, but they argue that she was deluded by her abusers, who pretended to conjure Satan in order to terrorize her. That both Smith and Pazder are self-deluded isn't viewed as a possibility, since to do so would be to admit that recovered memories can be false. Recovered memory therapists who do not believe in aliens use a similar logic to explain away recovered memories of molestation by aliens (discussed later). They assume that the molestation occurred but that parents rather than aliens were to blame. Patients who imagine that they were molested by aliens are said to be denying mistreatment by their parents.

Satan's Underground, which was first published in 1988, tells the story of Lauren Stratford, who claims to have recovered memories of abuse by Satan-worshipping pornographers that began when she was seven and continued after school and on weekends through her college years. Like Michelle Smith, Stratford recovered memories of ritual murder and infant cannibalism, and even of having borne three infants, one of whom was killed in a ritual and two of whom were killed in pornographic snuff films. The notion that someone can repress knowledge of three pregnancies and deliveries while maintaining a normal daytime life as a college student seemingly stretches the concept of repression past its breaking point. Nonetheless, three repressed memory therapists, including the well-known Los Angeles psychologist Catherine Gould, wrote an afterword endorsing *Satan's Underground* and cautioning readers against excessive doubt.[48] Like Pazder and Smith, Stratford believes in the devil and in the efficacy of the rituals she describes, and she credits Jesus with having helped her escape from the coven that had abused her.

As these books suggest, the satanic abuse story has been fueled in large part by religious feelings. Jeffrey Victor, a sociologist at the State University of New York, observed that allegations of satanic abuse are concentrated in areas with dense evangelical and fundamentalist populations, in other words, where many people believe in the literal existence of the devil.[49]

The religious and the therapeutic are hopelessly intermingled in the work of those pastor-therapists who employ the language and tools of recovered memory therapy for religious ends. A film by Anthony Thomas, produced in 1993, presented the work of one such pastor-therapist, Doug Riggs, of the Morningside Testimony Church, of Tulsa, Oklahoma.[50] In marathon therapy sessions, lasting up to 19 hours, Riggs contacted his parishoners' "dissociated" personality fragments, each of which carried memories of childhood satanic abuse, murder, and cannibalism. On film, Rigg's therapy sessions look as much like exorcisms as recovered memory sessions, and, in fact, some of the alters evoked seem to be thought of as real demons and are cast out in Jesus' name. The contortions and cries of parishoners during therapy sessions are thought of as "abreactions"; they supposedly represent bodily memories of tortures inflicted by satanists. By the time he was filmed, Riggs had verified satanic abuse in 14 of his parishoners, several of whom had more than 1,000 alters.

One parishioner, Pam, the daughter of a salesman from Omaha, Nebraska, had no memory of being abused before being treated by Riggs. When the abuse came to light, following Riggs's instructions, Pam cut off contact with her parents and with those in her family who denied that she had been abused. For some reason, Riggs believed that Pam's father, who had never traveled abroad, was an international satanist leader in charge of a project to gain "ritual control" of the American, English, French, and Russian governments, as well as of the Vatican. Although they had been raised in different parts of the country, each of the remaining 13 parishioners, including Pam's husband, Dan, who recalled being abused, claimed that Pam's father had been their chief abuser. When asked how so many people abused by one man from Omaha had come to attend the same small church in another state, parishioners claimed that Jesus had caused them to come together so that they could be healed by Riggs.

An especially interesting aspect of Thomas's film, which illustrates how a role can be used for social control, featured a young woman, Cynthia, whose religious, elderly parents also lived in Tulsa, where Cynthia had been raised. Cynthia's husband, Brad, explained to the interviewer that sexual problems had arisen in the early days of their marriage and that these indicated to him that "something had happened" to Cynthia. Cynthia, Brad complained, was also too close to her parents and overly influenced by them. In fact, Cynthia had been so strongly programmed that, even after receiving treatment from Riggs and becoming aware of abuse, part of her still loved her parents and wanted to see them again. It had taken a lot of treatment to break her of seeing her parents. In an emotional interview, Cynthia's parents explained how they had tried to resume contact with their only daughter, only to be frustrated by Riggs and by Cynthia's husband's influence. From the point of view taken here, Cynthia's husband used the social control of the church group to force Cynthia to separate from her parents. Once in treatment with Riggs, Cynthia could either adopt or refuse to adopt the survivor role Riggs demanded. In the first case, she would be choosing to cut herself off from her parents; in the second case, she would be choosing to give up the love of her group and possibly also her marriage. Riggs, after all, could declare that she was denying abuse and hence could not be cleansed of demonic influence. Cynthia chose to give up her parents rather than to endanger her marital and church ties, but, in talking about her ostensible programming by her parents, Cynthia hinted at insight into the bind she was in. "Sometimes it gets very confusing," she said, "as to . . . who is actually messing with my brain."

In the late 1980s, satanic abuse allegations made in the context of therapy created an epidemic of claims of current satanic abuse of children, especially in day care centers.[51] For one thing, it seemed logical to think that if people had been abused by well-organized cults 20 or 30 years previously, children would currently be at risk of such abuse. In addition, some misguided recovered memory therapists, thinking perhaps that catching satanic abusers "red handed" would give recovered memories of such abuse more credence, contributed to the fervor. As in the infamous McMartin Preschool case, such claims have never been backed by much in the way of hard evidence. What evidence has been produced appears to result from suggestive and even coercive interviewing techniques applied to very young children, who are thereby induced to be witnesses. A few unfortunate day care workers have been convicted by uninformed juries on the basis of such tainted evidence, but, in most cases, as in the original McMartin case, the charges have had to be dropped. A study by J. S. La Fontaine of cases of alleged satanic abuse of children in the United Kingdom found no evidence at all of organized abuse by satanists.[52]

The close link between recovered memory therapy and allegations of current satanic abuse is illustrated by *Satan's Underground*, which provides a list of "behavioral changes" that parents can look for to determine whether their children have fallen prey to satanists outside their homes.[53] Many of these putative signs of satanic abuse are sufficiently common in children that parents who believe in satanists will find some cause for alarm. Unwed mothers considering giving their infants up for adoption are warned of the risk of unwittingly turning their infants over to satanists; satanist couples pretend that they want to adopt an infant but are really just looking for victims to be used in satanic rites.

The Alien Abduction Syndrome

In recent years a new mental disorder has appeared, the signs and symptoms of which are attributed to abduction and sexual molestation by extraterrestrials.[54] Like patients who report having been ritually abused, most patients said to be suffering from alien abductions recall their traumas only after having been in therapy and often with the aid of hypnotic memory recovery techniques. However, patients who recall being abducted by aliens tend to be less troubled than those who claim to have been victims of human abuse. Claims of satanic abuse often complicate other illness roles, like multiple personality, or are made by individuals with severe personality or emotional problems, while claims of abduction most often appear in more normal settings.

Although the alien abduction syndrome, by which I refer to a constellation of psychological and physical complaints attributed to extraterrestrial abductions, is extremely rare, it illustrates in the clearest possible form basic findings common to several of the illness roles discussed thus far. It is therefore worth reviewing in some detail, in spite of its rarity. The findings it illustrates are (1) that the signs and symptoms of an illness role are shaped by culture-specific developments and may be further refined by therapists who train patients how to be ill; (2) that those who play an illness role must have certain requisite abilities and have something to gain by taking on the illness role, including group affiliation and special status; and (3) that therapists may have incentives to diagnose the illness and shape it if necessary. After describing the alien abduction syndrome and typical abduction memories, I show how this syndrome illustrates each of these several points.

In 1993, I attended the fourteenth Annual Rocky Mountain Conference on UFO Investigation, a meeting of abductees and their therapists in Laramie, Wyoming. The Rocky Mountain Conferences were started by Leo Sprinkle, an educational psychologist at the University of Wyoming who had been hypnotized and remembered being abducted by aliens. He began counseling other victims and started the annual conferences to provide a support group for them. An earlier annual conference had been described in the *Atlantic* by James Gordon, a Duke University psychiatrist with an interest in religious groups.[55] At the Rocky Mountain Conference and at other similar conferences I have attended since then, I had a chance to talk with numerous abductees. In the following section, I refer to some of these individuals and to their experiences, taking care to preserve their anonymity.

The Classical Abduction

What signs and symptoms precede memories of abductions? According to David Jacobs, a historian at Temple University who argues for the reality of alien abductions, abductees experience disturbing and otherwise inexplicable thoughts, feelings, and behaviors.[56] The severity of the impairment differs from case to case; most abductees are able to maintain their everyday lives, but others can no longer function. Some of the signs and symptoms Jacobs lists suggest anxiety or depression. Abductees have trouble sleeping and wake up during the night. They fear that someone will enter their room at night or that something will happen while they are asleep. They sleep with the lights, radio, or television on and frequently insist on locking their bedroom doors. Children insist on sleeping in their parents' room. When awake, abductees fear being left alone, especially in open places, and panic attacks may limit their activities outside the home. Sadness and tearfulness may lead to withdrawal from friends or even to suicidal gestures. Other abductees have mood instability; sometimes they feel euphoric, at other times they are depressed. They may have inexplicable feelings of anger toward others.

Some of the symptoms are sexual and may or may not be caused by anxiety or depression. According to Jacobs, some abductees report complete loss of sexual interest, while others report sadistic or masochistic fantasies. Some men become impotent or cannot ejaculate, while others become compulsive masturbators. Women fear visits to their gynecologists. Men and women alike feel sexual shame and guilt.

A third group of symptoms might be construed as positive evidence that abductions occur were it not for the fact that many of those who present with these symptoms have been exposed to abduction accounts in the popular media. According to Jacobs, many abduction victims report vivid dreams that feature alien beings or wide-eyed animals. Some are attracted to sexual partners who "look like" aliens, that is, who are short and dark. Some become obsessed with reading about UFOs. Even though they don't remember their own abductions, they experience strong emotions when reading about those of others. They experience memory lapses and cannot account for their whereabouts at certain critical times. Thinking about this upsets them.

Signs and symptoms cited by other authors include troubled relationships with spouses or with children, difficulties in the workplace, generalized feelings of dread, and feelings of persecution or of influence by others.[57] There are also widely cited physical signs of abductions. These include nosebleeds, aches and pains in the morning, and mysterious scoop-shaped scars (discussed later).

A patient with some of these symptoms may knowingly or by chance begin treatment with a therapist who specializes in alien abduction syndrome. Most of the patients described by John Mack, a Harvard psychiatrist who has written a book on abductions, were cognizant of his interest in abductions and chose him for that reason.[58] One patient, for instance, chose Mack after watching a CBS miniseries on abductions that portrayed a character based on Mack as a hero. Another patient chose Mack after learning about him through a UFO organization. Most of the abductees with whom I have spoken first learned of the syndrome from popular books and movies and then specifically sought out specialists in the field. Some, however, picked a therapist at random and later considered themselves fortunate to have happened upon one of the few clinicians aware that alien abductions are occurring.

The specialist in abductions begins by seeking evidence that favors an abduction.[59] The patient is closely questioned about the symptoms I have described. If the patient does not report them, the clinician repeatedly questions the patient about memory lapses, fears of being alone, sexual problems, nightmares about creatures or animals, or interests in UFOs. Questions are also asked about nosebleeds, which are considered significant even if they occurred only when the patient was a child. The patient is encouraged to carefully survey his or her skin, in the hopes of finding small scars he or she cannot account for. Children are given toy figures of extraterrestrials. Their play with these is scrutinized for evidence of abductions. Drawings of extraterrestrials are shown them to gauge their reactions. If need be, patients are given written materials explaining the signs and symptoms of alien abduction syndrome. Picture books are also available for children.

Patients who come seeking treatment for abduction syndrome will, of course, be happy to cooperate in this scenario by reporting lost time, dreams of aliens, and so on. However, even patients caught unawares by this line of questioning are likely to comply at least partially with the clinician, who after all is an authority figure and who speaks with some confidence about matters beyond the patient's knowledge. The specialist also conveys the promise of rewards for playing the abductee role (discussed later). In either event, the next step is hypnotic regression to recover memories of lost time periods. Most patients who are still cooperating by this point are sufficiently compliant to be hypnotized and to recover the requisite memories of abduction. If the patient is not hypnotizable, however, some therapists are willing to enter a trance in his stead, "telepathically" relive his abduction experience, and report it to him. This is considered hard work, though, and therapists prefer that patients relive their own abductions.

Here is the typical memory recovered using hypnosis: The patient recalls waking up in his bedroom or driving on a lonely country road. Peculiar lights appear through the windows or in the sky. If the abduction occurred at home, a dog may bark or whimper. If it occurred while the patient was driving, the car will begin to malfunction, and then the motor will die. Slender, humanoid aliens standing four feet tall appear in the room or on the road ahead. They have oversize heads and eyes, thin, straight lips, no ears or hair, and extremely long, graceful fingers. The victim may cry out, but others who are with him seem to be paralyzed. The humanoids touch the victim with a wand of some kind, leaving him unable to resist.

The victim then feels himself floating in the air and passing through walls and windows. As he rises up, he has a bird's-eye view of the surrounding area. Escorted by aliens, he enters a UFO. The walls are smooth and metallic, and the rooms most often lack corners. His clothes are removed, and he is made to lie naked on something like an operating table. Sometimes he is the only human in the room, but sometimes other naked people are seen on such tables. His hands and feet are restrained. Sometimes a taller alien with somewhat more human features enters the room at this point and appears to take control. He or the grays, as abductees call the smaller aliens, carry out what appears to be a detailed physical examination. Unfamiliar instruments and scanners are passed over the body. Some of these may give the aliens access to abductees' thoughts. Sometimes the aliens communicate with their victim by means of telepathy. They may try to reassure the victim that he will not be hurt.

A long needle with a small spherical object at the end may be inserted into the abductee's nose. Intense pain follows as the spherical object is pushed through the roof of the nasal passages into the brain. The aliens may explain that the spherical object serves to help keep them in touch. Abductees believe that these spherical objects are transmitters used by aliens to tag and follow their victims. This procedure causes the nosebleeds that suggest an abduction. Sometimes the spherical object is placed in the brain through the ear. Abductees sometimes report finding alien implants in their handkerchiefs after sneezing, and some of these implants supposedly have been scientifically analyzed. Some abductees have had brain scans to locate the alien implants and have tried to find neurosurgeons willing to remove them.[60]

Using a sharp, scooplike instrument, the aliens may take samples from the victim's skin. This is the cause of the scars sought by abduction therapists. Some sort of reproductive procedure usually follows. If the abductee is a woman, a tube may be inserted through the skin of her lower abdomen. Abductees believe this tube is used to examine the ovaries and perhaps to gather eggs. Some authors claim that abductees experienced such procedures long before physicians began using laparoscopes, but these claims are based on recently recovered memories. Alternatively, a probe may be inserted into the victim's vagina, or the victim may be raped by an alien being. If the abductee is a man, a hose may be placed on his penis to extract his semen. A few male abductees report having had sexual intercourse with female aliens.

When these procedures are finished, abductees are allowed to rise from the table, dressed, and floated back to their homes or cars. If he is returning home, the abductee immediately falls into a deep sleep. In the morning, he may be sore or bruised, presumably from being moved about by the aliens, but he has no memory of the abduction itself. If he had been abducted from his car, he will come to behind the wheel, only to realize later that an hour or two had passed of which he has no recall. The aliens are sometimes careless in dressing their victims. Some abductees, for example, have later found their underwear mysteriously reversed, or their shoes on the wrong feet.

In further hypnotic sessions, patients may recover memories of other abduction events. The aliens are believed to repeatedly abduct victims, whom they are able to locate by means of tracking devices, perhaps the small spherical objects placed in the victims' brains. Abductions usually start early in childhood and intensify when the victims reach reproductive maturity. Parents of abductees sometimes recover memories of being abducted themselves, leading to the widely held theory that abductions, like ritual abuse, run in families. The aliens are believed to have chosen whole families to study. In many cases, mothers have claimed that their children are offspring of alien fathers. These human-alien hybrids often report being abducted themselves to meet with their "off-planet" fathers.

A case described by a clinical psychologist at one conference illustrates multigenerational family abductions. The patient, a seven-year-old girl, was referred for psychological evaluation by school authorities after they noted that she was unusually withdrawn in her kindergarten classes. The parents also reported that their daughter had become more withdrawn over the preceeding two months. The psychologist, who was attuned to the danger of alien abductions, inquired about nosebleeds and unexplained skin lesions. The child had had a nosebleed several months earlier, so the psychologist gave her toy aliens to play with. The pattern of her play suggested that she had been traumatized by just such alien creatures. With hypnotic regression, the girl recalled being abducted and sexually molested by aliens.

The case was more complex than a simple abduction, however. The child was sensitive and liked to draw, and her therapist recognized these as characteristics of human-alien hybrids. Other widely cited characteristics of hybrids include telepathic abilities and knowledge of past lives. The child's parents were hypnotized, and soon they, too, recalled their own repeated abductions by aliens. The mother recalled having had intercourse with an alien nine months before the girl's birth. Family discussions soon led to the grandparents' involvement. They, too, were hypnotized and regressed to their own abductions. Both grandmothers remembered insemination by aliens before the birth of the parents. The young girl herself, therefore, was no more than one-quarter human! Discovery of this history apparently led to improvement in the girl's social behavior.

Not all hybrid children are raised on Earth, however. Female victims report being abducted early in the course of some hybrid pregnancies. The aliens abort the hybrid fetuses and raise them in liquid-filled capsules, which may be shown to the mothers. Sometimes women are shown alien-human children, which they are told are their own, from pregnancies years before. Unlike the Earthbound hybrids, the children abductees see on flying saucers tend to have delicate limbs, large heads and eyes, and thin hair. They appear to be true intermediates between abductees and their captors. Women report being told that these hybrids need human affection. They are asked to hold or hug them on these occasional visits. Some women claim to have numerous "off-planet" hybrid children. One young woman, for instance, claimed to have borne nine hybrids. None of these pregnancies had been diagnosed by physicians, nor, since the hybrids were taken early, had they had much adverse effect on her overall health. Other women report being told by their doctors that they were pregnant, only to have the pregnancy unexpectedly disappear. They understood the cause for the disappearance only years later with the aid of hypnotic regression.

Authors who believe that abductions are taking place claim that there are other, unpublished details of the abduction scenario.[61] When reported by putative abductees, these serve to confirm the reality of their abduction reports. In any event, the details released to the general public are sufficient to cause speculation that the extraterrestrials are engaged in cross-breeding experiments. That is, families appear to be chosen for breeding with aliens, and the results of cross-breeding are then raised on earth or in spaceships. Some abductees have been told by their alien captors that alien genes are needed to transform the human race. Others have been told that the aliens are changing themselves in order to inhabit Earth. In either case, abductees carry an urgent message back to humankind.

The Cultural Setting of the Alien Abduction Syndrome

A complete cultural history of the alien abduction syndrome is beyond the scope of this book and of the author's skills. Suffice it to say that aliens have captured, if not our bodies, at least our imaginations. One measure of our fascination is the many popular movies, television shows, and books produced since the 1950s that feature aliens in one form of contact or another with humans. For example, the film version of *War of the Worlds*, released in 1953, was based on H. G. Wells's story of an extraterrestrial attack. *Invaders from Mars*, a 1953 release that was remade in 1986, showed aliens attempting to capture a small town. There are now three versions, produced in 1956, 1978, and 1994, of *Invasion of the Body Snatchers*, a story of alien entities who control human beings. *The Thing*, released in 1951 and remade in 1982, had a similar theme. *Close Encounters of the Third Kind*, released in 1977, showed aliens taking humans in their flying saucers. *E.T.*, released in 1982, showed a friendly extraterrestrial. *The Invaders*, a widely watched

TV show, aired for several seasons in the late 1960s. The hero of this series was aware that an extraterrestrial invasion of Earth was in progress but could not alert other people or trust the authorities. There have also been books on this topic. *Chariot of the Gods*, by the Swiss author Eric von Däniken, sold more than 50 million copies in the United States between 1970, when it was first released, and 1990.[62] According to von Däniken, superintelligent aliens landed on Earth between 10,000 and 40,000 years ago and mated with ancestral humans; many wonders of the ancient world were actually built by aliens, not by human beings. Von Däniken's book was the subject of TV specials.

Pilots in World War II sighted some oddly shaped vehicles, seemingly not made by humans, and reports of similar sightings continued after the war, when civilian pilots and passengers claimed to see flying saucers that sometimes showed up on radar. Official denials led to rumors of government coverups. UFO sightings were especially common around military bases and nuclear test sites. In July 1947, newspapers around the country reported the crash of a saucer near an airbase in Roswell, New Mexico. The air force quickly announced that a weather balloon had crashed, but the rumor that alien bodies had been recovered persisted. In 1980, a popular book documented an ostensible government coverup of the true facts of the incident.[63] Two movies, *Hangar 18*, released in 1980, and *Roswell: The UFO Coverup*, released in 1994, have been based on this book. Every president since Harry Truman has been asked to release information about the alien craft that supposedly crashed at Roswell. In response to pressure from a New Mexico congressman, the Clinton administration recently revealed that the material recovered at Roswell was from a type of balloon then under study for use in detecting nuclear weapons tests, but this revelation will certainly not satisfy believers. UFO buffs today believe that the U.S. government has made secret agreements to create alien bases in exchange for alien technical information. One such base, for instance, is "Area 51," a restricted military reserve north of Las Vegas, where stealth aircraft have been tested.[64] The television miniseries based loosely on *Intruders*, a popular book on abductions,[65] showed a psychiatrist based on the real-life John Mack defying an air force general who demands that he cease his studies of abduction victims.

Abduction reports grew out of this cultural interest in aliens, who for some people at least have taken the places of gods and spirits; that is, they are perceived as unseen movers responsible for great events.[66] The first abduction account was published in 1965 but ostensibly occured in 1957. A young Brazilian rancher, Antonio Villa-Boas, reported being forced aboard a flying saucer by four large-headed beings. They stripped him of his clothes and collected blood from a cut they made on his chin before leaving him with a small, naked female with thin blond hair, large eyes, and long, pointed hands. Villa-Boas had intercourse twice with this alien being and reported that he believed he had been used for breeding. A two-part story in *Look* magazine in 1966 revealed the abduction of Betty and Barney Hill five years earlier. According to this report, the Hills had been driving through the White Mountains, in New Hampshire, en route to their home in Portsmouth. Around midnight, they realized they were being followed by a white light in the sky. The next morning Betty called her sister, Janet, who suggested that she and Barney might have been exposed to radiation. When Betty discovered that a magnetic compass behaved erratically in the vicinity of their car, she began to read books about UFOs and government coverups of them. She contacted a UFO group, members of which spent 12 hours interviewing her and Barney and suggested to them that they had been abducted during a two-hour period they claimed they could not account for. There the matter rested until 1963, when the Hills consulted a psychiatrist in Boston to help them deal with emotional problems related to their interracial marriage. When hypnotized, Betty and later Barney recalled being abducted by aliens and subjected to the same kind of examinations now reported by others.

In October 1975 and again in September 1976, NBC aired a two-hour dramatization of the Hill abduction. This dramatization led to other reports of UFO abductions, the most famous of which was the case of Travis Walton, a young Arizona woodcutter. In November 1975, Walton was working in a remote region with five other men when a flying saucer landed nearby. Walton's coworkers fled and, when they realized he was missing, reported the incident to the local sheriff. Five days later, after a massive manhunt covered by national news organizations, Walton reappeared, claiming that he had been captured by extraterrestrial beings. Walton and his brother, who was among his coworkers, passed a lie detector test given them several months later. Travis Walton's account was the basis for the popular movie *Fire in the Sky*, released in 1993.

During the 1980s, two men in particular popularized the notion that humans are being abducted. Bud Hopkins, a successful sculptor and painter, had a longstanding interest in UFOs when he began to interview putative abductees. In his 1983 book, *Missing Time*, Hopkins insisted that abduction reports must be taken at face value, and he speculated that aliens create memory blocks to prevent their victims from telling others what has happened to them.[67] He called the abduction phenomenon an invisible epidemic. In response to his book and numerous talk show appearances, Hopkins received many calls and letters from individuals who believed that they, too, had been abducted by aliens. One of the people who wrote to Hopkins was Kathie Davis, whose experience Hopkins reported in his second book, *Intruders*, published in 1987.[68] Davis recalled being abducted by aliens, and she reported seeing some of her hybrid children on spaceships. The book featured photographs of ground markings left by spaceships and many of Davis's drawings of aliens. The CBS miniseries that was loosely based on *Intruders* and carried the same name was mentioned earlier.

Whitley Streiber is a successful writer of horror stories, several of which have been made into movies. In the best-selling 1987 book, *Communion*, he told the story of his own repeated abductions by alien creatures.[69] Streiber described a period late in 1985 during which he became irritable and confused, suffered from fatigue, was unable to sleep, felt watched and suspicious, and was often in despair. He had pain behind one ear and in his rectum, and he wondered whether he was mad or suffering from a brain tumor. After local UFO sightings were reported, he read a book on abductions and diagnosed his problem. The book mentioned Bud Hopkins, whom Streiber called for help. Hopkins recommended that Streiber consult a psychologist who specialized in abductions, but Streiber wanted a more objective investigation, so he went to see Donald Klein, a well-known research psychiatrist at New York State Psychiatric Institute. When hypnotized by Klein, Streiber remembered abductions that antedated his mental symptoms. His rectal pain, he learned, was caused by an alien probe. A magnetic resonance brain scan showed small lesions in the frontal and temporoparietal white matter. Such lesions are common in middle-aged patients, but Streiber apparently thought these might be probes in his brain. *Communion* ends with results of a polygraph test (Streiber passed) and with a statement by Donald Klein attesting to Streiber's sanity. According to Klein, Streiber is an "excellent hypnotic subject" who was not then suffering from a psychosis, anxiety, or a mood or personality disorder. Klein described Streiber as functioning well at a "high level of uncertainty."

In 1988, Streiber published a sequel, *Transformation*, in which he described still further interactions with aliens.[70] In *Transformation*, Streiber expressed the view that the aliens are the most powerful force now acting on human culture. He believes that they may be directing humankind's evolution; alternatively, they may represent an intrusion of another plane of reality into the mundane world. He described techniques for seeking and controlling alien contacts and endorsed the view, expressed by some other abductees, that the aliens' language may be a version of Gaelic.

Insofar as abduction reports reflect an American preoccupation with aliens, they should be limited to the United States. Until very recently, this has been the case. In other countries, moreover, reports of contacts with aliens have differed in fundamental respects from those of American abductees. The Brazilian rancher who had the dubious distinction of being the first abductee reported having intercourse with a small, blonde creature; in the United Kingdom, abductees report meeting tall, blond, blue-eyed aliens wearing animal skins. Abduction specialists have tried to account for such differences by claiming that different species of extraterrestrial beings have been active in different parts of the world.

Therapist Cues to Patients

Many of the individuals who seek treatment from alien abduction therapists do so with full knowledge of their special interest. They have been referred to these therapists by other abductees or by UFO or abductee organizations, or, in some cases, they have found their names in books. Most such patients are well read regarding abduction symptoms and need no coaching to provide abduction memories when suitably hypnotized.

Some patients, though, come to treatment without adequate preparation for the abductee role. They may have picked the therapist's name from the phone book, or they may have been referred by other professionals who had no knowledge of the therapist's interest in abductions. In discussions with therapists who specialize in abductions, I have heard them describe how they give such patients powerful role cues. Some therapists, for example, repeatedly ask about symptoms indicative of abductions, such as dreams of large-eyed animals, missing periods of time, or feelings of being watched at night, while steering attention away from other preoccupations. If the patient dwells too long on his earthly concerns—for instance, his marital problems—such therapists may suggest that apparently mundane problems can result from traumatic experiences the patient is not aware of. The therapist may give the patient reading material—for example, *Intruders* or *Communion*—after telling him that his symptoms resemble those of the abductees described in these books. This is a test suggestion, akin to tests for hypnosis. If the patient responds to the implicit role cue by agreeing that he might have been abducted, then he will likely recall his abductions when he is hypnotized. If he rejects the cue by saying he was not abducted or by making disparaging remarks, the therapist can still avoid a serious breach in their relationship by claiming that she gave it to the patient only because she thought he might be interested. Many such patients will later take up the implicit cue, in which case their early resistance is attributed to their defensiveness.

A few abduction therapists dispense with subtlety and simply tell patients the role that they expect them to play. They do so even when patients have given no clues at all that they are abductees. Such a therapist, for example, might tell a patient complaining of work-related anxiety that she has been abducted by extraterrestrial creatures and that she is to read all about it and come back the next week to be hypnotized. He might add that there are signs that she is an abductee and that, being highly experienced, he can save her the wasted expense of protracted evaluations. According to the therapists with whom I have spoken, surprisingly few patients approached in this way protest, and surprisingly many of them do their reading and return the next week, ready to play the role of an abductee.

These practices are not confined to poorly trained therapists but are typical of therapists throughout the abduction movement. Donna Bassett, a Boston writer, made up a story suggesting she might be an abductee and presented herself to John Mack, the Harvard psychiatrist who has championed abductees.[71] Mack, of course, could not distinguish her presentation or her faked hypnotic regressions from the equally fanciful accounts of his more sincere patients. Mack believed her story, even when she recounted meeting John F. Kennedy and Nikita Khrushchev on a spaceship during the Cuban missile crisis, sufficiently to place her in an abductee support group, of which she became the treasurer. More to the point, however, Mack gave Bassett reading material before her hypnotic sessions and asked obviously leading questions during her regressions. According to Bassett, it was clear what Mack wanted to hear from his hypnotized patients.

Role-Playing Abilities

Successfully playing an illness role requires that actors be able to ignore contradictory data. Victims of possession or MPD must somehow overlook the fact that they still have volition. Patients with conversion disorder must somehow overlook the fact that they can move, feel, see, or hear, depending upon their symptoms. At least some recovered memory patients must overlook the fact that their parents treated them well by many objective criteria. Persons who are unable to overlook contradictory data find it hard to mount convincing performances of any of these roles. The abductee role in particular seems fraught with contradictions. How, for example, can abductees have had multiple alien pregnancies without having menstrual problems? How are abductees removed when windows and doors are locked? How are abductees removed without their absence being noticed by others?

If need be, of course, abductees can fall back on ad hoc explanations. With respect to the questions I have just posed, for instance, abductees might claim that they have been programmed not to notice their missing menstrual periods, that the aliens pass through walls, and that observers are rendered unconscious. But, as I observed among those I met, abductees can also be careful to avoid facts that require such explanations. For instance, with the aid of hypnotic regression, one woman recalled having had a fetus taken from her when she was seven months pregnant with her oldest child, who was eight years old at the time of the hypnosis. She concluded that her child had a twin being raised on a spaceship. When asked if her obstetrician had known she was pregnant with twins and hence might have documented the disappearance of one of the fetuses, she stated that she had not had time to ask him about it. On the basis of recovered memories, another abductee reported stealing what appeared to be documents from aliens who had abducted him. On being returned to his house, he placed these documents in his dresser drawer, with the idea of hiding them should the aliens return. When asked to show these documents, he explained that he had since moved and that many of his papers and belongings were now in storage; he would have to search through hundreds of boxes in order to find them, something he had simply not found the opportunity to do. Other abductees report recovering alien probes from their nose or ears. Most of these putative probes look like dried mucous or ear wax. Few of the abductees tried to find out what they were.

Many abductees also appear to be fantasy prone. Readers will recall that fantasy-prone individuals are those who can readily substitute imagined events for reality (see chapter 4). Spanos and coworkers compared 49 subjects who responded to an advertisement seeking adults who had seen UFOs with 53 subjects who responded to an add for a personality study and with 74 psychology students at Carleton University.[72] Subjects were given structured interviews and various tests of imaginative propensities, including Wilson and Barber's fantasy-proneness scale. The UFO subjects were further divided into those who had seen lights or shapes in the sky (n = 18) and those who reported at least seeing craft close up (n = 31). None of the four groups of subjects (two UFO and two control groups) differed in fantasy proneness or on other tests of imaginative propensities. The researchers developed an index of UFO sighting intensity. At one extreme were subjects who had seen UFOs in the sky. At the other extreme were subjects who reported abduction scenarios like those described in this chapter. With the two UFO groups combined, the index of sighting intensity correlated significantly with measures of magical thinking and with fantasy proneness. The more complex reports of aliens were given by individuals who were more fantasy prone. The lack of difference between the four groups was probably a result of the dearth of subjects with complex reports. Of the 31 subjects in the more complex UFO group, only nine had three or more of the elements of an abduction. Spanos and colleagues suggest that less complex UFO sightings occur when individuals who believe in UFOs perceive ambiguous stimuli; fantasy proneness plays no significant role. Complex encounters with aliens, though, require fantasy proneness.

Benefits to Abductees of Playing a Role

In chapter 1, I argued that patients play illness roles because they have something to gain by doing so. The more difficult the role, the greater the gain must be to compensate for the effort. I have shown how some putative illness roles do serve functions for patients, as the role model suggests. These same functions are evident for the abductee role.

For example, illness roles can help patients explain their problems to themselves and to their families, while controlling to some extent the behavior of those around them. Consistent with this, one middle-aged abductee feared that his wife might leave him. His wife told me that, in spite of their frequent fights, she would not leave her husband while he was being abducted. She hoped that when the aliens stopped abducting him, the couple would once again get along. Another abductee's husband complained of his wife's sexual coldness. He stopped complaining when he learned that her sexual problems were caused by her past abductions, rather than by any lack of attraction to him. A young man reported that he had been failing his freshman college courses. He felt anxious and agitated, could not sleep at night, and was unable to concentrate on reading or lecture material. Having an interest in UFOs, he decided that his problems were caused by nighttime abductions, and he found a hypnotherapist to help him confirm his suspicion. The aliens apparently were wafting him from his dorm. He thought that other students were being abducted with him, but they were in "denial," so he could not talk to them about it. He felt less ashamed of himself now that he knew that his problems were not really his fault. An older man had never done as well in work as he or his family thought he should have done. He had held well-paying jobs, but he frequently fought with his bosses and was fired on several occasions. Discovery of his abductions accounted for his work problems. How could he get along with authority figures while he was being misused by powerful aliens?

The abductee role leads to membership in cohesive groups. Abduction therapists enroll patients in support groups, which, in many cases, serve as substitute families. Abductees I have met spend much of their time socializing with other abductees they have met in such groups or at local or regional conferences of abductees and therapists. Many of those in attendance at the Laramie conference, for example, come every year to renew their acquaintances with other abductees.

The abductee role stakes a claim to special knowledge and status. Through it, those who may feel like failures in their personal lives or at work become part of an exclusive group. Abductees view themselves as participants in the most important event in human history, our initial contact with aliens. They are privy to secrets the government is trying to cover up. Those who believe that the aliens are conducting genetic experiments believe that abductees are chosen for their genes. Multigenerational families of abductees are thought to have special genes, perhaps of alien origin, which presumably are superior to those found in other families.

Status competition between abductees is evident. Those who have merely been abducted are upstaged by those who discover that they are human-alien hybrids. Among the hybrids, those who claim their fathers are alien starship captains are upstaged by those who claim that their fathers command whole fleets. Abductees sometimes claim to have information from aliens, or to have been told that they will play special roles in human-alien intercourse or in human history. Some abductees, for example, claim to have been given alien engine designs and technical specifications. Several companies started by such abductees have sought venture capital. Others abductees report being told that Earth will suffer an environmental catastrophe unless humans change their ways. They report being shown this catastrophe on alien movie screens or by telepathy, and they claim that the aliens deemed them messengers to humanity. Others report being told that Earth will turn upside down on its north-south axis; the north pole will be where the south pole is and vice versa. In the course of this sudden disaster, California will break apart from the rest of the continent and sink into the ocean, and the Great Lakes will drain into the Gulf of Mexico, destroying much of the eastern United States. Three abductees I have met reported that they were told that they would play critical roles after this cataclysm. One man, an engineer, believed that he would organize housing for refugees in the Midwest. A woman believed that her warnings would save millions of lives. Another woman believed she would be taken aboard a saucer before the catastrophe. The aliens would later return her along with certain others to repopulate Earth. The millenarian roots of some such beliefs are obvious.

One group of abductees claims to be in telepathic communication with the aliens who abducted them. Some attribute their power to alien technologies—even to probes in their brains—but most believe their power derives from an internal source. Even "hard-nosed" UFO buffs are surprisingly credulous when it comes to abductee channels, as they call themselves. At one conference I attended, the audience listened attentively as an abductee read a message to conferees dictated by the commander of the "Ashtar fleet." The message urged conferees not to be discouraged by doubting Thomases like Carl Sagan, the well-known astronomer who criticized abduction claims. At another conference, two aliens who belonged to hostile races held peace talks through two abductees who acted as channels for them. These channels were thought to be helping to end a galactic war.

Insofar as some of these claims suggest that aliens are friendly, they undermine the view of abductees as traumatized victims. Therefore, they threaten to undermine the abductee illness role. In fact, abductees who make such claims sometimes say that abductions would not be traumatic at all if abductees could understand the good intentions behind them. They liken abductees' fear to the fear felt by animals being examined by veterinarians who have the animals' best interests in mind. Comparisons like this, of course, suggest that abductees who see no silver lining in the abduction experience are taking too parochial a view of their contact with aliens. More traditional abductees, who are anxious to maintain their traumatized status, sometimes respond by claiming that the aliens are deceitful. By tricking some abductees into saying nice things about them, the aliens hope to still humankind's sense of alarm. Not only are they not parochial; their opponents are just plain naive. At meetings of abductees, disputes over how to view aliens sometimes lead to open arguments and anger. The real issue, of course, is not who the aliens are but whether the abductee role is that of the traumatized victim or of the emissary from the extramundane.

In chapter 3, I alluded to data from I. M. Lewis showing that possession by ancestral or totem spirits may indicate one is chosen to be a "central" shaman, and to wield great moral authority by channeling such spirits.[73] Significantly, central shamans are frequently viewed as their spirits' spouses, and as parents of spirit children, or they may be viewed as the spirits' offspring in the material realm. Parallels with alien abduction are obvious. Some now see abduction as a painful process of contact with higher beings concerned with human morality. Some abductees believe they have children on alien ships, and some of them even see themselves as children of alien beings. The argument regarding aliens' moral status is really about the status of the abductee cult, that is, in Lewis's terms, which were cited in chapter 3, whether that cult is "central" or "peripheral."

Therapists' Gains from Treating Abduction Syndrome

The illness role model suggests that those who provide role cues must have motives for doing so. No one would bother to shape another person's behavior unless he or she expected to gain something from it. In fact, abduction specialists have many of the same motives for their behavior as do specialists in recovered memory therapy.

I will not dwell on financial motives for treating abductees. Suffice it to say that many abduction specialists are marginal mental health workers, such as hypnotherapists, whose practices might not be viable without such a specialization. As specialists in abduction, they advertise in local papers and on bulletin boards read by large numbers of people with unconventional views. For purposes of referrals, they also band together in networks of like-minded therapists. I am not aware of any data on how much they charge, but conversations with several abduction specialists lead me to think that their fees are generally as high or higher than is standard for other psychotherapists in their communities. They are certainly not treating patients just to learn about aliens. Even those at the pinnacle of the abduction field appear to be profiting from treating abductees. Leo Sprinkle, the counseling psychologist who organizes the Rocky Mountain UFO Conferences, offers hypnotic services to attendees for a fee. Donna Bassett, the Boston writer who presented herself to John Mack, reported that Mack billed insurance plans for hypnotherapy sessions conducted with abductees.[74]

For clinicians like Mack, however, financial motives are no doubt less important than status. Mack's 1994 book, *Abductions: Human Encounters with Aliens*, reveals the sense of importance Mack and others like him gain from treating abductees.[75] Mack's book is composed of 13 abduction case histories sandwiched between introductory and concluding chapters. Although he views abductions as causes of distress, he belongs in the camp that sees aliens as ultimately benign. He argues that abductees acquire alien knowledge concerning "the fate of the earth in the wake of human destructiveness."[76] Not only can abductions heal serious illnesses, like leukemia and paralyses, but many, if not most, abductees experience personal growth. They develop psychic powers and even become aware of "cycles of birth and death" previously known only to Tibetan monks.[77] They become more concerned with Earth and with all creatures on it. One abductee, for instance, feels a kinship with lions, while another abductee says deer are his "totem" creatures. Some have changed their jobs in order to help the environment. Mack believes abductions are intended to help human beings climb to the next higher step in the evolution of consciousness. Unknown cosmic dimensions will soon be available to us.

Seeing abductees as emissary prophets, Mack seems to view himself as midwife to a new epoch. In *Abductions* and elsewhere, he states that his job is to help abductees spread their message. To do this, he must be heedless of threats, reprisals and ridicule from those who oppose the new age. Individuals mired in the old forms of thought will resist higher consciousness as revealed by aliens. The CBS miniseries that portrayed a character based on Mack as a hero had nothing at all on Mack's own heroic pretensions.

Heroic themes are evident in discussions with other therapists who specialize in abductions. They believe they are privy to secrets and in danger from government agents. They see themselves as modern-day Paul Reveres, sounding an early warning against threats from space, or, like Mack, they see themselves as modern-day secular apostles. This is heady stuff, more akin to religion than to mundane professional practice.

Like therapists who specialize in recovered memories, those who specialize in treating abductees are eager to inflate the importance of what they do by showing that the syndrome in which they specialize is actually widespread. A Roper Survey conducted between July and September 1991 queried 5,947 individuals about whether they had ever seen ghosts, had out-of-body experiences, seen UFOs, woken up paralyzed with the sense that someone was in the room, felt as if they were flying through the air, experienced missing time, seen unusual lights or balls of light in a room, found unexplained markings or scars on their body, seen terrifying, inexplicable figures in their bedrooms, or had vivid dreams of UFOs.[78] Eighteen percent of respondents reported waking up paralyzed with the sense that someone else is in the room, 15 percent reported having seen terrifying figures in their bedroom, and 14 percent reported out-of-body experiences. Thirteen percent reported episodes of missing time, and 10 percent reported having seen a ghost. Eight percent had seen unusual lights or balls of light, 8 percent had found puzzling scars on their bodies, and 7 percent had seen a UFO.

A summary of this survey was distributed to mental health professionals throughout the nation. An introduction by Mack asserts that the survey indicates that "hundreds of thousands, if not millions, of American men, women and children may have experienced UFO abductions, or abduction related phenomena."[79] Hopkins, Jacobs, and Westrum, the latter a sociologist at Eastern Michigan University, assert that since 2 percent of the Roper correspondents reported at least four abduction-related experiences, it is likely that at least 2 percent of people have been abducted, or about 5 million people in the United States alone.[80] If a significant proportion of abducted persons suffer adverse effects, figures like these suggest that alien abductions are a major cause, if not the major cause, of mental health problems today. With this sort of data in mind, abduction therapists have urged the American Psychiatric Association (APA) to incorporate alien abduction syndrome into the DSM-IV, a request the organization has thus far politely declined.[81] As we have seen, this refusal is based on something less than insight into illness roles, since the APA endorses MPD. Instead, alien abduction isn't currently *à la mode*.

8

Self-Knowledge, the Unconscious, and the Future of Illness Roles

In chapter 2, I noted that beliefs and attitudes change when social roles are adopted. I described an early study, published by Janis and King, that showed that college students who acted the role of an advocate in giving a speech to others changed their opinions to be more consistent with what they had said in their speeches.[1] Subjects who heard these speeches also changed their opinions, but to a lesser extent. Role-induced attitude changes are robust and affect important behaviors, and they may be exploited commercially, by advertisers, for instance.[2] The effects of such attitude changes are clearly observed in cult groups, among other social settings (see chapter 2).

Numerous studies conducted since Janis and King's early work suggest that role-induced changes in attitudes and beliefs occur to reduce discrepancies between overt behaviors and internal cognitive states, if these can't be explained away. That is, if a subject's beliefs and attitudes don't jibe with the role he is playing, and he can't explain why he is playing a role he doesn't believe in, then he may change his attitudes and beliefs to reduce the discrepancy. In Janis and King's experiment, for example, subjects who found themselves striving to effectively advocate points they did not initially believe in, as judged by their responses on an "opinion survey" completed four weeks before, changed their opinions to be more consonant with their behavior.

An early study by Festinger and Carlsmith illustrates the research that supports this view of the function of belief and attitude change.[3] Male college students spent an hour performing repetitive, boring tasks, ostensibly for the purpose of allowing researchers to measure their performance. After an hour had passed, the subjects were given a rationale for telling a prospective subject, who was actually a confederate of the experimenters, that the tasks had been interesting. Some of the subjects were paid $20 for this deception, while others were paid only $1, a symbolic amount. After the subjects had lied to the "prospective subject," they were asked, in another setting, what they had really thought. Subjects who had not been asked to mislead another person served as a control group to allow the researchers to get an accurate measure of how the tasks were perceived in the absence of any role playing.

On the theory that attitude changes occur to reduce discrepancies between cognitive states and behaviors if these cannot otherwise be explained away, Festinger and Carlsmith reasoned that attitude change would occur in the role players who had been paid $1, but not in those who had been paid $20. Subjects paid $20, a lot in the late 1950s, could explain their role-playing behavior in terms of the payment expected. They were doing it for the money. On the other hand, subjects paid just $1 could not explain their role playing, $1 being inadequate to account for misleading behavior, and so had to change their attitudes toward the tasks they were describing.

These predictions were proven correct. Subjects paid $20 to lie to a "prospective subject" were like the control subjects in that they rated the tasks as boring and unpleasant. Subjects paid only $1, though, thought the tasks were fine and, unlike other subjects, were willing to do them again. Analysis of the audiotapes of subjects who were acting a role showed that the $1 subjects were no more convincing play actors than the $20 subjects. Hence, the difference between the groups in their ratings of boring tasks could not be explained by intrinsic differences in their acting.

In another well-known study, Freedman studied 89 second- to fourth-grade boys, who were individually tested at their local elementary schools.[4] The subjects were all told that it was "wrong" for them to play with an ex-tremely attractive toy robot. No explanation was given for why such play would be wrong. Some boys were also threatened with unspecified reprisals should they play with the robot, but other boys were not. Half the boys were given no chance to play with the robot unobserved, but the other half were exposed to temptation by being left alone in the room for a short time with the forbidden toy. The few subjects who took advantage of the short time alone to actually play with the robot were dropped from the rest of the study.

Three to nine weeks later, the remaining subjects were once again shown the toy robot, but this time they were given permission to use it. The robot was equipped with a sensor that informed the researchers if the subjects turned it on. Freedman hypothesized that the way the subjects were treated in the initial session would affect their decision whether to play with the robot when given permission to do so. Some subjects had wanted to play with the robot, but they had not been able to do so because they had never been left alone with it. Since there were no real discrepancies between these subjects' attitudes and their behaviors, and hence no need for them to change attitudes, Freedman predicted that these subjects would play with the robot readily when given the chance to do so. Boys who had been threat-ened with reprisals and then left alone with the robot could explain their failure to play with it when they had the chance by the great risk they would have been taking, and Freedman predicted that they, too, would readily play with the robot when given permission to do so. The boys who had the great-est problem were those who had been neither threatened nor continually observed. They had not played with the robot only because the experimenter had told them it was wrong for them to do so, without an explanation for why it was wrong and without any threat of punishment. In effect, they had acted as if playing with the robot were indeed wrong, as the experimenter had said, but they could not say why it was wrong or point to particular risks. Freedman concluded that boys in this group would be forced to change their attitudes; the robot would have to become a less desirable toy.

These predictions proved correct. Two-thirds of the boys who were not given a chance to play with the robot or who were given a chance to play with it but threatened with reprisals during the first session played with the robot when given permission to do so. By contrast, fewer than one-third of boys who had been tempted without being threatened during the first session chose to play with the robot during the second session. As Freedman had predicted, the boys with the greatest discrepancies in attitudes and behaviors apparently changed their attitudes; the robot was now seen as less desirable. Interestingly, the groups varied less in their ratings of the toy's attractiveness than in their decision whether to play with it. Freedman suggests that the boys who had been tempted but not threatened during the first session later chose not to play with the robot because they saw playing with it as wrong, as the first experimenter had told them, rather than simply because they saw the robot as unattractive. The attitude change, in other words, may have been partly moral, rather than purely a matter of preferences. Freedman suggests that the conditions for this particular group—in which compliance with an unexplained moral injunction was achieved without specific threat of punishment—may approach the ideal conditions for moral indoctrination.

Elkin and Leippe recruited 40 college student subjects for what the subjects were told was a study of physiological responses to various tasks.[5] After expressing their attitudes on various campus issues, including the issue of whether there should be fees for parking, students were asked to write an essay supporting such fees. Since few if any students supported parking fees, they were being asked to write an essay contrary to their own beliefs. Some of the subjects (the high-choice group) were led to believe that they had a choice and were writing the essay freely, while others (the low-choice group) were told they had no choice respecting their essay position. After writing their essays, all subjects were once again asked to give their real opinions on the issue of parking fees.

On the same theory that guided the investigations described earlier, Elkin and Leippe predicted that attitude changes, if any, would occur in the high-choice group. Instructions to low-choice subjects emphasized that their position had been assigned to them and might not reflect their opinions. Hence, they had no difficulty reconciling their opinions and their behavior. Elkin and Leippe's prediction was proven correct. Although no difference existed in attitudes toward parking fees on the original survey, the high-choice subjects had more favorable opinions of fees after writing their essays than did the low-choice subjects. The high-choice subjects had changed their opinions of parking fees to be more in line with the essay they had "voluntarily" written.

In Elkin and Leippe's study, some of the subjects were given an outline of proparking-fee arguments to guide them in writing their essays. Interestingly, whether or not such arguments were given to subjects had no effect at all on the subjects' subsequent attitude changes, in either the low-choice or the high-choice group. In other words, whether or not the proparking-fee role was scripted (outline of arguments given) or improvised (no outline of arguments given) did not matter; what mattered was whether the subjects felt they had played the role voluntarily and therefore had to reconcile their opinions with the role they had assumed.

A well-known study by Lieberman shows how adoption of roles in real-life situations is followed by attitude change consistent with role requirements.[6] Lieberman surveyed workers at a midwestern company regarding their attitudes toward the company and their union. Later, 23 of the workers were promoted to foremen, meaning that they had joined management and had to resign from the union. They were given the survey again some months after changing positions. Congruent with their new roles, the newly promoted foremen expressed more promanagement and antiunion sentiments than they had on their previous surveys. They now had the requisite attitudes for their management role. As Lieberman's luck would have it, an economic recession that hit shortly after the second survey caused eight of his foremen subjects to lose their management jobs. Lieberman administered the attitude surveys again. The foremen who kept their jobs had become still more promanagement, while those demoted to workers once again held the attitudes they had voiced before their promotions.

Role-induced attitude changes may be hard to contain, in the sense that a change in one attitude requires changes in others if there is to be some consistency. For example, once they changed their opinions about the repetitive tasks, Festinger and Carlsmith's $1 group of subjects also had to change their recollection of their feelings during the task. A subject who had spent the hour thinking of walking out of the experiment room would have had to forget what had been on his mind and, if necessary, substitute something else. A subject in Elkin and Leippe's high-choice group, who adopted a profee opinion, would have had to forget that her opinion had been different before the experiment or adopt the belief that the process of writing an essay had changed her mind. If she saw herself as an anarchist, she might have had to change her self-image in order to take a position in favor of fees imposed by a government body. If she thought the university was already very wealthy, she might have had to change this opinion along with her view on fees. There are, in short, an indeterminate number of corollary beliefs and attitudes that may require adjustment once the process is set in motion.

Two experiments show that something like this occurs when attitudes change in response to external social events. The first study, by Bem and McConnell, used male college students who were taking introductory psychology classes.[7] An initial session was spent filling out attitude surveys on a number of campus issues. When asked the question "How much control should students have over the kinds of courses offered by the University?," more than 90 percent of subjects gave answers above the midpoint on a 61-point scale, indicating that they thought students should have at least some control over courses. Subjects whose answers on this item were below the midpoint were dropped from the rest of the study. At the next session, one week later, the remaining subjects were asked to write essays against student control over courses. Some of these subjects (the high-choice group) were led to believe they were choosing to write against student control, while others (the low-choice group) were led to believe they had no choice in the positions they were to take in their essays. After the essays were written, half of the subjects in each group were asked for their current opinion on the issue of student control, using the same scale as had been used the week before. The other half were asked to recall the answers they had given on the issue the week before.

A control group was also created, consisting of subjects not asked to write essays. At the second session, half of the control subjects were asked for their current opinion on the issue of student control, using the same scale that had been used the week before, and the other half were asked to recall the answers they had given on the issue the week before. At the end of the experiment, all subjects who recalled their opinions were asked for their current opinions on the issue of student control. Also, all subjects were asked whether their opinions had changed in the course of the study.

Consistent with subjects in the studies described earlier, Bem and McConnell's high-choice subjects changed their opinions to be more consistent with the essays they had written, while the low-choice subjects did not. In addition, errors in recalled opinions closely matched attitude changes; that is, high-choice subjects recalled their initial positions as having been consistent with their later essays, and therefore with their current opinions, while low-choice and control subjects recalled their initial positions correctly. Consistent with the hypothesis that subjects would distort their earlier attitudes to match their present ones, recalled attitudes among the subjects who wrote essays correlated nearly perfectly with the subjects' final attitudes ($r = .98$ for high-choice subjects; $r = .96$ for low-choice subjects). Out of 62 subjects who wrote essays and whose attitudes had changed over the course of the study, only nine subjects correctly reported that change in response to the poststudy question.

Goethals and Reckman gave 74 junior or senior high school students of both sexes an attitude test, which included a question on school busing to achieve racial integration.[8] Later, groups of two to four subjects with similar opinions regarding school busing were assembled to discuss the issue. Unbeknownst to the real subjects, a student research confederate, selected for his high status in their school, was added to each group. The confederate came armed with arguments intended to sway the other students to a position opposite from the position they shared in common. Thus, in a group of pro-busing students, the confederate would voice well-crafted arguments against busing; in a group of antibusing students, the confederate would voice well-crafted arguments in favor of busing. The researchers arranged for the confederate to be the first to speak in each discussion group.

Following the discussions, which lasted up to 20 minutes, the subjects were given forms on which they were asked to indicate their current attitude toward school busing. Subjects were also asked to recall, as accurately as possible, the attitude they had expressed on the original survey. The experimenter made clear that their answers that day would be checked against their original surveys.

A control group was also created, consisting of subjects who did not take part in the discussion groups. At the second session, these subjects were simply asked to recall their answers on the earlier survey.

As expected, the high-status, well-prepared confederate was highly effective in swaying students' opinions on busing. Following the discussion groups, the probusing students were more opposed to busing and the antibusing students more in favor of it than they had been before. These changes were so large that the two groups of subjects actually reversed their positions on busing: On the postdiscussion measure, initially probusing subjects expressed more antibusing sentiment than did subjects who were initially opposed to busing.

As Goethals and Reckman predicted, when subjects were asked to duplicate their earlier survey responses, those who had changed their opinions distorted their earlier answers to make them more consistent with their current positions. Thus, initially probusing students who later were more antibusing recalled their initial opinions as having been antibusing; initially antibusing students who later were more probusing recalled their initial opinions as having been probusing. Control students, on the other hand, accurately recalled their initial opinions. Postdiscussion opinions on the busing question and recalled opinions on busing were highly correlated ($r = .86$), suggesting that, as in Bem and McConnell's experiment, the subjects' current opinions determined what they recalled. Yet, when asked about it, Geothals and Reckman's subjects denied that the discussion groups had in fact changed their opinions. When they were told that they had changed their positions quite markedly and that they had misremembered their answers on the survey forms, the subjects seemed dubious. Believing perhaps, that they were being misled, some even asked to see their answers.

Distortion of past attitudes and beliefs so that they are more in line with present ones occurs in real-life settings. Collins and colleagues, for instance, surveyed high school students about their use of alcohol and other drugs.[9] Subjects were resurveyed two and half years later. In the course of the later surveys, the subjects were asked to recall their earlier patterns of use. Subjects whose use of substances had changed in the time between the surveys recalled their earlier patterns of use inaccurately to make them more consistent with their later patterns. In another study, Marcus surveyed a large number of high school students on a wide range of issues, such as women's rights and legalization of marijuana.[10] The subjects were surveyed again eight and 17 years later. At the 17-year follow-up, subjects were asked to recall their responses nine years earlier. Subjects whose attitudes had changed between the eight-year and the 17-year follow-ups recalled their earlier attitudes as consistent with their later ones, rather than as they really were.

Insofar as role-induced changes in one belief or attitude may entail changes in others, then those who are highly attuned to inconsistent thoughts will be at a disadvantage in playing new social roles. For them, adopting a social role, along with its mental concommitants, requires that they examine all aspects of their prior beliefs for possible discrepancies that require resolution. In contrast, those who are able to ignore inconsistent thoughts will be able to slip in and out of new social roles more readily; such a subject who finds himself, in Elkin and Leippe's study, professing to favor fees may not have to bother to change his self-image as an anarchist, an opponent of rules in general and of fees of all kinds in particular. Some evidence does exist that hypnotizable subjects, who are highly responsive to role cues, can withdraw their attention from stimuli, perhaps including existing attitudes and beliefs, that would distract most people (see chapter 4). We have already seen how several of the illness roles in this book tend to occur in highly hypnotizable people. In a classic book on the psychology of personality disorders, the psychoanalyst David Shapiro argued that hysterical personalities are characterized by a global, diffuse cognitive style.[11] The style described by Shapiro would favor ignoring discrepancies among disparate beliefs, perceptions, and attitudes and, therefore, perhaps role playing. Hysterical personality, of course, is a term that was formerly applied to self-dramatizing, histrionic patients prone to illness roles, such as conversion or somatization disorder, as discussed in the previous chapters.

The Limits of Self-Awareness

Experiments like those reviewed in this chapter produce seemingly paradoxical situations, in which the researchers know something about subjects' attitudes and beliefs that the subjects profess not to know. Subjects' lack of awareness of their own attitudes and beliefs cannot be explained by forgetting. Instead, it is part and parcel of their lack of awareness of the falseness of their own behavior, the extent, that is, to which they are playing roles. Consider, for example, a typical subject in Festinger and Carlsmith's $1 subject group. In light of the control subjects' ratings, the researchers knew with some confidence that this individual hadn't enjoyed the boring tasks assigned while he was actually doing them. Yet, when asked to rate these tasks after misleading a confederate, he claimed he did enjoy them. He could not have simply forgotten that he did not enjoy the tasks. Too little time had elapsed, and in any event, memory loss cannot account for the observed group differences. The researchers also knew that typical $1 subjects had given good reports of the tasks to the research confederate because they were asked to do so by an authority figure. To the degree that the typical subject believed he had enjoyed the tasks, he was spared the knowledge that he had lied in order to please an authority. His belief in his new attitude was linked to his lack of awareness of the fact that he had played a false role with the research confederate.

To give another example, consider a typical high-choice subject in Bem and McConnell's study. After writing the required essay, this subject reported that she was against student choice, or at least less strongly in favor of it than the researchers knew her to have been. She could not have simply forgotten what her position was. Again, little time had elapsed, and forgetting could not account for the observed group differences. Typical high-choice subjects wrote essays against student choice because they were compliant. To the extent that the typical subject believed that she opposed student choice, she would not be aware of the false role that she played in complying.

The typical subject in Goethals and Reckman's discussion groups claimed to have had a different prediscussion opinion on the busing issue than in fact he had had. Once again, he could not simply have forgotten what his position had been. Too little time had elapsed, and forgetting could not account for the observed group differences. Typical subjects, in fact, had been swayed by the high-status research confederate in their group. To the extent that the typical subject believed he had not changed opinions, he remained unaware of the fact he conformed with the high-status student, that is, that he played a role.

There are several views of the strange findings of studies like these. One such view is suggested by Nisbett and Wilson in their paper cited in chapter 2.[12] As the reader may recall, Nisbett and Wilson hypothesized that people lack access to knowledge of the causes of many of their own behaviors, for which they wind up inventing plausible explanations. Subjects in experiments like those cited here may not perceive that they are responding to social pressure. When they find themselves making statements with which they don't agree for reasons they don't understand, they may change their attitudes to explain what they cannot perceive. The Bem and McConnell study was designed with this view in mind. If subjects deduce their own attitudes by observing their own behavior, then their memories of attitudes previously held may change with their current behavior. A subject who finds himself acting one way today is likely to deduce that he has always held a belief consistent with that behavior.

Another view is that subjects in experiments like these are embarrassed that they played a role and are trying to salvage their self-esteem and self-presentation by changing their opinions and attitudes.[13] For example, Festinger and Carlsmith's subjects lied to the confederate because they were asked to do so, in other words, to please an authority figure. This would have been most evident to the $1 group subjects. Since "brown-nosing" is an especially unacceptable trait for typical college-age males, they may have preferred to believe that they had not lied at all. They could maintain this fiction by believing that they had liked the tasks. In Elkin and Leippe's experiment, the instructions given to high-choice subjects made it harder for them to ignore the fact of their own compliance. They could deny this compliance by "owning" the essay position. In Bem and McConnell's study, and in Goethals and Reckman's, too, subjects who distorted their previous attitudes and beliefs could thereby avoid acknowledging that they had changed their positions to comply with and conform to others.

If the view derived from Nisbett and Wilson's work is more "cognitive," then the alternative view is more "psychodynamic," in the sense that the purpose of attitude change is to protect self-esteem and self-presentation. While people play social roles that they have reason to believe will please or appease others or be rewarded in some way, they generally don't want to think of themselves, or to be seen, as cowardly, pliant, or opportunistic. They therefore obscure the fact that they are playing a role. This is an area in which clinical observations can contribute to social psychology (discussed later).

In either case, the ability to play a role convincingly may depend on some degree of role-induced attitude change. Those who believe in their roles may be less likely to betray self-doubt in stressful situations or when facing opposition.[14] Role-induced attitude change may be an essential contributor to human "political" skills, conceived in the broadest terms.[15]

Limited Self-Awareness in Clinical Situations

The seemingly paradoxical situations that result from social psychological experiments like those I have described will seem familiar to psychotherapists, who are often in the same position *vis à vis* their patients as the researchers in such studies are with respect to their subjects. That is, psychotherapists often deduce facts about their patients' attitudes and beliefs that the patients profess not to know. The patients' lack of awareness of their attitudes and beliefs cannot be explained by forgetting but instead is part and parcel of their self-presentation. Although most psychotherapists don't use the language of social roles to describe self-presentation, the basic concept of roles is also familiar to them: They observe patients shaping behavior to meet expectations of others, to appear more desirable, or to hide their motives.

Insofar as there are differences between researchers performing studies like those I have described and therapists dealing with patients, they reside in the source of their knowledge about their subjects' or patients' attitudes and beliefs and in the resulting assumptions clinicians are forced to make. Concerning the first, researchers know that their subjects have had role-discrepant attitudes and beliefs because they measured these before the new roles were adopted. Clinicians deduce their patients' role-discrepant attitudes and beliefs by slips in the patients' facades, which reveal these attitudes. To draw a theatrical analogy: Researchers know that an actor is someone other than Hamlet because they observed the actor before he went on stage. Clinicians deduce that the actor is someone other than Hamlet by looking for flaws in his performance that suggest he is acting a part.

The notion that clinical practice consists of noting slips in the role the patient is playing and deducing role-discrepant attitudes from these slips can be traced back to Freud, who invented this type of detective work. In a famous passage from the case of Dora, Freud put the matter succinctly. Freud had suggested to Dora that she had once masturbated. Although she denied masturbation, Dora came to a subsequent session with a small draw-string purse at her waist and proceeded to open and close it, inserting and removing her fingers, as she spoke to Freud. She had never before worn this purse, nor did she do so later. Freud interpreted Dora's play with her purse as a pantomimed statement of her wish to masturbate and made the following widely quoted aside:

> When I set myself the task of bringing to light what human beings keep hidden within them . . . I thought the task was a harder one than it really is. He that has eyes to see and ears to hear may convince himself that no mortal can keep a secret. If his lips are silent, he chatters with his finger-tips: betrayal oozes out of him at every pore.[16]

Concerning clinicians' assumptions, most social psychologists are little concerned with the status or fate of attitudes that are or become role discrepant. Nisbett and Wilson's position implies that these attitudes no longer exist, and Bem and McConnell's findings were interpreted in this light. Therapists, by contrast, make their living inferring such attitudes and so must assume they exist, if only in some special state from which they produce flawed performances. Clinicians influenced by Freud call the special state of such attitudes the "unconscious," and the mechanisms that render attitudes unconscious "defenses," defined as cognitive processes that serve to hide mental contents.[17] In the language of social roles, one might suggest the defenses hide attitudes and beliefs discrepant with the current roles the patient has chosen to play.

A famous case described by Wilhelm Reich illustrates the extent to which clinicians influenced by Freud have traditionally concerned themselves with what we might call role-discrepant attitudes. Reich was a student of Freud's whose early work laid the basis for later psychoanalysis and hence for some of the psychotherapies widely practiced today. Reich was especially important for the emphasis he gave to the study of "character," and indeed the present case was published as part of a book called *Character Analysis*, which remains his best-known work.[18] By "character," Reich meant something akin to a social role that serves strategic goals, albeit not simply interpersonal ones. Hence, Reich's case is especially easy to translate into the language of social roles, without the conceptual confusions that often result from translating clinical cases from one framework to another.

The patient described by Reich was a 24-year-old bank employee with a fear of mental illness, anxiety attacks, and a greatly inhibited sexual life. Regarding his fear of illness, the patient believed that he would become mentally ill and die in an asylum. This fear was not unfounded: His paternal grandfather and father had both had syphilis, which was then thought to be passed to heirs, a paternal uncle was anxious and an insomniac, his mother was very anxious, a maternal great-aunt was manic-depressive, and his maternal grandfather and a maternal uncle had both committed suicide. His anxiety attacks were accompanied by palpitations and what Reich called a "paralysis of all volition." The patient's anxiety attacks had started in childhood; as a child, he remembered being frightened by talk of the end of the world, the result of a falling comet. As for his sexual life, the patient rarely masturbated and had recently been impotent with a prostitute. He professed not to need much sex and not to be bothered by his impotence.

Of more immediate interest than the patient's anxiety, Reich diagnosed what he called a "passive-feminine" character, the description of which makes it obvious that the patient was playing a role characterized by greatly exaggerated expressions of deference. According to Reich:

> his demeanor was always excessively friendly and humble; he was forever excusing himself for the most trifling matters. Both when he arrived and when he departed, he bowed deeply several times. In addition, he was awkward, shy, and ceremonious. If he were asked, for example, whether he had any objection to rescheduling his hour, he would not simply answer "no." He would assure me that he was at my service, that everything was quite agreeable with him, etc.[19]

In his desire to please, and knowing that Reich was a Freudian, the patient also reported dreams with Oedipal themes, but Reich saw through these at once. Regarding these dreams, Reich hypothesized that even unconscious material might be strategically used in the service of abnormal character, or what we would call a role.

Confronted with this seemingly deferential patient, Reich proceeded by pointing out cues that the patient possessed attitudes, such as distrust, other than simple deference. The patient, for instance, reported the following dream to Reich: "My handwriting is sent to a graphologist for an expert evaluation. Answer: this man belongs in an insane asylum. Deep despair on the part of my mother. I want to make an end of my life. I wake up."[20] In connection with the graphologist, the patient thought of Freud, who, before referring him to Reich, had told him that his illness could certainly be cured by analysis. Reich pointed out that the dream suggested a lack of confidence in the result of his treatment. On another occasion, the patient reported a dream in which he was implicated in a crime, possibly murder. Reich observed the fear of detection evident in the dream and suggested to the patient that his demeanor implied that he was hiding something. In response to a similar dream, Reich suggested that the patient was feigning his trust in his analyst and actually had a bad conscience. It turned out the patient had lied to Reich when they had set Reich's fee. The patient had more resources than he had disclosed. In yet another dream, the patient's father laughed derisively at Freud. Reich suggested that the patient himself had derisive thoughts.

Not eager to give up his role as the perfectly deferential gentleman, the patient responded to Reich's interpretations by professing all the more trust and regard for Reich and by redoubling his efforts to please him. For instance, when Reich pointed out that the dream of the graphologist implied that he lacked faith in Reich, the patient insisted he had full confidence in his analysis. When Reich suggested that the patient distrusted him in regard to a particular matter, the patient "returned on the same day very much upset. He could not, he said, endure the thought that his analyst regarded him as distrustful, and he repeatedly begged forgiveness in the event he had said something that might have caused me to make such an assumption."[21] When told he was feigning good feelings, the patient began to produce hysterical movements and seizures, the enactment of which he imagined would somehow placate Reich.

It took months of therapy, during which Reich was "careful not to miss any indications of distrust" or animosity, before the patient began to drop his deferential role.[22] He came to perceive his exaggerated friendliness as something alien to him, and he became less obsequious and more overtly critical, both with Reich and with others. He even began to have intercourse, apparently with a prostitute.

There are several respects in which Reich's analysis of this case seems narrow and problematic from the social role viewpoint. For example, Reich thought that the ultimate motive for the patient's deference was castration anxiety. That is, the source of the patient's fear of others was his fear of his father. From a social role viewpoint, though, the deferential role could have reduced anxiety generated by any of numerous sources. This patient, especially, had a genetic risk for an anxiety disorder, one manifestation of which might have been fear of social censure. The patient's resistance to change signified to Reich that his deferential character was defensive. In Freudian terms, this means that the patient's character served to suppress his unconscious conflicts and attitudes. From the social role viewpoint, though, the seeming resistance was merely continued behavior *en role*. Insofar as Reich's patient was in the position of an actor playing Lear, Reich himself was a spectator calling out, "You're not Lear, you're just an actor." What is an actor to do, except to keep on performing as best he can, given the circumstance? Finally, Reich understood the eventual change in the patient's behavior to mean that his abnormal character or, in our terms, his social role was fully psychoanalyzed. From a social role viewpoint, though, the patient may have adopted a new, more manly role in order to please Reich, not because his old role had been deconstructed.

It is easy to see from this case why clinicians, unlike social psychological researchers, are forced to conclude that role-discrepant attitudes really exist and feel the need to name the special state of such attitudes. Something, for instance, was causing Reich's patient to slip out of role, if only to the extent of reporting dreams that could be interpreted as suggestive of distrust or derision or of making Freudian slips. Furthermore, by following up on such leads, Reich uncovered others of the patient's behaviors, such as his cheating on fees, that indicated these same attitudes. Yet, the patient professed that these attitudes were the farthest things from his mind. Whether or not "unconscious" is an apposite term for the special status of attitudes discrepant with current social roles, the need for some such construct is clear from the clinical data.[23]

Illness Roles versus Feigning

Past and present diagnostic schemes require clinicians to read their patients' minds to diagnose illness roles like those described in the previous chapters. The DSM-IV, for instance, requires that patients said to have conversion disorder have a "symptom or deficit [which] is not intentionally produced or feigned."[24] Malingering, by contrast, is characterized by "the intentional production of false or grossly exaggerated physical or psychological symptoms."[25] Likewise, a distinction is commonly drawn between somatization disorder on the one hand and malingering on the other, or between malingering and multiple personality. But how can psychiatrists tell if symptoms—physical, mental, or both—are intentional if patients with intentional symptoms mislead them on that score?

Since clinicians cannot read minds, such diagnostic distinctions are made on other, equally unreliable grounds. For example, patients who stand to gain money or to get out of work as the result of their symptoms are more likely to be diagnosed as malingerers than patients whose benefits are purely interpersonal. Yet, interpersonal benefits, such as care or attention from family, are just as powerful motives as money or work entitlements. Also, money or work entitlements are often themselves interpersonal, in the sense that they confer special standing with friends and family or enable patients to escape from awkward work situations. Likewise, patients who seem manipulative are more likely to be diagnosed as malingerers than are patients who seem more sincere. Yet, the impression of being manipulative may reflect poor role-playing skills and a lack of interpersonal subtlety as much as insincerity, and in any event such judgments are often in the eyes of the beholder. Finally, patients who give inconsistent performances are more likely to be diagnosed as malingerers than patients whose symptoms are constant. However, within certain limits, the degree to which symptoms are constant reflects patients' understanding of the roles they are playing, not whether they are playing it sincerely. Insofar as patients perceive consistency as the sine qua non of an illness, they will take care to achieve it, whether sincerely or not. Except in rare cases, such as when a patient who claims to be paralyzed is seen running into the clinic, the constancy of symptoms is a poor guide to the patient's state of mind in complaining.

A social role view of the disorders described in this book argues against distinctions based on inferred intentions. An illness role can be adopted for all kinds of motives and reasons, ranging from the financial to the interpersonal, and can be accompanied by various degrees of attitude change, from none at all to extensive. Furthermore, the motives may change over time, and so may the patient's attitudes. A patient who starts a role to get more attention from family may later discover that the role serves functions at work, as well. A patient who starts a role because he's involved in a lawsuit may continue it after a settlement for reasons entirely different. A patient may start a role aware that it is mostly volitional, only to later believe in the role he is playing. Or the opposite may occur: A patient may play a role in which he believes completely, only to find that his attitudes have become role discrepant. Pat Burgus, who was described in the preceeding chapter, is a case of this type.

Some clinicians may think that distinctions based on patients' intentions correlate with the presence or absence of various antisocial behaviors. Patients with intentional symptoms, for instance, are thought to be likely to lie, cheat, and steal, while those who are more sincere about their symptoms are thought to be less likely to engage in such behaviors. However, all illness roles, sincerely played or not, are inherently antisocial compared to other social roles. Also, patients with illness roles that are considered sincere, such as MPD, conversion, or somatization, are known to engage in antisocial activities.

The antisocial behaviors of patients with illness roles judged sincere were evident in many nineteenth-century cases. Genevieve, one of Charcot's most famous grand hysterics, was promiscuous and manipulative and was once even banned from the Salpêtrière.[26] She left one of her newborn children to die of exposure. Louis Vivet, whose case was described in chapter 6, was repeatedly charged with stealing. His many incarcerations led to the diagnosis of his alter states. Today, a large proportion of patients who play the illness roles described in the previous chapters, most of whom are presumed to be acting these roles sincerely, are said to have either antisocial or borderline personality disorders, the two personality disorders most associated with disregard for social norms. The reader may recall, for example, that about a third of patients said to have MPD meet the diagnostic criteria for antisocial personality disorder, and more than half of patients said to have MPD meet the diagnostic criteria for borderline personality disorder. Individuals with antisocial personality disorder (ASP) fail "to conform to social norms with respect to lawful behaviors."[27] They perform criminal acts, lie, use aliases, con and manipulate others, and lack a sense of remorse. Patients with borderline personality disorder are manipulative and attention seeking and are prone to lying and stealing and other social infractions.[28] About one-quarter of patients with borderline personality disorder also meet the diagnostic criteria for antisocial personality disorder, and, in fact, the overlap of the two syndromes is sufficiently broad that some authors have suggested that borderline personality is a variant form of ASP, one seen predominantly in females.[29] Criminal or antisocial acts in the setting of MPD are typically blamed on the alters. Indeed, escaping blame for such behaviors may be a major function of MPD for some patients. In chapter 6, for instance, I described Colin Ross's patient, Jenny, who met Ross after returning from a trip to Vancouver. While in Vancouver, she had stolen and spent several thousand dollars of her boyfriend's money. An alter, Sally, took the blame for this crime.

Among bodily illness roles, Briquet's syndrome and somatization disorder, in which physical symptoms are generally thought to be unfeigned, have also been shown to be linked to antisocial and borderline personality disorders. Researchers at Washington University, in St. Louis, for instance, have shown in a series of studies that women with Briquet's or with somatization disorder are more likely to have antisocial personality disorder and to report having committed more delinquent or antisocial acts in comparison with other women. They have also found that Briquet's syndrome is common among female felons.[30] Furthermore, studies show that this linkage may be genetic: Relatives of patients with Briquet's syndrome, especially if they are male, are at increased risk of ASP, and female relatives of male felons have a high incidence of Briquet's.[31] On the basis of these studies, these researchers hypothesized that Briquet's syndrome and antisocial personality disorder are caused by the same factors but that women with these factors are more likely to have Briquet's syndrome than typical ASP.[32]

The same researchers also studied 75 patients with borderline personality disorder who had been treated at the Washington University psychiatry clinic and at another St. Louis hospital and found that 63 percent of them met the diagnostic criteria for probable or definite Briquet's syndrome.[33] Thirty-six percent met the DSM-III-R criteria for somatization disorder, and 45 percent met DSM-IV criteria for somatization disorder.

Actually, not just Briquet's syndrome but conversion symptoms per se are associated with antisocial or borderline personality disorders. Of a group of 500 psychiatric outpatients studied by the Washington University group, 118 had a history of at least one conversion symptom, and 48 had more than one.[34] Antisocial personality disorder was significantly more common in patients with conversion symptoms, and especially in patients with more than one conversion symptom, than in patients without such symptoms. Rechlin and colleagues studied 18 patients with prolonged pseudoseizures who had been treated at a German University clinic between 1988 and 1992.[35] All of these patients, some of whom had been intubated and placed on respirators because they seemed to be convulsing, met the DSM-III-R criteria for conversion disorder. Ten of the patients met the DSM-III-R criteria for borderline personality disorder, two met the criteria for antisocial personality disorder, and three met the criteria for histrionic personality disorder. Histrionic personality disorder is yet another socalled cluster B personality disorder, in the same category as borderline and antisocial personality disorders.[36] While other cluster B patients manipulate persons for gain, histrionic patients manipulate them for attention.

Obviously, the extent to which those who play illness roles are generally antisocial will vary, depending on social and cultural circumstances. For example, in highly male-dominated societies, women who take on illness roles tend to be less antisocial. In such societies, illness behavior is literally the only available means by which these women can exercise a measure of social control. This is no doubt the case in most traditional societies, and it was also the case for many nineteenth-century hysterics, if the detailed case histories available from that time are any guide. In societies that are more open and egalitarian, illness roles are the venue of those who lack the skills required to play more constructive roles, or of those who are antisocial in a more general sense, for whom illness roles are just another manipulation. In our own society, those who play illness roles, however sincere, are probably heterogeneous; many in fact are handicapped, some are antisocial, and some appear to be both.

Is There a Sense in Which Multiples Do Have Alters?

That beliefs and attitudes sometimes follow behavior, rather than vice versa, has important implications with respect to the illness roles described in this book. It suggests, for example, that patients who act out conversion symptoms may come to believe they are paralyzed, anesthetic, or having seizures in spite of the fact that their symptoms are formed and maintained by social rewards. Patients who invent false memories may come to believe in them, in spite of the fact that these memories are really instrumental. Patients who complain of chronic fatigue may feel exhausted and weak, in spite of the fact that their illness occurs in pursuit of a goal.

The social psychological studies cited earlier show that belief and attitude change is greatest in subjects who can't otherwise explain their own behavior. For such subjects, new beliefs and attitudes serve to account for their behavior, thereby giving the subjects the false impression that they know why they acted as they did. Subjects in Festinger and Carlsmith's experiment who were paid $20, and hence given a clear reason for misleading a confederate, knew that they had lied, while subjects paid only $1 claimed to have really enjoyed the boring, repetitive tasks. The control group data, of course, proved that this wasn't the case. Subjects in Elkins and Leippe's experiment who were "assigned" to write an essay in support of parking fees did not change their antifee sentiments, while subjects encouraged to think they had chosen to write similar essays did change their positions. The boys in Freedman's experiment who were explicitly threatened if they dared to play with the robot still seemed to like the toy, while subjects who were not threatened explicitly later seemed to dislike it. Insofar as these studies are guides to clinically relevant situations, they suggest that those patients who act ill and who don't know their motive for doing so may come to believe they are ill and acting in accordance with they way they really feel, while those who act ill but know their motive for doing so will not reach such a conclusion.

In other words, the difference between the malingerer and the patient who sincerely acts an illness role may be less a matter of the latter's relative honesty than of his relative lack of insight. An insightful patient, who understands the instrumental reasons for his acting, will not conclude he's ill and therefore will be a malingerer. An uninsightful patient will come to believe he is ill and therefore will be acting sincerely. The reader may recall that research cited by Nisbett and Wilson in their 1977 paper shows that people can be unaware of the real causes of their behavior, even when these causes seem obvious to outsiders.[37] Hence, the proportion of patients with illness roles who are acting sincerely may be greater than we might think on the basis of how obvious their motives seem to us. Also, for any given illness role, the relative proportion of patients who are malingering, or insincerely acting, will be determined by the ease of insight into the motives and rewards that typically sustain that role. Some contingencies are more readily perceived than others. The proportion of insincere actors may therefore be very different for different illness roles.

Insofar as beliefs can rapidly track behavior, we may be faced with a paradox respecting illness roles—such as possession, dual personality, and MPD—that entail playing the part of one or more alter personae: Not only may patients believe that they are acting sincerely, but in fact they may have real alters or be, in a sense, possessed. Consider, for instance, an East African woman mistreated by her husband and subsequently possessed by an evil *Sar* spirit. In the role of the possessed host, she may come to believe that she is amnesic for periods of her life during which she is possessed. In the role of the possessing spirit, she may come to believe that her behavior is sincere, that is, that she is really a *Sar* spirit, that she views the host objectively, and that the demands she is making are not on the host's behalf. When playing the host, in other words, the possessed woman may believe herself to be the host, and when playing the spirit, she may believe herself to be the spirit. But this type of dual belief structure, if in fact it is achieved, is a kind of real possession, even if only the result of acting and subsequent attitude change.

Consider a patient who, for reasons she cannot articulate, begins to enact an alter personality. In the role of the host personality, she may come to believe that she is amnesic for periods of her life, during which the alter is "out." In the role of the alter personality, she may come to believe that her behavior is sincere, that is, that she is really someone other than the host, that she views the host objectively, and that her behavior is not in the host's behalf. When playing the host personality, in other words, the patient may believe herself to have symptoms of dual personality, and when playing the alter, she may believe herself to be the alter. But this type of dual belief structure, too, if in fact it is achieved, is a kind of real duality, again even if only the result of acting and subsequent attitude change.

With MPD, of course, several sets of beliefs and attitudes have to be rapidly juggled if the patient really is to sincerely enact each of her roles. This may not be possible for most patients. There may be some maximum rate at which beliefs can change, and it seems plausible that this is below the maximum rate at which role switching can occur. The latter maximum rate is very high indeed, judging by some multiples. Also, since, as the number of alters grows, less time can be spent enacting a particular alter role, at some point beliefs and attitudes have to follow on mere shreds of behavior, which may go beyond what is possible. On the other hand, the behaviors that changed beliefs in the psychological studies—such as writing an essay or deceiving a confederate—took a matter of minutes, so time may be less important than the fact of role playing per se. Possibly, some patients with MPD sincerely enact some of their alters, while others of their alters are purely facades, without any underlying complex or stable attitudes.

With this type of speculation, we complete a full circle begun with cases like that of Ansel Bourne. As Ellenberger observed, nineteenth-century students of the mind counted dual or, after Louis Vivet, multiple consciousness as perhaps their greatest discovery.[38] The study of patients like Estelle, the nine-year-old paralyzed girl whose double could walk and run and, unlike Estelle, ate heartily, or Felida X., whose double was gay and vivacious and enjoyed better health than Felida, convinced Despine and Azam and numerous other physicians that consciousness could be split, a potential that had not previously occurred to men of science. Through works like *Dr. Jekyll and Mr. Hyde*, the idea of split consciousness caught the popular imagination, too, and has since became part of the folk psychology of Western culture. Everyone raised in the West and in touch with its cultural currents since the late nineteenth century "knows" in some sense that the mind is capable of division, regardless of whether he has seen a particular instance. Ensconced in the cultural mainstream, and of not much concern to science, split consciousness came to the fore again as a matter of real debate only after 1980, when the MPD epidemic described in chapter 6 began to appear in earnest.

This time around, the reception given the seeming evidence for split consciousness has been even more mixed than it was in the nineteenth century. Although some observers believe that cases of MPD seen in their clinics today prove the existence of dual or, more commonly, multiple consciousness, many others doubt that anything has been shown. Modern clinicians, for one thing, are forewarned by numerous studies performed in the past 50 years that show the power of influence, suggestion, and role playing over human behavior. These studies prove Bernheim correct in his high estimation of role cues in the shaping of illness roles. The reader will recall that by claiming that grand hysteria resulted from cues given to patients in the Salpêtrière, Bernheim set in motion the Battle of the Schools between him and his followers in Nancy and the Salpétrists in Paris (see chapter 5). Informed modern clinicians are also more skeptical of hypnosis, and of its various products, including alter states, than their nineteenth-century counterparts; at the least, they know that just because something occurs while a subject is hypnotized does not prove it is real. Finally, the fact that MPD is now epidemic has undermined the claim that it reflects human nature rather than social fads. Due to modern mass media and widely read medical journals, medical fads can develop at a far faster rate than was possible 100 years ago. A faster-spreading fad is more easily revealed as such. In chapter 6, I outlined the conventional skeptical view of split consciousness as embodied by MPD. From my own experience, I believe that more clinicians accept some view like this than take MPD at anything like face value.

Yet, when the question of thought in relation to social role is considered and the modern studies I have cited are reviewed, the matter seems more complex. Role playing and split consciousness are not, in fact, mutually exclusive. At least in theory, split consciousness might occur as the result of enactments that purport to rely on such splitting. Split roles, in other words, may split the mind, as well. Whether and to what extent they really do so in a particular case is something we cannot know; this may not be stable or constant and therefore should not figure in our diagnostic system.

Looking to the Future

Whenever they can, humans give special attention, privileges, and care to their ill or disabled, often for very long periods of time. Care for the ill and disabled most likely evolved from what evolutionary theorists call kin altruism, or the evolutionarily advantageous tendency to aid those who carry one's genes by virtue of common descent.[39] Certainly, in modern human societies, caretaking behaviors are shown most strongly by families of origin. Studies of nonhuman primates and of fossil human remains suggest that caretaking behaviors toward the ill or injured are among the most ancient aspects of human nature.

As we have seen, the care, attention, and privileges lavished on the ill or disabled motivate illness roles and render them intelligible.[40] Since illness or disability leads to special care, privileges, and attention, some otherwise healthy persons, especially those who are socially disadvantaged, are tempted to play roles like those described in previous chapters. Many of these persons come to believe they are ill. In the most general sense, illness roles are a consequence of the care given to the ill and disabled. Given the ancient provenance of care of the ill and disabled, it seems likely that illness roles existed in the earliest, now unknown human societies.

Moreover, insofar as illness roles result from the provision of care to those who are really ill, and insofar as care is an aspect of human nature, no system of medical practice will ever completely eliminate illness roles. As one illness role falls under suspicion or becomes untenable due to technological or scientific advances, another will take its place. For example, as modern brain imaging and nerve conduction studies have made neurological diagnoses more objective, conversion disorders have been replaced by other illness roles, such as chronic fatigue or multiple chemical sensitivity, the symptoms of which lack objective, testable correlates.[41] The illness roles of the future are hardly imaginable now, but patients and healers, physicians or otherwise, will undoubtedly one day invent them.

The damage created by illness roles may be lessened by careful study of their causes and natural histories. It is fitting to end this chapter by enumerating several useful directions suggested by the theatrical model developed in this book.

First, clinical education should be modified to provide at least rudimentary knowledge of illness roles. As is evident from earlier chapters, some physicians and even psychologists are blind to illness roles. Unaware of the power of social roles in general, physicians have contributed to the spread of chronic fatigue syndrome and multiple chemical sensitivity; reifying illness roles and "dissociation," psychologists and psychiatrists helped spread multiple personality disorder, alien abduction syndrome, and false "recovered" memories. Clinical training curricula are already overcrowded, but the essentials of illness roles could be conveyed succinctly and to great effect, once a consensus emerges that such roles pose a problem. A discussion of grand hysteria, for example, combined with a review of pertinent social psychological experiments, would suffice to impress most students with the importance of roles in clinical practice.

Second, material in this book points to the potential value of a public health approach to illness roles. Illness roles are contagious. Just as nineteenth-century urban living conditions contributed, via particular vectors, to the spread of tuberculosis and other infectious diseases, so the modern environment may be conducive to the spread of illness roles. Mass media, in particular, disseminate knowledge of illness roles on a scale previously impossible. We have already seen how the media played a major part in the epidemics of multiple personality disorder and alien abduction syndrome. A public health approach to illness roles would entail ongoing efforts to monitor the media responsible for their spread, especially movies and television shows, along with alerts to clinicians akin to those currently issued with respect to infectious diseases. Just as it reports on sampling of deer ticks for lyme disease, the Centers for Disease Control could note that a possible illness role has been featured on prime-time TV, thereby alerting physicians to its potential spread. Public health officials could encourage the media to take a more responsible, balanced view of illness roles. If certain movies and TV shows had noted that doubt exists concerning the reality of multiple personality disorder or ritual abuse, many fewer cases might subsequently have appeared, and many fewer patients and families might have been harmed. Above all else, illness roles must be legitimized; balanced, objective portrayals may forestall some cases.

Of course, public health measures presuppose the existence of criteria for objective identification of illness roles. Throughout this book, I have suggested such criteria, including localization, rapidly increasing incidence, comorbidity with other illness roles, and connection to other role-playing behaviors, such as hypnosis. Yet, the problem of identifying illness roles remains quite difficult. Certain illness roles, such as chronic fatigue and Gulf War syndromes, may "piggyback" on real disorders so that some of the patients are playing roles and others are really ill. Also, many of the criteria I have offered for illness roles, such as rapid spread, are clearly recognizable only after illness roles have become epidemic. Research into objective identification of illness roles will therefore be intrinsic to public health measures against them.

Fourth, recognition of illness roles as a distinct class of syndromes should encourage focused research into clinical methodology. The theatrical model suggests that treatment depends on understanding the life needs served by illness and on helping patients address such needs in less destructive ways. Unfortunately, our means for understanding the needs served by illness behavior and for solving real-life problems are currently underdeveloped. Much research should go into learning how to identify problems that lead to illness behavior, remediation of handicaps in adaptive approaches to problems, and effective counseling regarding real-life problems. Dealing with real-life problems is unglamorous work, and research into helping patients deal with such problems is less exciting by far than the biological research that dominates modern psychiatry. Yet, the model developed here suggests that it should proceed if therapists hope to effectively treat patients who present with illness roles.

Finally, as I have shown in this chapter, recognition of illness roles and their social psychology should prompt a new look at some traditional psychiatric concepts, such as the "unconscious" and "defense mechanisms." Many of these concepts were invented to account for illness roles, such as hysteria, that were common at the end of the nineteenth century, so it is fitting to update them in the context of illness roles today. Armed with relevant experimental findings, we can breathe new life into seemingly stale concepts, while helping to eliminate those that are obsolete. Revitalization of concepts related to illness roles is likely to be of clinical use in managing such roles, and it no doubt would benefit treatment of patients with other disorders. I have tried to show that illness roles are "natural experiments" that throw certain aspects of human behavior and the human psyche into sharp relief seldom achieved outside the laboratory. The most important benefit of studying illness roles may be a more refined knowledge of human nature.

Notes

1. With respect to spirit possession, see S. Mulhern, "Embodied alternative identities: Bearing witness to a world that might have been," *Psychiatric Clinics of North America* 14 (September 1991): 769. With respect to mesmerism, see A. Winter, *Mesmerized: Powers of Mind in Victorian Britain* (Chicago: University of Chicago Press, 1998), and N. P. Spanos, *Multiple Identities and False Memories: A Sociocultural Perspective* (Washington, D.C.: American Psychological Association, 1996). With respect to the hysterias, see M. Borch-Jacobsen, *Remembering Anna O.: A Century of Mystification* (New York: Routledge, 1996); M. S. Micale, *Approaching Hysteria: Disease and Its Interpretation* (Princeton, N.J.: Princeton University Press, 1995); C. Smith-Rosenberg, *Disorderly Conduct: Visions of Gender in Victorian America* (New York: Knopf, 1985); and T. S. Szasz, *The Myth of Mental Illness: Foundations of a Theory of Personal Conduct* (New York: Hoeber-Harper, 1961). With respect to multiple personality disorder, see Spanos, *Multiple Identities and False Memories.* Brown (quoted in Spanos, p. 226) observed that "the psychology of acting will probably give considerable help in the ultimate solution" of the problem of MPD.

2. See Micale, *Approaching Hysteria,* p. 198.

3. F. de Waal, *Chimpanzee Politics: Power and Sex among Apes,* rev. ed. (Baltimore: Johns Hopkins University Press, 1998).

4. The theory of kin altruism is reviewed in R. Trivers, *Social Evolution* (Menlo Park, Calif.: Benjamin Cummings, 1985). See also I. Eibl-Eibesfeldt, *Human Ethology* (New York: Aldine de Gruyter, 1989); for information on how chimpanzees care for one another, see J. van Lawick-Goodall, *In the Shadow of Man* (Boston: Houghton Mifflin, 1971).

5. E. Trinkaus and P. Shipman, *The Neandertals: Changing the Image of Mankind* (New York: Knopf, 1993).

6. American Psychiatric Association, *Diagnostic and Statistical Manual of Mental Disorders, 4th ed.* (Washington, D.C.: American Psychiatric Association Press, 1994).

7. According to Ian Hacking, a well-known philosopher and medical historian, even Pierre Janet, who worked with Charcot in the Salpêtrière and "invented" dissociation, some years later considered his concept outmoded (*Mad Travelers: Reflections on the Reality of Transient Mental Illness* [Charlottesville: University Press of Virginia, 1998]). Hacking laments that psychiatry has failed to follow Janet, except in his early errors.

8. A. Kleinman, *Social Origins of Distress and Disease: Depression, Neurasthenia, and Pain in Modern China* (New Haven: Yale University Press, 1986); and A. Kleinman, *The Illness Narratives: Suffering, Healing, and the Human Condition* (New York: Basic Books, 1988).

9. The term "idiom of distress" is originally from M. Nichter, "Idioms of distress: Alternatives in the expression of psychosocial distress: A case study from South India," *Culture, Medicine and Psychiatry* 8 (1981): 379.

10. Hacking, in *Mad Travelers,* addressed this point in relation to fugues, which abruptly became epidemic in France in the 1880s. Hacking's findings are cited in chapter 6.

11. See T. Parsons, *Social Structure and Personality* (New York: Free Press, 1964); and "Illness and the role of the physician: A sociological perspective," in *The Talcott Parsons Reader*, ed. B. S. Turner (Malden, Mass.: Blackwell, 1999); H. E. Sigerist, "The special position of the sick," in *Henry E. Sigerist on the Sociology of Medicine*, ed. M. I. Roemer (New York: MD Publications, 1960).

12. Hacking, *Mad Travelers.*

13. I. M. Lewis, *Ecstatic Religion: A Study of Shamanisn and Spirit Possession,* 2nd ed. (New York: Routledge, 1989).

Chapter 2

1. See, for example, R. B. Cialdini, C. A. Kallgren, and R. R. Reno, "A focus theory of normative conduct," *Advances in Experimental Social Psychology* 24 (1991): 201; and R. B. Cialdini, R. R. Reno, and C. A. Kallgren, "A focus theory of normative conduct: Recycling the concept of norms to reduce littering in public places," *Journal of Personality and Social Psychology* 58 (1990): 1015.

2. M. Sherif, "An experimental approach to the study of attitudes," *Sociometry* 1 (1937): 90.

3. S. E. Asch, "Studies of independence and conformity: A minority of one against a unanimous majority," *Psychological Monographs* 70 (1956): No. 416.

4. S. Milgram, "Some conditions of obedience and disobedience to authority," *Human Relations* 18 (1965): 57, and S. Milgram, *Obedience to Authority* (New York: Harper and Row, 1974).

5. See P. G. Zimbardo, "A Pirandellian prison," *New York Times Magazine*, April 8, 1973, 38. A videotape on this study is also available (*Quiet Rage: The Stanford Prison Experiment* [HarperCollins College Publishers, 1992]).

6. J. M. Darley and B. Latané, "Bystander intervention in emergencies: Diffusion of responsibility," *Journal of Personality and Social Psychology* 8 (1968): 377; J. M. Darley, A. I. Teger, and L. D. Lewis, "Do groups always inhibit individuals' response to potential emergencies?" *Journal of Personality and Social Psychology* 26 (1973): 395; B. Latané and J. M. Darley, "Group inhibition of bystander intervention in emergencies," *Journal of Personality and Social Psychology* 10 (1968): 215; B. Latané and S. Nida, "Ten years of research on group-size and helping behavior," *Psychological Bulletin* 89 (1981): 308.

7. R. E. Nisbett and T. D. Wilson, "Telling more than we can know: Verbal reports on mental processes," *Psychological Review* 84 (1977): 231.

8. See, for example, D. J. Bem, "Self-perception theory," in *Advances in Experimental Social Psychology, Vol. 6,* ed. L. Berkowitz (New York: Academic Press, 1972).

9. For example, self-attribution theory predicts that subjects who perform

tasks without reward will come to believe they enjoy the tasks they have been given because they know that people work at tasks either because they enjoy them or because they are rewarded. In a classic study, Lepper and colleagues gave children colorful felt-tip pens (M. R. Lepper, D. Greene, and R. E. Nisbett, "Undermining children's intrinsic interest with extrinsic reward: A test of the overjustification hypothesis," *Journal of Personality and Social Psychology* 28 [1973]: 129). One group of children were promised a reward for using the pens. Other children were allowed to use the pens but were not promised or given a reward. Several days later, the children were given the pens again. The children who had received no rewards spent twice as much time drawing as the rewarded children. The rewarded children, in other words, no longer enjoyed the pens. Other studies have shown that rewards for learning tasks may decrease students' stated enjoyment of schoolwork, their willingness to tackle more complex tasks and problems, and the creativity and quality of their work. S. T. Fiske and S. E. Taylor, *Social Cognition,* 2nd ed. (New York: McGraw-Hill, 1991), cite this work under the rubric of "overjustification."

10. See, for example, P. R. Sanday, *Fraternity Gang Rape* (New York: New York University Press, 1990); B. Buford, *Among the Thugs* (New York: Norton, 1991).

11. M. Galanter, "The 'relief effect': A sociobiological model for neurotic distress and large-group therapy," *American Journal of Psychiatry* 135 (1978): 588; see also M. Galanter, *Cults: Faiths, Healing, and Coercion* (New York: Oxford University Press, 1989).

12. For a review of these studies, see B. Wenegrat, "Religious cult membership: A sociobiologic model," in *Cults and New Religious Movements: A Report of the American Psychiatric Association*, ed. M. Galanter (Washington, D.C.: American Psychiatric Press, 1989).

13. M. Galanter, ""Psychological induction into the large group: Findings from a modern religious sect," *American Journal of Psychiatry* 137 (1980): 1574.

14. For a review of the following findings, see Wenegrat, "Religious cult membership."

15. See J. S. Gordon, *The Golden Guru: The Strange Journey of the Bhagwan Shree Rajneesh* (Lexington, Mass.: Stephen Greene Press, 1987).

16. See C. Goldberg, "Courage and fanaticism: The charismatic leader and modern religious cults," in *Psychodynamic Perspectives on Religion, Sect, and Cult,* ed. D. A. Halperin (Littleton, Mass.: John Wright, 1983), D. Layton, *Seductive Poison: A Jonestown Survivor's Story of Life and Death in the People's Temple* (New York: Anchor Books, 1998); M. M. Maaga, *Hearing the Voices of Jonestown* (Syracuse: Syracuse University Press, 1998).

17. See N. Gibbs, "Oh, my God, they're killing themselves: Waco comes to an end," *Time*, May 3, 1993.

18. See W. Claiborne and W. Booth, "Cult members died in shifts over days," *Washington Post*, March 28, 1997.

19. See R. Lacayo, "Cults: In the reign of fire," *Time*, October 17, 1994; and M. S. Serrill, "Remains of the day: The leaders of the Solar Temple are among the dead in the mass murder-suicide, but many mysteries linger," *Time*, October 14, 1994.

20. I. L. Janis and B. T. King, "The influence of role playing on opinion change," *Journal of Abnormal and Social Psychology* 49 (1954): 211. Additional examples of this type of research are given in chapter 6.

21. One especially impressive study not cited in chapter 8 showed long-term decreases in smoking as the result of role-playing (I. L. Janis and L. Mann, "Effectiveness of emotional role-playing in modifying smoking habits and attitudes," *Journal of Experimental Research in Personality* 1 [1965]: 84; L. Mann and I. L. Janis, "A follow-up study on the long-term effects of emotional role playing," *Journal of Personality and Social Psychology* 8 [1968]: 339). Another such study showed that subjects who acted as if they were concerned about driving safety to the extent of posting a small sign in their window were later sufficiently "dedicated" to driving safety that they agreed to have highway-size billboards installed on their front lawns (J. L. Freedman and S. C. Fraser, "Compliance without pressure: The foot-in-the-door technique," *Journal of Personality and Social Psychology* 4 [1966]: 195). See also R. B. Cialdini, *Influence: The New Psychology of Modern Persuasion* (New York: Quill, 1984), and P. G. Zimbardo, E. B. Ebbesen, and C. Maslach, *Influencing Attitudes and Changing Behavior,* 2nd ed. (New York: Random House, 1977), which has a section entitled, "All the World's a Stage . . . and We Are Just Role-Players."

22. E. Goffman, *The Presentation of Self in Everyday Life* (Garden City, N.Y.: Doubleday Anchor, 1959).

23. D. Riesman, N. Glazer, and R. Denney, *The Lonely Crowd: A Study of the Changing American Character* (New Haven: Yale University Press, 1961).

24. The following findings on self-monitoring are reviewed by M. Synder, *Public Appearance/Private Realities* (New York: W. H. Freeman, 1987).

25. This and the following quote are from Snyder, *Public Appearance/Private Realities,* p. 178.

26. "Hypnotic virtuoso," a term coined by E. R. Hilgard (see E. R. Hilgard, "Suggestibility and suggestions as related to hypnosis," in *Human Suggestibility: Advances in Theory, Research, and Applications,* ed. J. F. Schumaker [New York: Routledge, 1991]), refers to individuals in the highest percentiles on hypnotizability scales. Hilgard likened the hypnotic talents of such subjects to the musical talents of concert-level musicians; hence the term "virtuosos." Spiegel and Spiegel refer to such individuals as "Grade 5" subjects and comment on their role malleability (H. Spiegel and D. Spiegel, *Trance and Treatment: Clinical Uses of Hypnosis* [New York: Basic Books, 1978]). In contrast, in a large sample, a group-administered scale of hypnotic responsiveness failed to correlate with self-monitoring scale scores (J. F. Kihlstron, W. A. Diaz, G. E. McClellan, P. M. Ruskin, D. O. Pistole, and R. E. Shor, "Personality correlates of hynotic susceptibility: Needs for achievement and autonomy, self-monitoring, and masculinity-femininity," *American Journal of Clinical Hypnosis* 22 [1980]: 225). Possibly, the self-monitoring scale measures a different type of role-cue responsiveness than the group hypnotizability scale Kihlstrom and his colleagues used, or perhaps only extreme hypnotizability is associated with role-cue responsiveness.

27. This issue and relevant data are reviewed in B. Wenegrat, *Illness and Power: Women's Mental Disorders and the Battle between the Sexes* (New York: New York University Press, 1995).

28. A. Kleinman, *Social Origins of Distress and Disease: Depression, Neurasthenia, and Pain in Modern China* (New Haven: Yale University Press, 1986); A. Kleinman, *The Illness Narratives: Suffering, Healing and the Human Condition* (New York: Basic Books, 1988).

29. American Psychiatric Association, *Diagnostic and Statistical Manual of*

Mental Disorders, 4th ed. (Washington, D.C.: American Psychiatric Association Press, 1994).

30. The classic critique of group-selection theory is G. C. Williams, *Adaptation and Natural Selection* (Princeton, N.J.: Princeton University Press, 1966). More recent arguments in favor of group selection are found in D. S. Wilson and E. Sober, "Reintroducing group selection to the behavioral sciences," *Behavioral and Brain Sciences* 17 (1994): 585; and E. Sober and D. S. Wilson, *Unto Others: The Evolution and Psychology of Unselfish Behavior* (Cambridge, Mass.: Harvard University Press, 1998).

31. S. Schachter, "Deviation, rejection, and communication," *Journal of Abnormal and Social Psychology* 46 (1951): 190.

32. American Psychiatric Association, *Diagnostic and Statistical Manual of Mental Disorders, 4th ed.*

33. See, for example, L. J. Siever, L. Friedman, J. Moskowitz, V. Mitropolou, R. Keefe, S. L. Roitman, D. Merhige, R. Trestman, J. Silverman, and R. Mohs, "Eye movement impairment and schizotypal psychopathology," *American Journal of Psychiatry* 515 (1994): 1209.

34. L. Wing, "Asperger's syndrome: A clinical account," *Psychological Medicine* 11 (1981): 115.

35. R. H. Dworkin, "Genetic Influences on Cross-situational Consistency," cited in M. Synder, *Public Appearance/Private Realities.*

36. S. Gangestadt, "On the etiology of individual differences in self-monitoring and expressive self-control: Testing the hypothesis of strong genetic influence," cited in M. Synder, *Public Appearance/Private Realities.*

37. H. J. Crawford, A. M. Brown, and C. E. Moon, "Sustained attentional and disattentional abilities: Differences between low and highly hypnotizable persons," *Journal of Abnormal Psychology* 102 (1993): 534.

38. M. Mesulam, *Principles of Behavioral Neurology* (Philadelphia: F. A. Davis, 1985).

39. F. X Castellanos, J. N. Giedd, P. Eckburg, W. L. Marsh, A. C. Vaituzis, D. Kaysen, S. D. Hamburger, and J. L. Rapoport, "Quantitative morphology of the caudate nucleus in attention deficit hyperactivity disorder," *American Journal of Psychiatry* 151 (1994): 1791.

40. See, for example, H. J. Crawford, R. C. Gur, B. Skolnick, R. E. Gur, and D. M. Benson, "Effects of hypnosis on regional cerebral blood flow during ischemic pain with and without suggested hypnotic analgesia," *International Journal of Psychophysiology* 15 (1993): 177.

Chapter 3

1. I. M. Lewis, *Ecstatic Religion: A Study of Shamanisn and Spirit Possession,* 2nd ed. (New York: Routledge, 1989).

2. Lewis, *Ecstatic Religion,* p. 64.

3. Lewis, *Ecstatic Religion,* p. 70.

4. Lewis, *Ecstatic Religion,* p. 71.

5. Lewis, *Ecstatic Religion,* p. 72.

6. Lewis, *Ecstatic Religion,* p. 72.

7. Lewis, *Ecstatic Religion,* p. 72.

8. Lewis, *Ecstatic Religion,* p. 72.

9. Lewis, *Ecstatic Religion,* p. 75. See also M. Nichter, "Idioms of distress: Al-

ternatives in the expression of psychosocial distress: A case study from South India," *Culture, Medicine and Psychiatry* 8 (1981): 379.

10. Lewis, *Ecstatic Religion,* p. 76.

11. Lewis, *Ecstatic Religion,* p. 76.

12. P. M. Yap, "The possession syndrome: A comparison of the Hong Kong and French findings," *Journal of Mental Science* 106 (1960): 114.

13. Lewis, *Ecstatic Religion*, p. 97.

14. L. L. Langness, "Hysterical psychosis in the New Guinea highlands: A Bena Bena example," *Psychiatry* 28 (1965): 258.

15. Lewis, *Ecstatic Religion.*

16. *Amok* may be less an illness role than ritualized murder-suicide, with roots in fighting tactics used by Malay warriors. For information on *amok,* see J. E. Carr, "Ethno-behaviorism and the culture-bound syndromes: The case of *amok," Culture, Medicine and Psychiatry* 2 (1978): 269; see also W. G. Ellis, "The *amok* of the Malays," *Journal of Mental Science* 39 (1893): 21; E. K. Tan and J. E. Carr, "Psychiatric Sequelae of *amok," Culture, Medicine and Psychiatry* 1 (1977): 59; J. I. Teoh, "The changing psychopathology of amok," *Psychiatry* 35 (1972): 345; F. H. G. Van Loon, "*Amok* and *latah," Journal of Abnormal and Social Psychology* 21 (1927): 434; J. Westermeyer, "On the epidemicity of *amok* violence," *Archives of General Psychiatry* 28 (1973): 873.

17. Though the Javanese are not the group in which *latah* and *amok* have been studied, they share common cultural features with all other Malay peoples. See C. Geertz, *The Religion of Java* (New York: Free Press, 1960); and C. Geertz, *Person, Time, and Conduct in Bali* (New Haven: Yale University Press, 1966).

18. Geertz, *Religion of Java;* see also J. E. Carr, "Ethno-behaviorism and the culture-bound syndromes"; M. G. Kenny, "*Latah*: The symbolism of a putative mental disorder," *Culture, Medicine and Psychiatry* 2 (1978): 209.

19. See Carr, "Ethno-behaviorism and the culture-bound syndromes"; Kenny, "*Latah.*"

20. C. Osgood, W. May, and M. Mison, *Cross-Cultural Universals of Affective Meaning* (Urbana: University of Illinois Press, 1975).

21. Carr, "Ethno-behaviorism and the culture-bound syndromes."

22. For information on *latah,* see Kenny, "*Latah*"; see also T. L. Chiu, J. E. Tong, and K. E. Schmidt, "A clinical and survey study of *latah* in Sarawak, Malysia," *Psychological Medicine* 2 (1972): 155; P. M. Yap, "The *latah* reaction: Its psychodynamics and nosological position," *Journal of Mental Science* 98 (1952): 33; F. H. G. Van Loon, "*Amok* and *latah.*"

23. Chiu, Tong, and Schmidt, "A clinical and survey study of *latah.*"

24. Yap, "The *latah* reaction."

25. N. S. Kline, "Psychiatry in Indonesia," *American Journal of Psychiatry* 120 (1963): 809.

26. See, for example, M. G. Kenny, "*Latah.*"

27. See Kenny, "*Latah.*"

28. Lewis, *Ecstatic Religion,* p. 38.

29. Kenny, "*Latah.*"

30. Chiu, Tong, and Schmidt, "A clinical and survey study of *latah*"; Yap, "The *latah* reaction."

31. E. A. Guinness, "Introduction," *British Journal of Psychiatry* 160 (suppl. 16, 1992): 4; E. A. Guinness, "I. Relationship between the neuroses and brief reactive psychosis: Descriptive case studies in Africa," *British Journal of Psychia-*

try 160 (suppl. 16, 1992): 12; E. A. Guinness, "II. Brief reactive psychosis and the major functional psychoses: Descriptive case studies in Africa," *British Journal of Psychiatry* 160 (suppl. 16, 1992): 24.

32. American Psychiatric Association, *Diagnostic and Statistical Manual of Mental Disorder, 4th ed.* (Washington, D.C.: American Psychiatric Association, 1994).

33. See also E. A. Guinness, "Profile and prevalence of the brain fag syndrome: Psychiatric morbidity in school populations in Africa," *British Journal of Psychiatry* 160 (suppl. 16, 1992): 42.

34. See Guinness, "II. Brief reactive psychosis and the major functional psychoses."

35. See, for example, M. H. Hollender and S. J. Hirsch, "Hysterical psychosis," *American Journal of Psychiatry* 120 (1964): 1066; S. J. Hirsch and M. H. Hollender, "Hysterical psychosis: Clarification of the concept," *American Journal of Psychiatry* 125 (1959): 909; L. L. Langness, "Hysterical psychosis: The cross-cultural evidence," *American Journal of Psychiatry* 124 (1967): 145; J. Modestin and K. M. Bachman, "Is the diagnosis of hysterical psychosis justified?: Clinical study of hysterical psychosis, reactive/psychogenic psychosis, and schizophrenia," *Comprehensive Psychiatry* 33 (1992): 17; H. E. Refsum, "Hysteric reactive psychoses: A follow-up," *Neuropsychobiology* 8 (1982): 172.

36. Hollender and Hirsch, "Hysterical psychosis."

37. D. Spiegel and R. Fink, "Hysterical psychosis and hypnotizability," *American Journal of Psychiatry* 136 (1979): 777.

38. See H. Spiegel and D. Spiegel, *Trance and Treatment: Clinical Uses of Hypnosis Hypnosis* (New York: Basic Books, 1978).

39. L. K. Suryani, "Culture and mental disorder: The case of *bebainan* in Bali," *Culture, Medicine and Psychiatry* 8 (1984): 95.

40. Suryani, "Culture and mental disorder."

41. See Nichter, "Idioms of distress"; A. Kleinman, *Social Origins of Distress and Disease: Depression, Neurasthenia, and Pain in Modern China* (New Haven: Yale University Press, 1986); A. Kleinman, *The Illness Narratives: Suffering, Healing and the Human Condition* (New York: Basic Books, 1988).

42. See P. J. Guarnaccia, V. DeLaCancela, and E. Carrillo, "The multiple meanings of *ataques de nervios* in the Latino community," *Medical Anthropology* 11 (1989): 47; P. J. Guarnaccia, M. Rubio-Stipec, and G. Canino, "*Ataques de nervios* in the Puerto Rican Diagnostic Interview Schedule: The impact of cultural categories on psychiatric epidemiology," *Culture, Medicine and Psychiatry* 13 (1989): 275; M. Oquendo, E. Horwath, and A. Martinez, "*Ataques de nervios*: Proposed diagnostic criteria for a culture specific syndrome," *Culture, Medicine and Psychiatry* 16 (1992): 367; A. Rothenberg, "Puerto Rico and aggression," *American Journal of Psychiatry* 120 (1964): 962; E. C. Trautman, "The suicidal fit," *Archives of General Psychiatry* 5 (1961): 98.

43. Rothenberg, "Puerto Rico and aggression."

44. Guarnaccia, DeLaCancela, and Carrillo, "The multiple meanings of *ataques de nervios* in the Latino community."

45. Guarnaccia, DeLaCancela, and Carrillo, "The multiple meanings of *ataques de nervios* in the Latino community."

46. Oquendo, Horwath, and Martinez, "*Ataques de nervios.*"

47. Oquendo, Horwath, and Martinez, "*Ataques de nervios.*"

48. Rothenberg, "Puerto Rico and aggression."

49. Guarnaccia, DeLaCancela, and Carrillo, "The multiple meanings of *ataques de nervios* in the Latino community."

50. American Psychiatric Association, *Diagnostic and Statistical Manual of Mental Disorder, 4th ed.*

51. L. Srole, T. S. Langner, S. T. Michael, M. K. Opler, and T. A. C. Rennie, *Mental Health in the Metropolis: The Midtown Manhattan Study* (New York: McGraw-Hill, 1962).

52. Guarnaccia, Rubio-Stipec, and Canino, "*Ataques de nervios* in the Puerto Rican Diagnostic Interview Schedule."

53. M. F. Wack, *Lovesickness in the Middle Ages: The* Viaticum *and Its Commentaries* (Philadelphia: University of Pennsylvania Press, 1990).

54. Wack, *Lovesickness,* p. 63.

55. Wack, *Lovesickness,* p. 63.

56. Lewis, *Ecstatic Religion.*

57. Lewis, *Ecstatic Religion.*

Chapter 4

1. See R. A. Baker, *They Call It Hypnosis* (Buffalo, N.Y.: Prometheus, 1990).

2. See W. C. Coe, "Hypnosis: The role of sociopolitical factors in a paradigm clash," in *Hypnosis: The Cognitive-Behavioral Perspective,* ed. N. P. Spanos and J. F. Chaves (Buffalo, N.Y.: Prometheus Books, 1989).

3. Baker, *They Call It Hypnosis.*

4. Baker, *They Call It Hypnosis.* See also G. F. Drinka, *The Birth of Neurosis: Myth, Malady and the Victorians* (New York: Simon and Schuster, 1984).

5. Baker, *They Call It Hypnosis.*

6. Drinka, *The Birth of Neurosis.* See also H. F. Ellenberger, *The Discovery of the Unconscious: The History and Evolution of Dynamic Psychiatry* (New York: Basic Books, 1970).

7. E. R. Hilgard, *Divided Consciousness: Multiple Controls in Human Thought and Action* (expanded ed.) (New York: Wiley, 1986).

8. For information on Mesmer, Puysegur, Barbarin, and Faria, see Baker, *They Call It Hypnosis.*

9. Coe, "Hypnosis."

10. See, for example, T. R. Sarbin and W. C. Coe, *Hypnosis: A Social Psychological Analysis of Influence Communication* (New York: Holt, Rinehart and Winston, 1972); and T. R. Sarbin and D. T. Lim, "Contributions to role-taking theory X: Some evidence in support of the role-taking hypothesis in hypnosis," *Journal of Clinical and Experimental Hypnosis* 11 (1963): 98.

11. E. Banyai and E. R. Hilgard, "A comparison of an active alert hypnotic induction with traditional relaxation induction," *Journal of Abnormal Psychology* 85 (1976): 218; and L. B. Glass and T. X. Barber, "A note on hypnotic behavior, the definition of the situation and the placebo effect," *Journal of Nervous and Mental Disease* 132 (1961): 539.

12. T. X. Barber, N. P. Spanos, and J. F. Chaves, *Hypnosis, Imagination, and Human Potentialities* (New York: Pergamon Press, 1974). For a scholarly sourcebook of hypnotism research motivated by the social psychological viewpoint, see N. P. Spanos and J. F. Chaves, eds., *Hypnosis: The Cognitive-Behavioral Perspective* (Buffalo, N.Y.: Prometheus Books, 1989).

13. See, for example, N. P. Spanos, *Multiple Identities and False Memories: A So-*

ciocultural Perspective (Washington, D.C.: American Psychological Association, 1996); A. Winter, *Mesmerized: Powers of Mind in Victorian Britain* (Chicago: University of Chicago Press, 1998).

14. See Winter, *Mesmerized.*

15. See L. D. Bertrand, "The assessment and modification of hypnotic susceptibility," in *Hypnosis: The Cognitive-Behavioral Perspective*, ed. N. P. Spanos and J. F. Chaves (Buffalo, N.Y.: Prometheus Books, 1989).

16. M. M. Gill and M. Brenman, *Hypnosis and Related States: Psychoanalytical Studies in Regression* (New York: International Universities Press, 1959).

17. E. R. Hilgard, *Divided Consciousness.*

18. Hilgard, *Divided Consciousness.*

19. Barber, Spanos, and Chaves, *Hypnosis, Imagination, and Human Potentialities.*

20. Bertrand, "The assessment and modification of hypnotic susceptibility."

21. Barber, Spanos, and Chaves, *Hypnosis, Imagination, and Human Potentialities*; see also C. S. Hendler and W. H. Redd, "Fear of hypnosis: The role of labelling in patients' acceptance of behavioral interventions," *Behavior Therapy* 17 (1986): 2.

22. Barber, Spanos, and Chaves, *Hypnosis, Imagination, and Human Potentialities.* For a review of modification of hypnotizability, see M. J. Diamond, "Modification of hypnotizability: A review," *Psychological Bulletin* 81 (1974): 180.

23. Hilgard, *Divided Consciousness.* See also N. P. Spanos and T. X. Barber, "Toward a convergence in hypnosis research," *American Psychologist* (July 1974): 500; S. C. Wilson and T. X. Barber, "The creative imagination scale as a measure of hypnotic responsiveness," *American Journal of Clinical Hypnosis* 20 (1978): 235.

24. S. C. Wilson and T. X. Barber, "The fantasy-prone personality: Implications for understanding imagery, hypnosis and parapsychological phenomena," in *Imagery: Current Theory, Research, and Application*, ed. A. A. Sheikh (New York: Wiley, 1983). In a related vein, Grabe and co-workers administered the Dissociative Experience Scale to 232 subjects, 191 of whom had psychiatric disorders. Dissociative experiences were associated with high "self-transcendance" scores on a Temperament and Character Inventory. According to the authors, persons with such scores are "creative, ingenious, and rich in fantasy" (H. Grabe, C. Spitzer, and H. J. Freyberger, "Relationship of dissociation to temperament and character in men and women," *American Journal of Psychiatry* 156 [1999]: 1811).

25. J. W. Rhue and S. J. Lynn, "Fantasy proneness, hypnotizability, and multiple personality," in *Human Suggestibility: Advances in Theory, Research, and Applications*, ed. J. F. Schumaker (New York: Routledge, 1991), and J. R. Hilgard, "Imaginative and sensory-affective involvement in everyday life and in hypnosis," in *Hypnosis: Developments in Research and New Perspectives,* ed. E. Fromm and R. Shor (New York: Aldine, 1979). Spanos, however, notes the weakness of data that suggest a link between childhood abuse and later hypnotic responsiveness (Spanos, *Multiple Identities and False Memories*).

26. A. M. Weitzenhoffer, "Hypnotic susceptibility revisited," *American Journal of Clinical Hypnosis* 22 (1980): 130.

27. See, for example, H. J. Eysenck, "Is suggestibility?" in *Human Suggestibility: Advances in Theory, Research, and Applications,* ed. F. F. Schumaker (New York: Routledge, 1991).

28. For this and the following point, see R. K. Moore, "Susceptibility to hyp-

nosis and suceptibility to social influence," *Journal of Abnormal and Social Psychology* 68 (1964): 282; K. R. Graham and L. D. Green, "Hypnotic susceptibility related to an independent measure of compliance—alumni annual giving: A brief communication," *International Journal of Clinical and Experimental Hypnosis* 29 (1981): 351; M. L. Shames, "Hypnotic susceptibility and conformity: On the mediational mechanism of suggestibility," *Psychological Reports* 49 (1981): 563; and P. Hajek and J. Spacek, "Territory, hypnotic susceptibility and social influence: A pilot study," *British Journal of Experimental and Clinical Hypnosis* 4 (1987): 115. See also G. F. Wagstaff, "Suggestibility: A social psychological approach," in *Human Suggestibility: Advances in Theory, Research, and Applications,* ed. J. F. Schumaker (New York: Routledge, 1991).

29. Spanos, *Multiple Identities and False Memories.* Spanos observed that the most hypnotizable subjects are those who are most "responsiveness to social communications" (p. 255). He cited studies showing that hypnotizability correlates with pantomime role-playing abilities and that people with backgrounds in drama tend to be hypnotizable (p. 258).

30. H. Spiegel and D. Spiegel, *Trance and Treatment: Clinical Uses of Hypnosis* (New York: Basic Books, 1978).

31. D. Shapiro, *Neurotic Styles* (New York: Basic Books, 1965).

32. American Psychiatric Association, *Diagnostic and Statistical Manual of Mental Disorders, 4th ed.* (Washington, D.C.: American Psychiatric Association Press, 1994).

33. Barber, Spanos, and Chaves, *Hypnosis, Imagination, and Human Potentialities.*

34. G. F. Wagstaff, "Forensic aspects of hypnosis," in *Hypnosis: The Cognitive-Behavioral Perspective,* ed. N. P. Spanos and J. F. Chaves (Buffalo, N.Y.: Prometheus Books, 1989).

35. Wagstaff, "Forensic aspects of hypnosis"; see also R. Buckhout, P. Eugenio, T. Licitra, L. Oliver, and T. H. Kramer, "Memory, hypnosis and evidence," *Social Action and the Law* 7 (1981): 67; P. W. Sheehand and J. Tilden, "Effects of suggestibility and hypnosis on accurate and distorted retrieval from memory," *Journal of Experimental Psychology: Learning, Memory and Cognition* 9 (1983): 283.

36. R. M. True, "Experimental control in hypnotic age regression states," *Science* 110 (1949): 583.

37. Barber, Spanos, and Chaves, *Hypnosis, Imagination, and Human Potentialities.*

38. M. Parrish, R. M. Lundy, and H. W. Liebowitz, "Effect of hypnotic age regression on the magnitude of the Ponzo and Poggendorff illusions," *Journal of Abnormal Psychology* 74 (1969): 693.

39. Barber, Spanos, and Chaves, *Hypnosis, Imagination, and Human Potentialities.*

40. J.-R. Laurence and C. Perry, "Hypnotically created memory among highly hypnotizable subjects," *Science* 222 (1983): 523.

41. These studies are reviewed in A. M. Weitzenhoffer, *Hypnotism: An Objective Study of Suggestibility* (New York: Wiley, 1953); and in M. T. Orne, "The mechanisms of hypnotic age regression: An experimental study," *Journal of Nervous and Mental Disorder* 46 (1951): 213.

42. D. N. O'Connell, R. E. Shor, and M. T. Orne, "Hypnotic age repression: An empirical and methodological analysis," *Journal of Abnormal Psychology* 76 (1970, Number 3, pt. 2): 1.

43. S. Troffer, *Hypnotic Age Regression and Cognitive Functioning,* unpublished doctoral dissertation, Stanford University, 1965.

44. Hilgard, *Divided Consciousness.*

45. See Baker, *They Call It Hypnosis,* ed. Spanos and Chaves; *Hypnosis: The Cognitive-Behavioral Perspective*; Barber, Spanos, and Chaves, *Hypnosis, Imagination, and Human Potentialities.*

46. M. Bernstein, *The Search for Bridey Murphy* (New York: Doubleday, 1956).

47. See M. V. Kline, ed., *A Scientific Report on the Search for Bridey Murphy* (New York: Julian Press, 1956).

48. J. S. Victor, *Satanic Panic: The Creation of a Contemporary Legend* (Chicago: Open Court, 1993).

49. Baker, *They Call It Hypnosis.*

50. See N. P. Spanos, "Past-life hypnotic regression: A critical view," *Skeptical Inquirer* 12 (Winter 1987–1988): 174.

51. M. T. Orne, "The use and misuse of hypnosis in court," *International Journal of Clinical and Experimental Hypnosis* 27 (1979): 311.

52. American Medical Association, "Council report: Scientific status of refreshing recollection by the use of hypnosis (August, 1985)," *International Journal of Clinical and Experimental Hypnosis* 34 (1986): 1.

53. H. Merskey also made this point about hypnosis with respect to hysterical symptoms in general. See *The Analysis of Hysteria: Understanding Conversion and Dissociation,* 2nd ed. (London: Gaskell, 1999).

54. N. P. Spanos, H. L. Radtke, and L. D. Bertrand, "Hypnotic amnesia as a strategic enactment: Breaching amnesia in highly susceptible subjects," *Journal of Personality and Social Psychology* 47 (1985): 1155. A study that purports to find a physiological correlate of hypnotic amnesia (S. LaBerge and P. G. Zimbardo, "Event-related potential correlates of suggested hypnotic amnesia," *Sleep and Hypnosis* 1 [1999]: 122) illustrates how difficult it can be to interpret physiological measures in the context of hypnosis. The authors measured late evoked brain potentials in response to words that subjects had been hypnotically instructed to forget. Subjects who reported ostensibly genuine posthypnotic amnesia for the words had larger late positive evoked brain potentials in response to these words than they showed in response to other words they had not been instructed to forget. This difference could not be explained by differences in overt responses to the two sets of words, nor did it occur in a group of subjects instructed to merely simulate posthypnotic amnesia. Other studies, however, show larger than usual late positive evoked brain potentials to stimuli connected with so-called guilty knowledge, or information the subject does not want to admit having. (See, for example, J. J. B. Allen and W. G. Iacono, "A comparison of methods for the analysis of event-related potentials in deception detection," *Psychophysiology* 34 [1997]: 234; L. A. Farwell and E. Donchin, "The truth will out: Interrogative polygraphy ["Lie Detection"] with event-related brain potentials," *Psychophysiology* 28 [1991]: 531). The stronger the incentive to hide such guilty knowledge, the larger the late positive potential to stimuli associated with it. Therefore, the study may prove only that subjects who are acting out the role of posthypnotic amnesia are especially eager not to acknowledge having information that they are supposed to have forgotten.

55. The historical observations in this section are from J. F. Chaves, "Hypnotic control of pain," in *Hypnosis: The Cognitive-Behavioral Perspective*, ed. N. P. Spanos and J. F. Chaves (Buffalo, N.Y.: Prometheus Books, 1989); Barber, Spanos, and Chaves, *Hypnosis, Imagination, and Human Potentialities*; and Baker, *They Call It Hypnosis.*

56. Chaves, "Hypnotic control of pain."

57. Barber, Spanos, and Chaves, *Hypnosis, Imagination, and Human Potentialities.*

58. Chaves, "Hypnotic control of pain."

59. N. P. Spanos, "Experimental research on hypnotic analgesia," in *Hypnosis: The Cognitive-Behavioral Perspective*, ed. N. P. Spanos and J. F. Chaves (Buffalo, N.Y.: Prometheus Books, 1989).

60. H. J. Stam and N. P. Spanos, "Experimental designs, expectancy effects, and hypnotic analgesia," *Journal of Abnormal Psychology* 89 (1980): 551.

61. E. R. Hilgard, J. R. Hilgard, H. MacDonald, A. H. Morgan, and L. S. Johnson, "Covert pain in hypnotic analgesia: Its reality as tested by the real-simulator design," *Journal of Abnormal Psychology* 87 (1978): 655; and E. R. Hilgard, A. H. Morgan, and H. MacDonald, "Pain and dissociation in the cold pressor test: A study of hypnotic analgesia with 'hidden reports' through automatic key-pressing and automatic talking," *Journal of Abnormal Psychology* 84 (1975): 280.

62. N. P. Spanos and E. C. Hewitt, "The hidden observer in hypnotic analgesia: Discovery or experimental creation?" *Journal of Personality and Social Psychology* 39 (1980): 1201.

63. N. P. Spanos, M. I. Gwynn, and H. J. Stam, "Instructional demands and ratings of overt and hidden pain during hypnotic analgesia," *Journal of Abnormal Psychology* 92 (1983): 479.

64. N. P. Spanos, H. P. de Groot, D. K. Tiller, J. R. Weekes, and L. P. Bertrand, "'Trance logic' duality and hidden observer responding in hypnotic, imagination control, and simulating subjects," *Journal of Abnormal Psychology* 94 (1985): 611.

65. H. S. Zamansky and S. P. Bartis, "The dissociation of an experience: The hidden observer observed," *Journal of Abnormal Psychology* 94 (1985): 243.

66. N. P. Spanos, D. M. Flynn, and M. I. Gwynn, "Contextual demands, negative hallucinations, and hidden observer responding: Three hidden observers observed," *British Journal of Experimental and Clinical Hypnosis* 5 (1988): 5.

67. Janet, Prince, Burnett and Hull are cited in Hilgard, *Divided Consciousness.*

68. Interference between suggested and ongoing activities can also be manifested in how these activities are performed, as well as in slower and less accurate performance. For example, if acts are being performed by separate mental subsystems, the component steps of one act should be temporally unrelated to the component steps of the other. Hilgard and colleagues, however, showed that this is not the case (V. J. Knox, L. Crutchfield, and E. R. Hilgard, "The nature of task interference in hypnotic dissociation: An investigation of hypnotic behavior," *International Journal of Clinical and Experimental Hypnosis* 23 [1975]: 305). Subjects were given suggestions to "unconsciously" press two keys. One key was pressed three times; then the other key was pressed three times, and so on. This task was performed while the subject named colors presented. Hilgard and colleagues found that simultaneous color naming led to more errors in the key-pressing task. They also found, however, that many subjects coordinated steps in the two tasks so as to minimize competition for limited cognitive capacities. Most subjects, for instance, gave color reports between the first and second depression of each key. Initiating the triplet apparently is incompatible with simultaneous naming of the presented colors. Subjects instead started the triplet and then used their mental capacity for the other task. Another com-

mon strategy was temporal segregation. Colors, in other words, were named between triplet depressions. In either case, there is evidence against independent subsystems.

If hypnosis cannot create independent mental subsystems, results like Janet's pose no problems for the social role view. In writing a letter while talking, Lucie was acting out the role of a hypnotic subject given the instructions she had been given by Janet. Nor is there evidence that hypnotic commands lead to less interference than waking instructions. In fact, studies performed by James Stevenson showed that subjects who simulated unconscious activities showed less interference with an ongoing task than did hypnotized subjects (J. H. Stevenson, "The effect of posthypnotic dissociation on the performance of interfering tasks," *Journal of Abnormal Psychology* 85 [1976]: 398). Stevenson argued that hypnotized subjects did worse because of the mental activity needed for dissociation. From a social role viewpoint, the hypnotized subjects may have done worse because of the mental demands of the role they were playing. The study by Hilgard and colleagues that showed coordination of component steps confirmed Stevenson's findings: Tasks were performed more successfully when both were admittedly conscious than when one was allegedly performed outside awareness.

In the studies cited here, subjects were told to do things that were difficult for them. They could not do two difficult tasks without one or both suffering. By contrast, some overlearned activities may be "routinized," which means they no longer impose significant cognitive strain. Routinization reduces interference with other tasks. To give a specific example, when driving a car for the first time it is hard to converse with someone; driving has not yet been routinized. Experienced drivers, though, can easily hold conversations while steering their automobiles; driving for them now requires little cognitive effort. Routinized tasks may require so little cognitive effort and ongoing attention that their execution is forgotten entirely. This is the cause of so-called highway hypnosis. Drivers with highway hypnosis arrive at their destination lacking clear memories of having driven there. Highway hypnosis is sometimes called dissociation, but, as in other instances where this term is used, it is hard to see what it really adds to our understanding, in this case of routinized actions.

69. C. L. Hull, *Hypnosis and Suggestibility: An Experimental Approach* (New York: Appleton-Century, 1933).

70. Weitzenhoffer, "Hypnotic susceptibility revisited."

71. See Barber, Spanos, and Chaves, *Hypnosis, Imagination, and Human Potentialities.*

72. For this and related studies, see Barber, Spanos, and Chaves, *Hypnosis, Imagination, and Human Potentialities.*

73. A. M. Weitzenhoffer, "When is an 'instruction' an 'instruction'?" *American Journal of Clinical Hypnosis* 22 (1974): 258.

74. S. J. Lynn, J. W. Rhue, and J. R. Weekes, "Hypnosis and experienced nonvolition: A social-cognitive integrative model," in *Hypnosis: The Cognitive-Behavioral Perspective*, ed. N. P. Spanos and J. F. Chaves (Buffalo, N.Y.: Prometheus Books, 1989).

75. Lynn, Rhue, and Weekes, "Hypnosis and experienced nonvolition'" p. 95.

76. N. P. Spanos, P. C. Cobb, and D. R. Gorassini, "Failing to resist hypnotic test suggestions: A strategy for self-presenting as deeply hypnotized," *Psychiatry* 48 (1985): 282.

77. Lynn, Rhue and Weekes, "Hypnosis and experienced nonvolition."

78. These studies are reviewed in Barber, Spanos, and Chaves, *Hypnosis, Imagination, and Human Potentialities*.

79. N. P. Spanos, M. W. Ham, and T. X. Barber, "Suggest ('hypnotic') visual hallucinations: Experimental and phenomenological data," *Journal of Abnormal Psychology* 81 (1973): 96.

80. A. E. Barbasz and C. Lonsdale, "Effects of hypnosis on P300 of olfactory-evoked potential amplitudes," *Journal of Abnormal Psychology* 92 (1983): 520.

81. D. Spiegel, S. Cutcomb, C. Ren, and K. Pribram, "Hypnotic hallucination alters evoked potentials," *Journal of Abnormal Psychology* 94 (1985): 249.

82. W. J. Jones and D. M. Flynn, "Methodological and theoretical considerations in the study of 'hypnotic' effects in perception," in *Hypnosis: The Cognitive-Behavioral Perspective*, ed. N. P. Spanos and J. F. Chaves (Buffalo, N.Y.: Prometheus Books, 1989).

83. T. X. Barber and D. S. Calverley, "Experimental studies in hypnotic behavior: Suggested deafness evaluated by delayed auditory feedback," *British Journal of Psychology* 55 (1964): 439.

84. See, for example, P. L Harriman, "Hypnotic induction of color vision anomalies: I. The Isihara and Jensen tests," *Journal of General Psychology* 26 (1942): 289.

85. S. M. Kosslyn, W. L. Thompson, M. R. Constantini-Ferrando, N. M. Alpert, and D. Spiegel, "Hypnotic visual illusion alters color processing in the brain," *American Journal of Psychiatry* 157 (2000): 1279.

86. M. T. Orne, "The nature of hypnosis: Artifact and essence," *Journal of Abnormal and Social Psychology* 58 (1959): 277.

87. According to Orne, trance logic differentiates real from faked hypnosis. In 1979, Orne was asked to evaluate Kenneth Bianchi, the alleged Hillside Strangler, who had murdered a number of women in the Los Angeles area (see Baker, *They Call It Hypnosis*). Bianchi based his defense on the claim that he had multiple personalities, one of whom had killed while in control of his body. To allow investigators to contact the hidden killer, Bianchi was hypnotized. While hypnotized, he revealed another side of himself, which went by the name Steven Walker, an alias Bianchi had once used for criminal purposes. To counter the hypnotic evidence, Orne was called in by the state attorneys. He reviewed video-tapes of Bianchi's hypnotic sessions and met with Bianchi himself, in the presence of Bianchi's lawyer. When Bianchi was hypnotized, Orne gave him suggestions to hallucinate his lawyer sitting in an empty chair. When Bianchi reported seeing the lawyer where Orne had suggested, Orne pointed out the real lawyer behind him. Bianchi said he could see his lawyer in only one place. On the basis of this and other failed tests for trance logic, Orne pronounced that Bianchi was faking his hypnotic responses.

Spanos, however, suggested that subjects instructed to fake hypnosis fail to show trance logic because they try to respond to suggestions completely (N. P. Spanos, "Hypnotic behavior: A social psychological interpretation of amnesia, analgesia and trance logic," *Behavioral and Brain Sciences* 9 [1986]: 449). Having said that they see a person sitting in a chair, they are loathe to contradict themselves by admitting that they see the chair, as well. By contrast, subjects who believe they are at least lightly hypnotized feel less pressure to give a perfect performance. Studies that employ as controls nonhypnotized, task-motivated subjects instructed to imagine objects or people as vividly as possible support this hypothesis. (See H. P. de Groot and M. I. Gwynn, "Trance logic, duality, and hidden observer responding," in *Hypnosis: The Cognitive-Behavioral Perspective*, ed. N. P. Spanos and J. F. Chaves [Buffalo, N.Y.: Prometheus Books, 1989]). See also Spanos, de Groot, Tiller, et al., "'Trance logic' duality and hidden observer." Subjects thought to be hypnotized and non-hypnotized, task-motivated subjects instructed to vividly imagine an image are equally likely to report seeing transparent images. A study by Spanos and colleagues also sheds light on this issue (N. P. Spanos, H. P. de Groot, and M. I. Gwynn, "Trance logic as incomplete responding," *Journal of Personality and Social Psychology* 53 [1987]: 911). Hypnotized subjects were given suggestions that they would be five years old and would see a stuffed toy. They were then queried for evidence of trance logic. Later, they were asked whether they had believed that the toy they had reported seeing was real. If trance logic characterizes highly hypnotizable subjects, as Orne argues, those who expressed the strongest beliefs in the reality of their hallucinated images should have shown the most trance logic. Inconsistent with Orne's hypothesis, Spanos and colleagues found that subjects who reported the least vivid hallucinations showed the most trance logic.

Spanos also observed that many of the behavioral signs of trance logic cited by Orne and said to distinguish hypnotized from simulating subjects have not been observed by other investigators (Spanos, *Multiple Identities and False Memories*, p. 27).

88. See G. F. Drinka, *The Birth of Neurosis: Myth, Malady and the Victorians* (New York: Simon and Schuster, 1984).

89. For discussions of "superhuman" feats, see Hilgard, *Divided Consciousness*, and Baker, *They Call It Hypnosis*.

90. M. Ullman and S. Z. Dudek, "On the psyche and warts: II. Hypnotic suggestion and warts," *Psychosomatic Medicine* 22 (1960): 68.

91. See, for example, O. S. Surman, S. K. Gottlieb, T. P. Hackett, and E. L. Silverberg, "Hypnosis in the treatment of warts," *Archives of General Psychiatry* 28 (1973): 439.

92. Reviewed in R. F. Q. Johnson, "Hypnosis, suggestions, and dermatological changes: A consideration of the production and diminution of dermatological entities," in *Hypnosis: The Cognitive-Behavioral Perspective*, ed. N. P. Spanos and J. F. Chaves (Buffalo, N.Y.: Prometheus Books, 1989).

93. N. P. Spanos, R. J. Stenstrom, and J. C. Johnston, "Hypnosis, placebo and suggestion in the treatment of warts," *Psychosomatic Medicine* 50 (1988): 245.

94. A. H. C. Sinclair-Gieben and D. Chalmers, "Evaluation of treatment of warts by hypnosis," *Lancet* 2 (1959): 480.

95. See, for example, Surman, Gottlieb, Hackett, et al., "Hypnosis in the treatment of warts."

96. J. D. Shea, "Suggestion, placebo, and expectation: Immune effects and other bodily change," in *Human Suggestibility: Advances in Theory, Research, and Applications*, ed. J. F. Schumaker (New York: Routledge, 1991).

97. Cited in Barber, Spanos, and Chaves, *Hypnosis, Imagination, and Human Potentialities*.

98. C. Graham and H. W. Leibowitz, "The effect of suggestion on visual acuity," *International Journal of Clinical and Experimental Hypnosis* 20 (1972): 169.

99. Cited in Barber, Spanos, and Chaves, *Hypnosis, Imagination, and Human Potentialities*.

100. Y. Ikemi and S. Nakagawa, "A psychosomatic study of contagious dermatitis," *Kyushu Journal of Medical Science* 13 (1962): 335.

101. Right-hemisphere activation during hypnosis is reviewed in Shea, "Suggestion, placebo, and expectation."

102. See Barber, Spanos, and Chaves, *Hypnosis, Imagination, and Human Potentialities*.

103. See Barber, Spanos, and Chaves, *Hypnosis, Imagination, and Human Potentialities*. See also Shea, "Suggestion, placebo, and expectation."

104. See, for example, P. J. Qualls and P. W. Sheehan, "Capacity for absorption and relaxation during electromyograph biofeedback and no-feedback conditions," *Journal of Abnormal Psychology* 88 (1979): 651.

105. See, for example, A. H. Roberts, D. G. Kewman, and H. MacDonald, "Voluntary control of skin temperature: Unilateral changes using hypnosis and feedback," *Journal of Abnormal Psychology* 82 (1973): 163.

106. Spanos, *Multiple Identities and False Memories*.

107. S. Fisher, "The role of expectancy in the performance of posthypnotic behavior," *Journal of Abnormal and Social Psychology* 49 (1954): 503.

108. R. St. Jean, "Posthypnotic behavior as a function of experimental surveillance," *American Journal of Clinical Hypnosis* 20 (1978): 250.

109. N. P. Spanos, E. Menary, P. J. Brett, W. Cross, and O. Ahmed, "Failure of posthypnotic responding to occur outside the experimental setting," *Journal of Abnormal Psychology* 96 (1987): 52.

110. Orne and colleagues conducted an experiment that is sometimes cited as evidence for hypnotic responding (M. T. Orne, P. W. Sheehan, and F. J. Evans, "The occurrence of posthypnotic behavior outside the experimental setting," *Journal of Personality and Social Psychology* 26 [1968]: 217). They gave 17 hypnotizable and 14 simulating subjects a suggestion to touch their forehead whenever they heard the word "experiment" during the next 48 hours. Responses were tested in the laboratory and by a secretary as subjects left the building and when they returned the next day. Five of seven of the most highly hypnotizable and none of the simulating subjects responded when tested by the secretary. Lynn, Rhue, and Weeks, however, observed that the secretary was not blind to most of the subjects' status and hence might have given some of them additional cues (Lynn, Rhue, and Weekes, "Hypnosis and experienced nonvolition"). Also, the five subjects who responded to the secretary failed to respond to the hypnotist's use of the cue word while discussing terminating the posthypnotic suggestion. The subjects indicated that they had jumped the gun in anticipating the removal of the suggestion.

Spanos cites additional studies showing that posthypnotic responding is intentional, rather than automatic (Spanos, *Multiple Identities and False Memories*. pp. 46, 48–49).

Chapter 5

1. The origin of this idea is described in M. S. Micale, *Approaching Hysteria: Disease and Its Interpretations* (Princeton, N.J.: Princeton University Press, 1995).

2. H. King, "Once upon a text: Hysteria from Hippocrates," in S. Gilman, H. King, R. Porter et al., *Hysteria beyond Freud* (Berkeley: University of California Press, 1993).

3. H. Merskey and P. Potter, "The womb lay still in ancient Egypt," *British Journal of Psychiatry* 154 (1989): 751. On a related theme, Ben-Yeong Ng ("Hysteria: A cross-cultural comparison of its origins and history," *History of Psy-*

chiatry 10 [1999]: 287) has reviewed references to hysteria-like syndromes in ancient Chinese medical texts. Although he finds reference to syndromes that in some ways resemble hysteria, that afflict mostly women, and that are sometimes attributed to female reproductive organs, he provides little evidence for a coherent syndrome. One group of patients suffered from what sounds like *globus hystericus* and may have had anxiety disorders, another group had fainting spells, a third group had a sensation of air rising from the abdomen to the chest, a fourth group yawned and stretched their limbs excessively, and a fifth group talked at night, as if conversing with ghosts. He mentions no references to conversion symptoms or seizures, the hallmarks of hysteria as it appeared in Europe. Significantly, ancient Chinese physicians were aware of the intentional aspects of such syndromes and even went so far as to threaten patients to get them to give up their illness.

4. Micale, *Approaching Hysteria.*

5. Micale, *Approaching Hysteria;* see also N. P. Spanos, *Multiple Identities and False Memories: A Sociocultural Perspective* (Washington, D.C.: American Psychological Association, 1996). Further information on Mary Glover is found in H. Merskey, *The Analysis of Hysteria: Understanding Converion and Dissociation,* 2nd ed. (London: Gaskell, 1999).

6. See Micale, *Approaching Hysteria.*

7. Micale, *Approaching Hysteria;* see also G. F. Drinka, *The Birth of Neurosis: Myth, Malady and the Victorians* (New York: Simon and Schuster, 1984).

8. L. J. Kirmayer and J. M. Robbins, "Introduction: Concepts of somatization," in *Current Concepts of Somatization: Research and Clinical Perspectives,* ed. L. J. Kirmayer and J. M. Robbins (Washington, D.C.: American Psychiatric Press, 1991), p. 1.

9. R. Kellner, "Somatization: Theories and research," *Journal of Nervous and Mental Disease* 178 (1990): 150; Z. J. Lipowski, "Somatization: The concept and its clinical application," *American Journal of Psychiatry* 145 (1988): 1358.

10. For a discussion of negative affectivity, see J. W. Pennebaker and D. Watson, "The psychology of somatic symptoms," in *Current Concepts of Somatization: Research and Clinical Perspectives,* ed. L. J. Kirmayer and J. M. Robbins (Washington, D.C.: American Psychiatric Press, 1991).

11. A. J. Barsky, "Amplification, somatization, and the somatoform disorders," *Psychosomatics* 33 (1992): 28.

12. See Kellner, "Somatization."

13. J. M. Robbins and L. J. Kirmayer, "Cognitive and social factors in somatization," in *Current Concepts of Somatization: Research and Clinical Perspectives,* ed. L. J. Kirmayer and J. M. Robbins (Washington, D.C.: American Psychiatric Press, 1991).

14. See J. I. Escobar, M. Swartz, M. Rubio-Stipec, and P. Mann, "Medically unexplained symptoms: Distribution, risk factors, and comorbidity," in *Current Concepts of Somatization: Research and Clinical Perspectives,* ed. L. J. Kirmayer and J. M. Robbins (Washington, D.C.: American Psychiatric Press, 1991).

15. Drinka, *The Birth of Neurosis*; Merskey, *The Analysis of Hysteria*; E. Shorter, *From Paralysis to Fatigue: A History of Psychosomatic Illness in the Modern Era* (New York: Free Press, 1992); and E. Shorter, *A History of Psychiatry: From the Era of the Asylum to the Age of Prozac* (New York: Wiley, 1997).

16. For a discussion of the neurological, as opposed to uterine, theories of hysteria, see Merskey, *The Analysis of Hysteria*; and Shorter, *From Paralysis to Fa-*

tigue. Shorter describes in detail the various dangerous treatments that followed from the reflex theory of hysteria.

17. Grand hysteria was rare even in the Salpêtrière. There were only 24 such patients, and as few as three actually manifested the full range of grand hypnotic phenomena (see Micale, *Approaching Hysteria*). Most Salpêtrière patients had more mundane petit hysterias.

18. Records show that most hysterical patients admitted to the Salpêtrière in the 1870s and 1880s were servants, laundresses, seamstresses, flower-sellers, and so on (See Micale, *Approaching Hysteria*). Merskey cites similar records from the Edinburgh infirmary (H. Merskey, *The Analysis of Hysteria*).

19. The following information on Darwin is from J. Bowlby, *Charles Darwin: A New Life* (New York: Norton, 1990).

20. See J. Strouse, *Alice James: A Biography* (Boston: Houghton Mifflin, 1980).

21. S. Butler, *Erewhon* (New York: Penguin Classics, 1872/1985); see also R. Rabkin, "Conversion hysteria as social maladaptation," *Psychiatry: Journal for the Study of Interpersonal Processes* 27 (1964): 349.

22. See F. M. Mai and H. Merskey, "Briquet's *Treatise on Hysteria*: A synopsis and commentary," *Archives of General Psychiatry* 37 (1980): 1401; Merskey, *The Analysis of Hysteria*; and Shorter, *From Paralysis to Fatigue*.

23. J. J. Purtell, E. Robins, and M. E. Cohen, "Observations on clinical aspects of hysteria: A quantitative study of 50 hysteria patients and 156 controls," *Journal of the American Medical Association* 146 (1951): 902.

24. M. J. Perley and S. B. Guze, "Hysteria—The stability and usefulness of clinical criteria: A quantitative study based on a follow-up period of six to eight years in 39 patients," *New England Journal of Medicine* 266 (1962): 421.

25. Perley and Guze, "Hysteria." See also E. Robins and P. O'Neal, "Clinical features of hysteria in children, with a note on prognosis. A two-to 17-year follow-up study of 41 patients," *Nervous Child* 10 (1953): 246.

26. American Psychiatric Association, *Diagnostic and Statistical Manual of Mental Disorders, 3rd ed.* (Washington, D.C.: American Psychiatric Association Press, 1980).

27. P. R. Slavney, *Perspectives on "Hysteria"* (Baltimore, Md.: Johns Hopkins University Press, 1990).

28. American Psychiatric Association, *Diagnostic and Statistical Manual of Mental Disorders, 3rd ed., rev.* (Washington, D.C.: American Psychiatric Association Press, 1987); and *Diagnostic and Statistical Manual of Mental Disorders, 4th ed.* (Washington, D.C.: American Psychiatric Association Press, 1994).

29. Escobar, Swartz, Rubio-Stipec, et al., "Medically unexplained symptoms."

30. Slavney, *Perspectives on "Hysteria."*

31. Purtell, Robins, and Cohen, "Observations on clinical aspects of hysteria."

32. M. J. Kaminsky and P. R. Slavney, "Hysterical and obsessional features in patients with Briquet's syndrome (Somatization Disorder)," *Psychological Medicine* 13 (1983): 111.

33. P. Chodoff and H. Lyons, "Hysteria, the hysterical personality and 'hysterical' conversion," *American Journal of Psychiatry* 114 (1958): 734.

34. American Psychiatric Association, *Diagnostic and Statistical Manual of Mental Disorders, 3rd ed.*; American Psychiatric Association, *Diagnostic and Statistical Manual of Mental Disorders, 3rd ed., rev.*; American Psychiatric Association, *Diagnostic and Statistical Manual of Mental Disorders, 4th ed.*

35. J. Morrison, "Histrionic personality disorder in women with somatization disorder," *Psychosomatics* 30 (1989): 433.

36. S. O. Lilienfeld, C. Van Valkenburg, and H. S. Akiskal, "The relationship of histrionic personality disorder to antisocial personality and somatization disorders," *American Journal of Psychiatry* 143 (1986): 718.

37. E. L. Bliss, "Hysteria and hypnosis," *Journal of Nervous and Mental Disease* 172 (1984): 203.

38. C. A. Ross, S. Heber, G. R. Norton, and G. Anderson, "Somatic symptoms in multiple personality disorder," *Psychosomatics* 30 (1989): 154.

39. K. Tomasson, D. Kent, and W. Coryell, "Somatization and conversion disorders: Comorbidity and demographics at presentation," *Acta Psychiatrica Scandinavica* 84 (1991): 288.

40. E. F. Pribor, S. H. Yutzy, J. T. Dean, and R. D. Wetzel, "Briquet's syndrome, dissociation, and abuse," *American Journal of Psychiatry* 150 (1993): 1507.

41. G. R. Smith and F. W. Brown, "Screening indexes in DSM-III-R somatization disorder," *General Hospital Psychiatry* 12 (1990): 148.

42. Pribor, Yutzy, Dean, et al., "Briquet's syndrome, dissociation, and abuse."

43. Morrison, "Histrionic personality disorder in women with somatization disorder."

44. Ross, Heber, Norton, et al., "Somatic symptoms in multiple personality disorder."

45. Pribor, Yutzy, Dean, et al., "Briquet's syndrome, dissociation, and abuse."

46. T. K. J. Craig, A. P. Boardman, K. Mills, O. Daly-Jones, and H. Drake, "The South London somatisation study: I. Longitudinal course and the influence of early life experiences," *British Journal of Psychiatry* 163 (1993): 579.

47. Kaminsky and Slavney, "Hysterical and obsessional features in patients with Briquet's syndrome (Somatization Disorder)."

48. Tomasson, Kent, and Coryell, "Somatization and conversion disorders."

49. J. M. Golding, K. Rost, T. M. Kashner, and G. R. Smith, "Family psychiatric history of patients with somatization disorder," *Psychiatric Medicine* 10 (1992): 33.

50. D. K. Routh, and A. R. Ernst, "Somatization disorder in relatives of children and adolescents with functional abdominal pain," *Journal of Pediatric Psychology* 9 (1984): 427.

51. Golding, Rost, Kashner, et al., "Family psychiatric history."

52. M. Hotopf, R. Mayou, M. Wadsworth, and S. Wessely, "Childhood risk factors for adults with medically unexplained symptoms: Results from a national birth cohort study," *American Journal of Psychiatry* 156 (1999): 1796.

53. S. B. Guze, C. R. Cloninger, R. L. Martin, and P. J. Clayton, "A follow-up and family study of Briquet's syndrome," *British Journal of Psychiatry* 149 (1986): 17.

54. Guze, Cloninger, Martin, et al., "Follow-up and family study." See also S. B. Guze, "Studies in hysteria," *Canadian Journal of Psychiatry* 28 (1983): 434.

55. Lilienfeld, Van Valkenburg, and Akiskal, "The relationship of histrionic personality disorder to antisocial personality and somatization disorders."

56. American Psychiatric Association, *Diagnostic and Statistical Manual of Mental Disorders, 4th ed.*

57. P. Draper and H. Harpending, "A sociobiological perspective on the development of human reproductive strategies," in *Sociobiological Perspectives on Human Development,* ed. K. B. MacDonald (New York: Springer-Verlag, 1988).

58. B. Wenegrat, *Illness and Power: Women's Mental Disorders and the Battle between the Sexes* (New York: New York University Press, 1995).

59. These histories are described in S. L. Zimdars-Swartz, *Encountering Mary: Visions of Mary from La Salette to Medjugorje* (New York: Avon Books, 1991).

60. American Psychiatric Association, *Diagnostic and Statistical Manual of Mental Disorders, 4th ed.*

61. Merskey cautions against assuming that cases of chronic pain syndrome are psychogenically caused. The psychological problems that are part of chronic pain syndromes may be caused by pain, rather than vice versa, and, as our understanding of the physiology of pain has improved, mechanisms for chronic pain syndromes have come to light. See, for example, H. Merskey, "Regional pain is rarely hysterical," *Archives of Neurology* 45 (1988): 915; "Psychiatry and chronic pain," *Canadian Journal of Psychiatry* 34 (1989): 329; "Psychological medicine, pain, and musculoskeletal disorders," *Rheumatic Disease Clinics of North America* 22 (1996): 623; and "Re: back pain in the workplace," *Pain* 65 (1996): 111. Also see R. W. Teasell and H. Merskey, "Chronic pain disability in the workplace," *Pain Research and Management* 2 (1997): 197. Nonetheless, as Merskey acknowledges, at least the expression of pain complaints is often under the control of social reinforcements and modeling, both in patients' families of origin and in their current environments. See, for example, A. R. Block, E. F. Kremer, and M. Gaylor, "Behavioral treatment of chronic pain: The spouse as a discriminative cue for pain behavior," *Pain* 9 (1980): 243; A. Cott, H. Anchel, W. M. Goldberg, M. Fabichi, and W. Parkinson, "Non-institutional treatment of chronic pain by field management: An outcome study with comparison group," *Pain* 40 (1990): 183; P. W. Edwards, A. Zeichner, A. R. Kuczmierczyk, and J. Boczkowski, "Familial pain models: The relationship between family history of pain and current pain experience," *Pain* 21 (1985): 379; W. Fordyce, R. Fowler, J. Lehmann, B. U. Delateur, P. L. Sand, and R. B. Trieschmann, "Operant conditioning in the treatment of chronic pain," *Archives of Physical Medicine and Rehabilitation* 54 (1973): 399; K. M. Gil, F. J. Keefe, J. E. Crisson, and P. J. Van Dalfsen, "Social support and pain behavior," *Pain* 29 (1987): 209; R. D. Kerns, J. Haythornthwaite, S. Southwick, and E. L. Giller, "The role of martial interaction in chronic pain and depressive symptom severity," *Journal of Psychosomatic Research* 34 (1990): 401; K. M. Prkachin and K. D. Craig, "Influencing non-verbal expressions of pain: Signal detection analyses," *Pain* 21 (1985): 399; S. N. Mohamed, G. M. Weisz, and E. M. Waring, "The relationship of chronic pain to depression, marital adjustment, and family dynamics," *Pain* 5 (1978): 285; and A. Violon and D. Giurgea, "Familial models for chronic pain," *Pain* 18 (1984): 199.

62. Dora's case is to be found in S. Freud, "Fragment of an analysis of a case of hysteria," in *The Standard Edition of the Complete Psychological Works of Sigmund Freud*, vol. 7, trans. J. Strachey (London: Hogarth Press, 1953–1974). See also C. Berheimer and C. Kahane, eds., *In Dora's Case: Freud-Hysteria-Feminism* (New York: Columbia University Press, 1985); S. R. Maddi, "The victimization of Dora," *Psychology Today*, September 1974.

63. Freud, "Fragment of an analysis of a case of hysteria," pp. 43–44.

64. American Psychiatric Association, *Diagnostic and Statistical Manual of Mental Disorder, 4th ed.*

65. See, for example, J. Ruesch, *Disturbed Communication* (New York: Norton, 1957); T. Szasz, *The Myth of Mental Illness* (New York: Hoeber, 1961).

66. M. Balint, *The Doctor, His Patient, and the Illness* (New York: International Universities Press, 1957).

67. See, for example, R. Rabkin, "Conversion hysteria as social maladaptation," *Psychiatry: Journal for the Study of Interpersonal Processes* 27 (1964): 349.

68. E. C. McCue and P. A. McCue, "Hypnosis in the elucidation of hysterical aphonia: A case report," *American Journal of Clinical Hypnosis* 30 (1988): 178.

69. F. O. Walker, A. G. Alessi, K. B. Digre, and W. T. McLean, "Psychogenic respiratory distress," *Archives of Neurology* 46 (1989): 196.

70. L. U. Thorpe, D. L. Keegan, and G. A. Veenan, "Conversion mutism: Case report and discussion," *Canadian Journal of Psychiatry* 30 (1985): 71.

71. See, for example, O. Kristenson and J. Alving, "Pseudoseizures: Risk factors and prognosis," *Acta Neurologica Scandinavica* 85 (1992): 177.

72. D. K. Ziegler and R. B. Schlemmer, "Familial psychogenic blindness and headache: A case study," *Journal of Clinical Psychiatry* 55 (1994): 114.

73. See, for example, P. Pérez-Sales, "Camptocormia," *British Journal of Psychiatry* 157 (1990): 765; M. Sinel and M. S. Eisenberg, "Two unusual gait disturbances: Astasia abasia and camptocormia," *Archives of Physical Medicine and Rehabilitation* 71 (1990): 1078.

74. See S. Fisher and R. P. Greenberg, *The Scientific Credibility of Freud's Theories and Therapy* (New York: Columbia University Press, 1985).

75. See G. J. Makari, "Franz Anton Mesmer and the case of the blind pianist," *Hospital and Community Psychiatry* 45 (1994): 106.

76. Chodoff and Lyons, "Hysteria, the hysterical personality and 'hysterical' conversion."

77. American Psychiatric Association, *Diagnostic and Statistical Manual of Mental Disorders, 4th ed.*

78. J. Kinzl, W. Biebl, and H. Rauchegger, "Functional aphonia: A conversion symptom as defensive mechanism against anxiety," *Psychotherapy and Psychosomatics* 49 (1988): 31.

79. R. Van Dyck and K. Hoogdiun, "Hypnosis and conversion disorders," *American Journal of Psychotherapy* 43 (1989): 480.

80. See Drinka, *The Birth of Neurosis.*

81. F. Bendefelt, L. L. Miller, and A. M. Ludwig, "Cognitive performance in conversion hysteria," *Archives of General Psychiatry* 22 (1976): 1250.

82. E. L. Bliss, "Multiple personalities, related disorders and hypnosis," *American Journal of Clinical Hypnosis* 26 (1983): 114; and E. L. Bliss, "Hysteria and hypnosis."

83. H. A. Sackheim, J. W. Nordlie, and R. C. Gur, "A model of hysterical and hypnotic blindness: Cognition, motivation and awareness," *Journal of Abnormal Psychology* 88 (1979): 474.

84. G. P. Holmes, J. E. Kaplan, N. M. Gantz, A. L. Komaroff, L. B. Schonberger, S. E. Straus, J. F. Jones, R. E. Dubois, C. Cunningham-Rundles, S. Pahwa et al., "Chronic fatigue syndrome: A working case definition," *Annals of Internal Medicine* 108 (1988): 387.

85. G. P. Holmes, J. E. Kaplan, L. B. Schonberger, S. E. Straus, L. S. Zegans, N. M. Gantz, I. Brus, A. Komaroff, J. F. Jones, R. E. DuBois, G. Tosato, N. A. Brown, S. Pahwa, and R. T. Schooley, "Definition of the chronic fatigue syndrome, in response [letter]," *Annals of Internal Medicine* 109 (1988): 512.

86. T. J. Lane, P. Manu, and D. A. Matthews, "Depression and somatization in the chronic fatigue syndrome," *American Journal of Medicine* 91 (1991): 335.

87. D. B. Buchwald, T. Pearlman, P. Kith, and K. Schmaling, "Gender differences in patients with chronic fatigue syndrome," *Journal of General Internal Medicine* 9 (1994): 397.

88. Reviewed in J. F. Jones, "Viral etiology of chronic fatigue syndrome," in *Chronic Fatigue and Related Immune Deficiency Syndromes,* ed. P. J. Goodnick and N. G. Klimas (Washington, D.C.: American Psychiatric Press, 1993).

89. See, for example, W. E. Dismukes, J. S. Wade, J. Y. Lee, B. K. Dockery, and J. D. Hain, "A randomized, double-blind trial of nystatin therapy for the candidiasis hypersensitivity syndrome," *New England Journal of Medicine* 323 (1990): 1717.

90. Reviewed in R. Patarca, M. A. Fletcher, and N. G. Klimas, "Immunological correlates of chronic fatigue syndrome," in *Chronic Fatigue and Related Immune Deficiency Syndromes,* ed. P. J. Goodnick and N. G. Klimas (Washington, D.C.: American Psychiatric Press, 1993). I am discounting here an even more recent theory; that CFS is caused by "Chiari-type" skull malformations. Chiari-type malformations are posterior skull deformities that cause pressure on brainstem structures, with consequent neurological symptoms. The *Wall Street Journal* (November 11, 1999) reported that three neurosurgeons, one in Chicago, one in North Carolina, and one at Johns Hopkins, have operated on dozens of CFS patients to correct putative skull malformations. According to the *Journal,* the procedure has been popularized by a physician with CFS, who, after undergoing surgery, became a crusader in patient groups and who advocates the practice. Specialists in Chiari-type malformations state that there is no evidence to link such malformations to CFS, and most neurosurgeons condemn the practice of operating on CFS patients.

91. See P. J. Goodnick and R. Sandoval, "Treatment of chronic fatigue syndrome and related disorders: Immunological approaches," in *Chronic Fatigue and Related Immune Deficiency Syndromes,* ed. P. J. Goodnick and N. G. Klimas (Washington, D.C.: American Psychiatric Press, 1993).

92. See, for example, C. Reynaert, P. Janne, A. Bosly, P. Staquet, N. Zdanowicz, M. Vause, B. Chatelain, and D. Léjeune, "From health locus of control to immune control: Internal locus of control has a buffering effect on natural killer cell activity decrease in major depression," *Acta Psychiatric Scandinavica* 92 (1995): 294.

93. P. J. Goodnick and R. Sandoval, "Treatment of chronic fatigue syndrome and related disorders: Psychotropic agents," in *Chronic Fatigue and Related Immune Deficiency Syndromes,* ed. P. J. Goodnick and N. G. Klimas (Washington, D.C.: American Psychiatric Press, 1993).

94. Merskey, for instance, takes the view that most patients with CFS do have real disease. See Merskey, *The Analysis of Hysteria.*

95. Buchwald, Pearlman, Kith, et al., "Gender differences in patients with chronic fatigue syndrome."

96. Lane, Manu, and Matthews, "Depression and somatization in the chronic fatigue syndrome."

97. M. J. P. Kruesi, J. Dale, and S. E. Straus, "Psychiatric diagnoses in patients who have chronic fatigue syndrome," *Journal of Clinical Psychiatry* 50 (1989): 53.

98. P. Manu, D. A. Matthews, and T. J. Lane, "The mental health of patients with a chief complaint of chronic fatigue," *Archives of Internal Medicine* 148 (1988): 2213.

99. P. Skapinakis, G. Lewis, and H. Meltzer, "Clarifying the relationship between unexplained chronic fatigue and psychiatric morbidity: Results from a community survey in Great Britain," *American Journal of Psychiatry* 157 (2000): 1492.

100. W. J. Katon, D. S. Buchwald, G. E. Simon, J. E. Russo, and P. J. Mease, "Psychiatric illness in patients with chronic fatigue and those with rheumatoid arthritis," *Journal of General Internal Medicine* 6 (1991): 277.

101. Lane, Manu, and Matthews, "Depression and somatization in the chronic fatigue syndrome."

102. Buchwald, Pearlman, Kith, et al., "Gender differences in patients with chronic fatigue syndrome."

103. Manu, Matthews, and Lane, "The mental health of patients with a chief complaint of chronic fatigue."

104. Katon, Buchwald, Simon, et al., "Psychiatric illness in patients with chronic fatigue and those with rheumatoid arthritis."

105. D. Buchwald and D. Garrity, "Comparison of patients with chronic fatigue syndrome, fibromyalgia, and multiple chemical sensitivities," *Archives of Internal Medicine* 154 (1994): 2049.

106. P. Manu, D. A. Matthews, and T. J. Lane, "Food intolerance in patients with chronic fatigue," *International Journal of Eating Disorders* 13 (1993): 203.

107. A. Stricklin, M. Sewell, and C. Austad, "Objective measurement of personality variables in epidemic neuromyasthenia patients," *South African Medical Journal* 77 (1990): 31.

108. See C. S. North, J. M. Ryall, D. A. Ricci, and R. D. Wetzel, *Multiple Personalities, Multiple Disorders: Psychiatric Classification and Media Influence* (New York: Oxford University Press, 1993), pp. 98–99.

109. Ross, Heber, Norton, et al., "Somatic symptoms in multiple personality disorder."

110. In an important series of studies, Westen and others have shown that the DSM-IV diagnosis of borderline personality identifies two separate subgroups. One subgroup suffers dysregulated affect and severe dysphoria, while another subgroup is better described as histrionic (see D. Westen and J. Shedler, "Revising and assessing Axis II, Part I: Developing a clinically and empirically valid assessment method," *American Journal of Psychiatry* 156 [1999]: 258; and "Revising and assessing Axis II, Part II: Toward an empirically based and clinically useful classification of personality disorders," *American Journal of Psychiatry* 156 [1999]: 273). Both groups are characterized by emotional intensity, but the first group perceives the intensity as being outside their control, while the second group perceives it as "ego-syntonic." In Westen and co-workers' studies, histrionic patients were characterized by dependence, intense attachments to others, a tendency to be suggestible or easily influenced, and exaggerated or theatrical emotionality, among other characteristics. In a study of borderline "identity disturbance," Wilkinson-Ryan and Westen showed that the histrionic subgroup of borderline patients tends to show role absorption, or over-identification with specific roles (T. Wilkinson-Ryan and D. Westen, "Identity disturbance in borderline personality disorder: An empirical investigation," *American Journal of Psychiatry* 157 [2000]: 528).

111. C. Millon, F. Salvato, N. Blaney, "A psychological assessment of chronic fatigue syndrome/chronic Epstein-Barr virus patients," *Psychology and Health* 3 (1989): 131.

112. S. E. Abbey and P. E. Garfinkel, "Neurasthenia and chronic fatigue syndrome: The role of culture in the making of a diagnosis," *American Journal of Psychiatry* 148 (1991): 1638. See also D. Greenberg, "Neurasthenia in the 1980s: Chronic mononucleosis, chronic fatigue syndrome, and anxiety and depressive disorders," *Psychosomatics* 31 (1990): 129.

113. Drinka, *The Birth of Neurosis.*

114. A. Young, *The Harmony of Illusions: Inventing Post-Traumatic Stress Disorder* (Princeton, N.J.: Princeton University Press, 1995).

115. See A. Kleinman, *Social Origins of Distress and Disease: Depression, Neurasthenia, and Pain in Modern China* (New Haven: Yale University Press, 1986); A. Kleinman, *The Illness Narratives: Suffering, Healing and the Human Condition* (New York: Basic Books, 1988).

116. I. B. Milner, B. N. Axelrod, J. Pasquantonio, and M. Sillanpaa, "Is there a Gulf War syndrome," *Journal of the American Medical Association* 271 (1994): 661; see also K. Fukuda, R. Nisenbaum, G. Stewart, W. W. Thompson, L. Robin, R. M. Washko, D. L. Noah, D. H. Barrett, B. Randall, B. L. Herwaldt, A. C. Mawle, and W. C. Reeves, "Chronic multisymptom illness affecting air force veterans of the Gulf War," *Journal of the American Medical Association* 280 (1998): 981; K. Kroenke, P. Koslowe, and M. Roy, "Symptoms in 18495 Persian Gulf War veterans," *Journal of Occupational and Environmental Medicine* 40 (1998): 520.

117. See, for example, R. W. Haley, T. L. Kurt, and J. Horn, "Is there a Gulf War syndrome?" *Journal of the American Medical Association* 277 (1997): 215; R. W. Haley, J. Hom, P. S. Roland, W. W. Bryan, P. C. Van Ness, F. J. Bonte, M. D. Devous, D. Mathews, J. L. Fleckenstein, F. H. Wians, G. I. Wolf, and T. L. Kurt, "Evaluation of neurologic function in Gulf War veterans: A blinded case-control study," *Journal of the American Medical Association* 277 (1997): 223; and R. W. Haley and T. L. Kurt, "Self-reported exposure to neurotoxic chemical combinations in the Gulf War," *Journal of the American Medical Association* 277 (1997): 231; NIH Technology Assessment Workshop Panel, "The Persian Gulf experience and health," *Journal of the American Medical Association* 272 (1994): 391; Persian Gulf War Veterans Coordinating Board, "Unexplained illnesses among Desert Storm veterans: A search for causes, treatment, and cooperation," *Archives of Internal Medicine* 155 (1995): 262.

118. M. R. Cullen, "Multiple chemical sensitivities," in *Public Health and Preventive Medicine,* 13th ed., ed. J. M. Last and R. B. Wallace (Norwalk, Conn.: Appleton and Lange, 1992).

119. See T. L. Kurt, "Multiple chemical sensitivities—a syndrome of pseudo-toxicity manifest as exposure perceived symptoms," *Clinical Toxicology* 33 (1995): 101.

120. References cited in G. E. Simon, W. Daniell, H. Stockbridge, K. Claypoole, and L. Rosenstock, "Immunologic, psychological, and neuropsychological factors in multiple chemical sensitivity: A controlled study," *Annals of Internal Medicine* 19 (1993): 97.

121. I. R. Bell, C. S. Miller, and G. E. Schwartz, "An olfactory-limbic model of multiple chemical sensitivity syndrome: Possible relationship to kindling and affective spectrum disorders," *Biological Psychiatry* 32 (1992): 218.

122. I. R. Bell, G. E. Schwartz, J. M. Peterson, and D. Amend, "Self-reported illness from chemical odors in young adults without clinical syndromes or occupational exposures," *Archives of Environmental Health* 48 (1993): 6.

123. For discussions of some of the practices of clinical ecologists, see American Academy of Allergy, "Position statements—controversial techniques," *Journal of Allergy and Clinical Immunology* 67 (1981): 333; T. M. Golbert, "A review of controversial diagnostic and therapeutic techniques employed in allergy," *Journal of Allergy and Clinical Immunology* 56 (1975): 170; M. H. Grieco, "Controversial practices in allergy," *Journal of the American Medical Association* 247 (1982): 3106; and T. E. Van Metre, Jr., "Critique of controversial and unproven procedures for diagnosis and therapy of allergic disorders," *Pediatric Clinics of North America* 30 (1983): 807.

124. A. L. Terr, "Clinical ecology in the workplace," *Journal of Occupational Medicine* 31 (1989): 257.

125. D. W. Black, A. Rathe, and R. B. Goldstein, "Environmental illness: A controlled study of 26 subjects with 'twentieth-century disease,'" *Journal of the American Medical Association* 264 (1990): 3166.

126. Simon, Daniell, Stockbridge, et al., "Immunologic, psychological, and neuropsychological factors in multiple chemical sensitivity."

127. A. I. Terr, "Environmental illness: A clinical review of 50 cases," *Archives of Internal Medicine* 146 (1986): 145.

128. Terr, "Clinical ecology in the workplace."

129. See S. Eneström and P. Hultman, "Does amalgam affect the immune system? A controversial issue," *International Archives of Allergy and Immunology* 106 (1995): 180.

130. See American Academy of Allergy, "Position statements—controversial techniques"; Golbert, "A review of controversial diagnostic and therapeutic techniques employed in allergy"; Grieco, "Controversial practices in allergy"; Van Metre, Jr., "Critique of controversial and unproven procedures for diagnosis and therapy of allergic disorders"; and D. A. Spyker, "Multiple chemical sensitivities—syndrome and solutions," *Clinical Toxicology* 33 (1995): 95.

131. Terr, "Clinical ecology in the workplace."

132. Black, Rathe, and Goldstein, "Environmental illness."

133. Terr, "Clinical ecology in the workplace."

134. C. M. Brodsky, "'Allergic to everything': A medical subculture," *Psychosomatics* 24 (1983): 731.

135. See Kurt, "Multiple chemical sensitivities."

136. Terr, "Clinical ecology in the workplace."

137. Simon, Daniell, Stockbridge, et al., "Immunologic, psychological, and neuropsychological factors in multiple chemical sensitivity."

138. G. E. Simon, W. J. Katon, and P. J. Sparks, "Allergic to life: Psychological factors in environmental illness," *American Journal of Psychiatry* 147 (1990): 901.

139. Black, Rathe, and Goldstein, "Environmental illness."

140. D. E. Stewart and J. Raskin, "Psychiatric assessment of patients with 'twentieth-century disease' ('total allergy syndrome')," *Canadian Medical Association Journal* 133 (1985): 1001.

141. See Kurt, "Multiple chemical sensitivities."

142. R. S. Schottenfeld, and M. R. Cullen, "Occupation-induced posttraumatic stress disorders," *American Journal of Psychiatry* 142 (1985): 198.

143. Spyker, "Multiple chemical sensitivities."

144. Simon, Katon, and Sparks, "Allergic to life."

145. See, for example, D. F. Klein, "False suffocation alarms, spontane-

ous panics, and related conditions," *Archives of General Psychiatry* 50 (1993): 306.

146. G. W. Small, M. W. Propper, E. T. Randolph, and S. Eth, "Mass hysteria among student performers: Social relationship as a symptom predictor," *American Journal of Psychiatry* 148 (1991): 1200. A similar incident and findings are documented in T. F. Jones, A. S. Craig, D. Hoy et el., "Mass psychogenic illness attributed to toxic exposure at a high school," *New England Journal of Medicine* 342 (2000): 96.

147. California Department of Health Services, "An investigation into an unusual outbreak of symptoms in staff members of a community hospital emergency room, Riverside, California," September 2, 1994.

148. Terr, "Clinical ecology in the workplace."

149. Simon, Daniell, Stockbridge, et al., "Immunologic, psychological, and neuropsychological factors in multiple chemical sensitivity."

150. American Psychiatric Association, *Diagnostic and Statistical Manual of Mental Disorders, 3rd ed., rev.* (Washington, D.C.: American Psychiatric Association Press, 1987); and J. I. Escobar, M. Swartz, M. Rubio-Stipec, and P. Mann, "Medically unexplained symptoms: Distribution, risk factors, and comorbidity," in *Current Concepts of Somatization: Research and Clinical Perspectives,* ed. L. J. Kirmayer and J. M. Robbins (Washington, D.C.: American Psychiatric Press, 1991).

151. Simon, Katon, and Sparks, "Allergic to life."

152. Stewart and Raskin, "Psychiatric assessment of patients with 'twentieth-century disease.'"

153. H. Staudenmayer, M. E. Selner, and J. C. Selner, "Adult sequelae of childhood abuse presenting as environmental illness," *Annals of Allergy* 71 (1993): 538.

154. Black, Rathe, and Goldstein, "Environmental illness."

155. Brodsky, "Allergic to everything."

156. Stewart and Raskin, "Psychiatric assessment of patients with 'twentieth-century disease.'"

157. R. E. Gots, "Multiple chemical sensitivities—public policy," *Clinical Toxicology* 33 (1995): 111.

158. Brodsky, "Allergic to everything."

Chapter 6

1. American Psychiatric Association, *Diagnostic and Statistical Manual of Mental Disorders, 4th ed.* (Washington, D.C.: American Psychiatric Association Press, 1994).

2. F. W. Putnam, J. J. Guroff, E. K. Silberman, L. Barban, and R. M. Post, "The clinical phenomenology of multiple personality disorder: Review of 100 recent cases," *Journal of Clinical Psychiatry* 47 (1986): 285.

3. C. A. Ross, G. R. Norton, and K. Wozney, "Multiple personality disorder: An analysis of 236 cases," *Canadian Journal of Psychiatry* 34 (1989): 413.

4. C. A. Ross, *The Osiris Complex: Case Studies in Multiple Personality Disorder* (Toronto: University of Toronto Press, 1994).

5. American Psychiatric Association, *Diagnostic and Statistical Manual of Mental Disorders, 3rd ed.* (Washington, D.C.: American Psychiatric Association Press, 1980).

6. American Psychiatric Association, *Diagnostic and Statistical Manual of Mental Disorders, 3rd ed., rev.* (Washington, D.C.: American Psychiatric Association Press, 1987).

7. American Psychiatric Association, *Diagnostic and Statistical Manual of Mental Disorders, 4th ed.*

8. D. Spiegel and P. McHugh, "The pros and cons of dissociative identity (multiple personality) disorder," *Journal of Practical Psychiatry and Behavioral Health* 1 (September 1995): 158, citation from p. 159.

9. Spiegel and McHugh, "Pros and cons of dissociative identity disorder," p. 164.

10. Ross, *The Osiris Complex*, p. ix.

11. See I. Hacking, *Rewriting the Soul: Multiple Personality and the Sciences of Memory* (Princeton, N.J.: Princeton University Press, 1995).

12. Putnam, Guroff, Silberman, et al., "The clinical phenomenology of multiple personality disorder."

13. Ross, Norton, and Wozney, "Multiple personality disorder."

14. For a complete outline of this theory, see, for example, F. W. Putnam, *Diagnosis and Treatment of Multiple Personality Disorder* (New York: Guilford Press, 1989).

15. Evidence for claims of this type are reviewed in R. Aldridge-Morris, *Multiple Personality: An Exercise in Deception* (Hillsdale, N.J.: Lawrence Erlbaum, 1989); C. S. North, J. M. Ryall, D. A. Ricci, and R. D. Wetzel, *Multiple Personalities, Multiple Disorders: Psychiatric Classification and Media Influence* (New York: Oxford University Press, 1993); and N. P. Spanos, *Multiple Identities and False Memories: A Sociocultural Perspective* (Washington, D.C.: American Psychological Association, 1996).

16. Abnormal EEGS are also frequently reported in conversion and hysteria generally. These may be due to the high proportion of patients with pseudo-seizures who also have real seizures. For a review of this literature, see H. Merskey, *The Analysis of Hysteria: Understanding Conversion and Dissociation,* 2nd ed. (London: Gaskell, 1999).

17. M. Mesulam, "Dissociative states with abnormal temporal lobe EEG: Multiple personality and the illusion of possession," *Archives of Neurology* 38 (1981): 176.

18. L. Schenk and D. Bear, "Multiple personality and related dissociative phenomena in patients with temporal lobe epilepsy," *American Journal of Psychiatry* 138 (1981): 1311.

19. Schenk and Bear's "Rebeccah" and Mesulam's Case 2 are both 21-year-old righthanded women with frequent *déjà vu* experiences. Both had previously found themselves with a bloody stick, next to an unconscious man, had held their psychiatrists for several hours at knifepoint, and showed predominantly right-sided bitemporal EEG spikes. Both patients' roommates had described two alter personae, a childish little girl and a tough, angry alter. Schenck and Bear's "Hilda" and Mesulam's Case 3 are both 27-year-old ambidextrous native German speakers with intermittent feelings of intense dread, epigastric distress, and olfactory hallucinations. Both had several alters, who were young girls of different ages of whom the host was unaware, who wrote and drew mainly with their left hands. spoke mostly German, and revealed themselves to their husbands. Schenk and Bear's "Dinah" and Mesulam's Case 1 are both left-handed women with absence attacks since childhood who spoke in a childish voice with

frequent verbal contractions. Both planned to become journalists and had two alters, one of which harmed animals, wrote with her right hand, and spoke in a guttural voice and the other of which was immature and vulnerable. Both hosts had apologized for missing an appointment kept by their aggressive alter.

20. D. F. Benson, B. L. Miller, and S. F. Signer, "Dual personality associated with epilepsy," *Archives of Neurology* 43 (1986): 471.

21. See, for example, G. L. Ahern, A. M. Herring, J. Tackenberg, J. F. Seeger, K. J. Oommen, D. M. Labiner, and M. E. Weinard, "The association of multiple personality and temporolimbic epilepsy: Intracarotid amobarbital test observations," *Archives of Neurology* 50 (1993): 1020; J. A. Cocores, A. L. Bender, and E. McBride, "Multiple personality, seizure disorder, and the electroencephalogram," *Journal of Nervous and Mental Disease* 172 (1984): 436; J. R. Hughes, D. T. Kuhlman, C. G. Fichtner, and M. J. Gruenfeld, "Brain mapping in a case of multiple personality," *Clinical Electroencephalography* 21 (1990): 200.

22. Putnam, *Diagnosis and Treatment of Multiple Personality Disorder.*

23. Putnam, *Diagnosis and Treatment of Multiple Personality Disorder.* See also North, Ryall, Ricci, et al., *Multiple Personalities, Multiple Disorders.*

24. Putnam, *Diagnosis and Treatment of Multiple Personality Disorder.*

25. R. J. Kohlenberg, "Behavioristic approach to multiple personality: A case study," *Behavior Therapy* 4 (1973): 137.

26. Spanos, *Multiple Identities and False Memories.*

27. A. Seltzer, "Multiple personality: A psychiatric misadventure," *Canadian Journal of Psychiatry* 39 (1994): 442.

28. See Spanos, *Multiple Identities and False Memories.* Spanos, too, compares MPD therapists with members of healing cults.

29. North, Ryall, Ricci, et al., *Multiple Personalities, Multiple Disorders.*

30. Actually, in calling herself (Eve) "Black," Sizemore, who was unhappily married, was using, and thereby symbolically reclaiming, her maiden name. This is what evolved into a second personality. See H. Merskey, *The Analysis of Hysteria.*

31. Prevalence data are reviewed in North, Ryall, Ricci et al., *Multiple Personalities, Multiple Disorders.*

32. B. G. Braun, "The transgenerational incidence of dissociation and multiple personality disorder: A preliminary report," in *Childhood Antecedents of Multiple Personality,* ed. R. P. Kluft (Washington, D.C.: American Psychiatric Press, 1985).

33. North, Ryall, Ricci, et al., *Multiple Personalities, Multiple Disorders.*

34. North, Ryall, Ricci, et al., *Multiple Personalities, Multiple Disorders.* p. 11.

35. Putnam, Guroff, Silberman, et al., "The clinical phenomenology of multiple personality disorder," p. 285.

36. See, for example, Putnam, *Diagnosis and Treatment of Multiple Personality Disorder.*

37. See, for example, E. L. Bliss, and E. A. Jeppsen, "Prevalence of multiple personality disorder among inpatients and outpatients," *American Journal of Psychiatry* 142 (1985): 250; C. A. Ross, "Epidemiology of multiple personality disorder and dissociation," *Psychiatric Clinics of North America* 14 (1991): 503.

38. Data on the geographical distribution of MPD are reviewed in North, Ryall, Ricci, et al., *Multiple Personalities, Multiple Disorders.*

39. Aldridge-Morris, *Multiple Personality.*

40. S. Boon and N. Draijer, "Diagnosing dissociative disorders in the Netherlands: A pilot study with the structured clinical interview for DSM-III-R dissociative disorders," *American Journal of Psychiatry* 148 (1991): 458.

41. S. Boon and N. Draijer, "Multiple personality disorder in the Netherlands: A clinical investigation of 71 patients," *American Journal of Psychiatry* 150 (1993): 489.

42. Adityanjee, G. S. P. Raju, and S. K. Khandelwal, "Current status of multiple personality disorder in India," *American Journal of Psychiatry* 146 (1989): 1607.

43. V. Sar, L. I. Yargiç, and H. Tutkun, "Structured interview data on 35 cases of dissociative identity disorder in Turkey," *American Journal of Psychiatry* 153 (1996): 1329.

44. H. Tutkun, V. Sar, L. I. Yargiç, T. Ozpulat, M. Yanik, and E. Kiziltan, "Frequency of dissociative disorders among psychiatric inpatients in a Turkish university clinic," *American Journal of Psychiatry* 155 (1998): 800.

45. Y. Fujii, K. Suzuki, T. Sato, Y. Murakami, and T. Takahashi, "Multiple personality disorder in Japan," *Psychiatry and Clinical Neurosciences* 52 (1998): 299.

46. Fujii, Suzuki, Sato, et al., "Multiple personality disorder in Japan," p. 300.

47. See, for example, S. Eguchi, "Between folk concepts of illness and psychiatric diagnosis: *Kitsune-Tsuki* (fox possession) in a mountain village of Western Japan," *Culture, Medicine and Psychiatry* 15 (1991): 421; S. Etsuko, "The interpretations of fox possession: Illness as metaphor," *Culture, Medicine and Psychiatry* 15 (1991): 453.

48. See, for example, Spiegel and McHugh, "The pros and cons of dissociative identity disorder."

49. I. M. Lewis, *Ecstatic Religion: A Study of Shamanisn and Spirit Possession,* 2nd ed. (New York: Routledge, 1989).

50. The following data are reviewed in North, Ryall, Ricci, et al., *Multiple Personalities, Multiple Disorders.*

51. See, for example, Putnam, *Diagnosis and Treatment of Multiple Personality Disorder.*

52. Putnam, *Diagnosis and Treatment of Multiple Personality Disorder.* See also North, Ryall, Ricci, et al., *Multiple Personalities, Multiple Disorders.*

53. North, Ryall, Ricci, et al., *Multiple Personalities, Multiple Disorders;* F. R. Schreiber, *Sybil* (Chicago: Henry Renery, 1973).

54. See Hacking, *Rewriting the Soul.*

55. Information and quote from H. Merskey, "The artifactual nature of multiple personality disorder," *Dissociation* 7 (1994): 173.

56. F. W. Putnam, *Diagnosis and Treatment of Multiple Personality Disorder*, discusses the use of hypnosis in diagnosis and treatment of MPD.

57. Cited in North, Ryall, Ricci, et al., *Multiple Personalities, Multiple Disorders,* p. 49.

58. C. A. Ross, S. Heber, G. R. Norton, and G. Anderson, "Somatic symptoms in multiple personality disorder," *Psychosomatics* 30 (1989): 154.

59. North, Ryall, Ricci, et al., *Multiple Personalities, Multiple Disorders.*

60. For data on personality disorders of MPD patients, see North, Ryall, Ricci, et al., *Multiple Personalities, Multiple Disorders,* p. 55; also P. M. Coons, "The differential diagnosis of multiple personality: A comprehensive review,"

Psychiatric Clinics of North American 7 (1984): 51; P. M. Coons, E. S. Bowman, and V. Milstein, "Multiple personality disorder: A clinical investigation of 50 cases," *Journal of Nervous and Mental Disease* 175 (1988): 519.

61. North, Ryall, Ricci, et al., *Multiple Personalities, Multiple Disorders.*

62. Studies cited in North, Ryall, Ricci, et al., *Multiple Personalities, Multiple Disorders*, p. 49.

63. See, for example, E. L. Bliss, "A symptom profile of patients with multiple personalities, including MMPI results," *Journal of Nervous and Mental Disease* 172 (1984): 197; Coons, "The differential diagnosis of multiple personality: A comprehensive review;" Coons, Bowman, and Milstein, "Multiple personality disorder: A clinical investigation of 50 cases"; and P. M. Coons and A. L. Sterne, "Initial and follow-up psychological testing on a group of patients with multiple personality disorder," *Psychological Reports* 58 (1986): 43.

64. See, for example, D. Keyes, *The Minds of Billy Milligan* (New York: Random House, 1981).

65. Kohlenberg, "Behavioristic approach to multiple personality."

66. See, for example, M. Smith and L. Pazder, *Michelle Remembers* (New York: Simon and Schuster, 1980).

67. Kohlenberg, "Behavioristic approach to multiple personality," p. 139.

68. See, for example, Putnam, *Diagnosis and Treatment of Multiple Personality Disorder.*

69. H. F. Ellenberger, *The Discovery of the Unconscious: The History and Evolution of Dynamic Psychiatry* (New York: Basic Books, 1970).

70. This and the following works are cited in Ellenberger, *The Discovery of the Unconscious.*

71. R. L. Stevenson, *Dr. Jekyll and Mr. Hyde* (New York: Bantam Books, 1981).

72. O. Wilde, "The picture of Dorian Gray," *Lippincott's Magazine*, July 1890; J. Conrad, "The secret sharer," *Harper's Magazine*, August-September 1910.

73. Mary Reynold's case is described in M. G. Kenny, *The Passion of Ansel Bourne: Multiple Personality in American Culture* (Washington, D.C.: Smithsonian Institution Press, 1986).

74. Merskey takes the view that Mary Reynolds had bipolar disorder, with alternating mood states rather than personalities, but this doesn't explain why her states changed with sleep. See H. Merskey, *The Analysis of Hysteria.*

75. Kenny, *The Passion of Ansel Bourne.*

76. Cited in Ellenberger, *The Discovery of the Unconscious.*

77. Cited in Ellenberger, *The Discovery of the Unconscious.*

78. See Kenny, *The Passion of Ansel Bourne.*

79. Kenny, *The Passion of Ansel Bourne.*

80. I. Hacking, *Mad Travelers: Reflections on the Reality of Transient Mental Illness* (Charlottesville: University Press of Virginia, 1998).

81. Cited in Hacking, *Mad Travelers,* p. 208.

82. Hacking, *Mad Travelers*, p. 40.

83. See Hacking, *Rewriting the Soul.*

84. Hacking, *Mad Travelers,* p. 41.

85. Hacking, *Rewriting the Soul*, p. 179.

86. Clara Fowler's case is described in Kenny, *The Passion of Ansel Bourne.*

87. Cited in Kenny, *The Passion of Ansel Bourne*, p. 143.

88. H. Merskey, "The manufacture of personalities: The production of multi-

ple personality disorder," *British Journal of Psychiatry* 160 (1992): 327.

89. Cited in Kenny, *The Passion of Ansel Bourne*.

Chapter 7

1. See, for example, R. P. Kluft, ed., *Childhood Antecedents of Multiple Personality* (Washington, D.C.: American Psychiatric Press, 1985); L. Terr, *Unchained Memories: True Stories of Traumatic Memories, Lost and Found* (New York: Basic Books, 1994).

2. See, for example, B. S. Brodsky, M. Cloitre, and R. A. Dulit, "Relationship of dissociation to self-mutilation and childhood abuse in borderline personality disorder," *American Journal of Psychiatry* 152 (1995): 1788; B. A. Fallon, C. Sadik, J. B. Saoud, and R. S. Garfinkel, "Childhood abuse, family environment, and outcome in bulimia nervosa," *Journal of Clinical Psychiatry* 55 (1994): 424; E. F. Figueroa, K. R. Silk, A. Huth, and N. E. Lohr, "History of childhood sexual abuse and general psychopathology," *Comprehensive Psychiatry* 38 (1997): 23; P. E. Mullen, J. L. Martin, J. C. Anderson, S. E. Romans, and G. P. Herbison, "Childhood sexual abuse and mental health in adult life," *British Journal of Psychiatry* 163 (1993): 721; M. R. Nash, T. L. Hulsey, M. C. Sexton, T. L. Harralson, and W. Lambert, "Long-term sequelae of childhood sexual abuse: Perceived family environment, psychopathology, and dissociation," *Journal of Consulting and Clinical Psychology* 61 (193): 276; M. C. Zanarini, A. A. Williams, R. E. Lewis, R. B. Reich, S. C. Vera, M. F. Marino, A. Levin, L. Yang, and F. R. Frankenburg, "Reported pathological childhood experiences associated with the development of borderline personality disorder," *American Journal of Psychiatry* 154 (1997): 1101.

3. See, for example, E. F. Loftus, "The reality of repressed memories," *American Psychologist* 48 (1993): 518; E. F. Loftus and K. Ketcham, *The Myth of Repressed Memory: False Memories and Allegations of Sexual Abuse* (New York: St. Martin's Press, 1994); E. F. Loftus and G. R. Loftus, "On the permanence of stored information in the human brain," *American Psychologist* 35 (1980): 409; E. F. Loftus, M. Garry, and J. Feldman, "Forgetting sexual trauma: What does it mean when 38% forget?" *Journal of Consulting and Clinical Psychology* 62 (1994): 1177; R. Ofshe and E. Watters, *Making Monsters: False Memories, Psychotherapy, and Sexual Hysteria* (New York: Scribner, 1994).

4. See, for example, S. Brandon, J. Boakes, D. Glaser, and R. Green, "Recovered memories of childhood sexual abuse: Implications for clinical practice," *British Journal of Psychiatry* 172 (1998): 296; F. H. Frankel, "Adult reconstruction of childhood events in the multiple personality literature," *American Journal of Psychiatry* 150 (1993): 954; Loftus and Ketcham, *The Myth of Repressed Memory: False Memories and Allegations of Sexual Abuse*; Ofshe and Watters, *Making Monsters*.

5. For the history of railway spine, see G. F. Drinka, *The Birth of Neurosis: Myth, Malady and the Victorians* (New York: Simon and Schuster, 1984); and A. Young, *The Harmony of Illusions: Inventing Post-Traumatic Stress Disorder* (Princeton, N.J.: Princeton University Press, 1995).

6. See H. Merskey, *The Analysis of Hysteria: Understanding Conversion and Dissociation,* 2nd ed. (London: Gaskell, 1999); M. S. Micale, *Approaching Hysteria: Disease and Its Interpretations* (Princeton, NJ: Princeton University Press, 1995); and Young, *The Harmony of Illusions*.

7. S. Freud and J. Breuer, "Studies on Hysteria," in *The Standard Edition of the Complete Psychological Works of Sigmund Freud*, vol. 2, trans. J. Strachey (London: Hogarth Press, 1953–1974).

8. M. Borch-Jacobsen, *Remembering Anna O.: A Century of Mystification*, trans. K. Olson (New York: Routledge, 1996).

9. H. Merskey argues that Anna O. was severely depressed at the time Breuer treated her. I have already noted the high rate of mood disorders among nineteenth-century hysterical patients. See H. Merskey, "Anna O. had a severe depressive illness," *British Journal of Psychiatry* 161 (1992): 185.

10. Borch-Jacobsen, *Remembering Anna O.*

11. J. M. Masson, *The Assault on Truth: Freud's Suppression of the Seduction Theory* (New York: Farrar, Straus, and Giroux, 1984).

12. For an excellent overview of shell shock, see Young, *The Harmony of Illusions*.

13. See J. Herman, *Trauma and Recovery* (New York: Basic Books, 1992).

14. See Young, *The Harmony of Illusions*.

15. Young, *The Harmony of Illusions*.

16. Merskey, *The Analysis of Hysteria*. Along the same lines, although childhood sexual abuse has been implicated as a cause of panic disorder (M. B. Stein, J. R. Walker, G. Anderson, A. L. Hazen, C. A. Ross, G. Edridge, and D. R. Forde, "Childhood physical and sexual abuse in patients with anxiety disorders and in a community sample," *American Journal of Psychiatry* 153 [1996]: 275), a study of 74 patients with panic disorder showed no association between derealization and depersonalization, the symptoms of panic most often considered dissociative, and childhood trauma (R. D. Marshall, F. R. Schneier, L. Shu-Hsing, H. B. Simpson, D. Vermes, and M. Liebowitz, "Childhood trauma and dissociative symptoms in panic disorder," *American Journal of Psychiatry* 157 [2000]: 451). Moreover, patients with depersonalization disorder, a rare syndrome charactized by repeated episodes of depersonalization, were found to have cognitive impairments in comparison with normal subjects (O. Guralnik, J. Schmeidler, and D. Simeon, "Feeling unreal: Cognitive processes in depersonalization," *American Journal of Psychiatry* 157 [2000]: 103). "Dissociation" here appears to be caused by brain disease!

17. J. B. Bryer, B. A. Nelson, J. B. Miller, and P. A. Krol, "Childhood sexual and physical abuse as factors in adult psychiatric illness," *American Journal of Psychiatry* 144 (1987): 1426.

18. Zanarini, Williams, Lewis, et al., "Reported pathological childhood experiences associated with the development of borderline personality disorder."

19. Brodsky, Cloitre, and Dulit, "Relationship of dissociation to self-mutilation and childhood abuse in borderline personality disorder."

20. Figueroa, Silk, Huth, et al., "History of childhood sexual abuse and general psychopathology."

21. Nash, Hulsey, Sexton, et al., "Long-term sequelae of childhood sexual abuse."

22. Nash, Hulsey, Sexton, et al., "Long-term sequelae of childhood sexual abuse," p. 282.

23. Fallon, Sadik, Saoud, et al., "Childhood abuse, family environment, and outcome in bulimia nervosa."

24. Mullen, Martin, Anderson, et al., "Childhood sexual abuse and mental health in adult life."

25. For example, Ruggiero and coauthors studied 200 male substance abusers admitted to the Bronx VA Medical Center (J. Ruggiero, D. P. Bernstein, and L. Handelsman, "Traumatic stress in childhood and later personality disorders: A retrospective study of male patients with substance dependence," *Psychiatric Annals* 29 [1999]: 713]. In this sample, patients who reported severe childhood sexual, physical, and emotional abuse had the most severe personality disorders, but patients with physical and emotional abuse alone, or severe neglect alone, also showed higher personality disorder scores in comparison with subjects who had not been maltreated. Patients reporting severe sexual abuse were more antisocial than others, raising the possibility that their reports were false or exaggerated.

Based on a study of women in the Virginia Twin Registry, Kendler and colleagues concluded that self-reported childhood sexual abuse is a risk factor for female depression, anxiety, bulimia, and drug and alcohol abuse (K. S. Kendler, C. M. Bulik, J. Silberg, J. M. Hettema, J. Myer, and C. A. Prescott, "Childhood sexual abuse and adult psychiatric and substance abuse disorders in women: An epidemiological and cotwin control analysis," *Archives of General Psychiatry* 57 [2000]: 953). When co-twins were asked to verify self-reported abuse, the associations remained, albeit in some cases weakened. However, the overall level of verification was modest (contingency coefficient = .50), and some verifications may have been artifactual: some co-twins may have been reporting what they were told. Since twins reporting sexual abuse showed more psychopathology than their co-twins without such abuse, Kendler and colleagues argued that sexual abuse per se, rather than family environment, was the cause of later disorders. However, the fully discordant twin pairs (one twin claiming to have been sexually abused and psychologically ill, the other claiming not to have been sexually abused and not ill) are precisely the pairs in which self-reports demand the greatest caution.

Bremmer and coauthors used "PET" scans, which measure cerebral oxygen consumption, in an attempt to show that childhood sexual abuse can cause changes in later brain functioning, at least in susceptible victims (J. D. Bremmer, M. Narayan, L. H. Staib, S. M. Southwick, T. McGlashan, and D. S. Charney, "Neural correlates of memories of childhood sexual abuse in women with and without post-traumatic stress disorder," *American Journal of Psychiatry* 156 [1999]: 1787). The subjects included 10 women (mean age 35 years) with post-traumatic stress disorder attributed to childhood sexual abuse and 12 women (mean age 32 years) without post-traumatic stress disorder who also reported childhood sexual abuse. Subjects were recruited through newspaper advertisements. No details are given as to whether memories of sexual abuse were "recovered memories" or not, or of whether and how they were verified. Each subject was read an account based on her description of her early abuse and asked to visualize the events described, while undergoing a PET scan to measure brain activity. While listening to these narrations, the subjects with PTSD showed greater oxygen uptake in prefrontal and motor cortex and decreased blood flow in hippocampus, fusiform gyrus, and other brain areas in comparison with subjects without PTSD. This study is too flawed to draw any useful conclusions: Aside from the fact that some of the "memories" may have been false, systematic differences unrelated to the specific memories but known to affect PET scans existed between subject groups. Eight of 10 subjects with PTSD had had major depressive episodes, compared to just three of the 12 subjects without PTSD.

Two of the PTSD group, but none of the comparison group, were depressed at the time of the study. Consistent with their inclusion in the PTSD group and their histories of emotional disorder, the subjects with PTSD developed emotional symptoms during the narrative readings; the subjects without remained calm. Since emotional state is reflected in oxygen uptake, the between-group PET scan differences are impossible to interpret.

Some data now suggest that psychiatrists may have confounded the effects of early adverse experiences in general and specific traumas, with temperamental factors leading to later pathology and adverse event construals. Thus, temperamentally vulnerable individuals may be more likely to later report early adverse events which, although they really occurred, played no causal role in their psychopathology (see, for example, J. Paris, "The primacy of early experience: A critique, an alternative, and some clinical implications," *Journal of Psychiatric Practice* 6 [2000]: 147; and J. Paris, *Myths of Childhood* [Philadelphia, PA: Brunner/Mazel, 2000]).

26. These are Brodsky, Cloitre, and Dulit, "Relationship of dissociation to self-mutilation and childhood abuse in borderline personality disorder"; Figueroa, Silk, Huth, et al., "History of childhood sexual abuse and general psychopathology"; Mullen, Martin, Anderson, et al., "Childhood sexual abuse and mental health in adult life"; and Nash, Hulsey, Sexton, et al., "Long-term sequelae of childhood sexual abuse."

27. L. M. Williams, "Recall of childhood trauma: A prospective study of women's memories of child sexual abuse," *Journal of Consulting and Clinical Psychology* 62 (1994): 1167. See also E. F. Loftus, M. Garry, and J. Feldman, "Forgetting sexual trauma: What does it mean when 38% forget?," and L. M. Williams, "What does it mean to forget child sexual abuse? A reply to Loftus, Garry and Feldman (1994)," both in *Journal of Consulting and Clinical Psychology* 62 (1994): 1182.

28. Williams, "Recall of childhood trauma," p. 1169.

29. Williams, "Recall of childhood trauma," p. 1170.

30. Loftus, Garry, and Feldman, "Forgetting sexual trauma: What does it mean when 38% forget?"

31. For studies of this effect, see S. J. Ceci and M. Bruck, "Suggestibility of the child witness: A historical review and synthesis," *Psychological Bulletin* 113 (1993): 403; also Loftus, and Ketcham, *The Myth of Repressed Memory*.

32. D. Della Femina, C. A. Yeager, and D. O. Lewis, "Child abuse: Adolescent records vs. adult recall," *Child Abuse and Neglect* 14 (1990): 227.

33. J. Briere and J. Conte, "Self-reported amnesia for abuse in adults molested as children," *Journal of Traumatic Stress* 6 (1993): 21.

34. J. L. Herman and E. Schatzow, "Recovery and verification of memories of childhood sexual trauma," *Psychoanalytic Psychology* 4 (1987): 1.

35. T. F. Nagy, "Incest memories recalled in hypnosis—a case study: A brief communication," *International Journal of Clinical and Experimental Hypnosis* 43 (1995): 118.

36. A. Martínez-Taboas, "Repressed memories: Some clinical data contributing toward its elucidation," *American Journal of Psychotherapy* 50 (1996): 217.

37. S. Duggal and L. A. Sroufe, "Recovered memory of childhood sexual trauma: A documented case from a longitudinal study," *Journal of Traumatic Stress* 11 (1998): 301.

38. Loftus and Ketcham, *The Myth of Repressed Memory*; Ofshe and Watters, *Making Monsters*.

39. For information on these allegations, see, for example, D. K. Sakheim and S. E. Devine, eds., *Out of Darkness: Exploring Satanism and Ritual Abuse* (New York: Lexington, 1992).

40. See K. V. Lanning, "A law-enforcement perspective on allegations of ritual abuse," in *Out of Darkness: Exploring Satanism and Ritual Abuse*, ed. D. K. Sakheim and S. E. Devine (New York: Lexington, 1992); J. S. Victor, *Satanic Panic: The Creation of a Contemporary* Legend (Chicago: Open Court, 1993).

41. Lanning, "A law-enforcement perspective."

42. J. S. La Fontaine, *Speak of the Devil: Tales of Satanic Abuse in Contemporary England* (Cambridge: Cambridge University Press, 1998).

43. The Burgus case was the subject of an NBC *Dateline* documentary (K. Smyser, "Devil's Advocate?") broadcast on October 27, 1998.

44. E. Bass and L. Davis, *The Courage to Heal: A Guide for Women Survivors of Child Sexual Abuse,* 3rd ed., rev. and updated (New York: HarperCollins, 1994).

45. M. Smith and L. Pazder, *Michelle Remembers* (New York: Pocket Books, 1980); L. Stratford, *Satan's Underground* (Gretna, La: Pelican, 1996).

46. Smith and Pazder, *Michelle Remembers*, p. 10.

47. Smith and Pazder, *Michelle Remembers*, p. 14.

48. L. Laboriel, C. Gould, and V. G. Costain, "Afterword," in L. Stratford, *Satan's Underground* (Gretna, La: Pelican, 1996).

49. Victor, *Satanic Panic*.

50. Andrew Thomas, *By Satan Possessed* (documentary film produced by Home Box Office, 1993).

51. For information about such cases, see S. J. Ceci and M. Bruck, "Suggestibility of the child witness: A historical review and synthesis"; and Victor, *Satanic Panic*.

52. La Fontaine, *Speak of the Devil*.

53. Stratford, *Satan's Underground*.

54. Information on alien abductions can be found in R. J. Boylan and L. K. Boylan, *Close Extraterrestrial Encounters: Positive Experiences with Mysterious Visitors* (Tigard, Ore.: Wild Flower Press, 1994); C. D. B. Bryan, *Close Encounters of the Fourth Kind: Alien Abduction, UFOs, and the Conference at M.I.T.* (New York: Knopf, 1995); E. Fiore, *Encounters: A Psychologist Reveals Case Studies of Abductions by Extraterrestrials* (New York: Ballantine, 1989); B. Hopkins, *Intruders: The Incredible Visitations at Copley Woods* (New York: Ballantine, 1987) and *Missing Time: A Documented Study of UFO Abductions* (New York: Ballantine, 1981); D. M. Jacobs, *Secret Life: Firsthand Accounts of UFO Abductions* (New York: Simon and Schuster, 1992); J. E. Mack, *Abduction: Human Encounters with Aliens* (New York: Scribner, 1994); E. Showalter, *Hystories: Hysterical Epidemics and Modern Media* (New York: Columbia University Press, 1997); W. Streiber, *Communion: A True Story* (New York: Avon, 1987) and *Transformation: The Breakthrough* (New York: Avon, 1988); and K. Thompson, *Angels and Aliens: UFOs and the Mythic Imagination* (New York: Fawcett Columbine, 1991).

55. J. S. Gordon, "The UFO experience," *Atlantic*, August 1991, p. 82; see also J. S. Gordon, *The Golden Guru: The Strange Journey of the Bhagwan Shree Rajneesh* (Lexington, Mass.: Stephen Greene Press, 1987), which was cited in chapter 1.

56. Jacobs, *Secret Life*.

57. See, for example, Hopkins, *Intruders* and *Missing Time*.

58. Mack, *Abduction*.

59. See, for example, Boylan and Boylan, *Close Extraterrestrial Encounters*.

60. See, for example, Streiber, *Communion*.

61. See, for example, Jacobs, *Secret Life*.

62. Cited in Thompson, *Angels and Aliens*.

63. C. Berlitz and W. L. Moore, *The Roswell Incident* (New York: Grosset and Dunlap, 1980).

64. For a wonderful ethnographic account of Area 51, see D. Darlington, *Area 51: The Dreamland Chronicles* (New York: Holt, 1997).

65. Hopkins, *Intruders*.

66. See, for instance, Thompson, *Angels and Aliens*.

67. Hopkins, *Missing Time*.

68. Hopkins, *Intruders*.

69. Streiber, *Communion*.

70. Streiber, *Transformation*.

71. See J. Willwerth, "The man from outer space," *Time*, April 25, 1994, p. 74.

72. N. P. Spanos, P. A. Cross, K. Dickson, and S. C. DuBrevil, "Close encounters: An examination of UFO experiences," *Journal of Abnormal Psychology* 102 (1993): 624.

73. I. M. Lewis, *Ecstatic Religion: A Study of Shamanisn and Spirit Possession,* 2nd ed. (New York: Routledge, 1989).

74. Willwerth, "The man from outer space."

75. Mack, *Abduction*.

76. Mack, *Abduction*, p. 395.

77. Mack, *Abduction*, p. 419.

78. B. Hopkins, D. M. Jacobs, and R. Westrum, "The UFO abduction syndrome: A report on unusual experiences associated with UFO abductions, based upon the Roper Organization's survey of 5847 adult Americans," in *Unusual Personal Experiences: An Analysis of the Data from Three National Surveys* (Las Vegas, Nev.: Bigelow Holding Corporation, 1992).

79. J. Mack, "Mental health professionals and the Roper poll," in *Unusual Personal Experiences: An Analysis of the Data from Three National Surveys* (Las Vegas, Nev.: Bigelow Holding Corporation, 1992), p. 7.

80. Hopkins, Jacobs, and Westrum, "The UFO abduction syndrome."

81. See Boylan and Boylan, *Close Extraterrestrial Encounters*.

Chapter 8

1. I. L. Janis and B. T. King, "The influence of role playing on opinion change," *Journal of Abnormal and Social Psychology* 49 (1954): 211.

2. See R. B. Cialdini, *Influence: The New Psychology of Modern Persuasion* (New York: Quill, 1984).

3. L. Festinger and J. M. Carlsmith, "Cognitive consequences of forced compliance," *Journal of Abnormal and Social Psychology* 58 (1959): 203.

4. J. L. Freedman, "Long-term behavioral effects of cognitive dissonance," *Journal of Experimental Social Psychology* 1 (1965): 145.

5. R. A. Elkin and M. R. Leippe, "Physiological arousal, dissonance, and atti-

tude change: Evidence for a dissonance-arousal link and a 'don't remind me' effect," *Journal of Personality and Social Psychology* 51 (1986): 55.

6. S. Lieberman, "The effects of changes in roles on the attitudes of role occupants," *Human Relations* 9 (1956): 385.

7. B. J. Bem and H. K. McConnell, "Testing the self-perception explanation of dissonance phenomena: On the salience of premanipulation attitudes," *Journal of Personality and Social Psychology* 14 (1970): 23.

8. G. R. Goethals and R. F. Reckman, "The perception of consistency in attitudes," *Journal of Experimental Social Psychology* 9 (1973): 491.

9. L. N. Collins, J. W. Graham, W. B. Hansen, and C. A. Johnson, "Agreement between retrospective accounts of substance use and earlier reported substance use," *Applied Psychological Measurement* 9 (1985): 301.

10. G. B. Marcus, "Stability and change in political attitudes: Observe, recall and 'explain,'" *Political Behavior* 8 (1986): 21.

11. D. Shapiro, *Neurotic Styles* (New York: Basic Books, 1965).

12. R. E. Nisbett and T. D. Wilson, "Telling more than we can know: Verbal reports on mental processes," *Psychological Review* 84 (1977): 231.

13. This view is sometimes described in terms of adherence to a so-called norm of rationality. See, for example, P. Rosenfeld, V. Melburg, and J. T. Tedeschi, "Forgetting as an impression management strategy in the forced compliance situation," *Journal of Social Psychology* 114 (1981): 69; B. R. Schlenker, D. R. Forsyth, M. R. Leary, and R. S. Miller, "A self-presentational analysis of the effects of incentives on attitude change following counterattitudinal behavior," *Journal of Personality and Social Psychology* 39 (1980): 553.

14. This is the view adopted by Robert Trivers, a well-known evolutionary biologist. See Trivers, *Social Evolution* (Menlo Park, Calif.: Benjamin/Cummings, 1985). Trivers thinks the capacity for self-deception may have evolved in humans, and possibly other primates, because self-deception makes it easier to hide hostile or egocentric motives from others. In general, persons who don't believe in their own self-presentations betray their insincerity through nonverbal channels, such as facial expressions, tremors, nervous tics, downward gaze, or changes in voice and posture, or by stilted or awkward language. People who do believe in their own self-presentations don't betray any uncertainty, even if these presentations are fundamentally false. Trivers reasons that individuals who are less cognizant of their own base motives can stage more convincing performances as beneficent persons than those with greater awareness. Trivers, in other words, sees self-deception as a method-acting device to make certain roles more convincing.

Although the roles Trivers discussed are broadly related to altruism, the evolutionary theory of which he has pioneered (Trivers, "The evolution of reciprocal altruism," *Quarterly Review of Biology* 46 [1971]: 35), his argument can be taken to apply to all social roles. In the most general terms, role-induced attitude change can be treated as self-deception in the service of better role playing. In this case, the link between attitude change and obliviousness to role playing, which is evident in the experiments cited in previous pages, goes to the heart of the function served by such attitude change. Attitude change is a step toward giving the best possible performance of any role.

15. For example, speaking of Theodore Roosevelt, H. W. Brands observed: "like most successful politicians, he possessed the gift of being able to believe the nasty things he found it convenient to say about his opponents—a happy

circumstance that made his attacks all the more effective." Brands, *T. R.: The Last Romantic* (New York: Basic Books, 1997), p. 303.

16. S. Freud, "Fragment of an analysis of a case of hysteria," in *The Standard Edition of the Complete Psychological Works of Sigmund Freud*, vol. 7, trans. J. Strachey (London: Hogarth Press, 1953–1974), pp. 77–78.

17. Randolph Nesse, a well-known evolutionary psychiatrist familiar with psychodynamic theories, argued that the defenses as conceived of by Freud and others serve to achieve self-deception of the kind Trivers thought was adaptive (see note 14). R. Nesse, "The evolutionary functions of repression and the ego defenses," *Journal of the American Academy of Psychoanalysis* 18 (1990): 260.

18. W. Reich, *Character Analysis,* 3rd, enlarged ed., trans. V. R. Carfagno, (New York: Simon and Schuster, 1972).

19. Reich, *Character Analysis,* p. 90.

20. Reich, *Character Analysis,* p. 94.

21. Reich, *Character Analysis,* p. 91.

22. Reich, *Character Analysis,* p. 94.

23. This is in contrast to the view of several influential authors, who cite recovered memory therapy as evidence that the concept of the dynamic unconscious is inherently unscientific and hence should be discarded. See, for example, F. Crews, *The Memory Wars: Freud's Legacy in Dispute* (New York: New York Review of Books, 1995); and E. Watters and R. Ofshe, *Therapy's Delusions: The Myth of the Unconscious and the Exploitation of Today's Walking Wounded* (New York: Scribner, 1999). The issue might be avoided by coining a new term, such as "unacknowledged role-discrepant attitudes," to describe the disavowed attitudes discussed in this section, but I have chosen instead to emphasis the connection between such attitudes and the traditional interests of psychodynamic therapists. Nor is clear that a new term would do much to mollify critics.

24. American Psychiatric Association, *Diagnostic and Statistical Manual of Mental Disorders, 4th ed.* (Washington, D.C.: American Psychiatric Association Press, 1994), p. 457.

25. American Psychiatric Association, *Diagnostic and Statistical Manual of Mental Disorders, 4th ed.,* p. 683.

26. G. F. Drinka, *The Birth of Neurosis: Myth, Malady and the Victorians* (New York: Simon and Schuster, 1984).

27. American Psychiatric Association, *Diagnostic and Statistical Manual of Mental Disorders, 4th ed.,* p. 650.

28. American Psychiatric Association, *Diagnostic and Statistical Manual of Mental Disorders, 4th ed.*

29. See, for example, J. G. Gunderson and M. C. Zanarini, "Current overview of the borderline diagnosis," *Journal of Clinical Psychiatry* 48 (August 1987): S5; J. J. Hudziak, T. J. Boffeli, J. J. Kriesman, M. M. Battaglia, C. Stranger, S. B. Guze, and J. J. Kriesman, "Clinical study of the relation of borderline personality disorder to Briquet's syndrome (hysteria), somatization disorder, antisocial personality disorder, and substance abuse disorders," *American Journal of Psychiatry* 153 (1996): 1598.

30. See, for example, C. R. Cloninger and S. B. Guze, "Psychiatric illness and female criminality: The role of sociopathy and hysteria in the antisocial woman," *American Journal of Psychiatry* 127 (1970): 303; S. G. Guze, R. A. Woodruff, and P. J. Clayton, "Hysteria and antisocial behavior: Further evidence of an association," *American Journal of Psychiatry* 127 (1971): 957.

31. See, for example, O. Arkonac and S. B. Guze, "A family study of hysteria," *New England Journal of Medicine* 266 (1963): 239; S. B. Guze, E. D. Wolfgram, J. K. McKinney, and D. P. Cantwell, "Psychiatric illness in the families of convicted criminals: A study of 519 first-degree relatives," *Diseases of the Nervous System* 28 (1967): 651; P. I. Woerner and S. B. Guze, "A family and marital study of hysteria," *British Journal of Psychiatry* 114 (1968): 161.

32. See, for example, C. R. Cloninger, T. Reich, and S. B. Guze, "The multifactorial model of disease transmission, III: Familial relationship between sociopathy and hysteria (Briquet's syndrome)," *British Journal of Psychiatry* 127 (1975): 23; S. B. Guze, C. R. Cloninger, R. L. Martin, and P. J. Clayton, "A follow-up and family study of Briquet's syndrome," *British Journal of Psychiatry* 149 (1986): 17.

33. Hudziak, Boffeli, Kriesman, et al., "Clinical study of the relation of borderline personality disorder to Briquet's syndrome (hysteria), somatization disorder, antisocial personality disorder, and substance abuse disorders."

34. S. B. Guze, R. A. Woodruff, and P. J. Clayton, "A study of conversion symptoms in psychiatric outpatients," *American Journal of Psychiatry* 128 (1971): 135.

35. T. Rechlin, T. H. Loew, and P. Joraschky, "Pseudoseizure 'status,'" *Journal of Psychosomatic Research* 42 (1997): 495.

36. American Psychiatric Association, *Diagnostic and Statistical Manual of Mental Disorders, 4th ed.*

37. Nisbett, and Wilson, "Telling more than we can know."

38. H. F. Ellenberger, *The Discovery of the Unconscious: The History and Evolution of Dynamic Psychiatry* (New York: Basic Books, 1970).

39. The theory of kin altruism is reviewed in Trivers, *Social Evolution*. See also I. Eibl-Eibesfeldt, *Human Ethology* (New York: Aldine de Gruyter, 1989); J. van Lawick-Goodall, *In the Shadow of Man* (Boston: Houghton Mifflin, 1971); E. Trinkaus and P. Shipman, *The Neandertals: Changing the Image of Mankind* (New York: Knopf, 1993).

40. As Merskey put it, "the ultimate paradigm [for hysteria] is of the small child . . . crying for his or her mother and protesting weakness and debility to secure love and affection." H. Merskey, *The Analysis of Hysteria: Understanding Conversion and Dissociation,* 2nd ed. (London: Gaskell, 1999), p. 393.

41. As A. J. Lewis ("The survival of hysteria," *Psychological Medicine* 5 [1975]: 9) observed, hysteria has outlived many a premature obituarist.

Index